THE NEW WORLD
OF
MICROENTERPRISE FINANCE

Kumarian Press Library of Management for Development

Selected Titles

Opening the Marketplace to Small Enterprise: Where Magic Ends and Development Begins, Ton de Wilde and Stijntje Schreurs, with Arleen Richman

Breaking the Cycle of Poverty: The BRAC Strategy, Catherine H. Lovell

The Challenge of Famine: Recent Experience, Lessons Learned, John Osgood Field, editor

In Defense of Livelihood: Comparative Studies on Environmental Action, John Friedmann and Haripriya Rangan, editors

Keepers of the Forest: Land Management Alternatives in Southeast Asia, Mark Poffenberger

Getting to the 21st Century: Voluntary Action and the Global Agenda, David C. Korten

Management Dimensions of Development: Perspectives and Strategies, Milton J. Esman

Tools for the Field: Methodologies Handbook for Gender in Agriculture, Hilary Sims Feldstein and Janice Jiggins, editors

Primary Health Care: Medicine in Its Place, John J. Macdonald

Transforming Humanity: The Visionary Writings of Soedjatmoko, Kathleen Newland and Kamala Chandrakirana Soedjatmoko, editors

Intermediary NGOs: The Supporting Link in Grassroots Development, Thomas F. Carroll

Democratizing Development: The Role of Voluntary Organizations, John Clark

Growing Our Future: Food Security and the Environment, Katie Smith and Tetsunao Yamamori, editors

Managing Organizations in Developing Countries: A Strategic and Operational Perspective, Moses N. Kiggundu

Toward a Green Central America: Integrating Conservation and Development, Valerie Barzetti and Yanina Rovinski, editors

Promises Not Kept: The Betrayal of Social Change in the Third World, Second Edition, John Isbister

Women at the Center: Development Issues and Practices for the 1990s, Gay Young, Vidyamali Samarasinghe, and Ken Kusterer, editors

Kumarian Press Books for a World that Works

Voices from the Amazon, Binka Le Breton

THE NEW WORLD OF MICROENTERPRISE FINANCE

Building Healthy Financial Institutions for the Poor

editors
María Otero
Elisabeth Rhyne

KUMARIAN PRESS

María Otero dedicates this book to Joe, Justin, David, and Ana Marisa.
Elisabeth Rhyne dedicates this book to Ed and Laura.

The New World of Microenterprise Finance: Building Healthy Financial Institutions for the Poor. Published 1994 in the United States of America by Kumarian Press, Inc., 630 Oakwood Avenue, Suite 119, West Hartford, Connecticut 06110.

Cover design by Beth Gorman

Production supervised by Jenna Dixon

Text design by Jenna Dixon
Copyedited by Linda Lotz
Typeset by ProProduction
Proofread by Karen Burnham
Index by Barabara DeGennaro

Printed in the United States of America on recycled acid-free paper by Thomson-Shore, Inc. Text printed with soy-based ink.

Library of Congress Cataloging-in-Publication Data

The New world of microenterprise finance : building healthy financial
   institutions for the poor / editors, María Otero, Elisabeth Rhyne
        p.   cm. — (Kumarian Press library of management for
   development)
    Includes bibliographical references and index.
   ISBN 1-56549-031-2 (alk. paper). — ISBN 1-56549-030-4 (pbk. : alk. paper).
    1. Financial institutions—Developing countries. 2. Small business—
   Developing countries—Finance. 3. Poor—Developing countries. I. Otero,
   María. II. Rhyne, Elisabeth. III. Series.
   HG195.N48   1994
   332.1'09172'4—dc20   93-47513

98   97   96   95   94   5   4   3   2   1

First printing, 1994

Contents

Tables

Foreword

"High interest rates are always immoral. It is better to deny credit than to let poor people employ themselves out of poverty."

"Since banks are the custodians of people's money, they should never finance poor people, regardless of repayment performance."

"Nonprofit organizations cannot prudently manage permanent capital."

"Poor people are not resourceful enough to survive and therefore cannot be entrusted with credit."

If we spoke this plainly, we might be better able to see the folly of some conventional wisdom. During the past twenty years, some visionary practitioners in business finance, banking, and poverty alleviation have challenged these truisms. They have created a highly profitable bank division with 10 million rural savers and 2 million rural business borrowers in Indonesia; used borrowing groups to cut transaction costs among the 1 million poor, self-employed female members of a bank in Bangladesh; and created a high-performing network of nonprofits in Latin America now striving to achieve $1 billion in new microbusiness loans in five years. Based on the economic impact of these innovations on local economies, the contributors to this book advance ideas that are remarkably different from the conventional wisdom. This is their logic:

1. Private banks gravitate to large transactions with affluent borrowers and probably should not be expected to deliver small-size financial services to low-income clients.

2. Banking institutions motivated by a longer-term vision of the common good can be capitalized for the primary purpose of entry-level economic development. By lowering information costs through specialization and innovation in delivery systems, they can operate profitably in markets with small transaction sizes and less affluent clients.

3. Poor entrepreneurs possess the same survival skills as affluent business operators. They save money, carefully apply their entrepreneurial energy, and repay debts as scheduled to maintain access to future loans.

4. Large-scale solutions are required to expand poor people's participation in their country's economy. Investment in self-sustaining institutions that finance poor residents is a comparatively cost-effective use of scarce subsidies.

5. An investment orientation is preferable to charity. Independently responsible borrowers and institutional managers perform better when there is risk involved. Enough is known about markets, self-interest, incentives, and disciplined structures to create systems that maximize borrower behavior.

6. Talent and energy are invaluable resources. Individuals possessing them can be attracted to both entrepreneurship and public-purpose banking, but only if given enough time and support to succeed. They will not risk their future on short-term or unpredictable bureaucratic support.

Debate about a link between banking and the poor elicits passion from all quarters. This book shares the perspectives of some of the most effective participants in the debate.

MARY HOUGHTON
President, Shorebank Corporation
Chicago, Illinois

Acknowledgments

This book was made possible through the GEMINI (Growth and Equity through Microenterprise Investments and Institutions) project, a microenterprise technical assistance project funded by the U.S. Agency for International Development (USAID) under contract No. DHR-5448-C-00-9080-00. The editors wish to express their appreciation to USAID and to Development Alternatives, Inc., which manages the GEMINI project. Special thanks go to Michael Farbman, who provided the original vision within USAID to address microenterprise development and supported our efforts to produce this book.

Our special acknowledgment goes to James J. Boomgard, the original director of the GEMINI project, whose insights, encouragement, and friendship enriched our work. He was instrumental in helping develop the point of view expressed in this book. We also want to express our gratitude to ACCION International, a collaborating agency in the GEMINI project.

Special thanks go to all the contributors for their thoughtful ideas and their support throughout this project. The effort of transforming their papers into a form appropriate for this book was a fruitful process that sharpened all our thinking. We especially appreciated their patience.

David Dumper, with the assistance of Kimberly Smith, managed the editing and preparation of the manuscript. Janet Craswell provided her excellent editing skills, and Timothy Wedding assisted on the logistical end. We express our great appreciation to them. Also, an expression of gratitude to Trish Reynolds, Kumarian's editor, who supported us enthusiastically.

Special recognition also goes to the many organizations across Asia, Latin America, and Africa that daily are carrying out this bold experiment and made their ideas and information available to these writers. We express enormous admiration for their work.

The contributors wish to acknowledge particular individuals and organizations, though, unfortunately, we cannot mention all the people whose assistance was appreciated.

Marguerite S. Robinson would like to thank the Indonesian Ministry of Finance; the Coordinating Minister for Economy, Finance, and Industry; the president, board of directors, and staff of the Bank Rakyat Indonesia (BRI); and the director and staff of the Center for Policy and Implementation Studies (CPIS).

Elaine L. Edgcomb and James Cawley would like to acknowledge the Small Enterprise Education and Promotion (SEEP) institutional development working group, which conceptualized and developed the institutional development framework that is the basis for their chapter. In addition to the authors, the group included Ross Croulet, Opportunity Industrialization Centers, International (OICI); Larry Frankel, CARE; and Larry R. Reed, Opportunity International. They also thank Suzanne Kindervatter, chair of the SEEP Network; Larry Cooley, Management Systems International; and Katherine Stearns, ACCION.

Shari Berenbach and Diego Guzman express their thanks to Lynn Bennett of World Bank, Sidney Schuler of John Snow International, and Barbara Durr of Community Economics Corporation for making available valuable information on microenterprise programs in Asia and Africa. They also thank Grameen Bank officials, who generously shared their insights.

John H. Magill wishes to thank the officers and staff of the World Council of Credit Unions (WOCCU).

Sharon L. Holt would like to acknowledge Lynn Bennett, the senior anthropologist from the World Bank's Women in Development Division, and recognize the valuable work of the organizations she observed, as well as their staffs.

Larry R. Reed and David R. Befus would like to express their appreciation to Don Mead, Katherine Stearns, Matthew Gamser, James J. Boomgard, and Mark King, who all provided helpful and insightful comments on early drafts of their chapter. They also want to express their appreciation to and their regard for the staffs and boards of Agence de Credit pour l'Enterprise Privee (ACEP), National Development Foundation of Jamaica (NDF/J), Instituto de Desarrollo Hondureño (IDH), Asociación para el Desarrollo de la Microempresa, Inc. (ADEMI), and the BRI Unit Desa.

James J. Boomgard and Kenneth J. Angell would like to express their gratitude to many individuals, including Kamardy Arief and other BRI staff; John Rogers, Shodan Purba, and Juanita Darmono from the USAID office in Indonesia; Richard Patten, Richard Hook, Don Johnston, and Ibu Noermaliah Saanin from the Harvard Institute for International Development (HIID); and David Lucock, Development Alternative, Inc.'s Chief of Party on the Financial Institutions Development I Project.

Amy J. Glosser wishes to acknowledge Riordan Roett, Johns Hopkins School for Advanced International Studies; Eduardo Bazoberry, Fundación para le Promocion y Desarrollo de la Microempresa (PRODEM); Pancho Otero, Miguel Taborga, and the entire BancoSol staff; and Rita Norman and Paul Norman.

Albert Kimanthi Mutua wishes to acknowledge Henry Oloo Oketch, senior research officer for Kenya Rural Enterprise Program (KREP), for his support in developing his chapter.

The opinions expressed in this book are the sole responsibility of each writer and are not necessarily those of the editors or any organization.

Contributors

María Otero is the associate director of ACCION International, a U.S.-based organization specializing in microenterprise development. Previously, she served as the director of the Honduran office of ACCION, as an economist for Latin America and the Caribbean in the U.S. Agency for International Development (USAID) Women in Development Office, and as a management training coordinator at the Centre for Development and Population Activities. She has written several articles and other publications, including a series of monographs on microenterprise development. Ms. Otero has an M.A. from the Johns Hopkins School for Advanced International Studies and an M.A. from the University of Maryland in literature.

Elisabeth Rhyne is an independent consultant specializing in small and microenterprise development and finance. Ms. Rhyne designed the GEMINI (Growth and Equity through Microenterprise Investments and Institutions) project and coordinated it from 1989 to 1992. She has worked as a private-sector officer for USAID in Kenya and as a financial economist for the Congressional Budget Office and Office of Management and Budget. She is the author or coauthor of books on the U.S. Small Business Administration and on government credit policy. Ms. Rhyne has a Ph.D. in public policy from Harvard University.

Kenneth J. Angell, a staff member of Development Alternatives, Inc., has sixteen years of international financial experience in commercial and development banking, project financing, investment promotion, and institutional development. He has worked in Asia, Africa, Eastern Europe, Latin America, and the Caribbean. For the past two years, Mr. Angell has applied his expertise in finance and private-sector development to microenterprise financial systems worldwide. Mr. Angell holds an M.B.A. in finance from the Wharton School at the University of Pennsylvania. He also has an M.A. in international relations and a B.A. in political science, both from the University of Pennsylvania.

David R. Befus has been working in development projects in Latin America since 1974. In 1979, he started a microenterprise project for what is now Opportunity International, a private organization that supports small-enterprise development agencies in twenty countries. He has been involved in business and job creation efforts as both a practitioner and an academic. He has an M.B.A. from the University of Michigan and a Ph.D. from the University of Miami. He currently lives in Costa Rica, where he is the Latin American regional director of a U.S. private development agency.

Shari Berenbach has worked with microenterprise programs for more than a dozen years as director of programs for Partnership for Productivity/International (1981–87), as a consultant for microenterprise program design and technical assistance for USAID and the World Bank, and currently as a consultant at the International Finance Corporation (IFC)/Business Advisory Service. She holds an M.B.A. in finance and international business from Columbia Business School and an M.A. in Latin American studies from the University of California–Los Angeles.

James J. Boomgard is the chief of party of the Agri-business Development Project in Indonesia and on the staff of Development Alternatives, Inc. He is an agricultural economist who has devoted his professional career to strategies that promote enterprise-based private-sector development. From 1989–92, Dr. Boomgard directed the GEMINI project, USAID's primary technical resource in small-scale and microenterprise development. He holds a Ph.D. in agricultural economics from Michigan State University.

Nan Borton is director of the Office of Foreign Disaster Assistance at USAID. She has over twenty-five years of program experience in assessing and addressing problems of poverty, discrimination, and human rights abuse in the United States and the developing world, including fourteen years' field experience in Asia. She served as the chair of the board of directors of both InterAction and Private Agencies Collaborating Together (PACT). She also served on the board of two refugee-serving agencies and is on the advisory committee of the Refugee Policy Group. Ms. Borton participated on teams investigating the condition of displaced persons in Central America and is a consultant to the U.S. government on job creation for minority persons. She served seven years as executive director of International Voluntary Services and most recently was senior vice president of Development Alternatives, Inc.

Carlos Castello is director of Centro Acción Microempresarial (CAM), which is responsible for coordinating and implementing technical assistance and training activities directed mainly toward ACCION International's affiliates. He has been with ACCION since 1985 as director for Colombia, providing technical support to twenty institutions in that country as well as to other ACCION affiliates throughout Latin America. Mr. Castello has twelve years' experience in the development field, particularly in the design, implementation, and evaluation of microenterprise programs.

James Cawley has twenty years of experience in the management of development projects and programs; organizational and human resource development; strategic and financial planning; and project design, implementation, monitoring, and evaluation. He served in the Peace Corps as a volunteer and on staff and was deputy director of International Voluntary Services, Inc. He works as a private consultant and is currently employed by the National Cooperative Business Association. He has been affiliated with the Small Enterprise Education and Promotion (SEEP) Network for eight years.

Rodrigo A. Chavez is a Ph.D. candidate in the Department of Agricultural Economics and Rural Sociology at Ohio State University. Mr. Chaves has researched depository financial intermediaries at both the theoretical and empirical levels. Before coming to Ohio State, he worked as director of savings mobilization for the Costa Rican Federation of Credit Cooperatives. His professional consulting activities have taken him to Bolivia, Costa Rica, Honduras, Nicaragua, the Dominican Republic, and Indonesia.

Elaine L. Edgcomb is the coordinator of the SEEP Network, an association of North American private development organizations supporting enterprise development in the South. She has written and consulted on evaluation, enterprise development, and institutional development, and for ten years she managed development programs in Central America and the Caribbean.

Amy J. Glosser is a joint degree candidate for an M.B.A. at the Wharton School of Business of the University of Pennsylvania and an M.A. from the Johns Hopkins School for Advanced International Studies. In addition to her work with Fundación para la Promocion y Desarrollo de la Microempresa (PRODEM) and BancoSol in Bolivia, Ms. Glosser has worked with ACCION International, the Ford Foundation in New York, and Fundación Arias para la Paz y el Progeso Humano in Costa Rica.

Arelis Gómez Alfonso is the director of international programs for the Foundation for International Community Assistance (FINCA) and has been a consultant to USAID for the past six years, concentrating in the field of small-enterprise development. She has conducted studies and evaluations of programs in various countries of Africa, Asia, and Latin America. She holds an M.A. in economics from the University of Santo Domingo and an M.A. in international development from American University, Washington, D.C.

Claudio Gonzalez-Vega is professor of both agricultural economics and economics at Ohio State University. Formerly, he was dean of economic sciences at the University of Costa Rica, where he received degrees in law and economics. He also holds degrees from the London School of Economics and Stanford University. He has published extensively in the areas of finance and development, rural financial markets, macroeconomic management and commercial policy in developing countries, and related topics. He has been a consultant for USAID, the World Bank, the International Monetary Fund, several United Nations programs, and governments in over two dozen countries in Latin America and Asia.

Diego Guzman is the associate director of Centro Acción, ACCION's regional training center for the development of microenterprise support institutions. From 1986 through 1991, he was a permanent consultant

with Asociación Grupos Solidarios de Colombia (AGS), the ACCION affiliate in Colombia, and provided technical assistance to microenterprise
programs throughout Latin America.

Sharon L. Holt has an M.A. in public affairs from Princeton University. She has been a consultant to the World Bank and USAID, doing applied
research on poverty issues, specifically as they relate to finance. She was a
contributor to the World Bank's *World Development Report* on poverty and
coauthored "Developing Financial Institutions for the Poor" with Helena
Ribe. Ms. Holt is currently a graduate student in agricultural economics at
the University of Wisconsin–Madison.

John H. Magill is a staff member of Development Alternatives, Inc.,
and specializes in financial and institutional support systems for
microenterprises. He received his Ph.D. in political science and Latin
American studies from the University of Wisconsin and has more than
twenty years of experience in the field of development as an officer of
USAID and as a staff member of the Credit Union National Association.

Albert Kimanthi Mutua is the managing director of Kenya Rural
Enterprise Program (KREP). He has been working with KREP since its
inception in 1984 in several capacities: finance manager, deputy director
of finance and administration, and deputy managing director. Before
joining KREP he was deputy chief accountant of the largest nongovernmental organization in Kenya. A financial analyst by profession, Mr.
Mutua's specialty is in management information systems and microenterprise credit program design.

Larry R. Reed is the Africa regional director of Opportunity International and currently resides in Harare, Zimbabwe. Mr. Reed has worked
with small and microenterprise programs for ten years and has an M.A.
in public policy from the John F. Kennedy School of Government at Harvard University.

Marguerite S. Robinson, a social anthropologist, is Institute Fellow at
Harvard Institute for International Development (HIID). She has worked
extensively in South and Southeast Asia on social and economic development and public policy, with particular emphasis on local finance, rural
development, and urban labor. Dr. Robinson served as consultant to the
Indonesian Ministry of Finance and to the Bank Rakyat Indonesia (BRI)
during the 1980s, the period when the Indonesian banking system discussed in her chapter was developed.

Abbreviations

ACCOSCA	African Confederation of Cooperative Savings and Credit Associations
ACCU	Asian Confederation of Credit Unions
ACEP	Agence de Credit pour l'Enterprise Privee
ACO	Area Credit Office (KREP)
ACTUAR	Corporación Acción
ADEMI	Asociación para el Desarrollo de la Microempresa, Inc.
AGS	Asociación Grupos Solidarios de Colombia
AGS-COOP	Cooperativa Grupos Solidarios de Colombia
APP	Asociation pour Productivite
ASSIST	Agency for the Selection and Support of Individuals Starting Trade (Jamaica)
BancoSol	Banco Solidario
BIMAS	Bimbingan Massal (Mass Guidance); Indonesia's rice intensification program
BKK	Badan Kredit Kecamatan
BRAC	Bangladesh Rural Advancement Committee
BRI	Bank Rakyat Indonesia
CAM	Centro Acción Microempresarial
CamCCUL	Cameroon Cooperative Credit Union League
CCCU	Caribbean Confederation of Credit Unions
CD	certificate of deposit
CDV	Centro de Desarrollo Vecinal
CEDLA	Centro de Estudios para el Desarrollo Laboral y Agrario
CIDES	Cooperativa Multiactiva de Desarrollo Social
CMMC	Corporación Mundial de la Mujer Colombia
COBANCO	Comite Promotor del Banco para la Microempresa; PRODEM steering committee
COLAC	Latin American Confederation of Credit Unions
CORFAS	Corporación Fondo de Apoyo de Empresas Asociativas/Nacional-Bucaramanga
CPIS	Center for Policy and Implementation Studies
CRS	Catholic Relief Services
DAI	Development Alternatives, Inc.
FAVDO	Forum of African Voluntary Development Organizations
FF	Fundación Familiar
FFH	Freedom from Hunger Foundation
FINCA	Foundation for International Community Assistance
FMM	Fundación Mundial de la Mujer
FMSD	Fundación Mario Santo Domingo
FUNDAP	Fundación para el Desarrollo Integral de Programas Socio-economicos

FUNDESPE	Fundación para el Desarrollo de la Pequeña Empresa
FUNDICAR	Fundación para el Desarrollo Industrial, Comercial y Artesenal de la Guajira/Riohacha
FUNTEC	Fundación Tecnica
FWWBC	Fundación Banco Mundial de la Mujer Colombia
GEMINI	Growth and Equity through Microenterprise Investments and Institutions
HIID	Harvard Institute for International Development
IDB	Inter-American Development Bank
IDH	Instituto de Desarrollo Hondureño
IFC	International Finance Corporation
IIC	Inter-American Investment Corporation
KIWA	Kikundi Cha Wanabiashara; thirty-member association that is part of Kenya's Juhudi Credit Scheme
KREP	Kenya Rural Enterprise Program
KUPEDES	Kredit Umum Pedesaan; BRI program of general rural credit offered at commercial rates
MFO	microenterprise finance organization
MUSCCO	Malawi Union of Savings and Credit Corporations
NDF/J	National Development Foundation of Jamaica
NGO	nongovernmental organization
OEF/ES	Organización Empresarial Femenina de El Salvador
OICI	Opportunity Industrialization Centers, International
PACT	Private Agencies Collaborating Together
PCRW	Production Credit for Rural Women (Nepal)
PDO	private development organization
PRIDE	Promotion of Rural Initiatives and Development Enterprises, Ltd.
PRODEM	Fundación para la Promocion y Desarrollo de la Microempresa (Bolivia)
PROSEM	Promoción de Servicios Empresariales
RESCA	regular (nonrotating) savings and credit association
RFI	rural financial institution
ROAA	return on average assets
ROSCA	rotating savings and credit association
SCF	Save the Children Fund
SED	small enterprise development
SEEP	Small Enterprise Education and Promotion (Network)
SGP	solidarity group program
SIB	Superintendent of Banks (Bolivia)
SIMASKOT	urban version of SIMPEDES
SIMPEDES	Simpanan Pedesaan; BRI's village (rural) savings program
TABANAS	national savings program administered by Bank Indonesia
TSPI	Tulay Sa Pag-Unlad, Inc.
USAID	U.S. Agency for International Development
WIB	Women in Business (pilot project of OEF/International)
WOCCU	World Council of Credit Unions
WWB	Women's World Banking

Introduction

FOR INCREASING NUMBERS of poor people, microenterprises are a source of income and employment where no other alternatives are available. Millions of people in developing countries produce a wide diversity of goods in makeshift shops or engage in small trading and retailing activities. They bang out pots and pans from scrap metal, make mops and brooms, shape pieces of furniture, or sell fruits and vegetables. In urban areas, a growing percentage of the working population—sometimes as high as 50 percent—is engaged in microenterprise activity. In rural settings, most families combine microenterprise activity with farming, and many depend on it as the main source of family income.

In order for their businesses to prosper, all microenterprises must have a sufficient supply of working capital for the purchase of supplies and inventories. As they expand, microenterprises also need to invest in assets such as tools, equipment, or improved premises. Lacking access to formal financial services, many microentrepreneurs must provide this financing themselves through their own savings, the help of relatives, or business profits; others turn to informal moneylenders, whose loans can be costly. Microenterprises often fail to secure the capital they need and miss opportunities for business growth.

In response to this problem, the field of microenterprise development began as a series of experiments to provide credit to impoverished entrepreneurs. During its first years, practitioners in programs scattered around the globe built a basic understanding of how to lend to microentrepreneurs and laid a strong foundation in this field.

More recently, the field of microenterprise finance has evolved in a pivotal way, toward larger scale and greater self-sufficiency. Significant experiments have been launched—and many have succeeded far beyond expectations. Taken together, these experiments and the lessons they provide constitute a "new world" of microenterprise finance. As they are widely applied, they have the potential to do in finance what the green revolution has done in agriculture—provide access on a massive scale to the poor.

Several ideas have been crucial to the transformation of microenterprise finance, and these ideas are the major themes of this book. New techniques for providing financial services to the poor have made it possible to achieve previously unthinkable scale and outreach while reaching toward financial self-sufficiency. In the process, the relationship

1

of programs and their beneficiaries has changed into a customer relationship. One aspect of that change is the recognition that savings services are as important as credit in meeting the financial needs of poor entrepreneurs. These changes have moved the microenterprise field from its starting point as a series of small, localized programs into contact with the financial system at large, bringing both the rewards of greater scale and sustainability and the responsibilities that accompany financial intermediation.

SCALE AND FINANCIAL SELF-SUFFICIENCY

Scale and financial self-sufficiency have become two organizing principles for addressing the needs of low-income microentrepreneurs throughout the world. Attention to scale is imperative because there are millions of entrepreneurs who lack access to financial services. If these millions are to be reached, then models for financing microenterprises must have design features that allow for continuing expansion. Ten years ago the standard microenterprise program reached only hundreds—at best, one or two thousand—microenterprises. Today, many programs reach tens of thousands, and the stunning examples have surpassed a million.

Attention to financial self-sufficiency in extending financial services to microenterprises derives from the commitment to scale. The only way for institutions to grow and stay big is to become financially self-sufficient. The most successful examples of large-scale lending to microenterprises have been accomplished through specialized financial institutions that have been able to reach large numbers with few or no subsidies.

Further, self-sufficiency is a concept that emerged from a widespread change in attitude regarding subsidized lending and from the realization that large-scale lending cannot be accomplished through subsidies from grants. The prevailing sense among donor organizations has been one of dissatisfaction with small, subsidized programs and a need to find more viable alternatives.

NEW TECHNIQUES

Scale and self-sufficiency have become feasible only because of new techniques for reaching microentrepreneurs. These techniques are discussed more fully in Chapter 1 and are illustrated throughout Part II. Their development shattered the conventional wisdom of banking, which held that microenterprises were too risky and too costly for anyone to serve profitably. In fact, the earliest microenterprise credit programs tried to adapt techniques from commercial banking and made little headway until organizations such as Grameen Bank and ACCION International introduced techniques adapted from informal financial systems.

These innovations used nontraditional approaches to solve risk and cost problems. First, innovators found that they could reduce risk not by analyzing loans more thoroughly or requiring more collateral but by giving clients strong motivation to repay. Two of the most important motivating techniques are peer group lending, in which several people guarantee one another's loans (perfected by solidarity groups, as described in Chapter 7), and the promise of ongoing—and increasing—access to credit for borrowers who repay on time (used by Bank Rakyat Indonesia [BRI] and BancoSol, as described in Chapters 11 and 12, respectively).

Second, the innovators in microenterprise finance found ways to slash their administrative costs: They drastically simplified and decentralized loan application, approval, and collection processes. Solidarity group programs gave borrowers responsibility for much of the loan approval process. The function of loan officers was transformed so that each loan officer could handle many more clients—in some cases as many as 500.

Finally, innovators found that borrowers were willing and able to pay interest rates that covered the higher costs associated with providing credit in small amounts. Borrowers were able to pay more than commercial bank rates in order to gain access to credit that otherwise would have cost them far more through the informal system or would have been unattainable.

These three areas of innovation—repayment motivation, streamlined administration, and market-based pricing—laid the foundation for the self-sufficiency of microenterprise finance—and its expansion.

THE CUSTOMER RELATIONSHIP

As they introduced these new techniques, microenterprise programs were actually transforming their relationship to clients from one based on charity to a more commercial relationship based on mutual respect.

When programs viewed their clients as "beneficiaries," they tended to see them as relatively passive people and to picture microenterprise finance as a transfer of money from rich to poor. In such a context, decisions about what type of help to provide were made on the basis of what program designers thought would be "good for" the beneficiaries. At the same time, such programs spent a great deal of effort deciding which beneficiary groups were the most deserving of assistance and how to target them.

The new microenterprise finance programs look at clients as customers they wish to serve. This entails recognizing that every microentrepreneur is a financial manager of her or his enterprise and household. The entrepreneur makes an ongoing stream of decisions about when to buy, sell, save, borrow, and invest, often weighing several alternative sources. The earlier model was based on a one-time injection of funds that would transform the enterprise; the newer model centers on creating an extended relationship between client and service provider. The new model places fewer restrictions on use of the credit, recognizing that clients, not program administrators, know the best use of the money for their situations.

Programs that see their borrowers as customers seek to match their services with what the customers want. Some programs develop services by first doing extensive survey work among client groups, followed by pilot testing. The process BRI went through to develop its savings products is described in Chapter 2. Others, such as the village banking programs described in Chapter 9, give clients a share in decision making about the use of funds. Some of the results of tailoring products to meet client demand include shorter loan terms, quick turnaround of loan applications, and highly liquid savings services.

Finally, a customer orientation seeks to broaden rather than narrow the client base. For example, many programs moved away from their initial policy of "graduating" their most successful clients when they realized that good customers strengthen the lending institution. Others, recognizing that microentrepreneurs are integral parts of households and communities, have begun to develop products aimed at these markets as well, bringing microenterprise finance into the hub of broader-based financial services.

SAVINGS SERVICES AND THE FINANCIAL SYSTEM

Savings mobilization is an indispensable ingredient under this new model—one that is as important as credit. Saving is an essential and widely used component of the finances of poor households. When there is no institution available, poor people tend to save in other than financial form, such as in small livestock or jewelry. However, if they can determine that their assets are securely held, will maintain value, are relatively liquid, and are in a convenient location, poor people prefer to save in monetary form, as some of the most successful programs have demonstrated. Because saving is part of the liquidity strategy of most households, it is likely that more people will demand savings services than credit. This position discards the previous belief that the poor do not save or do not demand savings services. It is based on the experience of programs such as BRI, which in the last few years has demonstrated that properly designed savings instruments can elicit overwhelming demand among the poor.

For microenterprise programs, savings mobilization brings far-reaching changes. Once an institution captures savings, it becomes a financial intermediary. This transformation requires that the institution operate within the legal framework governing financial institutions in the country. At this point, the principles of regulation and supervision are introduced as essential ingredients.

The rise of financial institutions that specialize in reaching the poor opens a window for defining microenterprise finance as part of a broader financial system. It also forces a change in focus—from creating good projects to creating healthy financial institutions for the poor.

The evolution of these institutions moves microenterprise finance toward real financial intermediation and brings a new set of principles to guide future work and measure its success. Most importantly, it means that the funding base for microenterprise programs now must come from inside the financial system in each country. This shift in thinking introduces into the microenterprise field a series of new topics that now become part of the core of this evolving approach.

ORIGINS OF THIS BOOK

This book reflects the changes that are under way in the field of microenterprise finance. Its genesis was the GEMINI (Growth and Equity through Microenterprise Investments and Institutions) project, a five-year microenterprise development project funded by the U.S. Agency for International Development (USAID) and designed to advance the thinking in this field through experimentation, research, and technical support to microenterprise programs. In its emphasis on BRI and solidarity group programs it reflects the experience of two of the institutions that lead GEMINI—Development Alternatives, Inc., and ACCION International.

Under the thoughtful guidance of its directors, James J. Boomgard and later Matthew Gamser, GEMINI sought to develop an approach to microenterprise finance that recognized the importance of the five factors introduced above. In the process, GEMINI commissioned papers on topics that needed further exploration. The chapters in this book are distilled from those papers and together constitute a new approach to microenterprise finance. For this reason, this book is more than a collection of essays on microenterprise development: It is the result of taking a systematic view of all the issues in the field of microenterprise finance and integrating them into one approach.

WHO SHOULD READ THIS BOOK

This book is aimed in part at people involved in the microenterprise development community in developing countries as practitioners, donors, or researchers. It is invaluable for practitioners to be aware of the experiences of other programs and to apply these lessons to their own work. This book will also shed light on the subject for people who are moving microenterprise development into new territories, especially in the United States and Eastern Europe. Though conditions differ in these settings, many of the techniques and principles still apply.

This book is also intended for policymakers. High-level policymakers frequently view microenterprise finance as a small, subsidy-intensive activity with little relevance to the larger picture. This view cannot be held any longer; the experiences documented in this book demonstrate that microenterprise finance has the potential to enfranchise a major part of the population. In particular, people working on financial sector reform and those concerned with how structural adjustment and similar policies affect the poor will find suggestions for how economic reform can include the poor. Although the activities of microenterprises are not necessarily the key to economic transformation, they play a crucial role in providing income to the majority of the population. Providing microentrepreneurs with financial services is an important way to mainstream them into the economy and help decrease the existing polarity between rich and poor. The techniques described here also add a potentially useful perspective to the ongoing rural finance debate, a perspective based on financing the rural household through its microenterprise activities rather than through riskier agricultural crops.

HOW THE BOOK IS ORGANIZED

This book looks at the new world that is opening up for microenterprise finance. The first chapter lays out a vision for the future of microenterprise finance, guided by certain fundamental principles. This framework is amplified in the remaining chapters of Part I. Parts II and III present the basic methodologies of microenterprise finance and describe some of the institutions that have embodied and applied the new approaches.

The Challenge for the Future

The institutions discussed tell a story of dramatic progress in the microenterprise field during the past decade. One by one, new institutional forms and relationships are being created that can make microenterprise institutions part of a country's financial landscape. Progress is most notable in the evolution away from donor grants as the main source of funding toward funding from savings deposits and borrowing from banks—sources that are ultimately much more plentiful and reliable than donor funds.

Many nongovernmental organization programs have shifted to commercial bank financing—at first with guarantees, but later on the strength of their own credit histories. Most programs that have not yet borrowed from banks have moved from grants to loans, increasingly at market-based interest rates. Financing through savings deposits, although more difficult to arrange for, provides programs such as BRI, BancoSol, and credit unions with real independence. In a few experiments not documented here, commercial banks are developing their own microenterprise programs, and this trend promises to grow.

There are many institutional routes to creating financial services for the poor, all sharing the common principles articulated here. Applying these approaches to a greater number of institutions in more and more countries is the challenge of the next decade. It is a challenge that will require sustained commitment of technical expertise, political and institutional will, and financial resources. There are no guarantees of success, for financial institutions everywhere are fragile—hard to build and always vulnerable to risks.

The contributors to this volume seek a time when poor people throughout the world will have access to financial services. We believe that this goal is both near enough and important enough to give confidence to those who pursue the challenge.

PART I

PRINCIPLES AND INSTITUTIONS FOR MICROENTERPRISE FINANCE

CHAPTER 1 INTRODUCES the major ingredients necessary for the development of a financial systems approach. These permit the creation of microenterprise finance institutions that achieve scale and financial self-sufficiency and that operate as part of the national financial system.

One of the most important of these elements is savings mobilization, a topic that microenterprise finance has neglected too long. As Robinson says in Chapter 2, savings is the sustaining half of local finance. Her chapter illustrates the explosive growth of savings in Indonesia, made possible by the crafting of convenient, safe, and liquid voluntary savings instruments for the Bank Rakyat Indonesia's unit banking system.

Chapter 3, on financial sector regulation, is a companion to the discussion of savings. If microenterprise finance institutions are to begin accepting voluntary savings deposits, they—like any other deposit-taking institution—must be subject to regulation and supervision of some kind, for the protection of their depositors. Chaves and Gonzalez-Vega condense their extensive knowledge of financial market regulation and supervision into a primer for microenterprise professionals and sketch out how these issues may intersect with the special characteristics of microenterprise finance organizations.

Chapters 4 and 5 move inside microenterprise finance organizations to explore the institutional processes that must support the transition to scale and self-sufficiency. Edgcomb and Cawley, in Chapter 4, develop a framework for thinking through the key institutional challenges microenterprise development organizations face as they move from their initial planning into implementation, growth, and finally expansion. In Chapter 5, Otero takes up where Edgcomb and Cawley left off, focusing on those institutions that have reached the takeoff point and need to transform themselves into financial institutions—or at least take on many of the characteristics of financial institutions.

In Chapter 6, Rhyne argues that evaluations of microenterprise finance programs should reflect the new financial systems perspective. She lays out an evaluation framework that departs from the traditional concern with the impact on beneficiaries and advocates a focus on the quality of financial services and the capacity of institutions to achieve scale and self-sufficiency.

CHAPTER 1

Financial Services for Microenterprises: Principles and Institutions

Elisabeth Rhyne and María Otero

A NEW VIEW OF MICROENTERPRISE FINANCE

This chapter examines access to financial services—credit and savings—for the majority of poor entrepreneurs throughout the Third World. It considers the prospect of providing such services from locally generated funds, without external subsidies. Although presently elusive, this goal may be attainable, as suggested by the recent experience of microenterprise development programs.[1] We argue that institutions that adopt certain key principles of credit delivery and savings services demonstrate a promising strategy for providing wider access to financial services. These institutions, when placed in the context of the development of a financial system as a whole, are developing what we call a financial systems approach to microenterprises.

The principles behind the emerging techniques for offering financial services to the poor are the same as those found in any financial system and involve the following elements: a market perspective that understands the preferences of the client group and designs products to meet them; a recognition that savings can be as important as credit for microenterprises, financial institutions, and the economy; and insistence that financially viable institutions provide only financial services. These principles require the institution to break even or turn a profit in its financial operations and raise funds from nonsubsidized sources.

This perspective is a clear departure from the assumptions behind the vast majority of microenterprise programs financed by donors and governments during the 1970s and 1980s. The historically dominant approach involved the supply of an integrated package of credit and training with the goal of enterprise development. Further, it was assumed that serving microenterprises would require a continuing large subsidy.

The financial systems perspective, in contrast, shifts the terms of the discussion away from individual firms onto institutions and their

11

ability to provide services on a sustainable and widespread basis. This shift in perspective is made precisely because of the lack of sustainability and limited reach of the traditional model. In shifting focus, the financial systems approach necessarily relaxes its attention to "impact" in terms of measurable enterprise growth and focuses instead on measures of increased access to financial services. Chapter 6 presents a new way of addressing evaluation under this approach.

A financial systems approach would not be feasible without the development of a set of new techniques and their application in a number of institutions, such as the Grameen Bank in Bangladesh, the Bank Rakyat Indonesia (BRI), ACCION International in Latin America, the affiliates of the World Council of Credit Unions in many countries, and a growing host of other institutions. Various chapters in this book discuss the experiences of many of these institutions. The history and accomplishments of these institutions demonstrate the importance of addressing microenterprise credit and financial systems development together. If techniques exist to serve microenterprises on a basis that approaches commercial viability, it is important to foster conditions in which those techniques can be applied widely. Given the vast numbers of the poor who lack access to financial services, the application of these techniques could bring dramatic results.

This chapter first briefly reviews the nature of microenterprises as financial services clients. It then discusses the gap between the financial needs of microenterprises and the ability of the formal system to meet those needs. This discussion sets the context for the core of the chapter, which outlines the principles of lending and savings services that are the basis for the financial systems approach and the institutional requirements for supporting such services. Institutional issues include the potential for specialized operations to become commercially viable and gain access to funds and the policies needed to support the growth of such operations.

MICROENTERPRISES AS FINANCIAL SERVICES CLIENTS

Microenterprises usually have very small start-up capital requirements. Liedholm and Mead's (1987, 38) review of evidence in several countries found initial capital requirements ranging from $49 in Sierra Leone to $1,104 in Jamaica. In contrast, the requirements for working capital are likely to be relatively large, to cover raw materials and inventory. Most urban microenterprises operate on short-term planning cycles, often daily or weekly. In rural locations, business often varies with agricultural seasons. The population of microenterprises is in constant flux, with large percentages of enterprises starting and ending in any given year (Liedholm 1990). These findings suggest that short-term financing, in small amounts, is the greatest need.

Many, if not most, microenterprises are not autonomous economic units but are part of larger family or household units. The cash associated with one microenterprise is frequently mingled with that of other household activities, including other enterprises. Thus, the financial needs of families, or at least of individual entrepreneurs, are often not separable from the financial needs of the enterprises themselves. This is particularly true for enterprises owned and operated by women (Downing 1990).

The families that operate microenterprises typically lack assets, especially marketable assets. Family members who operate microenterprises, especially women, have serious time constraints because of household responsibilities. These characteristics require substitutes for formal collateral, rapid loan-processing procedures, and convenient locations for financial offices. Because of time and mobility constraints, microenterprises need services that are located close to their places of business and that can process transactions quickly.

Many of the financial needs outlined above can be met through savings services as well as through credit. As discussed in the chapter that follows, the ability to save money securely is important for the long-term financial health of households and as protection against illness, periods of unemployment, and the like. Savings are equally important for enterprise growth, for it is from savings that most investment in enterprises comes (Liedholm and Mead 1987, 38). Moreover, investments made through savings are paid for in advance, while those made through credit are paid for after the fact. The former is certainly preferable. A recognition of the importance of savings argues strongly that it should be given equal weight in microenterprise finance programs.

AVAILABILITY OF SERVICES TO MICROENTERPRISES

Mainstream financial institutions cannot easily serve microenterprises. Banks must process loans at a cost that can be covered by interest charges, and they must have confidence in the borrower's intent and ability to repay. The practices that most banks use to gain confidence in the quality of loans are expensive. They involve credit checks to gain information about the client's character, project appraisal to assess the client's business prospects, and formal collateral. These techniques cannot be used in microenterprise lending. Project appraisal is too expensive, and microenterprises do not keep records. Microenterprises have no established credit rating. They lack marketable collateral. These factors keep commercial banks out of microenterprise lending.

In response, donor-funded programs have stepped in. Rather than adopting new methods for serving microenterprises, they have tended to use commercial bank methods that emphasize project appraisal while relaxing collateral requirements and charging low interest rates. The resulting combination of costly services, poor security, and low revenues requires large subsidies. Such programs have constituted the major response of the formal sector to microenterprise credit needs.

On the savings side, many financial institutions provide deposit services to the poor. Commercial banks, government-owned post office banks, and other institutions take very small savings deposits. Few of these institutions return those deposits in the form of loans to the communities or client groups from which they draw them, however. In Kenya, commercial banks, with their extensive branch networks, gather savings in remote areas and lend them mainly in Nairobi and other major cities. The Malawi Post Office Savings Bank uses its small deposits to finance government-owned corporations. Thus, an imbalance often exists whereby the poor and microenterprises have greater access to savings than to credit services. Despite the wider availability of deposit services, however, large populations remain without such services or with services not adapted to their requirements.

An alternative source of both savings and credit for microenterprises is the informal financial sector. Informal systems are more available to microenterprises than are formal systems but are nevertheless regarded as inadequate due to their lack of depth of intermediation and very high interest rates. Informal financial flows that channel increased formal-sector liquidity into the microenterprise sector could serve as vehicles for financial deepening. That effect depends, however, on the existence of interactions between the formal and informal sectors. Further, a most commonly cited shortcoming of the informal financial sector is its segmentation from the financial mainstream, since much of its financial flow now enters the formal sector (Germidis, Kessler, and Meghir 1991).

Similarly, flows of trade and supplier credit could reach microenterprises. The limited evidence from a variety of countries suggests, however, that the linkages between microenterprises and larger businesses are weak, accounting for only a small fraction of microenterprise sales (Liedholm and Mead 1987, 48). Although some researchers advocate building greater links between informal and formal markets, systematic methods for doing so have not evolved.

One could conclude that both the formal and the informal financial systems, as presently constituted, offer few prospects for greatly increasing the availability of financial services to microenterprises. This chapter discusses a third alternative: specialized financial services based on proven principles for delivery of credit and savings services to the poor.

Principles for Financial Service Delivery to the Poor

Credit Principles

The technology for lending to microenterprises has improved greatly during the past decade, with the creation and evolution of the programs mentioned above. Microenterprise lending programs now operate in Asia, Latin America, and Africa. However much these programs differ from one another, beneath these differences is a common thread that makes them effective credit delivery systems. Some analysts have implied that the common element is the focus on the very poor (Biggs, Snodgrass, and Srivastava 1990). Others emphasize that these programs strip themselves of all services except lending and as such become "minimal" in their approach. Neither of these attributes reaches the heart of the matter, however.

What are the common threads among effective credit delivery programs for microenterprises? All have found ways to streamline their activities so that the costs of lending are commensurate with the small size of the loans being made. The techniques employed resemble, often by conscious adaptation, those that have developed in the informal financial sector over many years. The following three principles represent the core of the new techniques:

1. *Know the market—the poor are willing to pay for access and convenience.* The major service need among the poor is credit for liquidity and working capital, with loan terms of one year or less and with little attempt to direct credit to specific uses. Transaction costs for borrowers are lowered by locating lending outlets near the client, providing simple application processes, and disbursing quickly. Interest rates are high relative to prevailing rates in the formal financial system, but they are low compared with typical informal-system rates.

2. *Special techniques slash administrative costs.* The simplest procedures are used for the smallest loans. Loan applications are often no more than one page. Approvals are decentralized and are based on readily verifiable eligibility criteria rather than business appraisal. Borrower groups often handle much of the loan-processing burden.

3. *Special techniques motivate repayments.* Lenders substitute other techniques for security and loan appraisals, such as

group guarantees or pressure from social networks, the promise of repeat loans in increasing amounts, and savings requirements. Although programs dealing with larger microenterprises may require tangible collateral, most do not.

Application of these principles is the foundation for financial viability of a lending operation that serves poor microenterprises. The essence of the difference between these techniques and commercial banking practices is the use of a repayment incentive structure instead of costly information gathering. This substitution enables lenders to serve microenterprises at a reasonable cost.

Group formation is often employed by microenterprise programs, particularly for the poorest clientele (see Chapter 7). The group plays a role in reducing the cost of gathering information about the borrower, but its more important role is in motivating repayments through shared liability for default.[2] Lenders can shift some of the loan-processing and loan-approval tasks onto groups because the groups have better access to information on the character and creditworthiness of potential borrowers. When very poor clients care more about access to credit than the terms on which it is offered, groups can be used without significantly impairing demand.

SAVINGS PRINCIPLES

The financial systems approach to microenterprises recognizes that savings are as important a service for the poor as credit, and that savings are crucial in building self-sufficient financial institutions. Well-crafted savings services can encourage a move from nonfinancial savings into financial savings, with the advantages of safety and liquidity for entrepreneurs and the provision of funds for investment for society (Vogel 1984b, 251–52). To date, although many other programs have incorporated savings elements, only the credit union movement and scattered programs have embraced savings as equally important as credit for dealing with poor populations.

Just as there are proven principles of lending to the poor, there are principles of savings that have emerged from experiences in various places. Indications are that when savings are approached using the following principles, customers respond enthusiastically. First, the most widely desired savings instruments offer safety, convenience, ready access to money, and a positive real return. Second, more people want a good place to save than want loans. Thus, savings services can reach deeper into the community. The opportunity to save should not be limited to those who borrow. Last, lending to microenterprises can be financed to a significant extent by savings from the same communities, provided savings services are designed with customer needs in mind. Marguerite S. Robinson discusses these issues in detail in Chapter 2.

Traditionally, most microenterprise programs with savings elements used some form of compulsory savings, whereby borrowers were required to save a portion of the amount they borrowed.[3] Typically, under such programs, borrowers did not have access to their savings until their loan was repaid. The savings mechanism thus functioned as asset storage in a very illiquid form. A voluntary savings instrument, such as passbook savings with free access to deposits, better meets savers' requirements and has the potential to raise much larger amounts of funds. The BRI Unit Banking system in Indonesia, discussed in Chapters 2 and 11, is now fully savings financed, demonstrating this potential. Legal restrictions on the acceptance of deposits by nonbank organizations can limit the ability of microenterprise programs to introduce voluntary savings, as discussed below.

The principles outlined above for financial services to the poor represent significant achievements in the field of microenterprise development. The success of programs that have used these principles during the past decade provides the basis for building financial services for microenterprises into the financial system.[4] Nevertheless, the programs employing these principles should still be regarded as incomplete. Their full potential to grow, spread, and achieve greater financial self-sufficiency has not yet been reached. The following sections discuss the institutional requirements for expanding the use of these techniques, beginning with questions of internal financial self-sufficiency and then moving to the external institutional and policy settings.

INSTITUTIONAL REQUIREMENTS

FINANCIAL SELF-SUFFICIENCY

Financial self-sufficiency is a prerequisite for making financial services widely available to microenterprises. Yet debate continues on whether it is feasible for most institutions. A financially self-sufficient credit operation must cover the following through fees and interest charges: operating costs, including loan loss reserves; the cost of funds; and inflation. To achieve genuine commercial viability, it must also yield a profit to owners.

Institutional performance can be analyzed in terms of four distinct levels of self-sufficiency. The lowest level, level one, is associated with traditional, highly subsidized programs. At this level, grants or soft loans cover operating expenses and establish a revolving loan fund. When programs are heavily subsidized and performing poorly, however, the value of the loan fund erodes quickly through delinquency and inflation.

Revenues fall short of operating expenses, resulting in a continuing need for grants. Many microenterprise credit programs operate at this level.

Most programs that use the proven principles described here can attain the second level of self-sufficiency. At level two, programs raise funds by borrowing on terms near, but still below, market rates. Interest income covers the cost of funds and a portion of operating expenses, but grants are still required to finance some aspects of operations. Most programs at this level are quite proud of their breakthrough, as they should be, because the subsidy required is significantly smaller than the one required at level one. However, they should not be satisfied to remain at this level.

At level three, most subsidy is eliminated, but programs find it difficult to eradicate a persistent dependence on some element of subsidy. This is the level associated with most of the well-known credit programs, and it is probably necessary to reach at least this point in order to achieve large-scale operations (see Chapter 5). Programs at this level are rarely required to take the next step, because both they and their sources of support are pleased with performance at this level. The Grameen Bank, for example, retains two kinds of subsidy: Its cost of capital is several points below market, and it receives income from soft loan funds placed on deposit (Hossain 1988). The Badan Kredit Kecamatan (BKK) program has eliminated subsidy from its branch network but requires some grant support for supervision. ACCION programs in several countries have reached this level, but they must deal with the problem of maintaining the value of loan funds in the face of very high inflation and distorted prevailing interest-rate structures.

The final level of self-sufficiency, level four, is reached when the program is fully financed from the savings of its clients and funds raised at commercial rates from formal financial institutions. Fees and interest income cover the real cost of funds, loan loss reserves, operations, and inflation. The only major microenterprise programs to have reached this level are those of the credit union movement in certain countries and the BRI Unit Desa system in Indonesia.

The presentation of these levels as a progression is not meant to imply that programs should begin at the bottom and work up. Beginning at a higher level is far preferable to starting at level one, because fewer bad habits have to be shed. Nevertheless, for many programs, achievement of self-sufficiency involves moving through progressively more stringent levels of cost recovery. Programs should be judged less by their current level of achievement than by their progress toward higher levels.

The following discussion outlines the structure of costs faced and income enjoyed by credit programs at each of the four levels of self-sufficiency. By analyzing each type of cost as well as fee and interest income, we can determine how credit programs move from one level to the next.

OPERATING COSTS. Traditional credit programs at level one typically have very high operating costs; it is not uncommon for programs to spend a dollar to lend a dollar, particularly among smaller programs (see Kilby and D'zmura 1985; Tendler 1983). Programs at higher levels of self-sufficiency achieve most of their movement toward viability by using methods that cost far less, that is, by adopting the principles outlined above, which brings them to level two. Once these methods are adopted, however, changes come incrementally from increasing efficiency and scale economies in operations. Efficiencies may come from marginal improvements in processes, computerization of management information, improved financial management, and the like. Staffing and physical plant are major costs that must be addressed on a case-by-case basis. Therefore, continued streamlining is not the primary strategy for moving to higher levels of self-sufficiency.

When nongovernmental organizations (NGOs) move toward becoming financial institutions, differentiating between financial and nonfinancial services becomes an important consideration. Most microenterprise programs, at all levels of self-sufficiency, provide nonfinancial services in a nontraditional form. These services include preparing the borrower to manage and use credit, assisting in the formation of guarantee groups, training in areas related to production, and holding special meetings. These services prepare impoverished entrepreneurs to meet the requirements for lending.

One position argues that these nonfinancial services are a social investment in a poor population with a corresponding social cost. This cost, the argument goes, should be subsidized, since no provision of financial services, however efficient, can cover it. The counter position is that these services are a necessary cost of lending to the poor and therefore should be built into full-cost pricing.

LOAN LOSSES. Programs that have adopted the principles outlined here have achieved substantially better repayment rates than traditional programs, often reaching levels that compare favorably with commercial bank operations. One can observe many programs, particularly at levels two and three, that claim losses at or below 3 percent of principal. Delinquency and default cannot be eliminated, but they can be maintained at a level that does not threaten the financial integrity of the institution.

COST OF FUNDS. Lending operations must pay to raise funds, either by borrowing or by generating savings. Programs operating on grants and very soft loans are spared this cost: Donors bear it. Dependence on soft sources of funds is a limiting factor, as soft sources are in short supply. Institutions at level two may still use them, but by level three the transition to commercial or nearly commercial sources should have been made. This is, in fact, one of the key distinctions between the two levels.

INFLATION. All programs bear the costs of inflation, whether they recognize them or not. In a well-functioning financial system, the inflation factor is built into the interest rate paid on funds raised or offered to depositors. This practice returns the real value of the funds to the suppliers and therefore maintains that value in the financial system. However, when programs use concessional funds, they are not charged this inflation factor. Despite an appearance of self-sufficiency, the real value of the loan fund dwindles, and the programs are able to serve fewer clients. If hyperinflation sets in, virtually all progress toward self-sufficiency is destroyed. Microenterprise programs have a good chance of reaching levels three and four only if they operate in countries where inflation is kept to moderate levels.

FEE AND INTEREST INCOME. Traditional loan programs have been reluctant to charge full-cost interest rates to microenterprises. In many level-one programs, the rate charged is negative in real terms.

In most countries there is a large difference between commercial rates of interest and rates charged in the informal financial sector. Microenterprise programs can charge much more than formal financial institutions and still underprice informal-sector alternatives. Moreover, studies have shown that microenterprise borrowers are far more sensitive to the availability and convenience of credit than to the interest rate (Christen 1989). The nonfinancial transaction costs borrowers normally face dwarf interest costs. Recognizing this fact, most level-two and level-three programs charge what they consider to be commercial rates, or more.

To make the transition from levels two and three to full self-sufficiency at level four, programs must maintain full-cost pricing policies: Interest and fee income must cover *all* cost elements. If full-cost pricing is adopted, the resulting rates will be well above those generally charged by commercial banks. Despite indications that full-cost pricing does not inhibit demand, few institutions have been willing or able to adopt it. In more and more countries, interest rate ceilings in the mainstream financial system are being removed, or at least raised to positive real levels. Even in countries with fully deregulated interest rate regimes, however, microenterprise programs have been reluctant to charge full cost, either because they believe that higher-than-commercial rates are unfair to poor clients or because they want to avoid the appearance of being unfair. These attitudes may prove as difficult to change as the earlier regulatory constraints.

Complicating this picture is the need for microenterprise programs to raise funds for rapid expansion. Initiating services in new areas requires a greater degree of subsidy than providing ongoing services. Operating costs associated with starting new branches cannot easily be internally generated. The same is true for funds for lending. Programs undergoing expansion need to raise increasing amounts of funds. These funds are likely to come dearer than the grants and soft loans available on a smaller scale. Expanding programs must often struggle with using more costly funds even while engaging in high-cost start-up activities. Therefore, programs that are expanding rapidly may look less financially self-sufficient than they would at a steady state.

The achievement of complete financial viability by microenterprise programs depends on the inherent ability of the techniques discussed here to yield a break-even operation. We do not yet know whether these techniques can consistently support level-four operations. On the basis of current experience, it seems safe to say that well-designed and well-implemented programs can yield level-three operations in any country in which cultural, economic, and institutional conditions are reasonably favorable. We do not know about level-four operations largely because so few programs have been willing to charge the higher interest rates that level four would require. Therefore, the effect of the higher rates on client demand and loan performance has had only limited testing.

It is incumbent upon governments and donors that currently support microenterprise programs to demand movement toward viability. This will require program supporters to fashion assistance in ways that complement the move rather than provide alibis for it. For example, donors can require increasing percentages of funds raised from savings, can guarantee loans from commercial sources, or can provide equity capital. At a minimum, grant funds should be limited to supporting operating costs so that programs are forced to use borrowed or deposited loan capital. Donors should use the subsidies at their disposal to equip organizations to rely on nonsubsidized sources of funds. Commercial financial institutions should be brought into partnership with microenterprise programs as early as possible, to bring both the know-how and the resolve for commercial viability. Such a shift in perspective need not involve rigid requirements. In each case, donors should recognize the level at which a program is operating and plan for moving it to the next level.

APPROPRIATE INSTITUTIONAL STRUCTURE

The path to expanding financial services for microenterprises outlined above can be realized through any number of institutional arrangements. This section discusses three institutional models that can support such services and their prospects for expansion.

LINKING NONGOVERNMENTAL PROGRAMS TO SOURCES OF FINANCE. Many of the microenterprise credit programs run by NGOs are not in a position to become true financial institutions that finance their lending largely from deposits. They may face legal restrictions on deposit taking, or they may decide not to take on the added responsibilities that come with handling individual deposits. The future of such programs depends on their ability to forge funding relationships with formal financial institutions. Such links are particularly desirable when deposit services offered by formal financial institutions are already widely available to microenterprises. Through links to these institutions, microenterprise lending programs can recirculate the capital raised through deposits, thus completing the financial loop.

The simplest arrangement is for microenterprise programs to finance their lending by borrowing from commercial banks. In order to be able to borrow in this way, microenterprise programs must meet two stringent criteria. First, they must be able to repay borrowed funds at a rate acceptable to the bank. If a commercial bank regards a loan to a microenterprise program as a commercial transaction, it will charge, at best, the prime lending rate charged to its favored customers. Second, programs must be able to assure banks that they are creditworthy. Very few microenterprise programs have as yet been able to meet these tests on their own. A number of programs, including several affiliated with ACCION International, do borrow from commercial banks, with support from other sources. In order to meet the interest rate targets, they blend commercial bank funding with soft loans or grants. As they grow, they plan to reduce their reliance on these soft sources. In order to meet creditworthiness standards, they use guarantees supplied through ACCION's bridge fund and the loan guarantee program of the U.S. Agency for International Development (USAID). Over time, programs can earn recognition as creditworthy borrowers, which can eventually lead to their receipt of bank loans without external guarantees, using their own funds and loan assets as security. The success of early efforts along these lines suggests that commercial banks potentially can channel a significant amount of resources through NGOs.

In some countries, so-called second-level institutions are being created to relieve credit programs of the necessity of building relationships directly with individual banks. These institutions act as brokers or wholesalers between banks and NGO-based programs. They raise funds from commercial, governmental, and donor sources and supply them to individual microenterprise programs. This service is helpful to the microenterprise programs because it gathers funds from a number of sources, and it is helpful to commercial banks because it takes on the burden of supervision of the individual credit programs. The second-level institution must enforce performance standards that permit banks to have confidence in the loans they make. Second-level institutions exist, among other places, in Colombia through ACCION, in the Philippines through Opportunity International, and in the Dominican Republic through FONDOMICRO. Many issues surrounding these institutions are only beginning to be resolved, including their financial viability, the best ways for them to enforce performance by credit programs, interest rate spread requirements, and the best division of risks among the various parties.

If successful, present efforts will demonstrate to banks that resource allocation to poor microentrepreneurs need not mean a sacrifice of either income or safety in the name of good deeds. Only if banks are so convinced will they commit significant amounts of resources.

TRANSFORMING PROGRAMS INTO SPECIALIZED FINANCIAL INSTITUTIONS. Microenterprise programs are carried out by a variety of institutions, from grant-oriented NGOs to those striving for self-sufficiency. These institutions must undergo several changes to become financial institutions that engage in lending and capturing deposits.

At the structural level, these institutions must reorganize to provide both savings and credit in a manner that will allow for expansion. At the first opportunity, the organizational structure must be modified to support the capturing of deposits and the provision of credit. The functions and the makeup of each department, as well as the relationship among departments, must also be reorganized. For example, most microenterprise programs contain a large operations department that provides credit and a much smaller financial department that tracks the uses of resources from grants and soft loans. The addition of savings services would require fundamental changes in both operational and financial departments. If the organization were close to level four, it would likely have undertaken some of these changes already. Chapter 12 presents the case of BancoSol, a commercial bank that started as an NGO.

A second structural change required is for the organization to use some form of franchise or branch office system to continue expanding its operations. Therefore, the organizational structure would require information systems adequate for a decentralized operation.

Legal considerations are a key factor in defining how these institutions will change internally. The legal framework in a country determines whether an institution can take deposits. In some countries, the law permits organizations outside the banking system to capture savings directly. In most countries, however, this is not the case. Institutions may modify themselves in order to fit within the existing law, for example, by creating a cooperative or a credit union arm, as has the Association of Solidarity Groups in Colombia, discussed in Chapter 13.

When institutions capture deposits, they must comply with regulations that govern all banks. These regulations are designed to maintain the stability of the financial system. The ability of specialized microenterprise institutions to cope with these requirements is untested and is therefore a topic for further exploration.

SPECIALIZED OPERATIONS WITHIN COMMERCIAL FINANCIAL INSTITUTIONS. To date, only a handful of commercial banks have shown interest in taking on the microenterprise client group. Yet it is possible for such an arrangement to succeed, as demonstrated by the tremendous success of the BRI Unit Banking system, which is run by a large government-owned bank and serves over eight million savers and two million borrowers (see Chapters 2 and 11). Major advantages of placing microenterprise operations in commercial banks include the infrastructure available to banks through branch networks, access to liquidity, and commercial orientation. Banks must be educated in the special techniques described above, however, for no bank will succeed with microenterprises by applying its standard operating procedures. At this time, banks are generally unaware of these techniques, of the promise these techniques may hold for serving microenterprises commercially, and of the changes required to make microenterprise lending successful.

POLICIES FOR PROMOTING FINANCIAL SERVICES FOR MICROENTERPRISES

Governments in many countries are moving toward including informal-sector enterprises in their national agendas. Along the way, a number of policies will have to be reformulated. The actors that must review their policies include national, regional, and local governments; financial institutions; and multilateral and bilateral donor organizations.

Financial system policies should foster the processes of transformation that have been described above. They should:

- Make it easier for programs offering specialized financial services to microenterprises to become financially self-sufficient.

- Support the efforts of NGO-based programs to gain access to commercial sources of funds.

- Support the efforts of NGO-based programs to become specialized financial institutions.

- Encourage mainstream financial institutions to develop specialized microenterprise operations of their own.

In addressing each of these tasks, the first priority should be interest rate deregulation. The ability to charge full-cost interest rates is the best strategy microenterprise lending programs have for becoming financially self-sufficient, after they have adopted the lending techniques advocated here. The interest rates that microenterprises will have to charge will be substantially higher than what are now commonly thought of as market or commercial rates, because they must cover the high unit costs of administration of very small loans. Even under deregulation, however, self-imposed and political restrictions are likely to remain. Governments, lenders, and donors can lead the way in changing attitudes by making and following firm policy determinations to require full-cost pricing policies from any organization that requests financing or special assistance from them. Interest rates on deposits should also be allowed to rise, in order to provide appropriate incentives for microenterprises to use savings rather than credit to finance lending operations.

Regulations governing acceptance of deposits must also be reviewed, although this will be a thorny issue. In many countries, NGO programs are prevented from accepting deposits by banking laws. As Chapter 3 discusses at length, the main purposes of such regulations are to protect individual deposits and secure the health of financial institutions. Governments have a responsibility to both depositors and financial institutions to ensure that depositor confidence is not violated. Therefore, when nonfinancial institutions begin to accept deposits, governments are legitimately concerned.

But as this chapter argues, savings services are as important to microenterprises as credit services. Savings services are also important to the viability of the institutions serving microenterprises. A way must be found to support savings elements in microenterprise programs based in new types of financial institutions. One solution may lie in supervisory standards tailored to specialized operations or institutions. In many countries, credit union systems operate according to explicitly designed rules that are promoted worldwide through the World Council of Credit Unions (see Chapter 8). As increasing numbers of microenterprise credit programs transform themselves into financial institutions, they will have to come together to consider these issues and present joint proposals to governments. Second-level institutions can play a role in developing standards and supervision procedures for the individual programs they serve and in lobbying for changes in legislation where needed.

It is premature to prescribe government policy toward deposit taking by microenterprise programs, but possible elements of such a policy can be identified. Programs offering credit for microenterprises would be permitted to take deposits, provided they meet minimum equity requirements, have adequate loan loss reserves, place a limit on the percentage of deposits that could be lent, and maintain proper accounting standards. In order to prevent misuse of any special provision by individuals wishing to circumvent normal banking regulations, programs could be required to keep loan sizes small.

At the same time, governments should allow banks and other formal institutions to develop microenterprise programs using the new techniques. This may require that standards governing loan collateral, approval, documentation, and the like be adapted for microenterprise loans.

The success of these efforts to make policy more supportive of financial services for microenterprises will depend to a great degree on the general economic climate in which they take place. Services being developed in a growing economy have a much better chance of succeeding than those facing economic stagnation. Similarly, if microenterprise finance is to be integrated into the formal financial system, that system should not be laboring under credit constraints that dry up liquidity. It is particularly important for inflation to be controlled, as high inflation plays havoc with interest rate structures and can quickly ruin carefully crafted plans for financial self-sufficiency. These macroeconomic conditions should be taken into account when discussing policy toward microenterprise finance.

Finally, a word about the role of multilateral and bilateral donor organizations is warranted. Local forces tend to argue that financial self-sufficiency is either unattainable or unnecessary. Governments and even private organizations have long viewed microenterprise programs as, at best, an income-redistribution strategy or, at worst, a means to court political favor among the ranks of the poor. The donor organizations, together with successful microenterprise finance institutions, should take the lead in advocating a financial systems perspective toward microenterprise development by demanding better performance from the programs they fund, promoting learning across countries, and encouraging governments to adopt more supportive interest rate and regulatory policies.

The next decade may not see the realization of the goal described at the outset of this chapter, but if all parties pursue that goal under the framework outlined here, we may come surprisingly close.

NOTES

This chapter is reprinted from *World Development*, vol. 20, no. 11, pp. 1561–72, copyright 1992, with kind permission from Pergamon Press Ltd, Headington Hill Hall, Oxford OX3 0BW, UK.

1. The definition of *microenterprise* is always arbitrary. In this chapter, we use the term to refer to enterprises with up to ten employees. This definition spans the size range from part-time income-generating activities of individuals, through family-operated businesses, to very small enterprises employing hired labor. The majority of the enterprises in most developing countries fall in the lower end of this spectrum. On another continuum, the term *microenterprise* encompasses all types of urban and nonfarm rural activities, from manufacturing to commerce to transport.

2. Groups provide the opportunity in many instances for achieving nonfinancial objectives, ranging from social consciousness-raising to nutrition education. The complex relationships among individual clients, groups, and lenders involve information asymmetries and the principal-agent problem. Huppi and Feder (1990) have made a start at examining such questions.

3. Examples include the Grameen Bank, several programs of ACCION, and the Badan Kredit Kecamatan.

4. For a listing of some of the largest such programs and their achievements, see Holt and Ribe (1990).

CHAPTER 2

Savings Mobilization and Microenterprise Finance: The Indonesian Experience

Marguerite S. Robinson

SAVINGS AT THE LOCAL LEVEL: MYTH AND REALITY

Throughout the world and across many cultures and income groups, people save for varied purposes, including emergencies, investment, consumption, social obligations, education of children, pilgrimages, sickness, disability, and retirement.

Extensive household savings have been reported from developing countries around the world for at least three decades. A 1962 United Nations study showed that household savings made up one-half to two-thirds of total savings in seven Asian countries (United Nations 1962; see Adams 1978). During the 1970s and 1980s, substantial household savings were reported from rural areas of developing countries worldwide. Rural savings of various kinds (in rotating savings and credit associations [ROSCAs], in savings and loan associations, in nonfinancial forms, and so on) were widely documented from many areas of Asia, Africa, and Latin America.[1]

Households save, and they will save in a financial form if appropriate institutions and instruments are available. This message has been stated clearly, convincingly, and with increasing evidence since the 1960s. In their extensive writings on rural financial markets, Adams, Bouman, Vogel, Von Pischke, and others have suggested that appropriate savings instruments providing positive real rates of return can induce households to put more of their savings into financial form; this, in turn, "may increase the average rate of return realized by the household on its savings portfolio and induce the household to divert more of its income to S (savings-investment activities)" (Adams 1978, 550).

Households are not the only savers at the local level. Local enterprises, groups, organizations, and institutions also save. Such savings

27

are potentially available to financial institutions offering security, convenience, liquidity, and returns.

The arguments that financial markets influence the forms and the amount of savings have so far had relatively little influence on policy decisions affecting the development of local financial institutions (Adams 1978). Neither the reality of extensive liquidity among households in many rural and urban areas of developing countries nor the importance of savings mobilization for local financial markets and enterprise development has yet been sufficiently understood.[2] One consequence is that few financial institutions provide appropriate deposit instruments in rural areas of developing countries, and few policymakers or donor agencies have made savings mobilization at the local level a high priority for economic development. Savings has rightly been called the forgotten half of rural finance (Vogel 1984b; see also Adams and Vogel 1986).

THE MYTHS

Two widespread myths prevail with regard to household savings in developing countries, particularly in rural areas. The first is the myth of pervasive rural undersavings; the second is the assumption that demand for financial savings instruments is low in most rural areas of developing countries (Braverman and Guasch forthcoming).[3] Such misguided assumptions are often extended to middle- and lower-income urban households as well.

It has been widely assumed that low institutional deposits in rural areas demonstrate that rural households cannot save because they are too poor, will not save because they prefer to use their incomes for consumption, or choose to save in other forms. Since there is no significant demand for financial savings instruments, the argument goes, why develop financial institutions with savings programs?

The view that there is little demand for rural savings has, in fact, become a self-fulfilling prophecy. Financial institutions in rural areas of developing countries, with a few significant exceptions, have generally been unsuccessful in mobilizing savings:

> Commercial banks and state-funded institutions have not mobilized much rural savings. The estimate of the percentage of loanable funds from rural sources has ranged from 5 percent to 40 percent, with the median much closer to the former than the latter figure. (Braverman and Guasch 1986, 1256)

THE REASONS FOR LACK OF DEPOSITS. The reasons for low institutional deposits, however, are often neither undersavings nor lack of demand for financial savings instruments, but the structure of services and institutions. The majority of projects for local finance are still concerned only with credit, usually subsidized credit. The low interest rates that characterize subsidized credit programs discourage savings mobilization. Organizations dispensing subsidized credit normally either are forbidden to mobilize savings or do not collect voluntary savings because financial regulations make deposit mobilization unprofitable.

The problem can be summarized briefly. Subsidized lending programs provide a limited volume of cheap loans. As these are scarce and desirable, the loans tend to be allocated predominantly to local elites who have the influence to obtain them, bypassing those who need smaller loans (which can usually be obtained commercially only from informal lenders at far higher interest rates). In addition, there is substantial evidence from developing countries worldwide that subsidized rural credit programs result in high arrears, generate losses both for the financial institutions administering the programs and for the government or donor agencies, and depress institutional savings and, thereby, the development of profitable, viable rural financial institutions.[4]

Credit subsidies, however, are often viewed as a mechanism for obtaining support for the government in rural areas (see Blair 1984). The subsidies, which come to be expected by local elites, are difficult to dislodge once they are begun. The result is that the programs persist on a large scale and tend to prevent the growth of viable rural financial institutions, since these can be sustained only by raising deposits.

THE EFFECTS ON MICROENTERPRISES. The dearth of institutional deposit facilities at the local level has an adverse effect on savers in general and on small-scale entrepreneurs in particular. There are two main reasons.

First, self-finance of investment is especially important for small and microenterprises. However, options for informal financial savings at the local level tend to offer security or returns, but normally not both. Thus, opportunities for financial savings outside the formal sector are typically either (1) low risk with no, or very low, returns (for example, ROSCAs, various types of savings clubs, and deposits made to employers or commodity wholesalers for safekeeping); or (2) risky, but with a possibility of positive real returns (for example, some small-scale finance companies and "investment" groups). In addition, both types often place restrictions on liquidity, a crucial requirement for microenterprise finance. Deposit instruments for voluntary savings in formal institutions are often the only mechanisms that can provide the saver with a combination of convenience, security, liquidity, and returns. These are rarely available at the local level, however.

Second, small entrepreneurs are typically bypassed by subsidized credit programs, and nonsubsidized institutional credit is often not available to them. Therefore, one of the most important benefits of institutional savings for microenterprise finance is an indirect one.

Creditworthy small and microenterprises can benefit from the expanded volume of institutional lending made possible by deposit mobilization (larger enterprises are more likely to have financing already, often through subsidized credit programs). Substantial growth in institutional deposits can both significantly increase the amount of credit available to smaller entrepreneurs and provide loans at much lower interest rates than are otherwise available in the informal commercial market. This is especially true in the case of the trade sector, which has been ignored by most rural credit programs.

SHATTERING THE MYTHS

Indonesia's rural banking system recently demolished the myths concerning the difficulties widely believed to be inherent in mobilizing local savings in developing nations. Massive local savings mobilization has occurred in Indonesia since 1986. This became possible because, by the early 1980s, the country's economics ministers understood that the government's subsidized credit programs offered since the early 1970s were deficient. They were prepared to try a new approach.

Beginning in 1984, a program of general rural credit offered at commercial interest rates was introduced in combination with rural savings mobilization. Administered by the Bank Rakyat Indonesia (BRI), a state-owned commercial bank, both were later extended to urban areas. Because Indonesia's approach to rural financial intermediation has been so successful, reference is made in this chapter to various aspects of the savings component of this program. See Chapter 11 for a detailed discussion of the lending side of BRI's local-level banking system.

Before 1984, Indonesia's approach to financial intermediation at the local level was similar to that found in many countries today: Institutional credit was subsidized, losses were high, deposits were low. After more than a decade of offering savings accounts in the country's more than 3,600 "village banks" located nationwide at the subdistrict level, deposits in BRI's unit banking system (or Unit Desa system) totaled only $17.6 million in 1983.

The primary purpose of the unit banking system was to channel subsidized credit from the government to farmers, especially rice farmers, through BRI's unit banks; this was known as the BIMAS (an acronym for Bimbingan Massal, or Mass Guidance) credit program. Since BRI was required to lend at a 12 percent annual effective interest rate and to pay 15 percent annual interest on most deposits, there was no incentive within the bank to mobilize savings through the unit banking system. As one depositor complained to the author in 1983, "BRI gives beautiful calendars to its customers every year, but only to borrowers. As a saver, am I not also a customer?"

With the exception of a few high-level policymakers, however, the consensus was that the poor deposit record of the unit banking system could be attributed to rural undersavings and to the villagers' lack of trust in banks, their lack of education and consequent aversion to the use of financial institutions, and even their "psychological inability" to make use of banks (Bank Indonesia Jakarta 1987). These views persisted despite mounting evidence of extensive household savings. Since 1968, studies of household savings in Indonesia had found the marginal propensity to save to be between 10 and 20 percent (see Kelley and Williamson 1968, 390; World Bank 1983).[5] Yet these results were typically either ignored or disbelieved.

In 1983, however, the Indonesian government began a series of major financial reforms. The first of these, issued in June 1983, permitted banks to set their own interest rates on most loans and deposits. As expected, this deregulation of interest rates had immediate and far-reaching effects on local finance throughout the country.

In 1984, Indonesia introduced a program of general rural credit offered at commercial interest rates (known as Kredit Umum Pedesaan, or KUPEDES); this was complemented in 1986 by a new program of savings mobilization designed specifically to meet local demand. The spread between loan and deposit interest rates was set to enable institutional profitability, and both programs were offered nationwide through BRI's unit banking system. The system, which had previously generated considerable losses for both the government and the bank, became profitable in 1986; by 1991 it supplied over two-thirds of BRI's total profits.

The new savings program offers a mix of deposit instruments and features a liquid instrument, previously unavailable at the local level. The result of the new program was that village bank deposits increased from $17.6 million at the time of the financial deregulation in 1983 to $1.3 billion in 1991.

This dramatic growth in the mobilization of local deposits resulted from a combination of factors. The most crucial of these were (1) a spread that provided institutional incentives for savings mobilization and permitted the profitability of the system, (2) extensive study of local demand for financial services and systematic identification of potential savers, (3) the design of banking instruments and services to meet that demand, and (4) effective leadership in both BRI and the government.

Extensive discussions with household members, enterprise heads, and leaders of organizations in widely differing regions of Indonesia during the 1980s offered massive evidence for two conclusions.[6] First, economic growth and monetization of the economy in rural areas had created a large and predominantly unsupplied demand for banking facilities. As an Indonesian villager commented, "I used to save in goats, but goats take a lot of work. Now the shepherds are all in school and the parents have jobs. Now we have no time to save in goats. We prefer to save in the bank." Second, there was large demand at the local level for a liquid financial savings instrument. Although the discussion here concerns primarily rural Indonesia, fieldwork in the late 1980s indicated that the banking needs of middle- and lower-middle income neighborhoods in urban areas are similar in many respects to those of villages. In 1989, BRI began to open unit banks in urban areas; these became profitable rapidly.

Before starting its new savings program, BRI conducted extensive research into existing forms of savings in rural areas, both formal and informal. Common forms of savings and savers' views of them are discussed below. Although some of the specifics may be particular to Indonesia, the general principles illustrated by the findings of this research have widespread application for developing countries.

THE ROLE OF SAVINGS IN LOCAL FINANCIAL MARKETS

CASH AND NONFINANCIAL SAVINGS

CASH. BRI found a widespread view among households and enterprises: They kept more cash in the house than they considered desirable because they did not know what else to do with it. One reason for not wanting too much cash at home was security, which was considered a major problem. Equally important, however, was the view that if one had cash on hand, it would be difficult to avoid lending to kinspeople and neighbors. Holding some cash in the house, however, was considered important, primarily for use in emergencies. Also, for traders, businesspeople, and artisans, the opportunity to purchase supplies at low cost might come unexpectedly. Beyond such needs for ready cash, households and enterprises throughout the country said that what they wanted was a savings account from which they could withdraw on demand in a conveniently located and secure bank. Since this was not available, they kept their cash at home.

GRAIN. Attitudes toward saving in grain, particularly rice, were similar to those expressed about cash savings. Virtually everyone wanted to have enough rice on hand to meet a reasonable level of unexpected need above anticipated requirements, but very few wished to store grain beyond that. Unlike cash, few villagers actually stored excess grain (partly a result of the general availability of rice in the 1980s, combined with the problems of grain storage). In addition, there was a strong village ethic that if you had grain stored, you had to give or lend

it to kin and neighbors in the preharvest season. Except for some informal commercial lenders, villagers said that they were generally relieved not to have to give loans. There were analogous reasons
for wanting savings accounts: Villagers also tended to be relieved
not to have to borrow from relatives and friends because, except in special circumstances, intravillage borrowing tended to lower the borrower's status.

ANIMALS. In general, rural households preferred to have on hand a
few of the larger animals: goats, sheep, cows (and pigs in some non-
Muslim areas). Except for those who bred or traded animals profes-
sionally, however, most did not want to care for more than a few. They
perceived the opportunity cost clearly. Particularly in densely popu-
lated areas where grass was scarce and space limited, the care of such
animals was considered onerous and time-consuming. Villagers said
that although a number of goats could be exchanged for a cow, which
would require less care, this presented another problem: Cows were
less liquid than goats. As one man put it, "When you have to pay the
school fees, you cannot sell the cow's leg." Overall, the disadvantages
of saving in animals (opportunity cost for household labor, liquidity
problems, lack of space, and the risks of shareherding) were usually
considered to outweigh the advantages (relatively high returns given
normal propagation).

GOLD. In the early 1980s, it was believed by many government bu-
reaucrats and bankers that a savings account could not compete with
gold as a form of savings in the rural areas; villagers, however, usually
disagreed. They frequently said that although gold might be a good
long-term investment, it was not suitable for the needs of most families,
beyond the amounts worn as jewelry. The most important perceived
advantages of gold were its liquidity and its ability to serve as a hedge
against currency devaluation and inflation. There were two primary
disadvantages, which, taken together, were widely thought by most
households and local enterprises to outweigh the benefits. The first was
that gold prices were generally stagnant during the 1980s, and villagers
in various regions reported that when they sold gold, they took a 5 to
12 percent loss on the buying price. The second was that saving in gold
presented a serious security problem. It had to be hidden from both
outsiders who might steal it and insiders who might appropriate
it, claiming shared rights. "If we have gold in the house, we cannot
sleep peacefully."

LAND. Government and BRI officials also tended to assume, in the
early 1980s, that rural households wanted to use their savings to invest
in land, either through purchase or by renting land for cultivation. It
was true that land control was a high priority for many of Indonesia's
villagers. Under village conditions, however, there was usually more
excess liquidity at any given time than opportunity to purchase land

suitable for the needs of the particular buyer. Thus, although villagers often wanted to purchase or rent land, these goals were perceived not as contradictory but as complementary to the holding of financial savings. Families waiting for suitable land to become available for purchase, and farmers who calculated the risks of renting land as too high for a particular season or stage of the household cycle, could benefit from the use of appropriate financial savings instruments. Older couples whose children were employed in nonfarm activities might decide to retire from land management and prefer liquid assets. In addition, the medium- and long-term savings goals of some rural households were not focused on control of additional land but were aimed instead at trade and business expansion, construction, higher education, and so on.

In summary, rural households that could afford to do so usually kept some grain and cash, a few animals, and some gold on hand; they attempted to control land as appropriate for their resources and requirements. Yet many households and enterprises had excess liquidity (permanently, seasonally, or occasionally) beyond that which could optimally be kept in these forms. As one villager commented, "My investment opportunities are not the same throughout the year. I need a place to store money safely while I look for the right openings."

FINANCIAL SAVINGS AT THE LOCAL LEVEL

Household, enterprise, and group savings in financial form may be held in ways that are informal, quasi-formal, or formal. Informal financial markets are ubiquitous. Although they are largely unregulated and unreported, it has long been recognized that these markets are not unorganized. They form part of the local political economy; financial channels and market shares of lenders are inextricably related to the local distribution of wealth and power, market interlinkages, political alliances, information flows, and so forth.

Informal markets are linked in a variety of ways with the formal financial sector and with quasi-formal bodies. The latter are unlicensed and generally unsupervised financial intermediaries that may, nevertheless, operate under particular laws and regulations (for example, some credit cooperatives and credit unions). The formal-informal distinction is not a dichotomy but a continuum. Thus, various kinds of financial intermediaries (for example, pawnshops, small-scale finance companies, cooperatives, and credit unions) occupy positions on the formal-informal axis that vary from country to country, and sometimes even within countries (see Germidis, Kessler, and Meghir 1991).

The extent and character of the interactions among formal, quasi-formal, and informal financial markets in rural areas can vary considerably, depending on the degree of regulation in the formal sector; the extent of monetization in the rural areas; the public's confidence in the government in general and in the available financial institutions in particular; the ease of customer access to formal financial services; the activities of parallel and black markets (see Roemer and Jones 1991); and a variety of geographic, economic, cultural, and other factors.

Informal financial savings may be held in ROSCAs or in nonrotating or regular savings and credit associations (RESCAs) (see Bouman 1989), or they may be placed for safekeeping with local patrons. Savings are also held in quasi-formal bodies such as some credit cooperatives, credit unions, and various forms of credit societies. Savings in formal financial institutions may be forced savings (which often accompany subsidized credit programs) or voluntary savings. As discussed above, appropriate instruments for mobilizing the latter are not widely available at the local level in many countries. For savers, appropriately designed institutional deposit instruments usually provide the only opportunity to combine security, convenience, liquidity, and returns. For financial institutions, mobilization of voluntary savings is the key to long-term viability.

THE BENEFITS OF INSTITUTIONAL SAVINGS

Well-designed and well-delivered deposit services can simultaneously benefit households, enterprises, groups, the participating financial institutions, and the government. Good savings programs can contribute to local, regional, and national economic development and can help improve equity. The benefits from institutional savings at local levels may include the following; all have been realized in the Indonesian case.

BENEFITS TO HOUSEHOLDS. Institutional savings provide numerous benefits to households, including the following:

- *Liquidity.* Rapid access to at least some financial savings is considered essential by many households in monetized or partially monetized economies. Liquidity is crucial for mobilizing household savings. The demand for deposit instruments permitting an unlimited number of withdrawals is high because people save for emergencies and for investment opportunities, which may arise at any time. Thus, in areas characterized by economic growth and development and by a reasonable level of political stability, potential household demand for liquid deposit instruments in financial institutions may be unexpectedly high.

- *Returns on deposits.* Positive real returns on deposits are typically not available at low-risk outside financial institutions. When such institutions offer appropriate deposit instruments, the interest can be used by the household as an income flow or as savings. Fixed-deposit accounts featuring lower liquidity and higher returns, especially when held in conjunction with liquid accounts, are suitable in various ways for the types of savings mentioned below.

- *Savings for consumption.* Households with uneven income streams (from agriculture, fishing, and enterprises with seasonal variations) can save for consumption during low-income periods.

- *Savings for investment.* Saving for development of household enterprises is discussed below. Households also tend to save for other kinds of investment, such as children's education, house construction, and electrification.

- *Savings for social and religious purposes and for consumer durables.* Social ceremonies (birth, puberty rites, weddings, and funerals) and religious donations or pilgrimages are some of the long-term goals for which people frequently save. Others are consumer durables; depending on household income level, these vary from cooking pots to automobiles.

- *Savings for retirement, ill health, or disability.* Saving for old age or disability may take the form of building retirement savings or helping to establish junior members of the household, who will then have the responsibility of caring for their elders.

- *Savings instead of or in addition to credit.* Households save in order to self-finance investments and to avoid paying what are often very high interest rates in the informal commercial credit market. Self-financed investments are particularly important for middle- and lower-income households, which often do not have access to institutional credit. The interest rates charged by informal commercial lenders, typically flat rates charged on the original balance, are widely reported to range from 2 percent to over 35 percent per month, with rates between 2 percent and 10 percent per month especially common.[7] In general, the poorer the borrower, the higher the interest rate, since lower-income borrowers normally have fewer credit options. Many households hold savings accounts and loans simultaneously, especially if institutional loans are available to them. This strategy permits some savings to be held for emergencies, while loans, used for working and investment capital and in some cases for consumption, are repaid from income flows.

- *Savings to build credit ratings and as collateral.* Institutional savers may also use their deposits to build credit ratings and as collateral for loans. These features are especially important for those who do not own land.

BENEFITS TO ENTERPRISES. Many of the benefits gained from institutional savings by households are also applicable to enterprises (security, returns, self-finance of investment, and so on). Enterprises at all scales tend to have high demand for liquidity; many also have high demand for transfer facilities.

Household savings are typically the main source of small and microenterprise finance, but in many cases small entrepreneurs must also borrow on the informal credit market at rates that, in Indonesia, range from three to more than twenty times nonsubsidized bank rates. Therefore, small and microenterprises can benefit from institutional savings programs both directly, through the encouragment of self-finance of investment, and indirectly, through the expanded volume of institutional lending at much lower rates than are otherwise available.

As financial institutions become sustainable through local savings mobilization, institutional financing for small and microenterprises becomes feasible on a large scale. In Indonesia, many small and microenterprises have been financed by KUPEDES loans, including those in trade, agriculture, livestock, poultry, dairying, food processing, services, and manufacturing (for example, textiles, garments, leather goods, crafts, furniture, jewelry, and herbal medicines). The important effect that voluntary savings mobilization can have on such enterprises is demonstrated clearly by the Indonesian example discussed below.

BENEFITS TO LOCAL GROUPS, ORGANIZATIONS, AND INSTITUTIONS. Deposit instruments that permit savings to be held in the name of organizations and institutions provide significant benefits to the depositors. In Indonesia, the provision that savings accounts may be held in the name of a group, organization, or institution opened a large new market for rural deposits derived from village treasuries, government offices, schools, religious institutions, development programs disbursing funds for rural projects, and a plethora of local organizations (for example, employees', women's, youth, and sports associations; informal savings and loan associations; and voluntary agencies). Previously, the group's president or treasurer held the organization's funds; the members of many groups, although not necessarily the leaders, preferred the new arrangement (see Robinson 1992).[8] Although not yet common in other countries, group savings accounts in Indonesia have been reported to improve the financial security of the group, decrease opportunities for corruption, and improve the accountability and financial management of group funds. Institutional savings also provide groups with the opportunity to earn returns on their deposits.

BENEFITS TO FINANCIAL INSTITUTIONS. Deposits mobilized in conjunction with commercial credit programs enable sustainable financial institutions. As of December 31, 1991, BRI's KUPEDES program had 1.8 million loans outstanding that were fully financed by unit bank deposits from 8.6 million savings accounts. In 1983, none of BRI's over 3,600 unit banks was profitable; by 1991, nearly all—except for the recently opened units—were earning profits. KUPEDES supplies an increasing amount of the large demand for local credit at commercial interest rates. With deposit mobilization more than covering outstanding KUPEDES loans, the prognosis seems excellent for the long-term viability of the unit banking system. This appears to be the main factor differentiating BRI from other financial institutions that reach microenterprises.

BENEFITS TO THE ECONOMY, DEVELOPMENT, AND EQUITY. Local savings mobilization benefits the economy directly by increasing the resources available for productive investment. Effective savings mobilization is crucial for local development because it encourages self-finance of investments; it permits the supply of a large demand for credit at commercial interest rates, which typically range from 5 to 50 percent of the rates charged by informal commercial lenders; and it enables the growth of sustainable financial institutions.

In the early 1980s in Indonesia, BRI staff asked villagers why they did not make use of TABANAS (the national savings program administered by Bank Indonesia, the central bank); TABANAS had been available through BRI's unit banks since the mid-1970s. The replies were nearly unanimous. People from one end of the country to the other responded that TABANAS permitted withdrawals only twice a month, and that the restriction on withdrawals was unacceptable.

Indonesia's new savings program was designed, accordingly, on four main principles: (1) liquidity is the key to local savings mobilization, (2) convenience and security are crucial, (3) a mix of instruments is needed to meet varied local demand, and (4) a set of deposit instruments offering different proportions of liquidity and returns can simultaneously meet demand and, in combination with the KUPEDES program of general rural credit, permit institutional profitability. BRI's unit bank savings program, which mobilized deposits from both stocks and flows at the local level, has shown that an institution can profitably offer a set of deposit instruments for voluntary savings that provides the saver with convenience, security, liquidity, and returns.

Indonesia is an exception, however. Although the reality is that institutional savings, and consequently the development of sustainable financial institutions, are depressed by the ubiquitous subsidized credit programs of developing countries, both the myth of rural undersavings and the presence of subsidized credit programs persist. As Sideri put it:

> The special role of savings mobilization for the development process and its actual realization is barely treated in most of the relevant development literature. . . . Unlike Chaucer's character who "knew the taverns well in every town" development economists do not seem to know this one tavern, possibly because not in town. (Sideri 1984, 207)

Indonesia's success in local savings mobilization in the second half of the 1980s can be summarized succinctly: The spread was set to provide incentives for savings mobilization; the bank staff went into the villages regularly, studied local financial markets, and found the missing "tavern."

A CASE STUDY IN SUCCESS: FINANCIAL INTERMEDIATION AT THE LOCAL LEVEL IN INDONESIA

THE CONDITIONS FOR SUCCESS

Had BRI attempted to develop its rural banking system in the mid-1960s instead of the mid-1980s, it undoubtedly would have failed. With over 600 percent inflation in 1966 and sharply decreasing real per capita income, falling production and investment, and a massive budget deficit, a successful rural banking initiative would have been impossible.

Beginning in 1967 under General and then President Suharto's New Order government, however, stabilization and rehabilitation policies were given the highest priority. These were followed by over two decades of sustained emphasis on economic development, accompanied by political stability. A considerable share of the wealth gained from the oil booms of the 1970s was invested in the development of the country's rural areas, in turn creating rural demand for banking services. Those investments laid the foundations for the achievements of the 1980s, including the attainment of rice self-sufficiency, employment creation, real per capita income growth, and substantial rural development. During the 1980s, major financial deregulations and tax, trade, and investment reforms strengthened the economy while permitting the development of a profitable nationwide rural banking system.

BRI's unit banks, established nationwide in the early 1970s in order to dispense agricultural credit, made banking activities familiar to many rural people. Government deregulations in the 1980s permitted the introduction of banking instruments that could both meet local demand and permit bank profitability. Control of inflation and political stability contributed to the growing trust of the people in government banks. These were the conditions under which BRI's experiment in nationwide rural banking was undertaken.

BRI'S UNIT BANKING SYSTEM: OVERVIEW

BRI's special assignment as one of five state-owned commercial banks is to provide banking services to the rural areas, with particular emphasis on agricultural credit. In accordance with this mandate, BRI developed a rural banking network in the early 1970s.[9] Known as the BRI Unit Banking system, it was begun in Yogyakarta in 1969 as part of a pilot project for the national rice intensification program, BIMAS.[10]

Until the end of 1983, the unit banking system functioned primarily as a channeling agent for subsidized rural lending programs, especially the BIMAS credit program. Savings accounts were offered in the unit banks beginning in 1976; however, the annual interest rates set by the government at 12 percent for loans and 15 percent for most deposits provided a disincentive for the bank to mobilize savings. By June 1983, deposits in over 3,600 unit banks nationwide totaled only Rp 16 billion (U.S. $17.6 million). In 1983, BRI's unit banking system sustained a loss of Rp 25 billion (U.S. $27.5 million).

Between December 31, 1983, and December 31, 1991, however, BRI's unit banking system extended 10.1 million loans totaling Rp 7 trillion (approximately U.S. $3.6 billion in 1991 dollars) in its KUPEDES program of general rural credit. The KUPEDES annual effective interest rate is 33 percent for prompt payers (late payers are penalized). As of December 31, 1991, outstanding KUPEDES loans totaled U.S. $746 million, with a long-term loss ratio of only 3.29 percent; unit bank deposits totaled U.S. $1.30 billion on the same date.[11] Interest rates were set so that the spread permitted institutional profitability, and the new program proved to be effective both in meeting the varied local demand for financial savings instruments and in fully financing KUPEDES credit. KUPEDES began in 1984; BRI's unit banking system broke even by early 1986; by 1991, the system contributed over two-thirds of BRI's total profits.

MOBILIZING LOCAL SAVINGS

BRI's new savings program was designed to meet local demand for savings instruments that offer different mixes of liquidity and returns.

The program, designed after extensive fieldwork throughout the country, was based on studies of local financial markets and on the views of the participants in these markets. This methodology, in itself, was a major innovation, and one that paid off.

Four savings instruments, with different ratios of liquidity and returns, were made available at the unit banks during 1986 as part of BRI's new rural savings program. SIMPEDES, a deposit instrument that permits an unlimited number of withdrawals, was introduced as the flagship of BRI's new rural savings program, which was extended in 1989 to urban areas as well. TABANAS, the national savings program that had been offered since 1976, was continued. Deposito Berjangka, a fixed-deposit instrument previously available from BRI only through its branches, was now offered at the unit banks as well. The fourth instrument, Giro, a type of current account used primarily by institutions with special requirements, was also made available at the unit banks.

Unlike the KUPEDES program of general rural credit, the savings program was developed gradually. In the case of KUPEDES, the imminent termination of the BIMAS credit program, combined with the fixed costs of maintaining over 3,600 unprofitable unit banks, forced an all-or-nothing decision in mid-1983: The rice banks would either be closed or, beginning in 1984, be transformed into real banks, starting with a commercial lending program. With regard to rural savings mobilization, however, there was both less urgency and less information about demand. Fieldwork throughout the country beginning in 1982 had shown that there was extensive rural demand, in general, for financial savings and, in particular, for liquid savings accounts in which financial stocks (usually kept in the house) and savings from income flows could be safely deposited. In addition, many villagers wanted to convert some nonfinancial savings into institutional deposits if these could be held in liquid form.

The magnitude of the demand, however, was unknown in 1984. BRI decided, therefore, to proceed through a series of pilot projects under which different deposit instruments could be tested and local demand studied. Accordingly, SIMPEDES was introduced in a pilot project in Sukabumi district (West Java) in November 1984; the instrument was extended to twelve other district-level pilot projects in 1985 and became available nationwide in 1986.

The most important characteristic of SIMPEDES is its liquidity; in addition, SIMPEDES pays generally positive real returns except on very small accounts. TABANAS, the only savings instrument previously available at the local level, permits only two withdrawals per month. Also in contrast to TABANAS, SIMPEDES allows deposits to be made in the name of organizations and institutions. Other features of SIMPEDES are that interest is compounded and posted monthly, and that lotteries for SIMPEDES savers are held locally. The number of SIMPEDES lottery coupons a depositor holds is determined by the minimum monthly balance in his or her account. Lottery prizes (ranging from cars to clocks) are awarded in district-level ceremonies; the opportunity is used to involve local dignitaries and to provide, in a festive setting, information about BRI and its services. In contrast, TABANAS posts uncompounded interest annually and holds national lotteries.

As BRI discovered, the use of previous institutional savings performance as a predictor for future potential may be seriously misleading. The first pilot project in Sukabumi quickly showed evidence of massive demand for the liquid SIMPEDES instrument, which was offered at a 12 percent annual interest rate on the minimum monthly balance (a lower rate than the 15 percent annual interest rate then paid on TABANAS deposits of Rp 1 million or less). At the end of October 1984, after nearly a decade of collecting savings in its unit banks, there was a total of Rp 173 million (U.S. $169,000) in BRI TABANAS deposits in the unit banks in Sukabumi district. The pilot savings project began on November 1, 1984. Two months later, Sukabumi's unit bank deposits totaled Rp 471 million (U.S. $459,000), an increase of 172 percent. SIMPEDES accounted for 65 percent of the total. By December 31, 1990, deposits in BRI unit banks in Sukabumi district totaled Rp 8.5 billion (U.S. $4.5 million), of which SIMPEDES accounted for 91 percent.

While it rapidly became apparent that the Sukabumi pilot project would be successful in mobilizing funds, it also became clear that SIMPEDES, as implemented in the pilot project, was a labor-intensive and expensive way to raise funds (for a variety of reasons, including recording of numerous transactions, monthly posting of interest, activities related to the SIMPEDES lottery, and promotional efforts). As more SIMPEDES accounts were added daily, it seemed either that additional staff would have to be employed, raising costs, or that the workload would cut into KUPEDES lending, lowering income. Either way, the profitability of the Sukabumi unit banks would be negatively affected. It was decided, therefore, that the SIMPEDES instrument would have to be revised before it could be expanded to other areas; otherwise its success in mobilizing deposits might drive the unit banking system into bankruptcy.

In mid-1985, therefore, a second-stage pilot project was begun in the unit banks of twelve BRI branches on Java. A modified, lower-cost SIMPEDES instrument was introduced in those districts. Changes included a split interest rate, determined by the minimum monthly balance; holding lotteries semiannually instead of quarterly; and improving efficiency in administration. During 1985, the modified SIMPEDES instrument was adjusted further and adapted in various ways to rural conditions. The cost to BRI for the modified instrument was reduced to approximately the same level as the costs for TABANAS and Deposito Berjangka, the other savings instruments then offered in the unit banks

(2 to 3 percent above the 15 percent cost of loanable funds from Bank Indonesia in 1985). In April 1986, BRI began expanding the modified SIMPEDES instrument to other areas. By September of the same year, it was available through the unit banking system nationwide.

Annual SIMPEDES interest rates in 1986, based on the minimum monthly balance, were split: No interest was paid on accounts of Rp 25,000 or less; 9 percent was paid on those between Rp 25,001 and Rp 200,000; and 12 percent was paid on accounts above Rp 200,000. Over time, the rates for the larger accounts rose; in 1990, 14.4 percent was paid on accounts with minimum monthly balances from Rp 200,001 to Rp 750,000; 15 percent was paid on accounts over Rp 750,000. In 1989, an urban version of SIMPEDES (SIMASKOT) was introduced in the new unit banks opened in cities.

SIMPEDES was introduced as part of a set of four savings instruments designed to meet different types of demand. The SIMPEDES instrument was aimed at households, firms, and organizations that demanded liquidity in combination with positive real returns. SIMPEDES is especially attractive to traders because of its liquidity. BRI also found that it has a comparative advantage over other banks in obtaining accounts from large, urban-based corporations that conduct substantial business in rural areas. For example, some of the large companies engaged in national distribution of soft drinks, cigarettes, cosmetics, and processed foods demand SIMPEDES accounts into which their local distributors can make deposits and from which funds can be transferred to urban banks. Similarly, urban-based companies purchasing raw materials or goods wholly or partially produced in rural areas find SIMPEDES accounts useful for making payments to their suppliers.

Because SIMPEDES is labor-intensive, very small accounts are discouraged (through nonpayment of interest on accounts of Rp 25,000 or less). TABANAS provides a higher interest rate and pays interest on all accounts regardless of size; however, the number of withdrawals continues to be limited to two per month. Annual TABANAS interest rates in 1986, calculated on the minimum monthly balance, were 15 percent for accounts of Rp 1 million or less and 12 percent for accounts over that amount. By 1990, BRI's annual TABANAS interest rate had risen to 17 percent for all accounts, and withdrawal provisions had been liberalized. TABANAS is aimed at depositors who want middle levels of both liquidity and returns. Schoolchildren and other holders of small accounts are encouraged to save in TABANAS.

Deposito Berjangka, a fixed-deposit instrument, provides the highest interest rates and the lowest liquidity of the instruments offered at the unit banks. In 1986, Deposito Berjangka began to be offered in the unit banks for periods of one, three, six, twelve, or twenty-four months; the 1986 annual interest rates for these time deposits ranged from 13 to 16 percent. By 1990, the range of interest rates had reached 18 to 21 percent. Many Deposito Berjangka account holders also have SIMPEDES accounts. Deposito Berjangka is used by wealthier villagers, by firms that want to realize higher returns and can afford to save in nonliquid instruments, and by those saving for particular future goals (for example, building construction, land purchase, education, retirement, or pilgrimage).

The savings instruments offered in the unit banks since 1976 have generally provided positive real interest rates,[12] with two exceptions: small SIMPEDES accounts and Giro, a low-interest demand-deposit account designed primarily for specialized institutional purposes. During 1990 and 1991, however, the interest received by SIMPEDES depositors with accounts from Rp 25,001 to Rp 200,000 was approximately equal to the inflation rate. Smaller SIMPEDES account holders who wanted higher returns could switch to TABANAS, but few did so because of the high priority given to liquidity. All TABANAS and Deposito Berjangka accounts, and all SIMPEDES accounts with minimum monthly balances over Rp 200,000, provide positive real returns, even after the tax on the interest owed by the account holder. Interest is taxed by the government at 15 percent per year, with the exception that TABANAS accounts of Rp 1 million or less are exempt from tax. Deposits in all instruments are guaranteed by BRI.

As of December 31, 1991, SIMPEDES, with Rp 1.334 trillion, and its urban counterpart SIMASKOT, with Rp 284 billion, together accounted for Rp 1.618 trillion (U.S. $830 million), or 63.7 percent of total unit bank deposits (Rp 2.54 trillion, or U.S. $1.30 billion). Deposito Berjangka, with Rp 566 billion (U.S. $290 million), accounted for 22.3 percent; TABANAS, with Rp 218 billion (U.S. $112 million), accounted for 8.6 percent. The remaining 5.4 percent was in Giro and other instruments.

All KUPEDES borrowers are provided with unit bank savings accounts for voluntary deposits; unlike many banks, BRI does not require forced savings as a condition of KUPEDES loans. With 8.6 million savings accounts as of December 31, 1991, BRI's unit banking system served about 20 percent of Indonesia's households. SIMPEDES, SIMASKOT, and TABANAS, designed for smaller account holders, accounted for 97.1 percent of total unit bank accounts (by number) and 72.3 percent of the amount of unit bank deposits. Among these instruments, the average deposit as of December 31, 1991, was U.S. $113. It is clear, therefore, that a rapidly increasing number of households and household-financed enterprises are benefiting from BRI's unit bank savings program.

BRI's accomplishments were made possible by a number of specific changes carried out within the bank. These included:

1. A major reorganization of BRI management at all levels from the head office to the unit banks.

2. The high priority accorded at the head office to the management of the unit banking system.

3. Extensive reorganization and training of staff throughout the country.

4. Establishment of a system of promotion that incorporates the unit bank staff into the wider BRI personnel system, and the development of promotion criteria that reflect the new expectations for performance.

5. A fundamental revision of bookkeeping, audit, and supervision systems, which permitted the establishment of the unit banks as independent financial units (rather than branch windows) and made accountability and a sustained anticorruption drive possible.

6. The opening of new unit banks and the relocation of others to areas with high demand.

7. Attention to learning about rural financial markets and emphasis on using this information to avoid potential problems associated with moral hazard and adverse selection.

8. Crucial improvements in communications and computerization facilities.

9. A complete overhaul of BRI's public relations.

10. The implementation of an effective unit bank staff incentive system that rewards good performance.

Of course, the system has remaining problems and difficulties (and some new ones): Some "old culture" managers still remain; unit bank staff recruitment procedures are still inadequate; the new criteria for staff promotion are not fully developed or systematically implemented; and continued improvement is needed in such diverse areas as supervision, communications, facilities for transferring funds, relations between the branches and the unit banks, and data collection and analysis. What is different about the new culture, however, is that these difficulties are recognized by BRI's management, and their improvement is accorded priority.

The Indonesian experience shows that there can be extensive rural demand for general rural credit at commercial interest rates and that a large volume of credit can be financed through local savings. Low institutional deposits may be due to a lack of appropriate institutions and instruments rather than a lack of savings potential. BRI undertook its major initiative in rural savings mobilization despite considerable "expert" advice to the contrary. As unit bank deposits increased by seventy-three times from 1983 to 1991, an old proverb came to be quoted in BRI: "The person who says it cannot be done should not interrupt the person doing it."

POLICY ISSUES: LESSONS FROM THE INDONESIAN EXPERIENCE

The Indonesian experience provides a number of lessons. On the lending side, KUPEDES is attractive because the rates are far lower than those available from informal commercial lenders—usually the only competition. People repay primarily because, under these circumstances, they want to reborrow. On the savings side, the experience shows that households, groups, and enterprises are often relieved to save in financial institutions for several reasons. These include security, which is related not only to possible theft but also to the multiple claims on ready cash that exist in local settings; positive real returns; and financial savings as an appropriate way to hold funds from uneven income streams and to save money for specific purposes. The Indonesian experience also provides overwhelming evidence that deposits can be mobilized locally in ways that are profitable for the institution and beneficial for the savers, that sustainable rural financial institutions can be created and maintained, and that successful development of rural financial intermediation is possible on a large scale.

To what extent are Indonesia's achievements in this regard adaptable to rural financial markets in other parts of the developing world? It appears that some of the lessons are general and might be adapted to the conditions of other countries.

MACROECONOMIC MANAGEMENT AND RURAL DEVELOPMENT

Good macroeconomic management and rural development are requirements for the sustainable development of a successful rural banking system operating on a large scale. In Indonesia, rural banking followed the government's investment of oil wealth in rural development. A growing economy resulted in households and enterprises with potential financial savings that could be mobilized by a trusted, convenient institution with appropriate deposit instruments. With an appropriate spread between lending and deposit interest rates, BRI's unit banking system has become profitable and sustainable. The particular Indonesian pattern is not, of course, a necessary component of a successful rural banking system. Nevertheless, for an effective, large-scale rural banking system, there must be rural development, inflation must be controlled, deposits must be mobilized, and financial institutions must be permitted to set interest rates that will enable institutional profitability. In some circumstances, local financial institutions may function well in the absence of some of these criteria, but all are crucial for sustainable large-scale systems of rural banking.

POLITICAL STABILITY

A reasonable level of political stability is required so that people have trust in the broad continuity of institutions and policies. Although households and enterprises will take loans from institutions they may not trust, they will voluntarily deposit their savings only when they have trust in the institution (public or private) and in the broader political and economic system. Viable financial institutions serving the local level are dependent on savings mobilization, the success of which depends heavily on trust. Thus, reasonable macrostability is required for voluntary savings mobilization, which, in turn, is required for profitable rural banking.

SAVINGS MOBILIZATION

Rural undersavings is a myth; savings mobilization is both achievable and essential for sustainable rural financial intermediation. Despite more than two decades of evidence and much thoughtful literature to the contrary, savings mobilization is still the forgotten half of rural finance. This is one of the primary causes of often repeated, but seriously mistaken, policy decisions concerning the development of rural financial markets. Thus, it is still widely assumed that the poor savings record of many rural financial institutions in monetized or partially monetized economies demonstrates that the tendency to save in rural areas is low and that savers prefer to save in other forms. What it usually demonstrates, however, is the lack of appropriate institutions and instruments. This misconception, in turn, leads to severe underemphasis of the importance of building rural financial institutions. These, of course, can be viable only if they mobilize deposits, and this is usually assumed to be too difficult.

An important result of the neglect of savings is that the institutional loan funds available in rural areas generally cannot meet demand. In addition, villagers are deprived of the opportunity to save in a financial form with positive real rates of return (and the opportunity to build up credit ratings through savings accounts).

The lesson from Indonesia is crucial. As BRI discovered, the use of previous institutional savings performance as a predictor for future potential may be seriously misleading. The interest rate spread had provided a disincentive for savings mobilization, and TABANAS was insufficiently liquid for most village demand. BRI's impressive growth in unit bank deposits between 1983 and 1991 was accomplished in large part because the bank learned the importance of liquidity for voluntary savings mobilization; how to identify and contact potential sources of savings at the local level; how to design instruments to meet varied local demand from individuals, households, enterprises, organizations, and institutions; and the critical role of staff incentives for good performance.

MARKET ANALYSIS AND STAFF TRAINING

Analysis of rural markets and the training of institutional staff in understanding the markets they finance are essential for the design and implementation of successful financial instruments and services and for the development of sustainable financial institutions. Successful rural banking is founded on analysis of rural markets and their interlinkages, understanding rural behavior under changing social and economic conditions, and knowledge of the financial requirements and aspirations of villagers who control different economic resources and whose households are at different stages in the developmental cycle of domestic groups. Extensive studies of these types were carried out in Indonesia, with the result that the country now has a profitable nationwide banking system serving households, enterprises, and organizations.

As would be expected in a financial institution without large-scale subsidized local lending programs, BRI's unit banking system has many more savings accounts than loans; the ratio is nearly five to one. Under these circumstances, savers are not only a source of funds, they are also a source of information to the institution concerning local financial markets and the identification of low-risk borrowers.

LEADERSHIP

Effective leadership and management are essential for selection of the priorities required for the development of viable rural financial institutions and for the successful implementation of appropriate services and instruments. BRI's president director from 1983 to 1992, its director responsible for the unit banking system, and the other members of BRI's board of directors led the development of what they called BRI's new culture and Indonesia's new rural banking system. In order to accomplish a number of interlinked goals, they placed emphasis on the extensive restructuring of BRI's management from the head office to the unit banks; on the development of a system of training, incentives, and promotions that reflects and incorporates the new expectations; on the development of the technical capability needed for the design and successful implementation of the new banking programs; and on developing staff capability to analyze rural markets and their interlinkages. BRI's board was supported in its efforts by the Indonesian Ministry of Finance, by the Coordinating Minister for the Economy, Finance, and Industry, and by other high-level government policymakers.

BRI planned its lending and savings programs together, as well as the crucial changes in management, training, incentives, accounting, and supervision that would support the new unit banking system. Other priorities, such as relocation of unit banks, expansion to urban areas, computerization, communications improvement, and expansion of financial services, were phased in more gradually. Some (for example, staffing and recruitment procedures, relations between the branches and the unit banks, facilities for transfer of funds) have only recently been accorded high priority. BRI kept its goals in focus and selected well among options.

COORDINATED PLANNING

Lending and deposit instruments and the spread in their interest rates should be planned in conjunction with each other. These need not be implemented simultaneously (for example, an institution may need to build up trust through lending before mobilizing voluntary savings), but if one is planned without regard for the other, the system cannot be sustainable over the long term. Subsidized credit programs are a case in point. Beginning with the 1983 financial deregulations, BRI's unit banking system was planned as a sustainable nationwide system of local financial intermediation. For reasons relating to BRI staff capacity, the new savings program was begun nearly two years after KUPEDES started. Yet credit, savings, and the spread in interest rates were planned together. At the time, some had suggested that KUPEDES could become self-sustaining even without substantial rural savings; that approach was rejected. There were four primary reasons:

1. The idea behind KUPEDES was to meet the country's demand for general rural credit at commercial interest rates. It was correctly anticipated that this would eventually require a substantially greater amount of financing than had been required for the total amount of all previous rural

credit programs (for which the targets had been borrowers with particular kinds of productive enterprises).

2. The government, concerned in the early 1980s about the
possibility of a decline in the real value of oil revenues,
had begun to seek new sources of income growth, encourage private-sector savings and investment, and undertake
major financial reforms. Under these conditions, it was
decided that extensive long-term funding for a nationwide rural credit program could not be committed from
Bank Indonesia, the central bank. Emphasis was placed
instead on the encouragement of private-sector savings
and investment.

3. The risk was considered too high for long-term commitment of central bank funds. It was well known that many
government rural credit programs in Indonesia and in developing countries throughout the world had a history of
high arrears. No example could be found of a profitable
nationwide rural credit program in a major developing
country. Indonesia's economics ministers recognized the
potential for a large-scale rural banking system and supported its introduction with government funding; they also
recognized the importance of limiting government risk.

4. As part of a wider policy of encouraging private savings,
the government wanted to arrange for the supply of what
was accurately estimated as a large potential rural demand for savings in financial institutions. It was thought
that an approach that offered savings instruments designed to be appropriate for rural demand could generally provide villagers with positive real returns while also
building the long-term viability of the unit banking system. Both results would contribute to rural development,
a primary aim.

For these reasons, extensive rural savings mobilization became a crucial component of the overall plan for the unit banks.

RURAL-URBAN FINANCIAL INTERMEDIATION

In a country undergoing significant rural development, there is
likely to be substantial demand for rural-urban financial intermediation. In addition, banking instruments and services that work in rural
areas can be adapted for urban neighborhoods, and vice versa. Given

the recent large-scale rural-urban migrations and the widespread communications facilities that link urban and rural areas in Indonesia and in other developing countries, the economics of rural organization cannot be considered apart from the wider context. Under these circumstances, there is considerable opportunity for the expansion of successful methods of rural financial intermediation into urban areas.

Critics have sometimes said that BRI's unit banking system draws funds from rural to urban areas, thus contributing to urban bias. In fact, the unit banks may help counteract urban bias. In urban units, savings (35 percent of total unit bank deposits) were higher than KUPEDES loans outstanding (25 percent of total outstanding) as of December 31, 1990; the reverse was true in rural units. Although most of the deposits are in rural areas, the trend is changing (the new savings program began nationwide in rural areas in 1986 and in urban areas in 1989). Also, the prevalence of remittances from urban workers to their rural families suggests that some rural savings originate from urban sources.

SOCIAL AND ECONOMIC PROFITABILITY

It is not necessary to choose between the economic profitability of the financial institution and the social profitability to the country. A recent review paper on rural credit markets posed the question: "Should viability be understood in terms of economic profitability of the institution, or should it be understood as social profitability to the country? . . . Given the decision to intervene . . . the salient criteria for viability should be social profitability to the country" (Braverman and Guasch forthcoming).

The crucial point is that it may not be necessary to choose. Although circumstances vary in different countries and regions, the Indonesian case shows that there need not be a tradeoff between economic and social profitability. In fact, in Indonesian rural banking, the former is necessary for the latter. The Indonesian government could not possibly make available the large volume of credit needed to meet demand for the full development of its rural areas. However, the demand for credit for productive uses in rural areas can be met by profitable financial institutions, both government and private. These can, of course, be viable only if they mobilize deposits.

The sectoral lending programs of the 1970s could not meet most of Indonesia's rural demand for credit because the programs were subsidized and therefore rationed. In contrast, KUPEDES, supported by local savings, has driven the unit banking system to profitability while extending a much larger volume of credit to millions of borrowers throughout the country. It is, therefore, no longer necessary for many of Indonesia's local borrowers to pay the high interest rates of informal commercial lenders.

The unit banks have had a positive effect on both development and equity; this can be demonstrated in several ways. First, a large amount of funds has been provided for rural credit at substantially lower interest rates than had previously been available. Unlike subsidized credit programs in Indonesia and elsewhere, these loans are not rationed and, therefore, are not limited de facto to higher-income borrowers. Second, the savings instruments offered in the unit banks provide generally positive real returns to millions of customers. Third, both KUPEDES and SIMPEDES have been successful in reaching customers who had never before borrowed or saved in a bank. Finally, KUPEDES provides loans to a wide range of borrowers; 33 percent of the survey respondents reported monthly household incomes of U.S. $78 or less. There are still many potential customers who have not yet been reached by the unit banking system, but it is clear that the system plays an important role in rural development and assists in poverty alleviation. It has been recognized at the highest levels in Indonesia that, in meeting the widespread demand for rural banking, BRI's unit banks help in maintaining social stability as well as in promoting economic development.

The Indonesian experience thus demonstrates that a spread between lending and savings interest rates can be set that permits bank profitability while offering loans at interest rates significantly below those of informal commercial lenders and providing savers with generally positive real rates of return on their deposits. The fundamental lessons from Indonesia are that institutional viability, rural development, enterprise finance, and improvement in equity can be achieved simultaneously; and this can happen only if savings mobilization is transformed from the forgotten half to the sustaining half of rural finance.

NOTES

The research on which this chapter is based was supported by the Ministry of Finance, government of Indonesia.

1. For discussion of rural savings in developing countries see, among others, Kelley and Williamson (1968); Adams (1973, 1978, 1984a, 1984b, 1984c, 1988); Howse (1983); Bouman (1977, 1979, 1984, 1989); Mauri (1977); Von Pischke (1978, 1983b, 1991); Lee, Kim, and Adams (1977); Von Pischke, Adams, and Donald (1983); Bourne and Graham (1980); Miracle, Miracle, and Cohen (1980); Sideri (1984); Adams, Graham, and Von Pischke (1984); Vogel (1984a, 1984b); Agabin (1985); Adams and Vogel (1986); Germidis, Kessler, and Meghir (1991).

2. For discussion of the problem of neglect of savings in local financial markets, see, among others, Adams (1978); Adams and Graham (1981); Vogel (1984b); Adams and Vogel (1986); Von Pischke (1991).

3. The author is indebted to the World Bank for permission to quote from the draft manuscript of Hoff, Braverman, and Stiglitz (forthcoming).

4. The 1984 World Bank agricultural sector policy paper reported that the average arrears rate for thirty-eight small farm credit institutions in Asia, Africa, and Latin America was 39.4 percent. For discussion of the problems of subsidized rural credit programs, see Adams (1971); Donald (1976); Gonzalez-Vega (1976); Lipton (1976); Vogel (1979); Bangladesh Bank (1979); Adams and Graham (1981); Eaton and Gersovitz (1981); Von Pischke, Adams, and Donald (1983); Adams, Graham, and Von Pischke (1984); Schaefer-Kehnert and Von Pischke (1984); Adams and Vogel (1986); Meyer (1985); Mosley and Dahal (1987); Adams (1988); Hossain (1988); Braverman (1989); Braverman and Guasch (1986, forthcoming); Von Pischke (1991); Floro and Yotopoulos (1991). See Vogel (1981) and Siamwalla et al. (forthcoming) for discussion of the implications of low delinquency rates in Costa Rica and Thailand, respectively. In the former case, the result was severe credit rationing; in the latter, loans are largely restricted in practice to supply of working capital to farmers with above-average incomes.

5. The World Bank's 1983 study of rural credit in Indonesia found rural savings propensity to be 20 percent.

6. The data reviewed here are drawn from unpublished reports by the Bank Rakyat Indonesia, Center for Policy and Implementation Studies, and Harvard Institute for International Development during the period 1980–90.

7. Interest rates in this range have been widely reported for rural areas of developing countries. See, for example, Reserve Bank of India (1954); Nisbet (1967); Ladman (1971); Bottomley (1975); Mundle (1976); Tun Wai (1977, 1980); Kamble (1979); Marla (1981); Adams and Graham (1981); Singh (1983); Wilmington (1983); Roth (1983); Chandravarkar (1987); Hossain (1988); Robinson (1988); Bouman (1989); Varian (1989); Von Pischke (1991); Germidis, Kessler, and Meghir (1991); Chen (1991); Floro and Yotopoulos (1991); Aleem (forthcoming); Braverman and Guasch (forthcoming); and Siamwalla et al. (forthcoming). For a classic study, see Darling (1978), first published in 1925. Interest rates lower than this range are also reported, and the rates in some areas have decreased over time; see, for example, Tun Wai (1977, 1980); Chandravarkar (1987); Fernando (1988); Bouman (1989); Von Pischke (1991). See Robinson (1992) for analysis of the reasons for the high rates prevalent in informal commercial credit markets.

8. On the day that the instrument permitting accounts to be held in the name of organizations was first introduced in a particular area of Indonesia, the author observed a street fight between members of the local horse-cart drivers' association and the treasurer of that organization. The former wanted the group funds deposited in the bank in the name of the association; the latter objected. When the members threatened to elect a new treasurer, the funds were deposited in the bank.

9. For the development of BRI's unit banking system, see Chapter 11; see also Suharto (1985, 1988); Robinson and Snodgrass (1987); Patten and Snodgrass (1987); Robinson and Sumarto (1988); International Labor Organization (1989); Sugianto (1989, 1990a, 1990b); Robinson (1989, 1991, 1992); Bank Rakyat Indonesia (1990); Afwan (1991); Holt (1991); Liong (1991); Moermanto (1991);

Patten and Rosengard (1991); Snodgrass and Patten (1991); Sartono (1991); Schmit (1991).

10. The term *unit bank* has a special meaning in Indonesia. BRI's subdistrict-level banks were originally called village units (unit *desa*); when urban units (unit *kota*) were added in the late 1980s, the term *unit bank* came to be used for all BRI's local banks, both rural and urban. Known as the unit banking system, it operates at the subdistrict *(kecamatan)* level, serving the villages of each sub-district and selected urban neighborhoods; the unit banks are under the super-vision of the BRI branch, regional, and head offices.
Improved national BIMAS was begun during the 1970–71 wet season.

11. BRI uses two measures of long-term arrears. Because portfolio status measures cumulative arrears as a percentage of current outstanding loans (which includes loans not yet due), the long-term loss ratio is considered the more accurate measure of the program's loan recovery. The KUPEDES long-term loss ratio was 3.28 percent and its portfolio status was 8.55 percent as of December 31, 1991.
December 31, 1991, figures are used where available. Where these are not available, earlier figures are used. It should be noted that the slow growth in KUPEDES lending during 1991 was caused primarily by credit restrictions in BRI resulting from the government's tight money policy in 1991 imposed in order to control inflation.

12. Annual interest rates were raised again in 1991: SIMPEDES rates reached 19 percent for accounts over Rp 2 million; TABANAS rates rose to 22 percent for accounts over Rp 10,000; and Deposito Berjangka rates ranged from 24 to 26 percent. Inflation was about 9.5 percent in 1991.

CHAPTER 3

Principles of Regulation and Prudential Supervision and Their Relevance for Microenterprise Finance Organizations

Rodrigo A. Chaves and Claudio Gonzalez-Vega

THIS CHAPTER OFFERS a discussion of some general principles of financial intermediary regulation and prudential supervision as well as an evaluation of how these issues are relevant for microenterprise finance organizations. It presents the state of the art as captured by the literature on regulation and supervision of depository institutions, interprets and further develops the necessary conceptual framework, and translates it for microenterprise finance agencies. Some definitions are provided first.

DEFINITIONS AND KEY CONCEPTS

Regulation refers most broadly to a set of enforceable rules that restrict or direct the actions of market participants and, as a result, alter the outcomes of those actions. In this sense, regulation may be performed by the market itself, without government intervention or participation of other external forces. Efficient markets regulate economic actors by rewarding or penalizing them for their performance. In principle, an efficient market guarantees that actors who make incorrect choices eventually go bankrupt.

The ability of markets to regulate actions and enforce contracts should be taken into account in the design of government regulation. The more regulation by governments imitates regulation by efficient markets, the more effective it will be. Optimal regulation seeks to replicate the mechanisms of a perfect market (Klein and Leffler 1981).

Enforceable public regulation substitutes the mandates of the government for market incentives. In this context, financial regulation becomes the coercive imposition of a set of rules that affect the behavior of agents in financial markets. The replacement of market incentives with government rules that restrict certain behavior may have either

55

beneficial or harmful effects on the performance of the economy. Since financial markets have been among the most regulated economic activities in every country in the world, it is easy to observe examples of both beneficial and harmful regulations on the basis of their effects on market efficiency.[1]

Prudential financial regulation refers to the set of general principles or legal rules that aim to contribute to the stable and efficient performance of financial institutions and markets. These rules represent constraints placed on the actions of financial intermediaries to ensure the safety and soundness of the system.

This type of government intervention should serve three basic policy goals. The first one, macroeconomic in nature, is to ensure the solvency and financial soundness of all intermediaries, in order to protect the stability of the country's payments system.[2] The second objective is to provide consumer (for example, depositor) protection against undue risks that may arise from failure, fraud, or opportunistic behavior on the part of the suppliers of financial services. The third goal of financial regulation is to promote the efficient performance of institutions and markets and the proper working of competitive market forces.

Achievement of the first two objectives of prudential financial regulation is simultaneous. Once the authorities provide depositors with reasonable protection, the stability of the payments system is guaranteed. The objective of promoting efficiency, however, implies increased competition and the possibility that inefficient firms will exit the market. This means, in turn, that some consumers may be exposed to deposit losses and that some degree of instability may arise. These seemingly conflicting objectives must be balanced in a system that allows the market mechanism to work while keeping the system safe.

We refer to *financial repression* as those forms of regulation that distort financial markets and reduce the efficiency of their performance (Shaw and McKinnon 1973). Financial repression encompasses the set of government-imposed rules whose purpose is to tax or to subsidize financial transactions, thereby redirecting resources away from market-determined uses.

Important tools of financial repression are confiscatory reserve requirements, interest rate ceilings, inflation tax, overvaluation of the domestic currency, and excessive restrictions on entry to the market. Other examples are credit subsidies, through loans granted at below-market interest rates; mandatory credit allocations that target loans for particular sectors; and usury restrictions. In some cases, small enterprises (though rarely microenterprises) have been the intended beneficiaries of such restrictions, to the detriment of the financial system as a whole and possibly to the detriment of the intended beneficiaries as well. The negative consequences of financial repression have been amply documented (Fry 1988).

Frequently, some of the most repressive regulations have been adopted with the best of intentions. In other words, badly conceived prudential regulations may become repressive. For instance, excessive barriers to entry into the financial industry are frequently raised with the intent of promoting a safe and resilient system. Such barriers may shield existing inefficient organizations from competition from new, more efficient intermediaries.

The observed negative consequences of financial market repression suggest that inappropriate regulation may frequently be more dangerous than no regulation at all.

Financial intermediary supervision consists of the examination and monitoring mechanisms through which the authorities verify compliance with and enforce either financial repression or prudential financial regulation. Supervision includes the specific procedures adopted in order to determine the risks faced by an intermediary and to review regulatory compliance. Supervision of compliance with rules that promote stability and efficiency is both desirable and a key component of financial progress.[3]

Internal control refers to the activities undertaken by the owners of a given financial institution in order to prevent, detect, and punish fraudulent behavior by the organization's personnel; to ensure that the financial policies adopted by the owners are properly implemented; and to ensure that the owners' equity is protected. Internal control activities are, in general, in the private interest of the intermediary's owners and normally should not be an overriding concern for the supervisory authorities. In the case of microenterprise finance organizations with member ownership or those structured as nonprofit organizations, their particular ownership arrangements may imply a special concern with internal control.

It is important to maintain the distinction among the concepts of regulation, supervision, and internal control, since each leads to separate policy issues. Regulation requires, in most cases, a legal framework. Once the appropriate regulation is in place, supervision may be more discretionary. Although these activities are complementary (regulation without supervision would be useless), one should be able to identify the separate virtues and defects of each set of activities in order to focus any corrective actions.

Microenterprise finance organizations (MFOs) are organizations that offer credit and sometimes savings services to microenterprises and others in poor communities. The main types of microenterprise finance organizations are discussed in the later chapters of this book and include nongovernmental organizations (NGOs) running solidarity group or transformation lending programs (Chapters 7 and 10); NGOs sponsoring village banking programs (Chapter 9); credit unions (Chapter 8); specialized government banks (Chapters 2 and 11); and private commercial banks (Chapter 12). Regulation and supervision of each of these MFOs depend first on the types of services they offer, particularly the nature of their savings services, and second on their ownership and management structure.

THE RATIONALE FOR REGULATING DEPOSITORY FINANCIAL INTERMEDIARIES

For the purposes of this chapter, we focus on the regulation of depository financial organizations. These are the most common type of formal financial institution in the developing world.

Depository intermediaries—banks—may be distinguished from other financial institutions by three characteristics.[4] On the liabilities side of the business, banks issue fixed-value claims, more commonly known as deposits, to their customers. They carry large amounts of debt, in the form of deposits, as compared to equity. On the assets side, banks hold a substantial portion of their portfolios as nonmarketable and risky securities, in particular business and personal loans.

The fact that fixed-value deposit claims are backed by risky loans makes the regulation and supervision of depository intermediaries necessary (all loans are risky by virtue of their nature as promises to deliver at a future date). Imperfections in financial markets arise from asymmetries of information among depositors, the financial institution, and borrowers about the likelihood of the promises being kept. Depositors cannot know as much as bankers about the safety of their deposits, and banks cannot know as much as borrowers about the likelihood of loans being repaid. Most if not all valid arguments in favor of the regulation of financial markets can ultimately be traced to combinations of these elements.

Excessive risks threaten some of the crucial functions of banks, including the safety of deposits, the allocation of credit in the economy, the management of the payments system, and the ability to provide portfolio management and risk-sharing services. Depository financial intermediaries are particularly important in developing countries, where other dimensions of financial markets are undeveloped or absent.[5]

The nature of the contracts between depositors and the owners of financial organizations provides ample occasion for opportunistic behavior by depository institutions. Banks can take advantage of depositors by, for example, investing in excessively risky loans. Once depositors have supplied the funds, bank managers and equity holders may be encouraged to greater risk taking, since they keep any extra rewards while depositors bear the additional risk. Because deposits carry fixed interest rates, the owners of the depository institution keep any extraordinary profits if the loans or investments turn out well, but they can go bankrupt and walk away from losses. This problem is referred to as *moral hazard*, which can be defined as the incentive by someone (an agent) who holds an asset belonging to another person (the principal) to endanger the value of that asset because the agent bears less than the full consequence of any loss.

This problem of moral hazard is also present between a bank and its borrowers. The same opportunity exists for the borrower to impose an unfair bet upon the bank (Stiglitz and Weiss 1981). This is precisely why banks impose requirements on their borrowers—an example of regulation through the market. These requirements are voluntarily agreed-to loan covenants designed to ensure—or at least increase the probability—that borrowers will behave responsibly. All forms of collateral are examples of such loan covenants. For microenterprises, regulation through the market often takes the form of collateral substitutes such as group guarantees, the promise of future loans, or the value of the borrower's reputation. These rules create incentives for the borrower to behave in ways that reduce the probability of default.

Similar market solutions to the problem of discouraging opportunistic behavior by banks are not available, however. Although banks find it profitable to invest large amounts of resources in loan screening and collection, individual depositors may find that similar efforts with respect to the bank are too expensive relative to their investment (their deposit). The market failure that results from the asymmetry of information between banks and depositors and the associated moral hazard on the part of banks is significant enough to warrant government intervention. The difficult question is how best to intervene.[6]

A second type of concern that originates from opportunistic or morally hazardous behavior relates to spillover effects that go beyond the direct (private) costs faced by the depositors and the owners of a failed depository intermediary to other depositors and other institutions. There are several ways these spillover effects can take place. For example, an intermediary that lends to very risky clients would be likely to charge and receive a high rate of interest on loans. This depository intermediary would, in turn, be willing to pay higher rates of interest on its deposits. In a competitive market, other intermediaries would be forced to match the increased deposit rates, covering the increase by higher interest rates on loans. This price race might escalate the level of risk in the system as a whole.

Alternatively, the failure of one intermediary may cause a panic or run on the deposits of other intermediaries that otherwise have healthy financial situations. Runs on deposits are sudden, massive, and unexpected withdrawals that endanger prudent and imprudent institutions alike. Even depositors who have informed themselves about the financial health of their intermediaries may find it rational to suddenly withdraw their deposits in the expectation that others are doing so or are about to do so.

The case for prudential financial regulation is almost complete. The question remains, however, why it is necessary to restrict potentially opportunistic behavior and other forms of mismanagement by depository institutions (preventive regulation) rather than punish them afterwards through the judicial system (remedial action), as is the case with most transactions in the economy.

The combination of the limited liability and high levels of financial leverage that characterize banks implies that the amount owners stand to lose is rather small, especially when compared with the size of potential damages (deposits lost). This supports the case for regulation. The case is even stronger when the costs from instability of the system are considered as well.

In addition, the lower the likelihood that remedial action will be taken by a court of justice, the more the system should rely on regulation (Shavell 1984). There will usually be a multitude of comparatively small depositors, who may find it too costly to organize together to bring suit. Moreover, the cause of morally hazardous behavior in bank failures may be difficult to establish in a court of law.[7]

From a macroeconomic perspective, if individual depositors perceive that, in order to protect the payments system, the government will be responsible for the safety of their deposits, the authorities may be called upon to engage in costly bailouts. This guarantee is usually not desirable, but if the government is committed to it, then preventive regulation is essential in order to minimize the cost of bailouts to the government.

When these general criteria for prudential regulation—from the point of view of consumer protection—are applied to MFOs, the argument for a solution closer to the preventive end of the scale is even stronger. It may even imply that some MFOs should be regulated more closely than other types of depository intermediaries. This is so because in some MFOs, those in control do not own the capital of the organization, and any negligent action on their part leading to the loss of deposits would be punished, at most, with the loss of their jobs.

PRINCIPLES FOR THE REGULATION OF DEPOSITORY FINANCIAL INTERMEDIARIES

There is a case for the prudential regulation of depository intermediaries. Much of the debate, however, is not about whether there should be regulation but about how much regulation and what kind. Economic theory has yet to offer standard principles for the determination of the optimal degree of regulation. The optimal type and degree of regulation may be very specific in terms of time, location, and institutional structure of the organizations to be regulated. The most that we can provide is a set of general principles or regulatory commandments.

Regulation should attempt to allow a competitive balance among financial intermediaries. This principle of competitive neutrality requires, among other things, that the regulatory environment provide all market players with a level playing field. No particular type of intermediary should be granted an advantage simply as a result of its classification.[8] Financial institutions operating under the same or different charters should be able to find their comparative advantages in serving all possible market niches.

The negative effects of regulation upon efficiency in the financial system should be minimized. Allocative efficiency requires that resources flow to the organizations that offer the highest prospective risk-adjusted rates of return. Operational efficiency requires that the costs of financial intermediation be as low as possible. Finally, dynamic efficiency requires intermediaries to adapt over time to the needs of the users of the system. Good regulation would minimize distortions in each of these areas.

The regulation of financial markets should not be used to promote the achievement of social objectives (for example, poverty alleviation) or to subsidize particular sectors of the population or priority industries. In most cases, regulation directed to achieve these objectives falls into the category of financial repression, because it taxes the financial system (or some of its participants) in order to subsidize other sectors of the economy. In practice, these regulations fail to achieve their objectives but impose high costs on all market participants. Worthy social and political objectives may best be achieved (in terms of both effectiveness and cost) through fiscal means, that is, government budgets (Gonzalez-Vega 1976).

The purpose of regulation and supervision should not be to avoid bank failures at all costs. Such a policy objective is not attainable, and to pursue it may induce severe negative effects. There is no purpose in allowing inefficient organizations to continue to operate. If an intermediary does not adapt to changes in the environment and does not react to competitive attacks from its rivals, or if its owners are not able to avoid malfeasance or incompetence by their staff, then the regulator must ensure that the owners of the intermediary replace the equity losses or exit the industry without damaging their depositors' interests or the stability of the market.

In effect, the policy of preventing bank failures, or of simply postponing them, has resulted in the reduction of competition and in the inefficiency of entire financial systems, while exerting significant pressure on public funds. The objectives of regulation and supervision should be to avoid unnecessary bank failures and to minimize the negative effects of failures that must take place.

Regulation must rely, as much as possible, on the self-interest of economic agents. Government regulation should simulate, as much as possible, the ability of the market to enforce contracts. In general, there are two possible ways to prevent opportunistic behavior. The first is to keep the discretionary powers of the intermediary within narrow and closely supervised limits. The second is to rely on the self-interest of the intermediary by introducing incentives that induce banks to reduce excessive risk taking. The second option relies on the possibility for external and internal discipline (Holstrom and Tirole 1990). Internal discipline would result, for instance, from a regulation that would require banks to keep a minimum amount of capital. External discipline is achieved by competition (for example, takeovers by other shareholders or the market to hire and fire agents).

The regulatory framework should not be static; it must recognize that there will inevitably be innovations adopted to avoid the original regulation. Efforts to alter market solutions through coercive regulation induce innovations to avoid the initial regulation, such as new products and services (for example, off–balance sheet liabilities) or product substitution. The efficiency of the process of prudential regulation is reduced as such innovations spread in the market.

Innovation tends to spread rapidly in financial markets, since financial products and processes are easily replicated by competitors. Products are openly available and are not protected by patents, while processes are copied through employee mobility or originate in widely available technology (computers, telecommunications). Regulation may become less effective in the presence of avoidance, and regulators tend to react to change more slowly than the organizations they supervise. Eventually, though, a process of re-regulation takes place and the cycle is repeated. This is what Kane (1977) identified as a process of regulatory dialectic.

The regulatory framework should be flexible enough to regulate different intermediaries in a different manner when necessary. The differences that may be important for regulatory purposes have to do with the environment in which the intermediaries operate, the market niches they serve, and their institutional design—property rights and rules of control over the organization's assets. For example, a cooperative's assets are controlled by the one-person-one-vote system, while the corresponding rule for a commercial bank is one share one vote.

The need for flexibility arises because such differences may imply different types of exposure to risk—idiosyncratic risks—for different intermediaries. There may be idiosyncratic risks that originate from the particular market segments or niches served by an intermediary.[9] Intermediaries specializing in the provision of housing loans would probably face consistently higher exposure to interest rate risk—as a result of their long-term, fixed-rate assets—than finance companies specializing in short-term lending. The regulatory framework must be flexible enough to accommodate such differences, in order to allow institutions that operate under different charters to find their comparative advantages in serving all possible market niches. Even intermediaries with the same charter should be able to find what sectors of the market they can serve at a lower cost and, therefore, more profitably than their competitors. The role of regulation is to ensure that the appropriate precautions are taken in each case.

Idiosyncratic risks may also arise as the result of the institutional design of the intermediaries. For example, some intermediary types, such as cooperatives or NGOs, have a diffused ownership structure, which may cause "owners" not to provide an optimal amount of oversight of their operations. Not only would prudential supervision be better—a lower probability of failure—but it would be more efficient as well as more cost-effective when these distinctions are recognized.

The fact that some idiosyncratic risks may call for differentiated regulation is not contradictory with the principle of competitive neutrality stated before. Equality of treatment is not assured by treating unequals equally. The idea is to allow for a diversity of organizations compatible with the diverse needs of the market, but at the same time to assign the regulatory burden with maximum efficiency.

FREQUENTLY ADOPTED INSTRUMENTS OF PRUDENTIAL REGULATION

The types and scope of government regulation of depository intermediaries vary significantly across countries. Preventive regulation attempts to control the risk exposure of the system in order to reduce the probability of failure in the aggregate. Protective regulation focuses on assuring depositors that they, as individuals, will not face losses if a particular intermediary experiences financial difficulties.

PREVENTIVE REGULATION

LICENSING OF FINANCIAL INTERMEDIARIES. Almost every government has restricted the entry of firms into the formal financial industry by requiring them to obtain a license or legal charter. Unfortunately, although promotion of the soundness of intermediaries is always the ostensible reason for restrictions to entry, the underlying purpose or effect is often to restrain competition and to influence the structure of the market by creating, through the barriers adopted, monopolistic rents for the industry's incumbents. From a purely regulatory perspective, the only purpose of any licensing requirement should be to ensure adequate capitalization and the availability of sound management (competence and moral standing), not to limit entry and reduce competition.

CAPITAL ADEQUACY. The first dimension of requirements dealing with capital adequacy is a preestablished minimum level of capital required for entry. This is an absolute amount of money. The second dimension is to require the maintenance of some solvency or leverage ratio; this is a minimum proportion of the assets of the intermediary.

Capital adequacy regulations are probably the most important component of any regulatory framework because of capital's key role in the operation of a financial intermediary. The most elementary definition of equity capital is the amount of money left for the owners of the intermediary in the event the organization is dismantled, after all creditors have been paid off.[10] Equity capital cannot be withdrawn by the owners and does not receive a fixed or contracted return.

As such, capital plays two roles. The first one is to absorb losses on the income account. For moderate losses, capital would allow depositors to redeem their claims at full value. Nevertheless, due to high levels of debt relative to capital on the liability side of depository intermediaries, capital does not represent a significant protection. Even losses that are small as a percentage of assets may wipe capital out.

The second, authentic function of capital in terms of consumer protection is to perform the role of a deductible, in the sense of an insurance policy. Equity capital is the amount that would be lost by the owners of the bank in the event of bankruptcy. The larger the deductible (expected owner losses), the more cautious the behavior of the intermediary (less risk assumed). In short, from a regulatory perspective, the main function of equity capital is to induce compatibility of incentives (that is, reduce moral hazard) between the depositors and the owners of the intermediary. Given a sufficiently large deductible, the interests of owners and depositors would be similar, and the former would behave accordingly.

Capital adequacy regulations in the form of some minimum solvency or maximum leverage ratio create good incentives. This makes for sound regulation. But capital adequacy requirements as an absolute minimum amount of equity to enter the industry are, conceptually, anticompetitive. The only justification for this latter type of regulation is a pragmatic one that has to do with the difficulty of supervising large numbers of intermediaries with small-scale operations.

There are two general problems with the practical implementation of capital adequacy ratios. The first problem has to do with the definition of capital and with its measurement. Capital as deductible should include all hidden reserves, including the value of the charter or franchise of established firms under restricted competition, as well as an appropriate market valuation of assets.

The second problem is the appraisal of the intermediary's off–balance sheet liabilities. These are usually contingent liabilities, such as guarantees or related contracts, that have not affected the organization's balance sheet yet but that may generate a claim on the assets of the organization in the future. These commitments represent actual contractual obligations that imply risks. Off–balance sheet items are one of the most common instruments of avoidance of capital adequacy requirements.

One of the interesting challenges in the regulation of MFOs is that some of these organizations have property rights structures that preclude accounting capital from performing the function of a deductible. This is so because these intermediaries do not have owners in the traditional sense. This may suggest the need for a different type of regulation for some MFOs.

PROHIBITIONS ON LOANS TO INSIDERS. One common and very important regulation of financial intermediaries is to limit the amount of loans that may be granted to bank insiders (large shareholders, related companies, employees). The usual argument for this regulation is that such credit may not meet the same standards as loans extended to other borrowers (Polizatto 1989). Insider loans are usually not properly collateralized. More importantly, credit to insiders may be used by the intermediary's owners to recapture their equity capital, thereby eliminating its function as a deductible. In the event that insiders receive loans equivalent to a large portion of their capital, they are able to escape their share of the losses from bankruptcy by falling in default on the loans they have received. Restrictions on credit to insiders are necessary for the successful enforcement of any capital adequacy regulation. The general rule should be that a bank cannot lend to its owners. This is one of the regulatory challenges, however, in the case of client-owned depository intermediaries (for example, credit cooperatives, village banks), since these organizations lend mostly to their owners. This represents one example of the need for idiosyncratic regulation.

DIVERSIFICATION RULES. This regulatory constraint is aimed at preventing an intermediary's loan or investment portfolio from being concentrated around a few individual customers or a group of customers that face similar economic risks, such as farmers growing the same crop. In such a situation, many investments or loans may fail at the same time, causing sudden deep losses to a system designed to cope with small, regularly occurring losses.

Although the precise form and content of this regulation vary significantly, it should stipulate limits on loans, investments, and exposure (for example, foreign exchange risks). The amount that any intermediary may risk in a single gamble or in a single risk group should be a function of its equity capital.

When institutions are restricted to certain geographic areas or certain client groups, they tend to be poorly diversified, and hence risky. This is a problem for the long-run stability of many MFOs.

REGULATIONS ABOUT ADMISSIBLE ACTIVITIES. Some countries have tried to separate banking activities from nonbanking areas of business. The practical implementation of the regulation has been to prohibit or restrict stock market and other equity investments by depository intermediaries. However, direct investment can also pose problems. Credit cooperatives in developing countries, for example, have invested in and managed all sorts of businesses (for example, grocery stores) side by side with their financial intermediation operations. This has been an important source of financial distress for these organizations. Multiple activities seriously endanger the effectiveness of supervision and risk assessment of financial intermediaries, and hence endanger depositors.

GENERAL POWERS FOR THE ENFORCEMENT OF REGULATIONS. The regulatory framework should provide the supervisory agency with enough authority to perform its mandate. Among the most frequently observed—and needed—general powers granted to regulators are the abilities to require standard formats for the reporting of financial performance, to restrict or suspend dividend payments, and to force intermediaries to create appropriate reserves.

PROTECTIVE REGULATION

The main purpose of protective interventions is to avoid runs on deposits by removing the incentive for a depositor to be the first one to withdraw funds from a troubled intermediary.

GOVERNMENT AS A LENDER OF LAST RESORT. Governments, most frequently through central banks, may intervene in financial markets to provide liquidity loans to troubled intermediaries. This is different from the open-market operations of the central bank aimed at increasing the liquidity of the entire system for macroeconomic reasons.

The idea behind the lender-of-last-resort facility is that there may be intermediaries that are temporarily illiquid but are solvent and fit for long-term survival. The implicit assumption is either that liquidity markets do not work properly or that the authorities have better judgment than the market about the soundness and possibility for long-term survival of individual organizations. In developing countries, liquidity markets may indeed be embryonic. With properly functioning markets, however, liquidity should not be a problem for solvent intermediaries.

DEPOSIT INSURANCE. The main purpose of deposit insurance is to remove the depositor's incentive to be the first one to withdraw funds from a troubled intermediary, thereby preventing mass runs by depositors. This is thought to increase the stability of the system. Deposit insurance may also imply, however, negative changes in the predeposit behavior of individuals. In particular, savers may have less incentive to verify the financial health of the intermediaries where they place their funds if they feel protected by the insurance.[11]

Protective regulatory interventions necessarily require an adequate framework of preventive regulations and an efficient system of supervision. For this reason, protective interventions should be the last step, if any role is assigned at all to them, in the development of a prudential framework. The establishment of protective measures in the absence of prudential regulation and supervision removes discipline from the market and encourages risks that may be greater than those resulting from the absence of regulation.

It is better to have no regulation than to adopt protective regulation alone. In particular, deposit insurance without a good supervisory system removes the cost for a bank to increase risk (it eliminates market discipline), making them less safe—exactly the opposite result sought by prudential interventions.

PRINCIPLES FOR THE PRUDENTIAL SUPERVISION OF DEPOSITORY FINANCIAL INTERMEDIARIES

Prudential supervision refers to the process of enforcing the regulatory framework. Efforts are aimed at monitoring and directing individual intermediaries to ensure that they obey regulatory requirements and do not behave imprudently. There is little advantage in having good regulatory policies in the absence of efficient enforcement mechanisms.

Since the main purpose of regulation is to reduce risk and its negative effects, the supervisory authority's practical challenge is to design indicators to measure these risks, to monitor and analyze the impact that external events might have on the performance of financial markets and intermediaries, and to make sure that the data fed into the monitoring system reflect the actual situation of the intermediary. The main goal of the supervisory system should be, therefore, to work as an early-warning mechanism about changes in the probability of an individual intermediary becoming illiquid, insolvent, or both.

The very nature of banking risks makes their measurement and prediction very difficult. Even well-trained and experienced supervisors issued positive reports on the Continental Illinois Bank only a few months before it had to be taken over by the Federal Deposit Insurance Corporation. There are, however, some basic principles, which will be called supervisory commandments.

Supervisory activities should not be used to enforce rules different from those related to prudential regulation. In some countries, bank supervisors are asked to verify compliance with tax laws, foreign exchange controls, central bank reserve requirements, and the like. Additional mandates affect the ability of supervisors to concentrate on their main task of risk assessment and control activities, while creating additional incentives for the regulated ones to hide information.

Supervisory authorities should not manage intermediaries. Supervisory activities and management tasks should be kept separate. Supervision should attempt to make intermediaries comply with a comparatively small number of clear rules. It should have nothing to do with personnel management, pricing policies, or even technical operational advice to financial intermediaries.

Supervision requires frequent monitoring. There should be no extended intervals between supervisory activities. Given that financial contracts involve maintaining and honoring promises over time, the risks involved in banking change constantly. Thus, the probability that an intermediary will be able to honor its deposits may change at any time. A single large loan or the adoption of a new foreign exchange position may dramatically change the financial position of an intermediary within hours of a supervisory visit.

Supervision of financial intermediaries should have a significant component of prediction. The assessment of the risk levels faced by an intermediary should not be based on past performance alone. Effective supervision requires a better predictive ability than that provided by the traditional methods of bank monitoring. One suggestion is to undertake simulations about the performance of intermediaries under different reasonable scenarios, such as changes in market interest rates.

Prudential supervision, as the process of enforcing the law and regulations, should show a high degree of flexibility and neutrality toward charter arrangements and the market segments served by particular intermediaries. Questions such as how does a bank examiner estimate the necessary provisions for loan losses in an intermediary whose portfolio is backed by character references only suggest the need to differentiate across organizations. Clearly, this evaluation process must be different from that of a commercial bank, whose loan portfolio is collateralized with marketable assets. Similarly, regulators should be flexible enough to understand that appropriate delinquency rates may vary with the nature of the clientele and the loan product.

THE METHODOLOGY OF SUPERVISION

An efficient mechanism for the surveillance of financial intermediaries should have two basic components. The off-site component should be an early-warning system based on analysis of data reported to the supervisory authority by the intermediaries themselves. Its main purpose is to provide a frequent depiction of the financial health and risks of each intermediary.

The on-site component involves actual visits to the intermediaries. On-site supervision is necessary to make those inspections that cannot be performed by an off-site analysis (for example, quality of internal control) and to verify that the data fed to the off-site surveillance system are correct.

RISKS OF FINANCIAL INTERMEDIATION

The dominant theme of this chapter has been the control and supervision of the risks assumed by depository financial intermediaries that can lead to insolvency. There are several common sources of insolvency for financial intermediaries.

CREDIT RISK

Whenever a financial intermediary acquires an earning asset, it bears the risk that the borrower will default, that is, not repay the principal and interest according to the contract. Credit risk is the potential variation in the intermediary's net income and in the value of its equity resulting from this lack of or delayed payment. Different types of assets exhibit different probabilities of default. Typically, loans carry the greatest credit risk.

INTEREST RATE RISK

This risk results from the potential variability in income and equity capital due to changes in the level of market interest rates. Interest rate risk, together with lack of appropriate diversification, is the most common source of bank failure in developed countries. This risk originates from the mismatch of the term to maturity of assets and liabilities with fixed interest rates (that is, from term transformation). When interest rates rise, intermediaries must pay more for deposits and short-term liabilities while not necessarily being able to raise their income on longer-term loans or other long-term assets.

LIQUIDITY RISK

Liquidity refers to the owner's ability to convert assets into cash with minimal loss, that is, the ability to sell an asset quickly without incurring significant losses. Typically, liquidity is needed to meet variation in depositor demand for withdrawals.

INTERNAL CONTROL OR FRAUD RISK

Internal control risk refers to the variation in income and equity capital that results from misappropriation of, theft of, or processing errors against the intermediary's assets by a customer or employee.

SPECIAL RISKS ASSOCIATED WITH DONORS

Excessive levels of the risks described above are the most frequently observed causes of failure among traditional financial intermediaries, as widely discussed in the literature on finance (Maisel 1981). All these risks affect traditional intermediaries and MFOs alike. The literature on finance does not recognize, however, risks that are characteristic of organizations supported by external donors.

One example that is frequent in MFOs but hardly observable in traditional intermediaries is what may be called subsidy-dependence risk.[12] Such a risk occurs in an MFO that is largely dependent on subsidies but mobilizes savings from the public as well. The problem, from a supervisory perspective, is that reductions in the annual flow of subsidies may endanger the stability of the intermediary and, therefore, the savings of its depositors. The supervisor should be concerned with the degree of dependence that a given intermediary has on volatile and uncertain subsidies (for example, government transfers and donor grants) and with the potential impact of their reduction or elimination.

In this sense, the supervisor need not be concerned with equity or capital transfers from donors, because they do not increase the risks faced by the intermediary, although they may discourage savings mobilization. Rather, the supervisory authority should be concerned, for example, with budget transfers to cover staff expenses or with below-market sources of loan capital.

Another example of these differences in risk between MFOs and traditional intermediaries is the result of the external influence exercised by donors or governments. MFOs are often flooded with cheap donor funds, accompanied by demands that these funds be allocated quickly. Frequently, donors target particular clientele without concern about creditworthiness, severely reducing the organization's degree of freedom in credit screening. All this imposes severe credit risks on the organization as it has to abruptly increase its pool of borrowers, frequently from a narrowly defined subset of the population. Rapid and disproportionate growth in the number of borrowers is highly correlated with portfolio losses from default.

Formal intermediaries experience portfolio growth in a more gradual fashion. Time allows them to adjust their loan-screening techniques gradually, and the development of bank-client relationships strengthens their customer base. Some MFOs, because of either choice or donor influence, have not diversified their loan portfolios or have not been able to select among all possible borrowers. These requirements have made MFOs the victims of the equivalent of repressive regulation.

REGULATION OF MICROENTERPRISE FINANCE ORGANIZATIONS

Depository institutions are defined in terms of the structure of their liabilities (for example, large debt as compared to equity), the fixed-value nature of their debt (for example, deposits), and the predominance of nonmarketable loans among their assets. Clearly, whenever microenterprise finance organizations introduce significant savings elements, they resemble depository financial intermediaries and share many of the characteristics that make regulation necessary. Thus, as MFOs seek to enhance their savings mobilization efforts, they must prepare themselves to be regulated and seek dialogue with regulators concerning appropriate forms of regulation. Changes will be needed on both sides.

This chapter has stressed the need for regulatory flexibility in the face of varying types of financial institutions and the varying market niches they serve. MFOs have a series of special needs arising first from the type of financial services they offer and to whom, and second from their institutional structures.

COLLATERAL AND CREDIT RISK

Many microenterprise loan programs do not require formal collateral. Instead, character-based loans, group loans, and the promise of subsequent larger loans are the main motivators for repayment. Well-performing microenterprise lending operations, such as PRODEM (see Chapter 12), have shown that individual credit risk can be effectively controlled by these techniques. Regulators would have to seek alternative means of valuing portfolios comprising such loans. Instead of collateral, the best indicators of portfolio value would be past performance of the portfolio and current status of arrears. Recent experience has shown that sound microenterprise loan operations need not generate high delinquency or default rates, but allowable levels of delinquency and default may need to vary from those sought in more standard commercial lending. If this method is to work, accurate measurement of portfolio quality is essential. Most microenterprise lenders require vast improvement in the quality and timeliness of their delinquency and default information.

INSUFFICIENT DIVERSIFICATION

Most MFOs have found it necessary to specialize in providing one loan product to a limited client group. Specialization has helped MFOs hone their programs to reach greater operational efficiency, but specialization may also increase risk, particularly in areas where geographic coverage is limited and risks are highly synchronized. However, even a broad mix of microenterprise clients will be dependent on the same underlying business conditions and therefore will be exposed to the same risks at the same time, especially if they live close together. Village banking programs are highly exposed to this type of risk, followed closely by credit unions (which are not quite as limited in terms of number of members and which offer loans for a wide variety of purposes). Large national MFOs, such as the Bank Rakyat Indonesia's unit banking system, are in the best position, as they can diversify risk across the nation. (See Chapter 9 on village banks, Chapter 8 on credit unions, and Chapter 11 on Bank Rakyat Indonesia for further discussion of these issues.) MFOs can also diversify slightly by serving a wider range of clients and by offering a slightly wider range of loan products. The benefits of such diversification must be balanced against the increased difficulty of managing a wider array of activities. In general, the best way for regulators to deal with the difficulty of diversifying in most microenterprise programs is to require higher emergency reserves than would be required for standard bank lending.

OWNERSHIP AND CAPITAL ADEQUACY

As discussed above, equity capital plays the central role in ensuring that owners have a stake in the solvency of the financial institution, and hence in the safety of deposits. In a very real sense, equity capital is the magic key that qualifies the bearer to accept deposits from the public. MFOs that are structured as nonprofit organizations have no equity capital, however. Even if an NGO owns funds that capitalize its loan program, these funds are not owned by investors who stand to lose their money. Thus, the capital can act as emergency reserves but cannot ensure prudent internal control by the directors or managers of the NGO. In most countries, lack of investor capital prevents NGOs from taking savings (other than limited forced savings from borrowers). This restriction should probably not be relaxed unless NGOs are required to maintain extraordinarily high capital reserve-to-asset ratios that can protect against large losses and are subject to stringent monitoring of their internal controls.

For credit unions and village banks, the ownership issue is different. In these organizations, capital is jointly owned by all members. However, as discussed in the chapters on these types of organizations, the different interests of savers and borrowers have been the source of conflicts. Particularly when borrowers are the dominant force, decisions may be made that are in the short-term interest of borrowers, but because they discourage savers, they work to the long-term detriment of all parties and may threaten the viability of the financial institution. These conflicts may make these organizations particularly unstable (Poyo 1992). Regulators have tended to allow member-owned organizations to govern themselves to a greater degree than investor-owned banks, on the presumption that members will look after their own best interests. Although this is true to some degree, there are sufficient problems—as testified by the history of the credit union movement—to warrant outside regulation and supervision.

LIQUIDITY RISK

Small MFOs are likely to be exposed to high levels of liquidity risk, particularly seasonal liquidity risk. If they are financially solvent and operating in a relatively healthy financial system, they should be able to deal with this risk through short-term borrowing and lending. Noncreditworthy MFOs will not be able to solve liquidity problems. Regulators must ensure that MFOs permitted to accept deposits are able to handle liquidity risks.

COSTS AND INFORMATION

Practical problems surrounding regulation of MFOs may be serious. They include the need for regulated MFOs to provide regular, high-quality financial information and the high cost of supervision (relative to assets protected) of MFOs.

DONOR-RELATED RISKS

As discussed above, MFOs receiving grants or concessional loans from donors are exposed to special types of risk, including those arising from subsidy dependence and donor influence.

This list of potential regulatory issues facing MFOs suggests that many MFOs need to implement significant structural and operational changes before accepting deposits. It also suggests that some MFOs should decide not to become depository institutions. As more MFOs reach this threshold, regulatory authorities will also need to consider the changes they can safely make to respond to the special characteristics of microenterprise finance.

As experience accumulates and it is interpreted from the perspective of the conceptual framework developed by this chapter, useful empirical generalizations will be found. It is important to protect microentrepreneurs who trust the organizations that mobilize their funds and grant them loans. Another objective is to promote healthy financial markets where the niche of providing credit to small borrowers and depository services to small savers becomes sufficiently attractive. In particular, it is important to avoid policy backlashes that might result from the failure of MFOs and other intermediaries that were not correctly regulated and supervised. Such failures and backlashes would jeopardize any progress in the achievement of the objective of improving access to financial services for microentrepreneurs.

NOTES

1. Although this chapter emphasizes the effects of regulation on market efficiency, beneficial and harmful outcomes may be identified with respect to stability, equitable distributions, and other policy objectives.

2. The basic assumption is that an efficient payments system is a key determinant of processes of economic growth and of efficiency in resource allocation. Low-cost operation of the payments system is based on the public's trust, which, in turn, depends on perceptions about the stability and solvency of the institutions that manage the system.

3. Similarly, highly efficient supervision efforts directed at enforcing financial repression packages will be damaging. We focus here on the dimensions of supervision that seek the enforcement of legitimate financial regulation.

4. For expository purposes, the term *bank* is used to denote any formal depository intermediary.

5. In economies with low per capita incomes, open markets for common stocks, bonds, mortgages, or even commercial bills are typically insignificant. Instead, private financial savings are largely currency and deposits (McKinnon 1989). Banks thus become the main formal source of funds.

6. In some instances, the costs of these interventions may be too high compared with their expected benefits. For example, if it would cost $1 million to supervise small intermediaries whose total assets amount to $500,000, it would be better to leave the market alone.

7. In developing countries, the court system may be prohibitively expensive, corrupt, or inefficient, further reducing the probability of successful contract enforcement.

8. For example, in several countries, cooperative banks are subject to less strict capital adequacy requirements than equivalent intermediaries, for entirely "political" reasons.

9. Sometimes, consistent risk differentials are the result of bad regulation itself, such as rules that force certain intermediaries to grant credit only in specific geographical locations or for specific purposes (for example, the savings and loans industry in the United States). These regulations do not allow intermediaries to diversify their risks sufficiently.

10. Under a regime of limited liability, this amount is the maximum loss that may be incurred, since the owners do not have a personal liability beyond their equity stakes in the firm.

11. As Kane (1985) has shown, in the presence of deposit insurance, the owner-managers of banks may assume higher risks than otherwise as well.

12. This risk explains much of the recent difficulty experienced by public development banks, particularly those that had not actively mobilized deposits from the public (Gonzalez-Vega 1990).

CHAPTER 4

The Process of Institutional Development: Assisting Small Enterprise Institutions Become More Effective

Elaine L. Edgcomb and James Cawley

INSTITUTIONAL DEVELOPMENT HAS emerged as a key factor influencing the performance of private development organizations (PDOs) that implement small enterprise development (SED) projects. In instance after instance, in case studies documenting twenty-five PDOs, those that chose to solve critical problems by paying attention to their institutional needs were able to work through the problems and become more effective SED implementors. Those PDOs that ignored their institutional needs continually encountered stumbling blocks that inhibited effective or efficient implementation.

This chapter examines the intersection between institutional development and small enterprise assistance, arguing that a better understanding of the first is essential for PDOs seeking to become effective implementors of the second. We present a framework for analyzing the process of institutional development based on a synthesis of twenty-five organizational cases, revealing concepts that can guide others in improving their small enterprise performance. The chapter draws principally upon the experience of members of the Small Enterprise Education and Promotion (SEEP) Network, which represents thirty-one North American PDOs.[1]

Institutional development is a complex process touching on values, mission, program, and intended goals. Contained in its definition are four important concepts:

1. *Process.* Institutional development is not static. It is organic and evolving. It affects all facets of an organization and it implies learning, adaptation, and change.

2. *Capacity.* Institutional development involves human resources as well as organizational structure and systems. Both need to be strengthened in concert.

3. *Sustainability.* The aim of institutional development is an organization that can sustain the flow of valued benefits and services to its members or clients over time.

4. *Impact.* Institutional development is not a goal. It is a means to solve problems, create a more favorable economic or policy environment, and improve the quality of people's lives.

Many PDOs that have recently entered the small enterprise sector are emphasizing methodology: learning the what and how of delivering essential business services. But experienced agencies have learned that engaging in small enterprise activities also requires the more profound institutional change suggested by these definitions and concepts. By reviewing how twenty-five organizations responded to this challenge, this chapter provides a structured path along which others can compare their own progress.

FRAMEWORK FOR INSTITUTIONAL DEVELOPMENT

Institutional development is a dynamic process of becoming a learning organization capable of influencing and adapting to a continually changing environment . . . it is a two way street, strengthening both partner organizations . . . it leads to financial, material and human resource autonomy and self-reliance . . . by mutually supporting one another's institutional development NGOs build a strong international movement in solidarity with the oppressed (InterAction/FAVDO African Partnership 1990).

Institutional development is a complex concept because the life of an organization is a complex process. A framework that expresses the fundamental ideas and concepts and permits an analysis of the principal elements involved is a useful approach to addressing the complexity. The matrix in Table 4.1 was created as an organizing tool to explore and analyze SED case experiences and embodies two notions:

1. *Components.* Institutional development implies a process of achieving mastery in at least four distinct, but related, areas of endeavor.

2. *Stages.* The requirements for mastery change over time as organizations mature.[2]

Table 4.1   Institutional Development in the Small Enterprise Sector: A Framework

Components	Stages		
	DEVELOPMENT Start-up, design, testing, and implementation of methodology and structure. Become effective. — Preparation — Start-up — Implementation	**SUSTAINABILITY** Organizational growth and maturation. Institution advances toward efficiency and financial viability. — Implementation — Consolidation — Growth	**EXPANSION** Scale-up. Institution expands its program by increasing clients and/or geographic coverage. — Transformation — Expansion
VISION An organization's ability to articulate and generate commitment for its mission. Key factors are executive leadership, board of directors, strategic planning.			
CAPACITY An organization's ability to structure itself; to develop systems and to recruit and train staff. Key factors are organizational structure, information systems, personnel policies, staff development.			
RESOURCES An organization's ability to raise, manage, and account for sufficient revenue to cover expenses. Key factors are fund-raising policies and practices, credit policies, budgeting and financial projections, accounting, portfolio management.			
LINKAGES The ability to develop and maintain productive relationships with relevant organizations. Key factors are government relations, peer networks, international PDO and donor partners.			

COMPONENTS

VISION. Vision is the ability to think creatively and critically about the organization. Vision is guided and formed by basic principles and beliefs that define the mission and purpose of an organization. It articulates a picture of the world that would result from the successful achievement of an organization's goals. It is important that vision grow out of, and respond to, locally defined needs. It is also important that vision is compatible with the principles of SED programs.

A vision that follows SED principles should clarify the people the institution seeks to serve and why, and it should reflect an understanding of these people as clients, rather than beneficiaries, with whom it shares a set of mutual rights and responsibilities. Finally, it should reflect the social and moral principles that guide the PDO and contain principles of cost-consciousness, sustainability, autofinancing of credit, growth, and expansion.

CAPACITY. Capacity is the ability to move thinking to action. It is the institution's ability to organize itself to achieve its mission effectively and efficiently. Capacity requires:

- A structure through which people can channel their energy and creativity, which anchors the organization in the mold of the vision, supports the organization's activities, is responsive to program and client needs, ensures that decisions get made at appropriate levels, and engenders appropriate forms of participation.

- Systems and procedures that ensure that the structure operates smoothly, that there is a timely flow of accurate information, and that staff and clients are treated fairly.

- A staff with the skills and motivation to implement the programs and manipulate the systems to achieve the objectives of the organization.

- A methodology that is an organized set of tactical steps that allows the organization to carry out its mission.

RESOURCE CAPABILITY. Resource capability is the ability to earn or raise sufficient funds to cover expenses without compromising vision or program design. An organization operating efficiently has achieved an assured flow of money that matches client demand and operational need. In addition to acquiring funds, organizations must be able to do financial planning and management and ensure accountability. Key factors include fund-raising policies and practices, credit policies, budgeting and accounting systems, financial projection and cash flow analysis, and portfolio management.

LINKAGE. Linkage is the ability to develop productive relationships with a wide variety of organizations. Linkage includes regular communication, interaction, and exchange of information and resources (Esman and Uphoff 1984). To be an effective implementor of SED activities, an organization must be perceived by the community in which it works, and by external entities, as carrying out activities that meet community needs in socially and culturally appropriate ways. Additionally, it must be seen as contributing to the overall improvement of the community. This legitimacy strengthens an organization and further supports the accomplishment of its mission.

Each component of the framework represents a distinctive organizational ability and involves an integral set of roles, policies, procedures, and tasks that need to be accomplished in systematic ways. The nature of the issues faced in each component and their importance to and impact on the organization change over time and thus require constant attention. Failure to appropriately address any of these issues has the potential to seriously weaken an organization and reduce its ability to serve its client population.

STAGES

The three stages identified in the framework present new challenges to be mastered.

DEVELOPMENT STAGE. The development stage begins at the initial point when an organization decides to undertake a small enterprise activity. During this stage, the organization makes major strides in crafting its methodology and begins structuring itself to carry out its mandate. The discussion of this stage is relevant for both new organizations in the process of establishing themselves and existing organizations incorporating SED into their mandates for the first time. This stage can be further divided into the preparation phase, during which planning is carried out and the foundation is laid for an organization and its program methodology; the start-up phase, when the program model is tested and modified; and the implementation phase, which involves the execution of a program ample enough to achieve visible levels of impact.

SUSTAINABILITY STAGE. This second stage is the period during which an organization achieves a certain amount of maturity, becomes an efficient implementor, attains a degree of financial viability, and can grow. It is during this stage that an organization makes the transition from effective implementation in accordance with predetermined impact targets, to a consolidation phase of more efficient delivery of services to clients, to a growth phase where the organization is increasingly capable of reaching larger numbers of clients with greater effect.

EXPANSION STAGE. In the expansion stage, an organization makes a structural transformation in order to scale up its operations to reach a significantly greater number of people. ACCION International, for example, identifies this stage with the capacity to reach 10,000 or more clients a year (Otero 1989a), though efforts of less magnitude may also qualify. Indicators that the threshold has been crossed include the clear existence of an organizational choice to reach larger numbers and the consequent decision to embark upon some form of structural change in the organization to make that goal a reality. Chapter 5 discusses the characteristics of organizations that enter the expansion stage.

This framework, like any analytic tool, is an abstraction of reality, reflecting and highlighting key elements to facilitate understanding. The actual process of institutional development is much less continuous than the logical progression the framework implies. The value of the framework is that it lays out the issues so that organizations can identify them, plan for them, recognize that these issues are not unique, and know that experience exists to address many of them. It is a tool that enables practitioners to analyze, understand, and do something about their organizations.

THE PROCESS OF INSTITUTIONAL DEVELOPMENT

Each stage of an institution's life presents central tasks to be accomplished and a number of characteristic stumbling blocks. In addition, each stage has its own particular quality or "emotional tenor" that is recognizably part of the process. This section addresses the key components of each stage, using examples from the twenty-five cases. Special attention is given to vision in the development stage, capacity in the sustainability stage, and linkage in the expansion stage. Resources, which require constant attention, are treated throughout.

DEVELOPMENT STAGE

For the development stage, the central task can be defined as establishing an effective program to mitigate or resolve a critical development problem. Viewed through the small enterprise lens, that critical problem reflects a pressing need for work and income on the part of large numbers of people. Two examples of problems addressed by SED activities are the increasing number of people working in the informal sector in large cities, trying to eke out a living by creating their own tiny businesses; and the pressing needs of low-income women displaced by political strife and violence.

To respond to problems such as these, there are a number of tasks an emerging organization (or program) needs to undertake. Most critically, it needs to:

- Generate a vision that articulates an achievable and motivating goal and links that goal to philosophic principles that express the institution's worldview and development approach.

- Develop the leadership to convey that vision to staff members and organize their efforts to bring it to fruition.

- Create or choose a methodology appropriate to the problem, then test and refine it to the point where impact can be achieved.

- Generate sufficient resources to support the organizational structure needed to make the program work.

As it works on these tasks, the organization passes through three phases of activity. In the preparation phase, the groundwork is laid. Initially, vision comes either from a leader seeking to make some kind of change or from a group of people seeking to solve a common problem. Vision is expressed differently, depending on local needs. For example, in Bangladesh, the vision of the NGO Proshika is to organize marginal classes for the structural transformation of society; in Guatemala, Fundación para el Desarrollo de la Pequeña Empresa (FUNDESPE) set out to promote the development of the western region through private initiative and small enterprise.

The locus for vision in an organization is, first and foremost, its leadership and board of directors, who use strategic planning to shape concrete goals, approaches, and resource requirements. Leadership is often embodied in the charismatic person who gave rise to the organization. In addition to vision, the leader is expected to be responsible for guiding the tasks that need to be done in the preparatory and start-up stages. A board of directors assumes the responsibility of governance of the institution. An effective board can gain access for, and enhance the legitimacy of, the organization at appropriate levels of government, with donor agencies, and in the private sector. As Chapter 5 discusses, this is particularly important when an organization decides to expand.

In some cases, board development precedes the formation of an organization. Opportunity International spent a year on the development of the Tulay Sa Pag-Unlad, Inc. (TSPI) board, which established a vision, developed policies, set program goals, and selected and supervised the executive director. Opportunity Industrialization Centers, International (OICI) is another North American PDO that invests heavily in assisting its local partners develop boards.

Although organizations such as TSPI and OICI pay particular attention to board development, generally PDOs are relatively unskilled in this area. A weak or ineffective board often hampers an organization's ability to operate efficiently, enter the sustainability stage, or expand. The Asociación para la Organización Empresarial Femenina de El Salvador (OEF/ES) assembly, for example, elected a board but paid little attention to its development. One of the challenges now facing OEF/ES is how to garner more support from the board and guarantee at least a quorum at meetings (Bath and de Sanchez 1990).

It is important to note the special challenge organizations face when they try to incorporate SED into a previously established mission (see Chapter 14). One PDO ran into obstacles when some of the Christian principles that formed its vision seemed to contravene sound SED practices such as charging market interest rates or applying sanctions for late repayment or nonpayment. Contradictions between an older vision and a new SED mission need to be conscientiously resolved by PDOs aspiring to be successful SED promoters.

Strategic planning provides the opportunity for an organization to think critically about its mission and purpose and how they will be achieved. A successful organization works from an internally driven strategy that grows out of locally identified needs and is sensitive to local environment and culture. Its plans reflect the capabilities of the organization and its commitment to cost-consciousness and self-financing.

Cameroon Cooperative Credit Union League (CamCCUL), for example, develops five-year plans with realistic and measurable objectives. In addition to setting the agenda for the organization, the level of detail makes these plans virtual project proposals. CamCCUL uses its plans to demonstrate to donors where it is going, how accomplishments will be measured, and what is needed from donors to achieve objectives.

The importance of the preparation phase to the future success of a small enterprise organization cannot be underestimated. ACCION International has found that the work involved can require one to two years without a single implementation step being taken. Similarly, Opportunity International's work with TSPI, the partner it helped establish in the Philippines, required a year's effort devoted to the identification of committed board members, the creation of a shared vision, the development of the initial operating systems of the organization, and an explicit understanding of the roles and responsibilities to be assumed by the local and international partners.

Settling on an appropriate methodology is critical. This task is simpler if an organization has access to a tested methodology that meets its clients' needs and can be adapted to local conditions. For example, ACCION's solidarity group methodology has been a source of training materials, operational manuals, control mechanisms, and evaluation for partners elsewhere, as discussed in Chapter 7. Other programs have found useful methodologies within networks such as the Pan American Development Foundation, Opportunity International, the World Council of Credit Unions (WOCCU), or programs applying the community bank model of the Foundation for International Community Assistance (FINCA). Of the twenty-five cases examined, fifteen have adapted methodologies from external sources in one form or another.

The second phase, start-up, covers the initial experience with implementation on a pilot or model basis. This is when the methodology is tested and adapted to meet client need. OEF/International's Women in Business (WIB) pilot project, undertaken simultaneously with the preparation steps surrounding the formation of OEF/ES, is an example. WIB demonstrated receptivity and demand for a program that provided accelerated training and credit for individually owned microbusinesses. It was four times more cost-effective than the previous approach, which focused on cooperatives, and it had 100 percent loan repayment. It became the core of the methodology adopted by the new institution.

During the preparation and start-up phases, organizations must begin to develop financial management systems that are flexible and expandable. Otherwise, an organization will quite likely find itself stymied by systems that lack the sophistication required to handle a larger operation. If possible, financial management systems should be computerized at the outset to avoid disruptive data transfer; to enable the institution to track income and expenses; to input data once for all levels of analysis; and to generate key reports on disbursements, repayment, delinquency, interest earned, and the performance of fieldworkers and offices (see Otero 1989a for more on this issue).

It is in the third phase of the development stage, implementation, when institutions begin to make a visible difference and demonstrate effectiveness. In ACCION-affiliated programs, where reaching a large number of clients is key and the experience base high, the model moves seamlessly into full implementation and reaches a large number of clients in the first year of operation (Otero 1989a). For other small enterprise programs, the move into fuller implementation is not characterized by high numbers but by gradual increases in the targets reached as experience is gained and the operation reaches a certain level of effectiveness. When the Agency for the Selection and Support of Individuals Starting Trade (ASSIST) entered this phase, it moved from serving a handful of small and medium-size businesses to serving sixty. OEF/ES reached an active portfolio of 199 loans and a total of 463 low-income women (and men) assisted.

There are three major stumbling blocks a small enterprise organization may face during this first period of organizational growth:

CRISIS IN LEADERSHIP. The cases show that leadership is sometimes exercised by a charismatic leader (Bangladesh Rural Advancement Committee [BRAC], CamCCUL, and the OICI movement) and sometimes by a group that forms the board (TSPI and Malawi Union of Savings and Credit Corporations [MUSCCO]). ASSIST's progress was minimal until the right mix of individuals was found for the board, which then located a dynamic, capable executive director. Instituto de Desarrollo Hondureño (IDH) was formed with the notion that the board need not be primarily responsible for resource mobilization. The result was a board formed of small businesspeople and white-collar professionals— sufficient for management, but not for growth.

METHODOLOGICAL PROBLEMS. OEF/International's striking success with the El Castaño Cooperative of tomato processors led it to concentrate on a method that incorporated intensive training, cooperative formation, ongoing technical assistance, and credit. The benefits that resulted in the first instance never materialized to the same degree in the next five replications. The match between the needs of displaced women and the service package was not quite right. It took the WIB pilot program to identify the adaptations that needed to be made.

RESOURCE SCARCITY. Successful small enterprise organizations stand on their own feet and are capable of raising the funds required to mount their programs and maintain their organizations. This is the lesson that Opportunity International's partners (TSPI and IDH), blessed with endowments, had to learn over the course of their relationship. OEF/ES had to learn it sooner, as it was born during a funding crisis that affected the U.S. parent organization and the local group. In many ways, the struggle for survival in its early development made OEF/ES a strong and resourceful institution. It strengthened the commitment of the staff, honed the fund-raising skills of the executive director, and forced cost-conscious management of the program. Security and continuity in resource flows can make a big difference in the ease with which an organization sets about its tasks, but an organization that has surmounted the challenges of resource mobilization early on leaves the development stage well prepared for the tasks of the next stage and its phases of consolidation, sustainability, and growth.

Finally, what does an organization at this stage look like, feel like? One that is working well is characterized by high motivation, a "mission mentality" that joins leadership and staff together and enables sacrifices of time, energy, and resources to be made in behalf of the common goal. Because staff is small, structure may be fairly loose;

systems are more personalized than standardized. As the OEF/ES case suggests, it is a time when personal loyalty and camaraderie can help a young group surmount the early challenges to create something more permanent and powerful.

SUSTAINABILITY STAGE

For reaching sustainability, the second major stage in our framework, the central task is to establish a mature organization with a program that achieves impact at a reasonable scale of operation and has satisfactorily addressed the issues of financial and technical viability. This stage implies generating a regular flow of benefits to clients on terms increasingly favorable to them and the PDO. Sustainable SED organizations can and must meet 100 percent autofinancing for their credit operations and establish a diversified funding base for other operational expenses not directly linked to credit. The base should include local funding as well as external support.

Unlike the phases of the development stage, the phases of consolidation and growth cannot be as readily divided, at least in terms of the case pool examined here. Consolidation implies efforts directed toward delivering services more efficiently and reaching larger numbers with greater effect. Consolidation has to do with systems and procedures, information management and computerization, staff development and incentives, and other cost-reduction measures. Growth pivots on organizational decentralization, methodological adaptation, and resource mobilization. Both were present simultaneously in the organizations studied.

The consolidation phase sometimes implies a slowdown in the tempo of an organization. There is a rush of activity as an organization begins implementing its program. With initial success the pace continues as organizations seek legitimacy, bring in new clients, orient staff, and demonstrate their effectiveness. During the consolidation phase, the focus is on modifying and adjusting so that an organization can achieve efficiency.

There are five tasks within two key components—capacity and resources—that require particular attention during this stage. Under capacity, the tasks are focused on staff, systems, methodology, and organizational structure. Under resource mobilization, the task is to achieve financial viability that allows growth and self-sufficiency.

STAFF. Attention to staff, systems, and structures is critical to an organization's consolidation and growth. A drop in repayment rates may signal that work needs to be done in one of these areas. Building institutional capacity means recruiting and nurturing a competent, committed staff, which requires attention to three details:

1. *Recruitment.* Recruitment processes must be developed that can detect individuals with the right mix of social and economic aptitudes and identify new staff members with the increasingly sophisticated financial skills required to manage programs at this level.

2. *Training.* Training is an important vehicle to integrate new staff members into the spirit and operations of the agency. Training also serves to upgrade the skills of long-time employees and to maintain motivation.

3. *Compensation.* Compensation is an important issue for sustainable organizations. Idealism can carry a staff only so far. In terms of both fair treatment of employees and getting results from staff, a program cannot effectively and efficiently deliver services at the long-term expense of its staff.

SYSTEMS AND POLICIES. At this stage, organizations need to regularize systems and policies for personnel, administration, and finance. Save the Children Fund (SCF)/Lebanon provides an example of the efforts required to make program operations and decision making systematic. Such ordered procedures increase in importance as staff size swells and programs grow geographically. SCF/Lebanon improved the efficiency of its program by developing a set of policy and procedure manuals. They were designed to detail all the procedure and policy areas that a commercial bank might require. They were written in clear, lay language so that they could be understood and used at all levels of the program. These policies included borrower selection criteria, interest rates and fees, repayment policies, delinquency policies, and loan terms and amounts. Procedures included planning, loan application, loan evaluation, loan approval, loan release, and loan maintenance.

METHODOLOGY. At the sustainability stage, a program fine-tunes its methodology to achieve greater efficiency and respond to evolving client needs. SED methodologies are neither static nor pure in their implementation. If a program works well for clients, their businesses grow in terms of assets, profits, employees, and borrowing needs. A lending strategy that worked at an earlier stage may no longer suit their needs. Among the methodological changes made by Asociación Grupos Solidarios de Colombia (AGS) were fixed-asset loans to solidarity groups that had been assisted for more than a year. Fixed-asset loans were also provided to individuals, maximum loan amounts were increased, and two programs were established to finance new microenterprises. Organizations that once served principally street and market vendors now finance neighborhood stores and other services as well as small-scale producers.

Meeting the needs of clients has led OICI to add small business to its training and job placement program. BRAC has responded to client needs by developing new production technologies and marketing ventures. The African credit union movements offer small enterprise lending windows for their clients. A sustainable program is far from static. Keeping up with client needs is a constant challenge.

STRUCTURE. The task is to institute a management-organizational structure that can efficiently implement and control a growing program. Organizations at the sustainability stage require business-minded, results-oriented management. They also need to delegate responsibility to middle-level managers. As organizational differentiation occurs, informality must give way to formality and vision must be augmented with sound management. PDOs have tried different combinations of staff mix between "social development" types and "business managers." The AGS organizations have found that the board is the most effective "keeper of the vision" and the executive director is the key business manager. SCF/Lebanon turned to a Yale business school graduate to help when the program began to grow.

FINANCIAL VIABILITY. Essential to organizations at the sustainability stage is the need to implement a plan for financial viability. For organizations in the sustainability stage, budgeting and financial projections become more complex. Larger amounts of money are needed, primarily to support larger portfolios. Operating costs will also increase as organizations train staff and attempt to reach a more geographically diverse client base. Financial management demands more sophisticated portfolio analysis, and the credit component moves toward 100 percent autofinancing. The organization needs capital to support a growing clientele.

Credit services should be fully self-sufficient. The standard has been set by several of the case organizations that have achieved that goal. CamCCUL generated 109.6 percent of its operating expenses; four of the fifteen AGS institutions achieved operational self-sufficiency; Asociación para el Desarrollo de la Microempresa, Inc. (ADEMI) in the Dominican Republic covered 103, 100, and 128 percent of operating costs for 1986, 1987, and 1988, respectively (Otero 1989a). TSPI at 90 percent is very close. These organizations have demonstrated that programs with sufficient loan capital, a large client base that can generate timely repayment, streamlined operations, and constant attention to cost control can cover their cost of operations (not including the cost of capital), if not totally, at least to a significant degree. That is, they can at a minimum reach Rhyne and Otero's level two (see Chapter 1).

Once an organization has achieved a credit delivery system that is 100 percent autofinanced, the next challenge is financial self-sufficiency. Financial self-sufficiency implies that an organization is covering all current operating expenses and maintaining the real value of money against the effects of inflation. It involves the ability to obtain and cover the cost of loan funds provided at unsubsidized interest rates. There are no agencies covered by the case studies that have fully achieved this goal.

Sustainability does not mean 100 percent self-sufficiency in all program aspects. Training, business services, and other activities may continue to require a subsidy. In these areas, sustainability is determined by the ability to generate resources on favorable terms from a diversified, reliable set of sources. This includes local fund-raising from private and government sources, fund-raising from external donors, and internal income generation from interest, other client fees, and savings (when legally possible). Organizations such as the African Opportunity Industrialization Centers (OICIs) (which cover all basic expenses from government subsidies and secure project support from other donors) and BRAC, TSPI, and IDH (with multiple external donor relationships) offer examples of institutions that are successfully meeting the challenge of developing a diversified set of supporters.

Financial results are only one part of the sustainability equation. There are two other parts: achieving regular and significant results for the institution's clients and reaching enough of them to have an impact in the operational context, be it local, regional, or national. As an organization works to achieve these results, it moves from its initial phase of implementation through phases of consolidation and growth.

There are five stumbling blocks organizations are likely to face in the sustainability stage:

A DROP IN REPAYMENT RATES. A decrease in repayment rates was reported by IDH, TSPI, SCF/Lebanon, and some ACCION affiliates. There are several roots, all related to the struggle of managing a larger portfolio. All have internal rather than external roots: An enlarged and developed client base cannot be reached by the same size staff under the established methodology (TSPI); new staff members do not have the same understanding of program principles and requisites as more experienced staff do (also TSPI); the organization does not understand the lending requirements and pitfalls of new economic sectors (IDH); and program structure adversely affects outreach (SCF). Poor repayment can be devastating unless handled forcefully with the application of sound banking practices.

DONOR-DRIVEN TEMPTATIONS. Because resource acquisition is a constant struggle, it is easy for an institution to fall prey to a donor's vision and end up sacrificing its own. At least five cases refer specifically to difficulties in this area. IDH, for example, found itself administering an agricultural lending program for which it was technically unprepared. TSPI accepted the management of a relief program. Care must be taken not to compromise vision in the drive to acquire resources for a growing organization.

STAFF COSTS. Low salary levels hinder recruitment of highly qualified individuals and eventually become a disincentive, even for the young and committed. Staff development becomes a crucial mechanism to train people in the skills required, to serve as a vehicle for motivation, and as a nonmonetary reward for good performance. A number of organizations have paid particular attention to this area. Both BRAC and CamCCUL spend a sizable portion of their resources upgrading staff. This is an area that merits more exploration among institutions struggling with the issues of the sustainability stage.

ORGANIZATIONAL BLOCKAGES. As an organization grows, its staff increases and tasks develop greater complexity; there is a consequent need for greater structure (and more levels), more sophisticated management, and devolution of decision making from the executive to the midmanagement level. These changes require an emphasis on training existing staff members and recruiting high-caliber people for positions that cannot be filled from within. They also mean painful reshuffling of those who cannot master the changing requirements of their positions.

COMPUTERIZATION. The growth of small enterprise programs depends on establishing an effective, computerized management information system. This need is keenly felt at the sustainability stage, when agencies become awash with the record keeping required to monitor loan repayments by hundreds or thousands of clients. A computer will resolve only part of the problem. Computerized information is only as good as the underlying systems that produce the data. If these fundamental systems are not working, the computer will not help, and it may divert attention from the fundamental problems.

Inadequate planning at the time an institution decides to computerize often leads to decisions made on the basis of available hardware or software rather than on the practical needs of the institution. The results are that institutions cannot effectively use the equipment or integrate the systems into their own. The move to computers can be facilitated by outside technical assistance, especially at the planning stage.

In summary, an organization in the sustainability stage must be a problem solver in order to overcome the many hurdles to financial viability and growth. Unlike in the development stage, the organization's character is less like a missionary and more akin to a systems analyst, as it crafts the underpinnings to support its methodology and pull its movement forward.

EXPANSION STAGE

The central task of the expansion stage is to develop the capacity to affect the lives of significantly increasing numbers of people. It implies a structural transformation in the institution itself in order to increase dramatically the number of people affected. Structural transformation involves a significant change in the vision and mission of an organization. It means setting a new direction or adding a major new component to its current mission. Strategic planning is required to ensure that the organization has the will and capacity to carry out such changes.

The goal is to increase impact significantly, either directly by providing services to more clients or indirectly by creating a better policy environment in which small enterprise can flourish. In almost all cases, the impact established as the goal of the expansion stage is of high magnitude. The target for TSPI and its network-in-development is 25,000 borrower businesses and 150,000 new jobs by the end of eleven years. AGS has set its sights on 50,000 borrowers by the mid-1990s. MUSCCO aims to serve 240 local societies with 25,000 members and assets of over $4 million. These numbers reflect an intent to jump from consolidation and growth into another phase of operation and accomplishment.

The entry of an organization into the expansion stage, from the SEEP perspective, is characterized less by a numerical client threshold (is it 1,000, 5,000, or 10,000?) than by a large-scale vision and the decision to undergo some form of structural transformation to make that vision a reality. This can take many different forms:

- For TSPI, the vision shifted from job creation in metropolitan Manila to achieving an economic impact throughout the country, in the belief that free enterprise was an essential element of the transition from dictatorship to democracy. The transformation was from an urban-based small business development agency to an institutional development organization focused on creating a network of fifteen micro- and small-enterprise agencies throughout the country.

- For MUSCCO, the vision shift was more subtle: from supporting a unified, nationwide credit union movement to becoming a key financial engine for the country's economic development. This shift required the agency to change from an apex organization dedicated to promotion, formation, and education into a central financial facility providing bank services, risk management, auditing, and other support services for the system.

- For AGS, the vision was large scale: providing credit to the poorest people in the informal sector in Colombia. The transformation was from a network support office providing coordination and technical services to a financial intermediary leveraging grants and loans for the members.

- For TechnoServe in Ghana, the vision was to achieve significant impact on important economic subsectors, such as palm oil, that employ the poor. The transition was from a technical and management assistance agency to one that can also act as a policy formation organization.

Expansion, as defined here, should not be the goal for all PDO programs. Given the difficulties inherent in the sector, sustainable small enterprise organizations are a valuable asset in and of themselves. To develop a viable program and efficiently deliver services to large numbers of the poor is an accomplishment that needs to be replicated in a variety of locations. Not all organizations can or want to undergo the transformation implied by expansion, nor should they be expected to. Chapter 5 discusses the characteristics that institutions in the expansion stage should have.

There are several stumbling blocks organizations face in the expansion stage:

A CRISIS IN VISION. This is especially evident at the board level, where older members may not feel the urgency of expansion or understand its implications. For example, when the TSPI board decided on its expansion drive, it took on new members chosen for their capacity to develop external links. In other instances, there is a difference in outlook between those with a nonprofit mentality and those with a keener sense of the bottom-line thinking that expansion requires. In fact, some observers and practitioners have questioned whether a PDO can achieve expansion if the goal is not part of an institution's vision from the outset. For that reason, some international agencies have found it easier to create new local organizations rather than work with those already on the scene. Chapter 13 also addresses this issue of board involvement in creating a vision for expansion.

NEW ROLES VERSUS OLD ROLES. When the Asociation pour Productivite (APP) in Burkina Faso revamped its methodology as a first step toward developing its autonomy and expanding its impact, there was a shift in clientele from individual, "somewhat better off" clients to groups made up largely of the poor and women. As a result, field staff (who had been privileged with high salaries and other status perks) were transferred from regional centers to key villages, and high-status motorcycles were replaced with mopeds. Not surprisingly, "the degree of understanding and acceptance of these measures by the staff varied enormously" (Rippey 1989, 14).

TSPI management, board members, and staff, skilled at credit management, found themselves expected to act in the unfamiliar role of organizational development specialists. In another example, MUSCCO found itself involved in a sorting process of matching skills and aptitudes with the requirements of new positions. Tension and dislocation were the unpleasant companions of the task.

INAPPROPRIATE RESOURCE MOBILIZATION. Sometimes international PDO partners can lead affiliates astray. APP, encouraged by the Partnership for Productivity, invested heavily in developing and managing certain enterprises, including a garage, agricultural input stores, a bookstore, a tractor plowing program, a heavy equipment rental service, and seed production centers. "They were planned to create a source of services for the programs so that it could become self-sufficient, but the result was quite the opposite . . . they lost money consistently" (Rippey 1989, 4). Although some large institutions such as BRAC can manage large commercial enterprises and use the revenues to support their programs, it is perhaps too demanding to expect most agencies to be entrepreneurial and take on the challenge of a credit program at the same time.

Sometimes the expansion stage is a reprise of the mood of the development period. There is an excitement and drive that can propel an organization to take on too much too fast. The content of a strategic plan may not realistically match the capacity of the organization or the support it is likely to receive from local or external sources. This can force the institution to slow down and consolidate early gains before it takes the next step forward.

The cases show that institutional development—the strengthening of organizational capacity—is key to effective implementation of SED programs. Whether a new organization is created to deliver small enterprise development, such as services, or an existing institution initiates SED programs, there are ramifications for program design, vision, capacity, resources, and linkages. If improving organizational capacity is ignored, it can lead to stumbling blocks that compromise a program's financial stability and diminish its impact. PDOs need to ensure that institutional development is a consciously and conscientiously programmed component of their SED program efforts.

NOTES

1. Formed in 1985 to aggregate, study and articulate PDO experience in small enterprise evaluation, the network has evolved into a center for member collaboration across the spectrum of enterprise issues. This chapter is written from the perspective of these members and their national partners.

2. This matrix was developed by the Institutional Development Working Group of SEEP and was presented in May 1989 at a SEEP workshop.

CHAPTER 5

The Evolution of Nongovernmental Organizations Toward Financial Intermediation

María Otero

T HERE ARE A growing number of examples of microenterprise development organizations that have decided to move toward financial intermediation. The demand among the poor for financial services is so great that it requires a more effective response than small programs that depend on outside funds. The decision to engage in financial intermediation brings with it the need for a fundamental transformation in the approach to microenterprise development. The nongovernmental organizations (NGOs) that have made this decision believe that such a transformation is the only way to address the demand for financial services over the long term and in a viable manner.

Edgcomb and Cawley, in Chapter 4, discuss how nonprofit organizations develop their institutional capacity to move toward a more sustainable approach to microenterprise development. This chapter is concerned with the subset of those organizations that are entering or mastering the expansion stage, have chosen to expand by forging closer links with the financial systems in their countries, and are moving toward financial intermediation.

Financial intermediation is the route taken by NGOs that have decided to specialize in financial services, scale up their microenterprise lending activities, and reach tens of thousands of borrowers (Otero 1989a). Expansion of lending activities becomes the vision that drives these NGOs forward, influences their operations, and ultimately differentiates their work from that of other NGOs. These organizations become specialized lending institutions whose primary objectives are to improve the quality and efficiency of their lending operations and expand them significantly.

This chapter presents seven institutional and financial characteristics that microenterprise development organizations must display before developing links with financial systems. These are type of governance, number of clients reached, sources of funding, methodology, self-sufficiency, financial management, and staff development.

Although this discussion draws primarily from ACCION's experience in Latin America, the framework it suggests for identifying NGOs that can link to financial systems pertains to other developing regions as well. (The discussion in this chapter is based on the experience of the ACCION-affiliated network of over fifty NGOs in Latin America, which are in the process of moving toward financial intermediation. The experience of the most advanced in this network is discussed in Chapters 12 and 13.)

Once an NGO decides to follow this "expansion-led" approach, its potential area of coverage becomes the whole country. This redefinition of its role means that the NGO must not only seek financial sustainability at its current level of lending but also find the resources necessary for the planned expansion. At this point, these NGOs begin to build links with the financial system. They recognize that donor funding cannot provide the very large sums of money needed for lending. To succeed in building links, the organizations must improve their efficiency, use sound lending principles to guide their financial operations, and cut costs. If an organization can operate in this manner, then it should also be able to obtain capital from local financial-sector institutions.

Financial intermediation—the path the NGO is beginning to follow—has at its base the intermediation between savers and borrowers: The financial organization receives savings for capital accumulation, pays interest to savers, and makes loans, receiving interest from borrowers. In most countries, regulations prevent nonprofit organizations from capturing savings, an essential ingredient of intermediation. Given this barrier, NGOs are currently exploring other institutional frameworks for financial intermediation, including raising funds from institutions that take deposits (thereby furnishing an additional lending capability to complement the savings—completing the financial intermediation loop) and transforming themselves into another type of institution that can engage in savings as well as credit.

The expansion-led approach creates internal changes well before an NGO is prepared to change its institutional format. The NGO must hire staff with strong technical skills in financial management and credit operations and must train its current staff more rigorously in these areas. The composition of the NGO staff gradually changes to include disciplines necessary for financial intermediation. As a result, the salary structure changes because of the higher salaries that the market offers these professionals.

Efficient financial management of the lending operations and the organization becomes a priority. A growing program disburses thousands of loans a month and maintains portfolios of over $1 million, requiring sophisticated management information systems (MIS). Most NGOs make use of systems used in banks to generate the information needed for monitoring their credit portfolios. They invest heavily in systems—both hardware and software—and in staff hiring and training.

Attention to efficiency in delivering financial services becomes another priority concern. The systems for obtaining loan information, reviewing and approving applications, and disbursing and collecting loans must not only respond to the needs of the clients but also incur low costs of operation and allow expansion. It is in this area of financial management that these organizations least resemble other NGOs and more closely approximate a bank's operations.

FINANCIAL INTERMEDIATION: SEVEN CHARACTERISTICS FOR NGOs

The seven characteristics laid out in Table 5.1 define the direction that expansion-led organizations should follow as they prepare to enter the world of financial intermediation. NGOs must demonstrate a high level of accomplishment in the seven areas outlined here, since these are proposed as prerequisites to engaging in financial intermediation.

GOVERNANCE AND BOARDS

The governance function and the composition of boards under the expansion-led approach are crucial considerations because the board will decide whether the NGO should move toward financial intermediation. Key factors are at play in this decision, in particular the increased level of effort the board members must accept to make it happen and the much higher level of risk that they assume, both for themselves and for the institution.

Perhaps the first way in which NGOs link into the financial systems in their countries is by choosing private-sector individuals—businesspeople and bankers—as board members. If these people combine their knowledge and access with a clear sense of the social responsibility behind these programs, they become a priceless and essential resource for the expansion process.

Private-sector board members create access to institutions and sources of finance that are otherwise unreachable. They also outline a vision for the NGO that can take it toward financial viability and intermediation. They provide the technical financial expertise necessary to prepare for expansion and institutional transformation. All the ACCION-affiliated programs that have been most successful in expanding operations and in initiating links with the financial sectors in their countries have done so under the leadership of private-sector board members.

Ownership becomes important when an organization moves out of the nonprofit world to become a financial institution. The board no

Table 5.1 NGO Characteristics Necessary for Financial Intermediation

Characteristics	Expansion-Led Approach
Governance and board	The importance of an active, well-informed board with financial expertise becomes more of a priority. Private-sector individuals play a decisive role in obtaining resources and setting the vision for the organization. Boards assume additional risks by helping gain access to commercial money and investing in the organization.
Client population	Main emphasis is on scaling up the size of the program. Focus is on reaching tens of thousands or more microentrepreneurs. Borrowers are defined as "clients."
Sources of capital	Funding from grants, soft loans, and bank loans is blended, moving toward borrowing only from banks.
Methodology for delivering financial services	Use methods that have been fine-tuned. Specialize in financial services only. Do not experiment. Operate many thousands of transactions a month. Developing savings instruments becomes very important.
Self-sufficiency/ financial standing	Attaining operational and financial self-sufficiency becomes a requirement. Transaction costs decrease due to increased efficiency and scale. This is a key issue for NGOs that want to continue expansion.
Financial management	Effective financial analysis and more complete MIS become a priority. Financial projections are more sophisticated. Financial analysis is integrated into program implementation.
Personnel/staff development	Technical expertise in financial areas increases. Staff grows rapidly; more emphasis is placed on training the staff. Areas of emphasis are client relationship, portfolio management, planning, and institutional development.

Note: The characteristics of organizations in earlier stages of development are discussed in Chapter 4 and are omitted from this table.

longer plays only a governance role. Its responsibilities now include identifying responsible owners, building an equity base, and creating a permanent ownership structure that assumes accountability for the organization. The institution's operations are of greatest interest to the owners who have a stake in its performance. Board composition will be a determinant in ensuring that maximizing returns does not overtake the priority objective of reaching the poor.

CLIENTS REACHED

The scaling up of operations is the characteristic that most clearly differentiates the NGOs that are moving toward financial intermediation. Scaling up refers to gradual but consistent expansion of operations to reach thousands of small-scale entrepreneurs. Scaling up leads programs to develop a market perspective and to focus on financial services that respond to the preferences of their clients.

NGOs must maintain clarity about their ultimate objective: provision of services to the poor. Two indicators assist in determining whether they are lending to the smallest and neediest borrowers. The average size of a loan indicates who is borrowing. Small loans tend to reach smaller businesses. Gender is a second indicator. Those NGOs reaching a significant percentage of women are providing services to the poor, since women predominate at the bottom of the pyramid of microenterprise production.

PRODEM (Fundación para la Promocion y Desarrollo de la Microempresa) in Bolivia, discussed in Chapter 12, provides a good illustration. During July through December 1991, for example, the organization disbursed an average of $1.5 million each month to an average of 1,091 new borrowers and 4,100 second-time borrowers. The small size of the average loan—$289—indicates that socioeconomically the borrowers were poor. Not surprisingly, 74 percent of PRODEM's borrowers were women.

Effectiveness in lending—for example, reaching the desired target group—can be adversely affected by expansion. Factors such as transaction costs and perceived level of risk tend to pressure the NGO to lend gradually larger amounts to borrowers who are moving up the microenterprise pyramid and to shift slowly away from its original purpose of providing financial services for the poor.

A successful resolution to this problem is reached by programs that provide first loans to very small-scale producers but do not "graduate" those who have grown and need larger loans. These programs have expanded their target group to include those who, although producing on a larger scale, still have difficulty obtaining commercial loans. Asociación para el Desarrollo de la Microempresa, Inc. (ADEMI) in the Dominican Republic provides a good example. Its 1991 lending portfolio showed that of the 11,249 loans made, 82 percent were less than $800, and 60 percent were less than $400. The average loan size, at $681, was higher than PRODEM's, in part because the program made five loans of between $16,000 and $30,000.

Finally, the NGO's coverage must shift from local to regional and eventually, where feasible, to national. Most NGOs open branches or regional offices in different cities, developing decentralized systems of operation that resemble bank branches.

SOURCES OF CAPITAL

The shift from being a donor-funded organization to being one that blends grants and soft loans with funds borrowed from banks (moving from level one to level two in terms of Chapter 1) constitutes the most dramatic change for NGOs. The objective of these organizations is to eliminate subsidies gradually for their lending operations. NGOs moving in this direction currently borrow part of their funds from banks and still rely on grants and soft money. Expansion into new areas, for example, continues to require subsidized money.

There are no examples today of NGOs that operate exclusively on funds borrowed from commercial sources. In the most advanced examples, one notes a combination of grant funding with bank financing, though the ratio of borrowed to grant funds varies, depending on the financial standing and size of the operation. In the ACCION network, of the total 1991 portfolio estimated at $26 million, over 25 percent was financed through bank loans (ACCION International 1991).

Access to borrowed money and the capacity to use it fundamentally change the relationship between NGOs and donors and between NGOs and financial-sector institutions in their countries. The challenge for these NGOs is to find effective ways to link up with commercial sources of funds and to work with donors and commercial institutions to overcome the internal and external barriers that constrain NGOs from gaining access to adequate sources of capital (Drake and Otero 1992).

METHODOLOGY AND OPERATIONS MANAGEMENT

The techniques for providing financial services to the poor proliferated in the 1980s. Various NGOs demonstrated that one can lower transaction costs and maintain high repayment rates while reaching large numbers of people. To move toward financial intermediation, NGOs must perfect their lending methodology and concentrate only on financial services.

Chapter 1 outlines the lending principles that have proved effective. There are three indicators of the degree to which an NGO uses these principles: capacity to disburse large numbers of loans, capacity to incur low transaction costs, and ability to maintain a sound portfolio. As NGOs move toward financial intermediation, their objective is to improve efficiency and increase the size of their lending operations rather than experiment with new methodologies.

SELF-SUFFICIENCY AND FINANCIAL STANDING

NGOs on the expansion-led track are concerned not only with operational self-sufficiency—covering their costs with income earned —but also with taking on the financial costs of borrowed money. The high unit cost of making very small loans is reflected in the interest rates they charge, which in some successful programs is 10 to 12 percent above the market rate (Jackelen and Rhyne 1991). Organizations must also build loan loss reserve funds and maintain the real value of their portfolios. NGOs must be able to demonstrate a high level of self-sufficiency before they can engage in financial intermediation. Chapter 1 outlines four levels of self-sufficiency and suggests that level three—which still provides for a level of subsidy but moves organizations toward self-sufficiency—is the level institutions must reach before engaging in financial intermediation. The ability to operate at or near level three is one of the most important determining factors in an NGO's capacity to borrow from commercial sources.

FINANCIAL MANAGEMENT

For expansion-led organizations, investment in effective financial management is essential for continued growth and any move into financial intermediation. Information systems are at the heart of good financial management (Christen 1990). An NGO must allocate substantial resources so that its system provides timely and accurate information, conducts needed analysis of performance, and generates projections for future planning. These three functions of financial management cannot be met unless the information system generates these data and adapts to the information needs of a growing program.

An important issue in financial management is the degree of centralization required in the collection and analysis of information. As a program grows, it develops additional offices, each with its own portfolio, income, and expenses. Some suggest that the primary unit of field activity, whether it is a branch or a regional office, must operate with a significant degree of autonomy to allow it to carry out its responsibilities with authority (Patten and Rosengard 1991). Patten and Rosengard (1991) suggest that a unit should have its own balance sheet and income statement to enable the NGO to judge performance on both output and financial standing.

The difficulty is to generate consolidated financial statements that provide a view of the financial standing of the whole organization. NGOs often fall short by either disaggregating data to the point that the whole picture is unclear or aggregating them to the point that the inefficiencies of one unit are covered by the efficiency of another, a great disincentive for continued good performance.

Proper financial management remains a challenge for NGOs. The necessary mix of technology, expertise, and resources is difficult to assemble. Although there are principles and considerable guidance in this area, each NGO ultimately must develop its own system and must adapt existing software for its own needs.

PERSONNEL AND STAFF DEVELOPMENT

Staff training is essential to maintain clear objectives, motivate performance, and increase skills. The closer an NGO gets to financial intermediation, the greater the need to train its staff. Also, the NGO will have to combine staff from social science disciplines with finance professionals. Training must provide both the technical and the social framework to work with the poor in financial intermediation.

The most useful approach to staff training integrates training into ongoing operations to ensure that staff members receive training in a structured and systematic way. In addition to training staff on topics related to their specific responsibilities, the NGO should upgrade financial skills for all staff and improve their financial management skills. Financial intermediation requires all staff members to move up the learning curve in these areas.

Program expansion brings with it rapid growth in staff size. There are NGOs that in three to four years tripled or quadrupled their staff. ADEMI in the Dominican Republic has a staff of over 100 employees; PRODEM in Bolivia grew to more than 120 in four years. In order to incorporate new staff, maintain integration among staff, and undertake increased decentralization, staff must receive training in the principles of proper management and communication necessary for expansion. This training contributes to the creation of an institutional culture that is held in common by the staff and that allows for a smooth transition to financial intermediation.

ADOPTING THE EXPANSION-LED APPROACH AND TAKING ON FINANCIAL INTERMEDIATION: IMPLICATIONS FOR NGOs

The move toward financial intermediation takes NGOs along a new and difficult path. Three of the most important challenges along that path are considered here.

THE SOCIAL DEVELOPMENT VERSUS PROFIT DILEMMA

It is important to understand the ethos from which these institutions are evolving. Their work as development organizations is based on a strong foundation built on social development and equity considerations. Their priority continues to be increasing the poor's access to financial services. In the process, they are entering the world of financial intermediation in settings where financial systems lack the capacity to reach this population. By assuming this role, NGOs are incorporating the basic thinking of financial institutions—making loans while reducing risks and charging an interest rate that reflects the costs of lending—into their own social objectives of reaching the poor.

The conflict that arises is quickly apparent. These organizations seek to maintain their social development objectives and combine them with the profit objective of a financial institution. Although they make use of financial market tools for their lending—charging positive interest rates that are often higher than commercial rates, reducing risk, and increasing efficiency in their operations—they also target their credit to a poor population that appears risky and least able to repay. In this context, profits are seen as essential to long-run sustainability and expansion but not as ends in themselves.

The social agenda these NGOs pursue is the creation of access to financial services for a significant number of poor people. These organizations interpret their possible transformation into financial institutions as a way of changing the closed nature of lending in their own countries by opening the financial system to previously excluded populations. They wish to demonstrate that there is a market for these financial services and that the services can be provided in a sound financial manner.

One challenge for these organizations is to maintain the integrity of this duality of purpose and not allow one part to overtake the other. The ownership profile—who invests in these institutions and what values they bring as shareholders—will either safeguard or compromise the social commitment of the institution. A move toward financial intermediation could make an organization lose sight of its social objective, much as adherence to only the social agenda could make it ignore the steps necessary for long-term, unsubsidized viability.

NGOs that scale up their microenterprise programs and utilize financial principles for lending become specialized lending institutions. They gradually relinquish the familiar world of NGOs and assume a less predictable role as hybrid organizations that combine social objectives with financial viability. In this period of transition, the organizations do not quite fit in either world. Specialization under conditions that draw from two very different and apparently contradictory approaches—the nonprofit and the profit-making—suggests that each organization will undergo a difficult process of redefinition of organizational goals and objectives and will meet with criticism from both the world of NGOs it is leaving and the world of financial institutions it is approaching. One will deny the organization's commitment to social objectives while the other will maintain skepticism regarding its ability to become viable.

Clarity about these dual values is fundamental to the process of specialization and the subsequent institutional transformation these organizations undergo. Only when the organization's goals and objectives are clearly specified can the necessary changes in operations be identified and agreed upon. Each organization must also be able to explain its role convincingly to other institutions around it.

SAVINGS MOBILIZATION

Capturing savings is an essential part of financial intermediation. NGOs have not developed expertise in this area for two reasons. First, they have always conceived of their programs as lending operations and have concentrated on perfecting their methodology in this area. As Chapter 2 argues, savings has not been recognized as a financial service that the poor demand. Second, as mentioned above, regulatory policies in many countries prevent nonprofit organizations from capturing savings. Finally, some organizations believe that accepting savings should be a second step because an organization must first establish itself as a competent lender before it can safeguard the funds it accepts.

The experience of some successful programs shows that savings can be introduced as a compulsory feature of lending activity (Otero 1989b). The Grameen Bank requires borrowers to save an established percentage of the loan, which remains on deposit while they borrow from the program. PRODEM and some organizations in Colombia have also used this mechanism to generate savings from their borrowers, constituting a significant percentage of their portfolios (see Chapters 12 and 13). The incorporation of forced savings into lending programs helps the organization learn about the savings practices and needs of its borrowers. At a more advanced stage in their institutional evolution, these organizations will be better prepared to design the voluntary savings instruments that are essential for financial intermediation.

Savings mobilization must become an integral part of an NGO's move toward financial intermediation. Those institutions that for legal reasons cannot capture savings can nevertheless facilitate their clients' access to formal savings services. Those NGOs that choose to become financial institutions must recognize that savings should become their major source of capital (see Chapters 1, 2, and 11). The design of appropriate instruments for voluntary savings should begin early in the process.

INSTITUTIONAL SUSTAINABILITY

The long-term viability of an organization becomes much more difficult when donor funds are not the source of capital. Although all microenterprise NGOs aspire to sustainability, this goal is traditionally seen in the context of available donor monies. In the case of expansion-led organizations, however, sustainability must be discussed in the context of decreasing grant funding and increasing borrowed monies or deposits. If an NGO borrows money to lend, its continued operation will depend on its capacity to pay back its loans.

Very close supervision of lending operations becomes an important ingredient for institutional sustainability. Because an NGO's operations are not supervised by an outside national entity—and previously its accountability was primarily to its donors—the NGO must assume responsibility for appropriate supervision of its lending operations. Although there are shortcomings in supervising one's own work, periodic audits, reporting mechanisms, and other systems can highlight trouble areas before a problem becomes serious. The role of the board in this supervisory function is essential.

Table 5.1 builds on a new approach to microenterprise development that moves NGOs toward financial intermediation and toward becoming part of the financial system. The seven characteristics discussed here enable one to identify which NGOs are best suited to move in this direction. Among current NGOs, several are moving in this direction; however, most are at the early stages. The most advanced ones have already entered into relationships with banks and in many cases show better performance in all seven areas (Drake and Otero 1992).

CHAPTER 6

A New View of
Finance Program Evaluation

Elisabeth Rhyne

THIS CHAPTER ADDRESSES the evaluation of projects that offer financial services—credit and/or savings deposits—to poor clients and
microenterprises. The chapter presents a framework for evaluating
such programs that is in keeping with our current understanding of the
role of finance in economic development and the best practices in financial development programs. To understand why such a framework
is needed and why it differs from currently prevailing methods, it is
necessary to summarize the major debate about finance programs and
explain how that debate has been resolved. Following this introduction, the evaluation framework itself is presented.

During recent years, development institutions have increasingly
adopted a new view of credit and finance programs. This new view replaces an older approach in which programs funneled credit to particular
economic groups, using whatever institution offered the most competent
delivery mechanism. Development finance institutions, discounted lines of
credit, and nongovernmental organizations (NGOs) were all used to reach
target groups selected by governments and donors. The targets themselves
ranged from major industry to small farmers to microenterprises. Though
targets and mechanisms varied widely, the programs of the older approach shared an underlying set of motivations and working principles:

- They were conceived as efforts to generate economic
  growth in a target group designated as crucial for national
  development. In a sense, they were not finance programs
  but sector programs that used finance as a means of
  reaching the target population, predicated on the notion
  that they could release a binding "credit constraint."

- They assumed a static view of the mainstream financial
  system and consequently sought to compensate for the
  failure of the system to serve target groups by providing
  an alternative source of services.

- They were financed by donor or government funds rather than from within the financial system.

Such programs have been a mainstay of international development for decades and can be found in nearly every country.

A critique of this approach, first articulated in the early 1970s (USAID 1972), has now gained sufficiently widespread acceptance to be considered the dominant view in the field of international development finance. Among the leading proponents of this view, and responsible for much of the literature that articulates it, have been the financial economists of the Department of Agricultural Economics and Rural Sociology at Ohio State University.

This new view takes a radically different stance on each of the three points that characterize the old view. It argues first that the causal links between receipt of credit by individual borrowers and their subsequent economic growth are indirect, credit being but one factor in an extremely complex process of decision making by enterprises and households. Financial services are valued more for their general enabling effects across whole economic sectors rather than for the direct change induced by individual loans. Second, the new view argues that it is far better to build the capacity of the financial system than to provide a substitute for its inadequacies. By providing finance directly, often on a noncommercial basis, old-view programs reduced incentives for commercial lenders to innovate in areas where donors or governments already operated. Finally, the new view recognizes that, in the long run, nationwide financial services cannot be funded from limited donor or government coffers; a healthy, sustainable financial system must be based on mobilization of resources from the citizens of the country itself and through commercial sources. In short, the new view of finance emphasizes building financial intermediation systems that offer savings and credit services on a commercially sustainable basis.[1]

As a result of this shift in thinking, some of the major donors have reduced their use of development finance institutions and lines of directed credit. An increasing number of new programs are being developed using the new principles. However, a mix of approaches remains. At present, credit and finance programs can be found throughout the spectrum from targeted subsidized credit to pure financial system development.

In light of this new view of finance, methods of evaluation need to be rethought. For the most part, evaluations of credit programs are still based on the old view's ideas about causality. They are centered on the presumption of a direct causal link between receipt of credit by individual borrowers and a particular desired economic response, for example, changed borrower income resulting directly from receipt of a particular loan. In essence, these are still sector program evaluations rather than evaluations of financial system development.

There are two problems with the old evaluation model. First, the focus on the direct causal response to individual loans misses much of the richness of the effects of finance, which are generally diffuse rather than strictly linear. Second, evaluations that try to measure that response are, in effect, attempting to prove that financial services are valuable, a task that is better left to more general research that explores the relationship between the presence of a healthy financial system and economic growth. On the basis of what is already known about the value of financial services, one can be confident that wider availability of credit and savings services benefits the users, their communities, and their economic sectors. Additional knowledge about the benefits of financial services is needed, but it is best gathered in the context of a rigorous research effort that is not necessarily focused on individual loan programs. If program evaluations can be freed from the burden of proving that finance matters—a task for which they are not well suited—they can concentrate on evaluating the quality of the services and their institutional setting.

THE VALUE OF FINANCIAL SERVICES TO THE ECONOMY AND TO CLIENTS

Evaluations should use the current understanding of the role of financial services as their frame of reference. From an economy-wide perspective, financial economists agree that financial institutions contribute to economic growth by performing three crucial functions (World Bank 1989, 25):

1. Mobilizing a society's resources and allocating them to efficient uses (intermediation).

2. Helping the economy manage risk by diversifying it.

3. Facilitating transactions—providing "axle grease" to the economy.

Financial services do not create economic opportunities directly. Rather, they help people and enterprises position themselves to take advantage of opportunities. In general, goals for finance programs should be specified in terms of improving the ability of financial systems to perform these three functions or extending them to new areas or client groups. Evaluation should focus on indicators that reveal whether assisted institutions perform these basic financial functions well.

From the individual's perspective, access to financial services allows clients to:

1. Protect themselves and their families against bad times by building a stock of assets or by borrowing during emergencies.

2. Manage their enterprises and other activities more efficiently, for example, by purchasing inventory or inputs at advantageous times and prices.

3. Obtain capital for investment.

These three points have several further implications that are crucial for understanding how finance works. First, clients can use savings as well as credit to carry out these functions (Gadway, Gadway, and Sardi 1991). Many people prefer to save rather than to borrow. Thus a good finance project involves both credit and savings (or at least fits into a system that involves both). Second, any given transaction is only one event in an ongoing series of financial decisions that the client manages. A focus by evaluators on individual transactions misses much of the real story. Third, financial services are used for important functions other than growth-oriented investment, such as special family events, home improvement, or purchase of consumer durables. Planners and evaluators should understand these functions before specifying their own objectives, in order to avoid specifying objectives that do not adequately match client behavior.

Let us examine how an evaluation might be organized to build upon this understanding of the functions of financial services for individuals and the economy.

A FRAMEWORK FOR EVALUATING FINANCE PROJECTS

The evaluation framework described here has two levels, that of the client and that of the institution (see Table 6.1).[2] Before moving to an item-by-item discussion of the issues that evaluations should examine, a few general comments are needed on the characteristics of the proposed approach.

In keeping with the emphasis on building healthy financial institutions, the new view would consider market discipline to be one of the most reliable and relevant indicators of performance. Each of the two evaluation levels is associated with a strong commercial test. The service-client relationship is best measured by a market test of demand, or the willingness of clients to pay. If people pay full cost for a service on an ongoing basis, then evaluators can be sure that the service is valued at least as highly as its price. By their actions, clients reveal information

Table 6.1   A Framework for Evaluating Finance Programs

The client-service relationship
1. Outreach
    a. Number of clients; market penetration indicators
    b. Characteristics of clients: gender, location, income status, sector of enterprise
2. Quality of service, alternatives
    a. Market test: willingness to pay
    b. Client transactions costs: convenience and timeliness
    c. Service terms: price, loan sizes, maturity, collateral, access to deposits, eligibility requirements
3. Enlarging clients' decision-making options; how the service fits into the client's financial management process—liquidity, consumption smoothing, investment

Institutional viability
1. Financial self-sufficiency of service
2. Financial condition of institution
    a. Profitability or ability to break even
    b. Portfolio quality
    c. Liquidity
    d. Capital adequacy
3. Institutional strength and context

---

on the value of benefits, which is more credible than verbal responses to questionnaires.

The market demand test is less valid when services are underpriced or subsidized, because the price to clients does not include the cost of the subsidy. By buying the service, clients show that they value it as much as its price, but not whether they value it as much as its cost. This factor becomes more problematic the greater the subsidy.

At the level of the institution, the strong commercial test is financial self-sufficiency, or the ability to cover all costs from program revenues. These two tests, which are interdependent, make finance programs "self-evaluating."[3] The tests are easily verified and, if both are passed, evaluators can be confident that the program is successful.

A strict free-market evaluation might stop there, saying that a market-based service has no further burden of proof than showing that it yields a solvent commercial operation. More is needed, however, whenever a government or a donor becomes involved in supporting financial programs that serve marginal clients. The fundamental purpose for their involvement is to extend the frontier of the financial sector into sustainable, profitable activities through innovation and demonstration effects (Von Pischke 1991). Innovation is sought by introducing a new type of service or instrument to existing clients, introducing a new type of client to existing instruments, or both. This frontier orientation requires that evaluations concern themselves with the nature of the innovation. An evaluation should determine whether the frontiers have, in fact, shifted. This area of inquiry requires examination of the client group and the specifics of the services it receives.

In addition, evaluations should produce information that enables the financial institution to improve its performance by reaching new customers, offering better services, and operating more efficiently. Meeting this objective requires detailed information on clients—along the lines of market research—and on internal operations.

Use of such a framework blurs the traditional distinction between "management" evaluation and "impact" evaluation. One finds that information about clients can be significant for management decisions, and indicators of institutional performance, such as cost recovery, reveal a great deal about the achievement of ultimate objectives. With the framework proposed here it does not make sense to carry out management-only evaluations, confined to operations and administration, nor to allow evaluations of the impact on clients to stray very far from the interaction between client and service.

These principles become clearer as the following sections move point by point along the organizing framework shown in Table 6.1, describing the relevant indicators and their uses at each stage.

CLIENT LEVEL

At the level of clients, evaluations should substantially resemble market research. The main point of the research would be to understand the needs, preferences, and alternatives of the clients as they relate to the use of financial services generally and the offered services in particular. Such research should be highly useful to the institutions in refining current services and designing new ones.

CLIENT OUTREACH. Indicators of outreach include numbers of clients as well as information on their basic characteristics, such as gender, location, or type of business. Assessment of outreach responds to the strong interest that donors, sponsors, and financial institutions should have in understanding clients. If donors and sponsors want to know whether frontiers have shifted, and if institutions want to improve services, they can learn by adopting a marketing point of view that emphasizes knowing as much as possible about customers and focuses on certain customer groups. Good finance projects adopt this perspective from the planning stage and carry it through, just as private financial institutions survive by selecting target groups that they have a comparative advantage in serving. Knowledge of and focus on certain groups enable institutions to craft attractive services.

Very basic outreach information (for example, client location, gender, or category of business) can be incorporated into ongoing monitoring systems; more complex data are best gathered periodically through sample surveys. Two types of analysis should be performed on the outreach information to yield performance indicators. First, information on clients should be sorted to determine which categories of clients use specific types of services and which categories yield "good" clients (for example, who repay promptly, save regularly).

Second, information on clients should be compared with information about the general population of the area covered by the program, so that the function of the program within its context can be assessed. Market penetration ratios, for example, indicate whether a service is well-accepted and how much growth potential it has. Estimates of the percentage of female clients relative to the percentage of women in the service area can tell a program whether it needs to make a minor adjustment or start a completely new service in order to reach women.

QUALITY OF SERVICE. Evaluators should judge finance programs on the quality of services they provide. This emphasis on service quality is one of the clearest departures of the evaluation approach described here from the evaluation methods most often applied to donor-assisted finance programs. Quality should be judged in a way that respects the clients' preferences and decision-making positions. The strongest and simplest test of service quality, as stated above, is willingness of clients to pay, which serves as a basic indicator of the value or benefit of the service.

This market test should be supplemented with assessments of specific service features. This line of investigation is again very close to market research, and of similar value. The starting point should be the terms of the services. These terms—loan size, maturity, collateral, group guarantees, grace period, liquidity of deposits, and so on—should each be examined in light of the preferences of the clients. For example, the length of the loan and the repayment schedule should reflect the timing pattern of income from clients' businesses—perhaps longer for agricultural enterprises and shorter for retail establishments. Evaluators should ask whether the program has developed the right product or whether other products might have greater demand.

Another aspect of quality of service concerns transaction costs borne by clients, under the general headings of convenience and timeliness. As transaction costs can be a high proportion of total costs of financial services, particularly for poor clients and informal enterprises, the ability to minimize them is a crucial feature of good services. Transaction costs include both out-of-pocket costs involved in obtaining services, such as transport costs or legal fees, and the cost of time that must be diverted from the business in order to obtain services. For example, minimizing the time between loan application and loan disbursement greatly increases the service value to clients, as the opportunities for which clients borrow are frequently time-sensitive. Thus, time from application to disbursement is an important performance measure.

An additional concern, for both evaluators and clients, is the trade-off between service features and cost. Clients will be willing to pay more for services with desirable attributes such as low transaction costs. In situations where there is limited competition, however, clients may be paying unnecessarily high rates—in effect, subsidizing the inefficiency of the program. This appears to be the case in several well-known microenterprise credit programs.

Such a low-competition situation is one illustration of why programs should not be judged in isolation but in contrast to other available services. Attributes of a service can be interpreted only when they are compared and contrasted to the characteristics of the next best available alternatives. Many standard finance project evaluations implicitly assume that clients have no alternative source of finance. In fact, this assumption is likely to be mistaken. As more and more is learned about informal financial arrangements, we discover that alternatives are widely available. Evaluators should learn about the terms and the transaction costs associated with these alternative arrangements and should understand why and when clients select one or another option. The requirement to assess other sources of finance adds a significant information-gathering burden on evaluators, but it is an essential requirement if conclusions are to be useful.

Generally, information obtained from clients regarding their views on service attributes and alternative services is more credible than their reporting on sensitive and quantitative impact indicators such as changes in income. Clients have relatively little incentive to distort their responses. At present, however, few evaluators are familiar with techniques to elicit such information, particularly from poorer clients.

EFFECTS ON CLIENTS' RANGE OF DECISIONS. Donors and sponsors of finance programs are always intensely interested in the effect their efforts have on clients. Their ultimate motivation for becoming involved in finance—the new view of finance notwithstanding—remains a desire to increase the economic activity or improve the quality of life for direct clients and their families, employees, or customers. Evaluations are placed under great pressure to demonstrate such changes. However, the path from financial service to changed economic performance or quality of life is full of curves, bumps, forks, and even dead ends. It cannot be easily traced. The path is best understood not by examining the end points but by taking the perspective of the client as he or she negotiates it.

Evaluators must recognize three things that appear obvious to clients. First, economic and quality-of-life decisions are affected by a wide range of factors, of which finance is only one. Competition, markets, health, weather, and many other factors can all have an overwhelming direct effect. The effect of finance is not likely to be as clear-cut as the effect of these other factors. Second, clients use finance for a variety of purposes, as described above: protection against bad times, facilitation of efficient business operations (liquidity), and financing of investments. Third, use of financial services is not a single event but an ongoing process involving a series of decisions and a range of alternative sources. Tracing the effect of a finance program through all these processes is difficult for any evaluation. Therefore, when attempting to measure the effect of finance programs on clients, evaluations must recognize the limited role of finance, and particularly of specific transactions.

It is, of course, possible to distinguish the effects of any given variable, such as finance, from among a variety of contributing factors. Statistical techniques have been designed explicitly for that purpose. These techniques must be rigorously applied if they are to yield reliable results. Their application requires collection of data at two or more points in time as well as the use of control groups. For the vast majority of donor-assisted finance programs, such data are too expensive to collect, and evaluators fall back on measurement of subjective responses from clients and reliance on client memories. Such subjective responses, assuming they are positive, are of little value except for public-relations purposes.

More importantly, techniques designed to control for other factors are of little value if the ultimate indicators being examined are not the most relevant ones. This happens when evaluations employ a model of the role of finance that does not reflect the way clients actually use it. Typically, the evaluation assumes that financial transactions will be used for investment and therefore measures changes in return on investment. In such cases, all other uses of finance tend to be overlooked.

In order to avoid these pitfalls while still examining the effect of finance on clients, evaluations should stay close to the direct uses of finance. The basic question to be pursued is: How has the availability of this financial service changed the clients' decisions? In other words: What can clients do now that was not possible without the service? The aim is to explain how the service changed the strategies and options available to the client, and how those financial decisions affected other economic decisions. Questions should stay close to the direct and immediate uses of the services and examine how the stated use was satisfied before the service was available. Examples might focus on such changes as ability to purchase raw materials at cheaper prices or accumulation of enough savings to survive a drought year. The line of questioning may have to be as open-ended as are the strategies available to clients.[4] Rather than providing definitive "impact" results on predetermined indicators, such a line of questioning produces results that are indicative of the nature of the effect. Although they may seem less precise, such results are more likely to be accurate reflections of what the provision of financial services actually accomplishes.

INSTITUTIONAL VIABILITY

The new approach to evaluation is most novel in its client-level questions on outreach, service quality, and client options. When it comes to the financial institution, evaluations can rely mainly on standard financial analysis techniques. A shift in perspective is needed, however, away from a donor-centered examination of the use of donor funds, which is, in essence, an audit of the use of the funds. The center of the institutional portion of an evaluation must be the service and the institution, and particularly their financial self-sufficiency. Moreover, although standard techniques can be used, they need to be adapted to the special attributes of the service, particularly when the service differs significantly from standard commercial bank services.

SELF-SUFFICIENCY OF THE SERVICE. The basic question at issue here is whether the service really works from a commercial point of view. Does the service have the potential to survive and expand? The answer to this question is yes only if the income from the service covers its associated costs—both direct administrative costs and financing costs. It is important to examine the service separately before turning to the question of the viability of the sponsoring institution (except when the service is the only activity of the institution). The key indicators at this level are profitability of the service and, for credit, portfolio quality. In each of these areas, an overall assessment must be made, supplemented by a more detailed analysis using ratios and other tools, to ensure that reported findings are robust and to pinpoint the sources of problems. Some of these ratios will be strictly financial, such as the ratio of loans outstanding to total assets; others will be indicators of operational efficiency, such as the average number of clients per loan officer.

One problem facing evaluators, particularly for nonbank programs, is a lack of standards for services aimed at marginal groups. Programs tend to be evaluated without reference to "industry" norms or to the achievements of well-performing institutions. Indicators such as arrears, charge-offs, and operating margins vary widely from top institutions to the mediocre, and evaluators have little guidance to determine what levels might be considered standard. For example, administrative costs as a percentage of loan portfolio can vary by a factor of two or three among well-performing institutions serving microenterprises in different countries, because the cost structures these institutions face are so varied. Moreover, information is often kept in a form that prevents both accurate assessment and comparison across programs, especially in the area of portfolio quality. Evaluators should expect institutions to maintain portfolio quality information that shows arrears categorized by degree of delinquency, so that they can assess accurately the proportion of the portfolio at risk. Frequently, such information is not available.

Development of industry norms can be particularly useful in low-competition situations. Clients should be served at prices that reflect the full cost of providing a service, but they should not have to bear the consequences of inefficient service delivery. Competition can ensure that inefficient services are driven out of the marketplace, but financial services offered on the frontier typically lack competition. In the short and medium term, industry norms become crucial benchmarks of efficiency.

FINANCIAL CONDITION OF THE INSTITUTION. Just as important as knowing whether the service is viable is knowing whether it has a secure institutional base, and that requires a look at the financial condition of the institution as a whole. Methods for assessing financial condition are well established and widely known. They involve analysis of income statement and balance sheet information.

The indicators of financial condition used most often are:

1. Profitability, which measures the excess of income over expenses, both absolutely and in terms of return on equity.

2. Portfolio quality, which measures exposure of the institution to the risk of default.

3. Liquidity, which measures the ability of the institution to avoid interruption of lending due to lack of available funds or inability to meet demand for withdrawal of deposits. Liquidity is measured by the percentage of total assets held in liquid forms, such as cash or demand deposits.

4. Capital adequacy, which measures equity as a percentage of total assets. Financial institutions must have enough capital to ensure that investors will manage resources prudently and that the institution can weather unexpected risks.

Profitability must be assessed both from an operating standpoint (actual costs) and from a standpoint that takes subsidies into account. When grants or cheap capital make an operation appear more profitable, the subsidy must be corrected for when assessing financial self-sufficiency. In addition, the equity (or quasi-equity for a nonprofit) of an institution must bear a cost at least equal to the rate of inflation, in order to assess whether the operation can maintain its value. Yaron (1991a) constructed what he calls the subsidy dependency index to use as a tool in evaluating institutions; each institution's books are placed on a footing that allows comparison with other institutions.

Evaluations must recognize stages in the pursuit of self-sufficiency (see Chapter 1), including a start-up stage during which the goal is for income to cover operating costs, followed by a second stage in which income covers the real costs of capital at unsubsidized rates. One task is to examine which current subsidies are start-up subsidies and which are chronic. A program may be acceptable, even if it has not reached viability, if it shows a convincing trend toward smaller subsidies and eventual commercial operations.

INSTITUTIONAL STRENGTH AND CONTEXT. Although strong financial performance indicates a strong institution, qualitative assessment must supplement the quantitative indicators in order to gauge the institution's ability to sustain and expand achievements in the future or adapt to challenges or changing circumstances. Internal issues such as leadership, vision, and management must be examined. For example, do the board, management, and staff share the same organizational vision? Is there good information flow among all levels of the organization? Are there problems of staff turnover? Does the board play an appropriate policymaking and oversight role?

External issues are also important. These issues include the image of the institution among key entities such as clients, the business community, and political leaders, with analysis of potential political forces that may push the institution in various directions. They also include regulatory issues and the relation of the institution to the financial system. Examination of these qualitative questions informs decisions about future directions for the institution and its services.

Evaluations of finance programs based on the two-level framework described here provide a clear picture of program achievements and a useful market and service analysis for the assisted financial institution. They conform to an appropriate vision of what finance does and how finance programs should be conceived and implemented.

Implementation of this framework faces several challenges. Some may argue that this framework is appropriate only for programs conceived under the new view of finance, and that old-view programs should be evaluated using a more traditional framework, in keeping with original goals. This argument has some merit, as it is unfair to change standards midstream. Evaluations based on the framework provided here, however, can pave the way for such old-style programs to move toward a sounder future, if the evaluations are applied in a way that acknowledges performance vis-à-vis original goals as they rate the program against new goals.

NOTES

1. This is a highly abbreviated description of the debate on these issues. For a full elaboration of the old and new views, see Adams, Graham, and Von Pischke (1984).

2. Similarly, Yaron (1991a) proposes two measures for evaluation: outreach (clients) and profitability (institutions).

3. This term was originally applied to finance programs by Jackelen (1989).

4. See the example of Mrs. Kariuki in Von Pischke (1991, 84).

PART II

METHODOLOGIES FOR MICROENTERPRISE FINANCE

PART II CONSISTS of four chapters that examine several of the leading methodologies for providing financial services to microenterprises: solidarity group lending, credit unions, village banking, and transformation lending. Each of these chapters reviews the experience of a variety of organizations to assess the strengths and weaknesses of each methodology. When considered together with the discussion of the methods used by the Bank Rakyat Indonesia (BRI) unit banking system, discussed in Chapters 2 and 11, this set of chapters reflects a reasonably complete survey of the state of practice in microenterprise finance.

Readers will notice that the different methodologies are at different stages in their development. Solidarity group lending through the Grameen Bank and the ACCION network has become well established enough to make it the basis for large institutions. Innovations at those institutions are now focused outside the methodology itself, for example, on new institutional forms and on development of additional services. Village banking is at an earlier stage of development, where innovation is still focused on refining the methodology to a point where it is clearly sustainable and replicable. Credit unions face a different challenge: As a movement with more than thirty years of experience, credit unions must find a way to modernize their services and take advantage of what has been learned about microenterprise finance. Finally, although transformation lending has been around for some time, it is only beginning to be explored systematically within the framework of the financial systems approach.

These methodologies cover a wide range of client types. Village banking is aimed at the poorest clients, particularly women, carrying out the simplest enterprise activities. Solidarity group programs are aimed at slightly more established enterprises. Transformation lending serves a third tier of clients whose enterprises are becoming substantially more sophisticated. Yet the lesson from these chapters is not in the differences in clientele but rather in the fact that organizations must be free to select their own mix of clients, in response to their institutional needs (for example, for risk diversification) and to the needs of their clients (for example, for continued services as they grow). BRI and credit unions, for example, gain substantial strength from offering their services to the community at large, not just to microenterprises.

Some of the methodologies (BRI and village banking) were developed in mainly rural settings; others (solidarity groups) were born in urban areas. As they have grown, it has become obvious that the differences are not as great as might be supposed. Most methodologies have crossed over to be used in geographical areas different from those in which they began, with only minor modifications.

Across these varying methodologies one notes a common concern with finding ways to balance the need for decentralization with the need for control and maintenance of standards. Lending to microenterprises requires decentralization; the volume of individual transactions would clog any centralized system. Achievement of scale thus depends on the ability to establish small retail units that have responsibility for lending decisions and financial performance. In village banking and solidarity groups, a portion of this responsibility is moved to the clients themselves. Yet the center is still important for ensuring that the retail units perform well, spreading risks (for example, through maintaining a liquidity fund), and creating new retail units. The methodologies represented here incorporate different mixes of relative strength of the retail level and the center. Comparing these experiences can provide insight into the benefits of each.

CHAPTER 7

The Solidarity Group Experience Worldwide

Shari Berenbach and Diego Guzman

CREATING ACCESS TO reasonably priced financial services has been identified as an effective strategy to promote informal-sector firms or microenterprise growth. Informal-sector firms are excluded from the formal financial markets for reasons that have been well documented (Farbman 1981; Berger and Buvinič 1989). Financing from moneylenders, although available, in most instances is not an attractive financing source, given its high cost.

Recognizing this credit constraint, donors and governmental agencies have sought to make credit available to small borrowers. Peer group lending conducted by private nongovernmental organizations (NGOs) or poverty-oriented financial institutions is one successful model for financial service delivery widely introduced over the last decade. Commonly referred to as solidarity group programs (SGPs), this approach is distinguished by the following characteristics:

- Three to ten microentrepreneurs join together to receive access to credit and related services such as training and organization building.

- Group members collectively guarantee loan repayment, and access to subsequent loans is dependent on successful repayment by all group members.

- Loans are appropriate to borrower needs in size, purpose, and terms.

The solidarity group methodology adapts elements of the traditional model of rotating savings and credit associations (ROSCAs), which are widespread in the developing world. In ROSCAs, members contribute a regular amount each week or month, with group members taking turns collecting the full contribution of all members. In peer group lending schemes, members receive loans and then make regular weekly or monthly repayments, with group members providing a mutual guarantee for loan repayment. Peer group lending emerged during the 1970s in diverse settings such as PRIDECO/Fedeccredito in El Salvador, the Working Women's Forum in India, and the Grameen Bank in Bangladesh.

Since the 1970s, peer group lending programs have grown in number, size, and variety of settings. In Latin America, ACCION International called its peer group lending schemes solidarity groups. A similar mutual guarantee arrangement is conducted by the Grameen Bank of Bangladesh and is being replicated in more than six other countries in Africa and Asia. Today, solidarity group–type lending schemes are being used worldwide in twenty-four countries, serving more than a million borrowers. The diverse experience and sustained operation of these programs provide an important performance track record. Most significantly, the number of programs and borrowers has grown dramatically in the last five years. A growing number of SGPs are attaining economies of scale that contribute to their potential long-term financial viability and development impact.

This chapter updates existing documentation on the peer group lending guarantee method (Farbman 1981; Ashe 1985; Otero 1986) and explores its results and reproducibility in diverse settings. Focusing on the experiences of three Latin American group lending programs associated with ACCION International and on the Grameen Bank of Bangladesh, we argue that these organizations have become successful, client-centered lending institutions. The discussion addresses the substantial track record established and considers how these programs continue to innovate in areas such as the delivery of savings, training, and other client services. Finally, we examine how the experience of SGPs offers insights for sustainable microenterprise lending.

THE INTERNAL DYNAMICS OF SOLIDARITY GROUP PROGRAMS

The peer group lending programs examined here have three principal goals: to provide services to the poor, attain financial self-sufficiency, and reach large numbers. In normal banking practice, the goals of providing financial services to the poor and attaining financial viability are at odds. Poor people are usually considered problematic borrowers. Because the loan amounts they seek are small, the administrative cost per loan is high. Because they lack collateral or access to cosignatories to guarantee their loans, lenders perceive them as risky.

The group mutual guarantee method reduces risks and administrative costs per borrower. Solidarity groups have proved effective in deterring loan defaults, as evidenced by the loan repayment rates attained by the three ACCION-affiliated programs and the Grameen Bank examined here. In addition, working through groups enables the programs to reach more households. The credit administration cost of a loan is the same whether the loan is extended to an individual or a group.

Programs that use the mutual group guarantee method successfully have adapted other organizational features that enable them to attain their goals. Successful programs have a relentless commitment to management efficiency; they have tested, refined, and streamlined their credit delivery methods. Sophisticated management information systems have been introduced to track client and staff performance. The management feat of programs such as the Grameen Bank, with approximately one million loans outstanding, is exceptional even when compared with management achievements of leading private-sector firms.

Market responsiveness is another element of success. Programs that want to attract and maintain a large client base must adopt a package of services and a means for service delivery that satisfy client preferences.

The goals and means outlined above have generated significant outcomes. These programs provide financial services to a large number of the poor. Delivering financial services to a population that historically has been outside formal credit markets is a major accomplishment. The programs have also generated a climate of mutual accountability between the client and the program. Over time, there has been a subtle shift in the tone and demeanor of client-program relationships. Client capacities as microentrepreneurs and as participants in the credit screening process are respected, and the organizations define their responsibility as provision of a reliable service at a reasonable price. This mutual accountability has been essential in enabling these programs to attract and maintain a large client base.

Analysis shows that these programs have contributed to broader social benefits. The mutual trust arrangement itself, at the heart of the group guarantee, has had profound social implications. The solidarity group, because of its basis in mutual support, helps free borrowers from historically dependent relationships. Further, the peer group itself often becomes the building block to a broader social network. The social objectives of mutual self-help and poverty alleviation remain fundamental to the broader goals of these peer group lending schemes.

It is important to recognize that not all solidarity group lending programs have attained the results described here. Organizations that have not made an explicit commitment to attaining the goals described above (servicing the very poor, reaching large numbers, and attaining financial self-sufficiency) or have not pursued all the means discussed here (management efficiency, market responsiveness) have not achieved the same breadth and scope of outcomes.

FEATURES OF EFFECTIVE CREDIT DELIVERY IN SOLIDARITY GROUP PROGRAMS

The solidarity group methodology entails three main components: credit, training, and organization building. First presented in the solidarity group concept five years ago, these components continue to be central to this methodology. Although there is considerable variation in how these features are applied in different countries and regions of the world, the successful peer group lending schemes examined here have adopted certain common practices.

CLIENT POPULATION. Group members must have an ongoing microenterprise or must have demonstrated an ability to conduct their proposed business. The majority of group members are women. Activities include small-scale manufacturing, services, and trading, reflecting the mix of informal enterprises.

GROUP SELF-FORMATION. Groups are responsible for selecting their own members and leaders and receive orientation from the field extension workers. The self-selection feature is vital, because group members share collective responsibility. Groups are small, typically between three and ten members, and only one member of a family participates in the same group. The group's internal dynamic, beginning with self-selection, is the impetus for successful group lending.

DECENTRALIZED OPERATIONS. Program staff work out in the communities, marketplaces, and shops, reaching borrowers at their place of work. The field delivery capacity reduces the borrowers' transaction costs and overcomes cultural barriers that inhibit microentrepreneurs from approaching formal banks. Equally important is that by being in the communities and workplaces of borrowers, the extension agents become familiar with group members, knowledgeable about current business conditions, and aware of events that may influence borrower performance.

APPROPRIATE LOAN SIZES AND TERMS. Borrowers in the group decide how much each member needs; then the sum of each loan is approved by the institution and lent to the group as a whole. Loan amounts begin small with short payback periods, allowing the entrepreneur to gradually build up his or her business. In urban Latin America, loans of $50 to $250 for one to six months are lent to meet working capital needs. In other regions, such as rural southern Asia, loan amounts of $20 to $120 may be extended for a full year. The longer loan periods in southern Asia reflect the lower productivity of investments in these rural areas and therefore the longer period needed to gradually build an asset base and cancel the outstanding obligations. Loan terms are adjusted to fit the economic activities of the borrowers.

INTEREST RATES AND SERVICE FEES. Peer group lenders generate revenue from credit activities to cover their operating costs and to prevent decapitalization of their loan funds. The real charge to borrowers includes a combination of interest rates, service fees, and implicit costs of compulsory savings. Borrowing costs for solidarity groups are higher than those for commercial borrowers because, even with the cost savings associated with lending through groups, these operations are more expensive relative to loan sizes. On average, the operating costs of SGP lending range from 25 to 50 percent of the average portfolio. These rates remain affordable for short-term working capital loans, given the return on assets that can be earned in many countries; such rates are lower than those charged by moneylenders for comparable financial services.

SIMPLE LOAN APPLICATION AND RAPID REVIEW. Loan applications ask for simple, readily available information to assess the basic financial viability of the proposed activity, but they fall short of formal project credit analysis. Well-designed questionnaires, visits to workplaces, and qualified staff contribute to the effective application and review process. In communities that are largely illiterate, group lending decisions are based on oral assessments among members. With the backing of the solidarity group guarantee and the screening involved in group self-selection, loan review and approval can be performed quickly. The group approves the individual loan requests of each member; program staff decide to lend to each group. Loan turnaround time rarely exceeds seven days for first-time borrowers and one day for repeat loans.

ON-TIME REPAYMENT REQUIREMENTS. Peer group lending operations have developed a variety of incentives and sanctions to facilitate timely repayment. Group members are responsible for collecting the total loan, and no member is eligible for additional credit until the whole group has repaid its loan. Second and subsequent loans are made immediately and in larger amounts to groups that repay on time, offering an important incentive for on-time repayment. Successful group lending schemes develop a driving commitment to on-time repayment and maintain up-to-date credit administration systems that rapidly alert field agents to delinquencies. Staff may visit delinquent borrowers daily to impress on them the need to repay. In some instances, staff incentives reward extension agents whose portfolios perform well. In other programs, late payments are simply not considered an option.

LINKING CREDIT TO SAVINGS AND OTHER FINANCIAL SERVICES. Although most SGPs began by providing credit, several now also offer savings facilities. A safe and accessible savings facility is highly valued by group members. Savings, in the form of intragroup emergency funds, facilitate repayment by serving as a safety net; members can draw from the emergency fund to ensure on-time repayment in the case of personal crisis or problems. In some programs, member savings form part of the program's strategy to raise loan funds.

TRAINING AND ORGANIZATION BUILDING. Training and on-site technical assistance are integral to the solidarity group strategy. Cost-effective training allows group members to improve their existing management and administrative techniques. Training may entail required and elective components. In addition, SGPs may address members' social and economic needs.

BORROWER AND LENDER ACCOUNTABILITY AND MUTUAL RESPECT. Underlying the group lending mechanism is accountability between the borrower and lender. By trusting group members to manage their credit, meeting the clients' real business needs, and competently conducting the loan transaction, SGPs call on the group borrowers to fulfill their commitments. Over time, an atmosphere of mutual trust and respect emerges, which enables these programs to meet their goals.

SOLIDARITY GROUP LENDING PROGRAMS

ACCION INTERNATIONAL AFFILIATES

ACCION International affiliates lend to solidarity groups in ten Latin American countries and in the United States. In 1991, ACCION affiliate group lending reached almost 65,000 borrowers with $39 million; the average loan size per group member was $284. Among the countries where ACCION affiliates operate solidarity groups, three programs are highlighted in this chapter. These programs were selected because of their significant scale and stable performance over three years or more:

- *PRODEM (Fundación para la Promocion y Desarrollo de la Microempresa, Bolivia).* PRODEM, founded by a group of national business leaders in 1987, provides services to microentrepreneurs in La Paz, Santa Cruz, Cochabamba, and El Alto. PRODEM has demonstrated impressive growth. To meet demand and gain access to more attractive sources of loan funds, PRODEM established BancoSol, a bank for the informal sector, in 1991. Chapter 12 discusses the transformation of PRODEM into BancoSol.

- *AGS (Asociación Grupos Solidarios de Colombia).* AGS, the ACCION International affiliate in Colombia, is a consortium of twenty-one local NGOs founded in 1983. This intermediate-level organization provides services to its member groups in areas such as technical assistance, training, research, and evaluation. Chapter 13 provides an analysis of the AGS experience.

- GENESIS *and* PROSEM *(Promoción y Servicios Empresariales) Guatemala.* FUNTEC (Fundación Tecnica), a local private voluntary organization made up of business leaders dedicated to technology transfer, operates the GENESIS solidarity group program. GENESIS works in Guatemala City and twelve other cities. FUNDAP (Fundación para el Desarrollo Integral de Programas Socio-economicos) specializes in rural enterprise development and runs PROSEM to provide microcredit in the highlands for off-farm activities. Both programs began in 1988.

CLIENT CHARACTERISTICS. In the three ACCION programs, borrowers' economic activities included furniture and clothing manufacturing, equipment repair, restaurants, and street vending. Manufacturing activities engaged about one-third of the borrowers, with the remaining two-thirds participating in commerce or service enterprises (Table 7.1). Contrary to widely held misconceptions, solidarity group lending is not specifically designed for market vendors. Strong demand is also expressed by small manufacturers and service firms. On average, 52 percent of all clients were women, although the rate of women's participation varied from 71 percent in Bolivia to 35 percent in Guatemala. The high rate of participation by women in Bolivia is attributed to the explicit goal of that program to reach the poorest of the economically active.

LOAN FEATURES. The average loan for a new solidarity group member was $180, ranging from $87 to $205 (see Table 7.1). Almost all loans were extended for working capital purposes. Most loans were made available for three to nine months; some loan terms were as short as one month, with loan terms extended with each subsequent loan.

Nominal interest rates varied but were positive even in environments where the commercial rate was negative. Effective interest rates (incorporating fees and charges for additional training and technical assistance services) were 42 percent in Colombia (1990 annual inflation of 27 percent) and 45 percent in Guatemala (annual inflation of 30 percent). These rates appear high compared with standard commercial interest rates in stable economies. As the strong demand for these loans demonstrated, however, these interest rates were affordable for the microentrepreneurs.

PERFORMANCE LEVELS. The number of new borrowers for 1991 ranged from 3,635 in Guatemala to 20,851 in Colombia. The ACCION-affiliated programs have been growing rapidly, with the number of borrowers nearly doubling in three years. This dramatic growth was accompanied

Table 7.1   Selected Performance Indicators for Three ACCION
International Affiliates as of December 31, 1991[a]

Performance Indicator	Bolivia	Colombia	Guatemala
Client Characteristics			
Women	71%	49%	35%
Commerce/service	66%	65%	63%
Manufacturing	34%	35%	37%
Loan Features			
Average beginning loan size	$87	$176	$205
Interest rate (annual)	48%	42%	45%
Borrowers Reached			
Total active members	19,901	33,871	9,436
Annual membership growth rate	52%	62%	40%
Loan Funds			
Active portfolio	$4,561,775	$3,979,515	$1,426,714
Turnover[b]	4.2	2.9	5.0
Growth rate of portfolio 1990–91	87%	37%	55%
Repayment Performance			
% arrears 30 days	0.2%	4.0%	8.0%
% default	0.0002%	0.18%	0.68%

[a] Data are derived from ACCION (1991).
[b] Turnover is defined as total loan funds disbursed over the average loan
portfolio. Average loan portfolio is calculated as: (year-beginning + year-end
portfolio)/2.

by an increase in field offices or local affiliates through which the programs extend their services. These programs anticipate sustaining this
growth rate, given the unmet demand for their services and the standardized field delivery system, which can be easily replicated.

The annual volume of funds lent ranged from $14.8 million in Bo-
livia to $5.9 million in Guatemala and has been increasing rapidly. The
active portfolios at the end of 1991 were approximately $4.5 million in
Bolivia and $4.0 million in Colombia, with the Guatemala affiliate port-
folios around $1.5 million (see Table 7.1). Portfolio turnover ranged
from three to five, reflecting the short maturities and diverse trends.
With the projections for portfolio growth, these programs will face an
increasing need to raise sufficient capital to meet their lending targets.

Loan defaults—the value of uncollectible loans written off, expressed as a percentage of the active portfolio—were negligible in all
programs. For example, in Bolivia, the default rate was less than 0.1

percent, with only $500 written off out of a total active portfolio of $2.5 million. Arrears—the rate of payments outstanding more than thirty days, expressed as a percentage of the portfolio—stood at 8 percent in Guatemala and 4 percent in Colombia. Bolivia, which has established a "total quality" commitment for on-time repayment, has less than 1 percent of its total portfolio in arrears. This low default rate is considered exceptional when compared with commercial banks and development financial institutions.

FINANCIAL PERFORMANCE. Despite the similarity in methodologies used by the ACCION International affiliates, an analysis of recently audited financial statements indicates considerable variation in their financial strategies. Table 7.2 presents a financial analysis of the affiliates examined, highlighting one program per country. Bolivia's PRODEM and GENESIS of Guatemala have adopted a conservative capital structure, with capital-to-asset ratios of 50 percent and 90 percent, respectively. Corporación Acción por Bogotá (ACTUAR/Bogotá), an AGS member, borrowed a substantial share of the funds available for lending, with a capital-to-asset ratio of 8 percent. ACTUAR/Bogotá's capital structure more closely resembles that of a commercial bank, which would typically have capital levels between 4 and 10 percent.

All organizations examined are nonprofit institutions. The return on year-end assets of 3 to 9 percent is not inconsistent with the organizations' goals. Higher levels of returns, however, would allow these programs to finance their own growth.

In comparing these programs, one should note that ACTUAR/Bogotá has broken out its training revenues. Although training income was far less than interest income, greater training expenses probably explain why ACTUAR/Bogotá's other costs were greater than those of the other programs. Further, unlike the other programs examined, ACTUAR/Bogotá is paying substantial finance charges for its borrowed funds. Financial costs rose to 21 percent of the value of the portfolio. The other programs, which rely on donations to capitalize their loan funds, have not had significant financial costs (1 to 5 percent). Typically, the difference between the interest earned and interest paid constitutes a spread available to lending institutions to cover their operating expenses, loan losses, and profits. The spreads earned by these programs, 1 to 29 percent, reflected the operating costs associated with this lending methodology. For PRODEM and GENESIS, this spread is likely to narrow as the programs raise funds for on-lending requiring financial obligations.

SOLIDARITY GROUP LENDING IN ASIA AND AFRICA

GRAMEEN BANK. The Grameen Bank of Bangladesh stands out as the most significant peer group lending program in the world. It is significant

Table 7.2   Financial Analysis of ACCION Affiliates Using Audited Financial Statements[a]

Indicators	Bolivia	Guatemala	Colombia
Average total portfolio[b]	7,001,124	2,737,608	794,939,418
Total funds lent[b]	26,240,628	15,195,282	4,198,293,590
Nominal portfolio growth 1989–90	157%	105%	269%
Capital-to-asset ratio	50%	90%	8%
Return on assets	3%	9%	6%
Return on capital	6%	10%	78%
Total revenue[c]	33%	36%	68%
Interest income	23%	30%	22%
Other income	10%	6%	41%
Training income	NA	NA	5%
Total costs	28%	35%	58%
Financial costs	5%	1%	21%
Personnel costs	12%	20%	21%
Other costs	11%	14%	16%
Interest income–Financial cost spread	18%	29%	1%
Total revenue–Total cost spread	5%	1%	10%

NA = not applicable.

[a] In an effort to arrive at reliable, comparable data, audited statements from one program per country were used: PRODEM of Bolivia (1990), GENESIS of Guatemala (1990), and ACTUAR/Bogotá of Colombia (1991).

[b] Local currency units.

[c] Expressed as a percentage of the average portfolio.

because of its size, well-honed field delivery methods, charismatic leadership, and efforts to disseminate its lending methodology to other countries. The Grameen Bank began as an experimental project of the Chittagong University in 1976. Based on this initial experience, the bank was established in 1983 with government support. Today, the Grameen Bank is mostly privately owned, with its member borrowers making up the largest shareholder group.

The Grameen Bank's operations are extensive. In 1988 the bank employed 7,026 staff members, 78 percent of whom were located in regional branch offices, with only 10 percent based in the capital city headquarters. With growth, the bank has continued to decentralize its operations; all loan decisions are made at the branch or regional office level.

For several reasons, it is difficult to compare the financial profile of the Grameen Bank with those of the ACCION programs discussed earlier (Table 7.3). The Grameen Bank's capital-to-asset ratio is more in line with commercial banking conventions, but it is low even by those standards. The profitability of the Grameen Bank is also very low. For a nonprofit organization, such returns are not particularly problematic; however, this financial strategy leaves little room for flexibility.

The revenues earned by the Grameen Bank, when expressed as a percentage of the average assets, are not significantly different from those of the ACCION programs. What is important to recognize, however, is that interest earnings from the loan portfolio ranged from 13 to 17 percent, or approximately half the interest earnings generated by the ACCION-affiliated programs. Excluding ACTUAR/Bogotá, which had significant training revenues and costs, the total costs of the Grameen Bank program were not far from those of the ACCION affiliates. The greater personnel costs of the ACCION programs were offset by the higher financial costs borne by the Grameen Bank.

The Grameen Bank draws earnings from portfolio investments in addition to interest earnings. In the years examined, the investment income was nearly the same as the income from interest on loans. Portfolio investment is an important element of the Grameen Bank's financial strategy. It should be noted that the investment portfolios of most banks are funded by the banks' borrowings or earnings; the Grameen Bank directly or indirectly draws on donor resources for an important share of this investment. This additional source of income available to the Grameen Bank helps explain how it and the ACCION affiliates have adopted such different strategies for pricing their services. The Grameen Bank offers its services at close to commercial rates, whereas rates charged by the ACCION affiliates are typically higher.

OTHER PEER GROUP LENDING ORGANIZATIONS IN ASIA. Numerous other organizations conduct peer group lending programs in Asia. The Working Women's Forum was one of the first organizations to use the peer group methodology. First established in 1978, the Working Women's Forum began by serving as an intermediary between commercial banks that were legally mandated to target a small portion of their portfolios for lending to disadvantaged sectors. The program organizes women in the community into groups of ten to twenty members. Loans are mutually guaranteed by all members of the group; if one member does not repay, the entire group does not qualify for future loans. By 1988, 32,303 members had been assisted in securing financing, with total disbursements reaching $1 million. The recovery rate varied across regions from 87 to 100 percent.

PROGRAMS IN AFRICA. Peer group lending programs in Africa are able to draw on the widespread practice of ROSCAs, also known as *tontines* or *susus*. Several development organizations have introduced group

Table 7.3   Grameen Bank: Financial Performance

Indicators	1985	1986	1987
Average portfolio	U.S. $7.4 million	U.S. $10.9 million	U.S. $15.23 million
% portfolio growth	39.0%	35.0%	95.0%
Capital-to-asset ratio	5.9%	4.2%	3.6%
Return on assets	0.1%	0.0%	0.0%
Return on capital	1.4%	0.9%	1.0%
Total revenue[a]	31.0%	27.6%	25.8%
Loan portfolio interest income	16.8%	13.4%	13.4%
Investment interest income	14.2%	14.1%	12.3%
Other income	0.0%	0.1%	0.1%
Total costs[a]	30.8%	27.5%	25.7%
Financial costs	14.0%	9.5%	7.1%
Personnel costs	12.2%	13.4%	13.4%
Other costs	4.0%	4.6%	5.2%
Loan portfolio interest income less interest expense	2.6%	3.5%	5.7%
Total interest income less interest expense	17.0%	18.0%	18.6%
Loan portfolio interest income less total costs	–14.0%	–14.5%	–12.9%
Total income less total costs	0.2%	0.1%	0.1%

[a] Expressed as a percentage of average assets.

lending schemes modeled on these indigenous practices. The South African Get Ahead Foundation, an NGO that supports local economic development, established the Stokvel Program, which is an adaptation of the traditional *stokvel* rotating savings groups. More than 12,000 households participated in the program between 1987 and 1992. Women constitute 92 percent of all participants, and more than half are market vendors. The average loan size is $175.

In recent years, several African initiatives have been modeled generally after the Grameen Bank. In Kenya, for example, PRIDE (Promotion of Rural Initiatives and Development Enterprises, Ltd.) began introducing modified Grameen Bank lending methodology in 1989. As of April 1991, PRIDE services extended to 1,600 participants who had borrowed $420,000 and saved $64,000. The Kenya Rural Enterprise Program (KREP), an umbrella organization that provides technical and financial support to local NGOs, has sought to disseminate the peer group lending approach among the different local NGOs it finances; it also established its own program, the Juhudi Credit Scheme (see Chapter 14). The Malawi Mudzi Fund is another recent initiative to replicate the Grameen Bank operation. The first years, however, have been problematic, as the local organizers attempt to adapt this methodology to the specific economic and cultural settings. During its first year, 1990, the Mudzi Fund screened an initial 2,285 groups. Only 485 people received loans, however, with total first-year disbursements of $130,000. Additional initiatives are under way in Sierra Leone, Togo, Burkina Faso, and Ethiopia.

INNOVATIONS IN SOLIDARITY GROUP METHODOLOGY

The solidarity group methodology has three main components: credit and other financial services, training and technical assistance, and the promotion of organization and social development. Although core features of the solidarity group lending approach have withstood the test of time, programs continue to refine and improve delivery methods. Field methodologies have been forged through a continual process of adaptation, testing, and dissemination. Presented below is a discussion of innovations that have emerged.

FINANCIAL SERVICE INNOVATIONS

LOAN SIZE AND PAYBACK POLICY. Peer group lending schemes follow the basic policy of requiring a client to cancel fully and satisfactorily his or her prior obligation before qualifying for a subsequent loan. Experience has demonstrated that when programs deviate from this basic policy, the quality of their portfolios declines.

Among the ACCION affiliates, a lively debate has emerged over the benefits of maintaining a strict, uniform policy for loan amounts and terms as opposed to a more flexible, responsive policy that tailors loan amounts and terms to the cash-flow requirements of the borrower groups. A general view on this debate is emerging at ACCION that involves a uniform lending policy for the client's first twelve to eighteen months of borrowing. Loan periods and a payback schedule are applied to all businesses regardless of their type and working capital needs. Solidarity groups begin with a first loan of a set amount, a slightly larger second loan, and an increase in loan size for each subsequent loan. All loans are extended for a set period of time, usually about three months, and maintain an established repayment schedule. The uniformity in terms is consistent with the practice of the Grameen Bank, which extends nearly all loans for the same term and repayment schedule.

For both the ACCION affiliates and the Grameen Bank, the uniform lending formula has proved beneficial. The programs operate in a straightforward manner that is widely understood by staff and clients and is easy to administer. This initial period of strict and uniform lending policies is an important training phase, preparing group members to be responsible borrowers. Over time, the responsible borrowing behavior establishes a foundation that can lead to larger loans lent on terms that are more conducive to the growth requirements of the particular business.

UPPER LOAN-SIZE LIMITS. When SGPs first began, most of them specified an upper limit on loan size, intended to encourage successful borrowers to graduate to the commercial banking system. Today, ACCION-affiliated SGPs no longer have upper loan limits. Clients can elect to seek financing from commercial banks or remain with the microcredit program. Repeat clients who have demonstrated a reliable track record are now considered very attractive loan candidates. SGPs have responded by creating additional financial services (individual working capital or fixed-asset loans) to keep these valued customers.

FIXED-ASSET LENDING. To address the need for capital formation, several ACCION affiliates have introduced fixed-asset loans. Initially, fixed-asset lending helped "associative enterprises" purchase common facilities or equipment (for example, purchase of a buttonhole maker for a group of seamstresses). In practice, however, this approach proved problematic. Solidarity group members often were not engaged in the same industry. Adequate maintenance and time-sharing were difficult, and ownership controversies developed when groups disbanded. The requirement to use the fixed-asset credit line for common facilities was subsequently abandoned.

In Colombia, as of December 31, 1991, AGS members had 324 fixed-asset loans outstanding for a total of $200,000. Loan terms averaged one year, with a maximum term of eighteen months; funds were used to purchase equipment. Of the borrowers, 61 percent were manufacturing firms. The fixed-asset loan is extended to an individual borrower and does not carry the guarantee of the solidarity group members. A member must demonstrate a borrowing history, however, and this is often done through prior group loans. Group members are asked to endorse the request for the fixed-asset loan even though this is not a full legal guarantee obligation. The equipment serves as the loan collateral. There has been minimal delinquency in loan payments (under 5 percent) and not a single loan default.

SAVINGS. Group savings or emergency funds have become increasingly vital for peer group lending schemes. The savings are usually held in a savings account in the name of the group, similar to the compensating balances required by commercial lenders. Although interest earnings accrue to the group, group members may have to seek permission from the program to use the savings. Among the ACCION programs examined, savings constituted 12 to 24 percent of the value of the active portfolio.

Initially, savings were considered part of a strategy to encourage enterprise capitalization and as a financial cushion that indirectly served as a loan guarantee. If loan payments were not forthcoming, the program or solidarity group members could liquidate savings to cover such outstanding obligations.

The savings requirements have become increasingly important. As the volume of savings has grown, programs have used these funds as a negotiating tool for leverage with local financial institutions. With these savings, the programs can negotiate more favorable terms for credit lines with financial institutions that are eager to bolster their levels of demand deposits. In some instances, these savings have been held on deposit, serving as a source of guarantee, thereby opening access to commercial lines of financing two or three times the face value of the savings.

Client savings are increasingly central to an organization's ability to expand its source of funds and reach more clients. Programs now recognize that through financial intermediation—that is, through taking deposits and lending them out—programs that already have a large number of clients can attract funds at lower rates. Most SGPs do not have the legal authorization to act as deposit-taking institutions. Programs are expressing increasing interest in taking the necessary steps to satisfy regulatory requirements (see Chapter 3) and in transforming group lending development programs into banks. The Grameen Bank in Bangladesh and BancoSol of Bolivia are examples of group lending programs that have endeavored to establish commercial banks. The long-term viability and growth of these SGPs will depend on their mobilizing savings as a source of funds for their own lending activities.

EMERGENCY FUNDS. Because they are administered by the groups themselves, emergency funds provide an important support to the lending institution, ensuring that clients will be able to make their payments even if they experience unforeseen problems such as theft, fire, or domestic calamities. Among the ACCION affiliates, the groups formed in the Guatemalan markets can open an emergency fund with an initial contribution of $5 per group member or $25 per group. The savings contribution is collected weekly and turned over to the group treasurer, who is responsible for depositing the funds in the bank. As a measure of control, withdrawals from the solidarity group accounts must be countersigned by both the treasurer and the group leader.

In the case of the Grameen Bank, emergency funds also perform the vital function of ensuring the bank's resilience. The Grameen Bank operates two levels of emergency funds. The Group Fund operates similarly to the emergency funds described above. The Grameen Bank Emergency Fund is controlled by the bank and is tapped at times of natural disasters, such as the floods in 1989 or the cyclone in 1991. When such disasters destroy the productive assets of whole communities, the Grameen Bank draws on the emergency fund to support its solvency until the economic environment is stabilized and loan repayments are resumed.

LIFE INSURANCE. Life insurance was originally used by ACCION affiliates for purposes similar to those of standard financial institutions. A life insurance policy is taken out over the life of the loan and is intended to guarantee payment in the case of the death of the borrower. The SGPs initially served as the intermediaries between the life insurance companies and the borrowers, including collecting the insurance payments along with loan repayments. The programs realized that rather than hand over the payments to a life insurance company, they could collect these funds and establish their own insurance funds. The Fundación Mario Santo Domingo (FMSD) in Barranquilla, for example, conducted an actuarial analysis, taking into consideration the total value of the payments made and claims collected, and decided to manage the insurance funds itself. In this way, it was able to provide new services for its clients at lower cost than insurance companies and use part of the returns from the investment of insurance funds to organize a funeral service that provides adequate burials for the deceased.

INNOVATIONS IN TRAINING AND TECHNICAL ASSISTANCE

During the formative years of ACCION-affiliated SGPs, training and technical assistance focused on group formation, loan application development, and credit supervision. With the emphasis on credit delivery and the pressure on staff to meet credit volume targets, training and technical assistance were often overlooked or performed in a superficial manner. Nevertheless, most ACCION affiliates charged borrowers a distinct training fee. Staff within ACCION questioned whether participants received full value for their training fees. As effective interest rates crept upward, this concern became an issue of increasing importance. The increased efficiency in credit delivery methods and administrative systems of more mature programs allowed the affiliates to pay more attention to other facets of the program, including training and technical assistance.

TRAINING. A standardized training methodology is being developed among ACCION affiliates based on a series of training notebooks. A two-tiered training program has been developed that incorporates required and optional modules. Required training includes ten hours of training per group and addresses issues involved in the formation of lending groups and the functioning of loan programs. By strengthening and consolidating the groups, the required training modules support the credit component.

The elective tier of training responds to the requests of group members and includes management techniques appropriate to microenterprises. Among the ten training courses that have been developed are Management—Let's Get Organized, Marketing—Prosper as Producers, and Finance—Let's Begin Profiting.

Participants can attend any course and are not expected to attend sessions they do not consider necessary. Each workbook is designed to be self-teaching and self-evaluating. The workbook leads participants through a series of exercises that concludes with the elaboration of a specific plan for the client to implement in his or her own business. The workbooks are disseminated through the network of ACCION-affiliated programs, with each program adapting the approach to its environment.

Training activities have been attended by a significant share of all clients. In Guatemala, 74 percent of program clients attended at least one elective training session. At the Fundación Paraguaya, where a nine-module program is offered, the number of training participants was 8,131, meaning that, on average, each client attended two sessions.

TECHNICAL ASSISTANCE. Technical assistance in the form of one-on-one counseling is used to follow up on the training sessions. Advisers visit the client's business to reinforce the course material and assist the client in applying what was learned to his or her own business. For example, a simple bookkeeping system is taught in ten class sessions held once a week for one hour each session, with three sessions conducted by the technical adviser at the client's business location.

In the past, many ACCION affiliates did not distinguish clearly between credit supervision and technical assistance. To strengthen the technical assistance features, several steps have been taken, including the segregation of technical assistance from the credit component, the upgrading of field personnel to provide more valuable guidance to the microentrepreneurs, and the standardization of training materials to facilitate the delivery of technical assistance.

TRAINING AND TECHNICAL ASSISTANCE FEES. Given the importance of attaining self-sufficiency, fee structures are adjusted in two ways. First, programs are encouraged to break out the training fees as a separate component and not to lump them together with the interest rate charged for the loan. Second, programs are changing the way in which the training fee is calculated. In the past, when programs charged a training fee, it was expressed as a percentage of the loan. As a result of this fee structure, clients with larger loans were paying a disproportionate share of the training costs. Instead, several programs are adopting a flat training fee that is charged to all borrowers. All clients receive the required training and have the option to receive elective training. Training fees, although not expressed as a percentage of the loan, are collected at the same time as the loan repayments.

Most importantly, by segregating training costs and fees, it is possible to avoid hidden subsidies; credit is not expected to cover the cost of inefficient training programs, and training operations are not being called on to subsidize cumbersome credit delivery methods. Unfortunately, segregation of training fees is relatively new and is not yet fully reflected in program financial records.

TESTING THE LIMITS OF INNOVATIONS

For all peer group lending programs, innovation is an iterative process. Adaptations to the methodologies are introduced and then tested to determine their effects. Careful supervision of and management controls over staff and client performance are needed at all times. Some programs have learned that certain features of the core methodology are essential for continued success. Features such as group members coming from more than one family and repeat loans that gradually grow in size over time remain fundamental to successful peer group lending. When these basic guidelines have been relaxed, there has been a rapid deterioration of portfolio performance. Despite the desire to increase the volume and value of loans, the need to maintain a quality portfolio requires that the programs not short-circuit the basic principles of successful group lending. Decentralized decision making has also challenged the management effectiveness of SGPs. In some cases, too much authority devolved to inexperienced regional officers or field supervisors has contributed to lax performance standards or poor leadership or judgment. Programs undergoing dramatic growth are most susceptible to these types of problems.

Given the vulnerabilities of peer group lending programs, well-developed management information systems are critical. With an adequate credit information system, slippage in portfolio performance can be quickly identified; poor performance can be traced to specific regions or staff. Recent innovations can be more closely examined to determine the underlying cause of performance problems. Time and again, when performance problems develop, they can be traced to sloppy adherence to the basic core model for solidarity group lending and basic staff management guidelines.

LESSONS FROM SOLIDARITY GROUP LENDING FOR DEVELOPMENT FINANCE

Over the past thirty years, international development agencies have made significant investments in development finance institutions. Solidarity group lending is a radically different approach to the development finance traditionally conducted by specialized, nonbank financial intermediaries. The approach differs by:

- Providing working capital rather than term lending; it finances existing businesses in all sectors and is not limited to start-up industrial establishments.

- Conducting limited project analysis.

- Targeting poor households, particularly women, with small loan amounts.

- Providing strong repayment incentives rather than relying on the success of the business venture for repayment.

Lenders focusing on somewhat larger enterprises can learn important lessons from the solidarity group lending approach. Several operating methods—not dissimilar from standard commercial banking practices—can be introduced as lenders administer medium-term project financing for industrial firms. Testing the reliability of borrowers through their responsible use of credit lines, evaluating debt service coverage in relation to the family group's personal and business revenue streams, and adopting a firm on-time repayment policy are examples.

ARE SOLIDARITY GROUPS A FORM OF MINIMALIST CREDIT?

Over the last five years, a debate has emerged over the relative advantages of different microenterprise promotion models. Tendler, in a study conducted for the Ford Foundation, noted the success of programs that focused on the delivery of credit, referring to this approach as "minimalist" credit delivery (Tendler 1989). Others have described the nonminimalist lending as "integrated approaches," stressing the link between financial services and other business and social support services. A careful examination of field methods, however, demonstrates that the distinction between the minimalist and integrated credit approaches is not easily drawn. For example, many have referred to solidarity group lending as minimalist credit, even though training and organization building are integral to this method. At the same time, financing is the predominant service provided by others that do not consider themselves to be minimalist lenders.

The debate between minimalist and integrated approaches has served as a proxy for a broader debate about basic approaches to development and the assumptions that underlie these different strategies. For example, traditional development models emphasized training. SGPs have demonstrated that credit provided to an existing entrepreneur can be used effectively without requiring numerous hours of training before credit disbursement. In some instances, however, this recognition was understood to imply that microentrepreneurs had no use for any training. Although demonstrating appropriate levels of skill and management sophistication, most microentrepreneurs could further refine their production methods or enhance their management abilities. Microentrepreneurs participating in most ACCION SGPs have demonstrated a keen interest in training programs made available on an elective basis.

The discussion of the minimalist credit strategy has also served as a proxy for a debate on the role of subsidies in development programs. SGPs adopted financial sustainability as an integral feature of their methodology. Debate continues, however, about the extent to which the training components associated with solidarity group lending can be fully self-financing or whether some form of donor support for these additional services is appropriate. Several ACCION affiliates are now able to fully cover the cost of training services through fees charged to borrowers. Although SGPs in urban Latin America may have the means to cover training expenses fully, this is not the case in all settings. In Bangladesh, donors have been willing to subsidize these additional services. Whenever and wherever possible, the same drive toward efficient delivery of services and full cost recovery should apply to training as well as credit delivery.

What is important, however, is that some programs have used the minimalist debate as a veil to divert attention away from their own highly cumbersome and inefficient operations. In so doing, such organizations have attempted to sidestep the issue of achieving financial self-sufficiency. Some organizations that label their operations as "integrated" or "transformational" may derive a large share of their costs from unrelated overheads and unnecessarily bureaucratic service delivery methods. In such a setting, the argument in favor of subsidy is unjustified. Whether training services or credit is being provided, the drive toward operational efficiency and the need to respond to market pressures remain. When a subsidy is introduced, it should be transparent.

A final related debate is raised by those who contend that as programs become more effective deliverers of financial services (credit and savings) they should limit the scope of their activities to financial services alone. The programs examined here, however, do not demonstrate this pattern. Instead, many programs began by focusing on the delivery of credit. Once this capacity was fully developed, these programs diversified in response to client requests and now provide additional financial and nonfinancial services. Paradoxically, rather than demonstrating a linear progression toward concentration on a single service, the programs examined here perceive nonfinancial services to be vital. The distinguishing feature of these financial institutions is not just that they lend to the poor but that they also respond to the diverse needs of their clients.

Underlying the service mix debate (financial services only or a combination of financial and nonfinancial services) are classic organizational tensions related to specialization versus diversification. These issues are not specific to microenterprise programs. Common sense tells us that it is easier to do one thing well. The programs examined here have demonstrated that although it is essential to concentrate on a single objective (such as credit delivery) at certain times in an organization's development, once certain performance standards have been attained, the programs can respond to diverse client needs. The correct balance of specialization and diversification is specific to each organization, reflecting the existing organizational capacity, management talent, and judgments of the board of directors.

The solidarity group methodology has proved during the past few years to be dynamic and responsive to the development challenges it faced. SGPs reconcile the competing pressures of serving the very poor, reaching large numbers, and operating in a self-sustaining manner. They have done this through the mutual guarantee mechanism, heightened attention to management efficiency, and responsiveness to the market they service. Moreover, these programs are building a sustainable basis for mutual accountability. In a field replete with development dinosaurs, this is no small accomplishment.

CHAPTER 8

Credit Unions:
A Formal-Sector Alternative for
Financing Microenterprise Development

John H. Magill

THIS CHAPTER EXAMINES one type of financial institution—the credit union—that is heavily involved in small-scale enterprise lending in nearly every developing country. Credit unions meet many of the criteria for financial system development outlined in Chapter 1. They are generally sustainable institutions that are financed from local savings and require little external subsidy. They perform an active financial intermediation function, particularly mediating flows from urban and semiurban to rural areas and between net savers and net borrowers, while ensuring that loan resources remain in the communities from which the savings were mobilized.

THE CREDIT UNION SYSTEM

Credit unions are cooperative financial institutions that began operating in developing countries in the 1950s. The credit union system that comprises the World Council of Credit Unions (WOCCU) is made up of four different types of institutions—credit unions, leagues, regional confederations, and the worldwide confederation—each of which has a specific role and purpose.

Credit unions, or savings and credit cooperatives, are the base-level financial institutions that provide savings and credit services to individual members.[1] As cooperatives, they are organized and operated according to basic cooperative principles: There are no external shareholders; the members are the owners of the institution, with each member having the right to one vote in the organization. The policy-making leadership is drawn from the members themselves, and in new or small credit unions these positions are unpaid. Credit unions are legally constituted financial institutions—chartered and supervised, for the most part, under national cooperative legislation.

Membership eligibility in a credit union has traditionally been defined in terms of a common bond that restricts membership to a group of people who have some natural affiliation with one another.[2] The argument is that restricting membership to people who are known to other members of the group reduces credit risks and provides peer-pressure incentives to meet loan payment obligations. Closed common bonds limit membership to a clearly defined group of people. Historically there have been two types of closed bonds—employment based, where only employees of a given company are eligible for membership, and associational bonds, where people affiliated with a specific group (such as teachers, members of a church, or small employers) are considered eligible for membership. Open common bonds draw members from a geographical area rather than a specific group. With few exceptions, credit unions have significant geographic coverage in developing countries. They are located in the major cities as well as scattered throughout towns and villages.

Individual credit unions may (or may not) choose to be affiliated with a national league.[3] These leagues exist in seventy-nine countries around the world—including in sixty-seven developing countries—for the purposes of representing credit unions at the national level, providing training and technical assistance to affiliated credit unions, acting as a central deposit and interlending facility, and, in the case of the developing country movements, channeling resources from external donors to the national credit union system. Affiliation involves purchasing share capital (usually non-interest-bearing) and paying annual dues to the national league. It permits the credit union to vote on national leadership and policies and to participate in nationally sponsored services and programs.

Confederations are regional associations of credit union leagues. There are currently four such confederations in the developing world—ACCU (the Asian Confederation of Credit Unions), ACCOSCA (the African Confederation of Cooperative Savings and Credit Associations), CCCU (the Caribbean Confederation of Credit Unions), and COLAC (the Latin American Confederation of Credit Unions). The regional confederations perform different functions. COLAC, for example, operates as an intermediary financial institution for the Latin American federations. It manages a portfolio of some $100 million in loan funds provided by the Inter-American Development Bank (IDB) and holds offshore reserves for the national federations. The other confederations do not have a financial intermediation role but concentrate on representation, education, promotion, and technical services.

The WOCCU is the apex membership organization of the worldwide affiliated credit union movement. WOCCU's role is to disseminate information, techniques, and resources across the regions.

The development of affiliated credit unions takes place within the context of a common structure—adaptable to local conditions—that is designed to ensure the continued growth and sustainability of credit unions throughout the world. Unlike banks and other formal-sector financial institutions, credit unions cooperate with one another, horizontally and vertically, and it is this cooperation that has permitted the system to grow to its present dimensions. This league-confederation-WOCCU network is designed to ensure that success can be replicated, that new services and concepts can be incorporated by credit unions within a single country and across national borders, and that credit unions and leagues experiencing difficulties can receive timely and effective support.

CREDIT UNION INVOLVEMENT IN MICROENTERPRISE LENDING

Estimating the extent of credit union involvement in micro- and small-scale enterprise lending is complicated by several factors: Loan purpose categories used by credit unions are not standardized; the credit unions themselves often do not keep detailed records on loan purposes; and there is no systematic compilation of loan purpose data at the league or confederation level.

The purpose of this section, therefore, is not to present a definitive estimate of credit union participation in the sector; the data simply do not permit that. Rather, it is to establish a preliminary range of estimates of such activity, based on aggregate data available through the WOCCU; detailed loan, savings, and membership data collected from a sample of credit unions in five countries;[4] and other information from individual credit union annual reports, special studies, and evaluations.

SIZE AND SCOPE OF THE AFFILIATED CREDIT UNION SYSTEM

According to statistics maintained by WOCCU, there are currently more than 36,000 credit unions in seventy-nine countries (WOCCU 1990, 35).[5] These credit unions have nearly 78 million members, $232 billion in member-owned savings and deposits, and $178 billion in loans outstanding to members. Most of these are concentrated in developed countries. Credit unions in the United States, Canada, and Australia, for example, account for 85 percent of the total membership and 97 percent of the total savings and loans in the system.

Table 8.1 provides data on credit unions of Asia, Africa, Latin America, and the Caribbean, which are the focus of this chapter. As of the end of 1989, there were over 17,000 credit unions, with approximately 8.7

million members, in sixty-seven developing countries. As of 1989, these credit unions had accumulated $1.8 billion in member-owned savings and had outstanding loans of nearly $1.4 billion (WOCCU 1990, 33–35). It is interesting to note that more than half the total number of credit unions are found in developing countries, but these credit unions have only 15 percent of the total membership, 3 percent of the loans, and less than 0.5 percent of member-owned savings.

The majority of credit union loans, in all countries, are for family expenses, home purchase and improvements, education, and health. Determining the extent of business and productive (as opposed to consumer) lending is difficult.

AGGREGATE COUNTRY DATA

A review of annual reports submitted by various leagues to WOCCU as part of a regular reporting system indicates that micro- and small-enterprise lending constitutes a small but consistent portion of the overall credit union portfolio. The percentage of the loan portfolio ranges from a low of 1.4 percent in Barbados (where the credit union, because of local banking restrictions, has a high percentage of its portfolio in vehicle loans) to a high of 42 percent in Colombia. Credit unions in most countries appear to have 10 to 20 percent of outstanding loans in small-enterprise activities.

The Honduras Credit Union Federation (1987) estimated that 17 percent of the movement's portfolio was invested in small-scale commercial ventures in 1987. According to the 1987 annual report of the Dominican Republic Credit Union League (p. 49), 10 percent of that movement's outstanding loans were for business purposes, including trade tools, huckstering, bakeries, auto mechanics, and furniture making. A review of the loan portfolios of Philippine credit unions in 1987 reported that 14.6 percent of the loans were to small businesses, and another 16.4 percent had gone to "productive" activities (WOCCU 1987, 186). Data from Cameroon indicated that as much as 8 percent of the number and 15 percent of the amount of loans in the credit union system supported small-scale trading activities (De Santis and Long 1989, 20). A study in Chile in 1985 pointed out that at least 10 percent of the movement's loan portfolio was in the form of loans to merchants and business, and another 25 percent had been used for the purchase of tools, equipment, and raw materials, some of which was for small-business operations (Campbell et al. 1985, 32).

The consistency of these reports and examples—across regions and countries, and independent of specific microenterprise programs—suggests that credit unions in the developing world are generally involved in small-scale enterprise lending activities. More extensive information

Table 8.1   Affiliated Credit Unions in Sixty-seven Developing Countries

Region	Countries	Credit Unions	Members	Savings[a]	Loans Outstanding[a]	Annual Microenterprise Loan Volume[a]
Africa	25	5,152	2,343,412	539.7	384.5	42.2–84.5
Asia	7	9,157	1,168,805	118.8	107.7	11.9–23.8
Caribbean	19	465	806,125	548.2	416.1	45.8–47.5
Latin America	16	2,364	4,340,376	600.0	486.8	53.6–107.1
Total	67	17,138	8,658,718	1,806.7	1,395.1	153.5–262.9

[a] In U.S. $ million.

on loan uses was collected from credit unions in four countries—Malawi, Togo, Bolivia, and Ecuador—to extrapolate a more accurate estimation of credit union involvement in microenterprise lending. The data from this review suggest that credit unions lend significantly to microenterprises. In only one of the credit unions for which data were available did microenterprise loans represent less than 10 percent of the outstanding loan portfolio. In most credit unions, the range was between 15 and 25 percent; in a few, the ratio of microenterprise loans to the total portfolio reached 50 percent.

One of the purposes of this chapter is to establish a preliminary range of activity from which we can determine whether credit unions should receive increased or decreased attention by the microenterprise development community. Projecting on the basis of only the most conservative of the estimates—that 10 percent of the members and 10 percent of the loan volumes are related to small-scale enterprises—a minimum estimate is that the credit union movement in the sixty-seven developing countries currently serves about 850,000 small-scale entrepreneurs with an annual loan volume of approximately $150 million. An upper-range figure of 20 percent of the members and 20 percent of the annual loan volume yields a projection of about 1.7 million small-scale entrepreneurs with an annual loan volume of $300 million. Even with the limited data available, therefore, it appears that credit unions represent one of the most important sources of financing for small-scale entrepreneurs in developing countries.

KEY CHARACTERISTICS OF THE CREDIT UNION APPROACH TO ENTERPRISE LENDING

It can be misleading to refer to a "credit union approach." Because of the variety of credit unions in developing countries, there is a great deal of variation in objectives, strategies, operations, and philosophies.

Nevertheless, there is a general credit union model that has been followed by most credit union systems. Understanding the underlying characteristics of this model, with its strengths and weaknesses, is important for assessing both the potential future role of credit unions in the micro- and small-enterprise field and the relevance of the credit union experience for other micro- and small-enterprise programs.[6]

CLIENT FOCUS. Credit unions in the developing countries tend to serve low-income and lower middle-income segments of the population. This low-income market niche of credit unions is a result of two different factors. First, many credit unions were established by socially oriented missionary and other groups that were working with a low-income membership base. Second, credit unions provide a basic set of services that low-income members find valuable, because they do not have access to these services through existing formal-sector alternatives. These services typically are not attractive enough to entice a more affluent clientele. Loan amounts are not large enough, interest rates and other terms are not favorable enough, and credit unions lack the legal power to provide some of the services (notably checking) that more sophisticated clients need.

Although there is certainly a temptation to assume that credit union members are different from the microenterprise clients of other programs, this does not appear to be the case. In Bolivia, for example, project designers could find little difference—in terms of assets, size of business, income, or other relevant criteria—between the microproducers served by credit unions and those clients served by Fundación para la Promocion y Desarrollo de la Microempresa (PRODEM), the program described in Chapter 12. The membership base of the credit unions is strikingly similar to the client base of the specialized microenterprise programs, representing a segment of the population that generates many of the microenterprises and small-scale businesses in the community.

SERVICES. For the most part, credit unions in the developing countries are single-purpose cooperatives that specialize in providing financial services to their members. Savings and relatively short-term installment credit are the two principal financial services offered by credit unions. Very few have developed more sophisticated services such as open-ended lines of credit, pension programs, checking accounts, or investment services. Although some have expanded to offer medical, dental, group purchasing, and other ancillary services, these are clearly secondary to and separate from the provision of financial services.

SAVINGS. Credit unions develop both a savings and a loan relationship with their members. The savings relationship is generally first and is the key to the eventual loan relationship. In most developing countries, members are required to establish and maintain regular savings programs before they become eligible for loans. This reduces risk by allowing the credit union to gain experience with the member before making a loan. It also creates an asset that can be used to partially guarantee the eventual loan.

Credit unions have not made the most of their savings services, however. Although savings have traditionally been the entry point for credit union members, provision of low-cost loans has dominated the credit union philosophy. As a result, savings policies and practices are skewed to support low-interest loan policies. Savings are made in the form of purchases of shares in the credit union. These can be redeemed only when the member withdraws from the credit union itself. Dividends, rather than interest, are paid on these shares, and only at the end of the fiscal year. Local policies and regulations in developing countries often prevent them from being paid at all. Interest rates are typically far below local inflation rates.

The only incentive to save in credit unions that have such policies is a desire to obtain a low-cost loan. This approach is often referred to as "forced" savings in the financial institutions literature. Potential loan recipients are required to maintain a savings balance in order to qualify for a loan. In the case of credit unions, loan-share ratios of two to one or three to one are common. This is not really a savings service but a cost associated with obtaining a loan (Gadway, Gadway, and Sardi 1991, 43). These "compensating balances" have the impact of increasing effective interest rates. As a result, in many credit union movements, savers subsidize borrowers.

Credit unions throughout the developing world, and particularly in countries facing high inflation rates, have begun to modernize their savings services. Regular savings accounts and deposits are being offered in addition to the traditional share savings accounts. Credit unions are paying interest that is closer to market rates on these new savings instruments and allowing greater flexibility for withdrawals. These changes will make credit unions more viable financial institutions (see Chapter 2).

Even micro- and small-enterprise clients are capable of generating sizable savings balances. In the sample of credit unions surveyed for this chapter, these members' savings averaged 65.7 percent of loans outstanding.

CREDIT. Credit unions follow a "minimalist" approach to credit delivery;[7] very rarely do they provide training, technical assistance, or ancillary services to their small-enterprise members. This approach assumes that the member is capable of running his or her own business and determining the need for financial resources. The role of the credit union is to attempt to serve the members' requests, not to evaluate those decisions—except as they relate to the members' ability to repay the loan.

Credit union financing serves the entire spectrum of member needs; it is not targeted toward specific ends or limited as to purpose. As pointed out in Chapter 1, microenterprises are not autonomous economic units but an integral part of the family itself. Demand for credit in such situations is inevitably a mixture of family and enterprise needs. Unlike specialized microenterprise programs aimed only at enterprise demand, credit unions legitimately respond to both sets of needs.

Credit unions are engaged in character-based lending. The member is known to the credit union because of the common bond of affiliation. Because loans tend to be small—even when used to finance small-enterprise activities—they can be treated as personal rather than business loans. Credit unions require little collateral. Most loans are limited to a multiple of the member's savings, so that at least part of the loan is guaranteed by the savings balance. The use of other members as cosigners is the other principal guarantee mechanism used in credit unions.

Credit unions seldom charge origination or other administrative fees, and interest is uniformly charged on the declining loan balance. Thus, the quoted interest rate is, in fact, the true annual percentage rate for the loan. As discussed above, however, the requirement that members maintain a permanent savings account to be eligible for a loan has the effect of increasing the real rate of interest charged on loans.

INSTITUTIONAL STRUCTURE. As cooperatives, credit unions are owned and operated by their members, who are also the beneficiaries or clients. The people who are saving in and borrowing from the institution are also those making the basic decisions on interest rates, terms, and other policies. This is significantly different from standard microenterprise programs, in which the institutions are established and staffed by outsiders to channel externally provided resources to local clients. Credit unions are local institutions, owned and operated by the local population and using locally generated resources within the community. In this way they are similar to the village banks profiled in Chapter 9.

FINANCIAL STRUCTURE. One key characteristic of credit unions throughout the developing world is that they operate on self-generated capital. The loans made by credit unions are almost entirely financed by member savings, not external donations or loans. Savings exceed loans outstanding in all regions. The same pattern holds true at the individual country level; in 1989, savings exceeded loans in fifty-one of the sixty-seven countries.[8] Even within individual credit unions there is very little dependency on external funding to finance loan portfolios.

In developing countries, credit unions depend on share savings as their primary source of funds. Because dividends on these shares are notoriously low, members have little incentive to save for reasons other than maintaining eligibility for loans.[9] As rates of inflation increase throughout the developing world, however, the tendency is to substitute interest-bearing, withdrawable savings and deposits for share savings as the primary source of capital. As this occurs, and as credit unions begin to pay competitive rates of interest to capture savings, incentives to save will gradually improve.

Finally, with only rare exceptions, credit unions are self-sustaining on the basis of operations; they are generally not dependent on operating subsidies or subsidized capital funds from either donors or governments.[10] As an analysis of credit unions in Malawi pointed out, "the cost of operating a local credit society is low. Except for one or two paid bookkeepers, management expenses are negligible. . . . It is thus possible for societies to be financially self-sustaining in terms of covering their operating costs from interest income if their arrearages are controlled" (Webster and Mooney 1989, 9). This has several important implications: It shows that it is possible to finance grassroots development through self-generated capital; it protects credit unions from the vagaries of international donors or government, and it yields a sustainable overall system.

MANAGING RISK

The credit union movement has developed numerous methods for minimizing credit risk. In employee-based credit unions, the credit union can have knowledge about the work history and salary of the member. Similarly, in association-based credit unions, the member is usually affiliated with the group that formed the credit union (such as a parish) and is known to the membership. Both cases lower information costs, reduce risk, and increase the rate of collections. Community-chartered credit unions have less knowledge of their members and have traditionally been weaker than either industrial or associational credit unions.

The pattern of membership—requiring an individual to be a regularly saving member for several months before becoming eligible for a loan—is another method of reducing risk. By the time the member applies for a loan, he or she has a track record with the credit union. This temporal relationship with the member reduces much of the need for credit checks, project appraisal, and collateral, which characterizes other programs.

Requiring minimum savings balances and tying loans to the amount of a member's savings is another risk-reducing mechanism. Credit unions in developing countries typically lend a member two to three times the amount of savings that he or she has accumulated.[11] The savings balance serves as a partial guarantee for the loan. With this policy, credit unions have created a tradeoff between risk reduction through compensating balances and maintaining incentives to save.

Another method for reducing risk is character-based lending. Although the loans may be used for productive activities (such as small businesses), the key to the amount of any loan is the ability of the member to meet the repayment schedule, not the underlying validity of the business enterprise or any projection of the business's profits. The credit union does not have to evaluate the viability of the proposed business activity to judge the creditworthiness of the individual. This reduces both the cost of processing loan applications and portfolio risks.

Finally, maintaining a diversified portfolio is another method for minimizing risk. Credit union loan portfolios are widely diversified. Since credit unions lend for a wide variety of purposes, the portfolio risk of specializing in a single type of activity is reduced.

MAJOR WEAKNESSES AND CONSTRAINTS

Several factors constrain the performance of credit unions in the developing world, particularly in the context of their ability to serve the enterprise sector.

Credit unions tend to be small. Many credit unions have very small memberships and are making only fifty to a hundred loans a year. Credit unions of this size cannot be expected to greatly expand their activities and could not assume the risk involved in developing or implementing specialized programs designed to reach large numbers of small-scale enterprises.

Because of basic inadequacies in credit union financial and interest rate policies in most countries—particularly the precedence of credit over savings—credit unions are not generating capital rapidly enough to meet member demand. The demand for loans exceeds the supply of savings, creating severe liquidity problems for most credit unions. Credit rationing, in one form or another, is the standard practice; it is carried out through queuing (in which loan applications are processed as funds become available) or limiting the member's loan to a relatively low multiple of the amount of savings.

Increased credit union participation in enterprise lending is also limited by the fact that most are conservative, highly traditional organizations that do not have a modern growth- and service-oriented philosophy. Credit unions have not aggressively pursued membership objectives in recent years and have not been at the forefront in designing new savings instruments or loan programs. The general lack of progressive marketing strategies—especially strategies to identify and meet member needs and target micro- and small enterprises—hampers the development and expansion of financial products and services.

Internal credit union policies and operating procedures need modernizing if credit unions are to significantly expand their role in small-scale enterprise lending. In particular, poor delinquency control and weak portfolio management capabilities limit the ability of many credit unions to expand loan portfolios or add new services. Management, operational systems, and even basic accounting systems need improvement, particularly in smaller credit unions.

Major Lessons from the Credit Union Experience

As institutions with a thirty-year history of providing financial services to relatively poor people in developing countries, and as institutions that have a major portion of their portfolios in small-scale enterprise lending, credit union experiences have considerable relevance to other institutional programs designed to help micro- and small enterprises. A number of lessons relevant to the financing of microenterprise development can be drawn from the credit union experience.

SAVINGS MOBILIZATION. Domestic savings mobilization is both possible and important. Poor people in developing countries are capable of generating large volumes of savings.[12] Although this may not be sufficient to meet all capital requirements, at least in the short run, the assumption that significant development cannot be financed from domestic savings (and the corresponding assumption that development requires external capital) is clearly false. Moreover, as Gadway, Gadway, and Sardi (1991, 42–48) pointed out, savings are an important alternative liquidity source for members that can substitute for, or reduce, the use of loans to finance small-business development activities. Microenterprise development programs could place greater emphasis on mobilizing domestic savings, both as a means of meeting local capital requirements and as a positive service for members.

FIDUCIARY RESPONSIBILITY. Managing savings implies a fiduciary responsibility. Unlike a program that manages only donor-provided credit, a program that accepts deposits and must maintain the value of savings requires a greater degree of sophistication and responsibility than typically exists in small-scale organizations and institutions providing support services to micro- and small enterprises. The fiduciary responsibility requires external regulation and supervision. As discussed in Chapter 3, unregistered, unsupervised savings institutions should be avoided at all costs.

SIZE-RELATED LIMITATIONS. Benefits are a function of scale. Small institutions and programs, with small client bases, can have only a minimal impact on their clients. Institutions with small memberships simply cannot generate sufficient resources to satisfy the financial needs of their membership and provide meaningful levels of credit to significant numbers of people.

DONOR SUPPORT. Credit union experience in many countries has shown that dependence on donor agency support can be destabilizing and constrain institutional growth. It is tempting for a relatively new institution to achieve scale by accepting externally provided resources. Credit unions in developing countries have a long history of relationships with various donor agencies—particularly the U.S. Agency for International Development and, in Latin America, the IDB. These external agencies were important in enabling credit unions to provide meaningful levels of services when they were still small. However, growth financed by low-cost donor funds, particularly in Latin America, permitted credit unions to avoid making necessary adjustments in savings and loan policies and interest rates, reducing their ability to capture savings. Programs focusing on a single loan purpose (such as small farmer credit) encouraged credit unions to abandon some of the basic criteria for success—particularly a diversified portfolio and membership base. Many leagues and confederations have had severe financial problems resulting from the premature termination of donor assistance, on which they had come to depend.

DIVERSITY. Successful financial intermediation requires a diverse client base. It requires a client base composed of both net savers and net borrowers—the savers to generate the resources used for loans to the borrowers. It also requires a clientele with different cyclical requirements, so that loan demand during peak periods does not exceed the institution's available liquidity. Both these criteria are likely to be missing in programs specializing only in small-scale enterprise credit, placing even further constraints on capital adequacy.

THE FUTURE ROLE OF CREDIT UNIONS IN SMALL-SCALE ENTERPRISE LENDING

Credit unions will continue to be a major source of small-scale enterprise lending in the developing world. Two key questions, however, are whether that involvement can increase and become more effective, and what types of actions might be required to help the credit union system expand its participation in the micro- and small-enterprise sector. At least two scenarios are possible:

1. Credit unions could continue to perform their traditional role of making small personal loans to members—many of which will support small-enterprise activities—with little or no relationship to other institutions involved in the sector.

2. Credit unions could become more active financial partners of the specialized microenterprise programs.

UPGRADING THE TRADITIONAL ROLE

With little outside assistance, credit unions can continue to perform their traditional role of providing financial services to their members, and a major portion of the credit union loan portfolio will continue to be invested in small-scale business activities. In this scenario, growth in credit union services to micro- and small enterprises is directly dependent on growth in the credit union system: As credit union membership increases, the number of micro- and small-enterprise clients will increase at least proportionately. Significant growth in the credit union systems of the developing world depends on major improvements in the credit unions themselves.

Credit unions need to improve their marketing capabilities, both to identify their prospective niche and to build on competitive advantages. This marketing effort must help credit unions identify potential membership growth opportunities and the types of services required to meet the financial needs of their existing and potential members. Based on this, credit unions need to develop modern financial services that meet a broader spectrum of member needs, including those of micro- and small-enterprise members. Modernization of credit union services should focus on:

- Developing a broader range of savings services, including long-term savings instruments, with different interest rates and maturities.

- Developing an expanded range of loan services designed to meet the needs of a wider variety of members.

- Pushing aggressively forward to offer quasi-transaction loan and share draft accounts to meet the transaction needs of their members.

A critical need in this area is for credit unions to develop a better understanding of their current and potential micro- and small-enterprise members. Customer analysis (marketing analysis) has seldom been employed by credit unions in the developing countries, and certainly not on micro- and small-enterprise members. The credit unions need to know more about the savings potential, loan requirements, and viability of this potential customer market so that they can plan and develop financial services that better meet the needs of this sector.

The entire credit union system needs to be strengthened, particularly in the areas of internal operations and procedures, delinquency control and reporting, financial and credit policies, and effective management information systems. Perhaps most important is that credit unions in the developing world desperately need to develop a growth mentality and a vision of the credit union as a modern financial-sector institution. Credit union movements in developing countries need to practice strategic planning that emphasizes growth (in terms of members, assets, and savings), open competition with the private banking sector for member business, and responsiveness to members.

Improving supervision, regulation, and monitoring systems would also benefit the credit union system and contribute to overall safety and soundness. Far too many national agencies responsible for supervising credit unions are not adequately prepared to administer modern financial institutions. ACCOSCA, in Africa, has initiated a program of regulator education to lead to a more standardized, higher-quality supervision.

With these changes, little outside assistance, and no coordination with other micro- and small-enterprise programs, the credit union system could play an increasing role in financing small-scale enterprise activities in the developing world. Expanding that role would require a better understanding of the current limitations on credit union growth and assistance programs designed to stimulate credit union development.

A FINANCIAL SYSTEM ROLE

Another interesting possibility, however, is that credit unions could fill existing gaps in financial service coverage for small-scale entrepreneurs. Should credit unions become the formal-sector financial institution targeted to receive graduating microenterprise clients from subsidized, specialized micro- and small-enterprise programs? Can credit unions become the financial partners (source of funding and other services) for specialized small-scale enterprise programs?

GRADUATION OF CLIENTS. Although graduation of clients from microenterprise development programs to formal financial institutions is a stated objective of many microenterprise programs, in practice this seldom occurs. Banks do not view small savers and borrowers as a market niche that they wish to serve.

Small savers and borrowers are, however, the primary client base of developing-country credit unions; that is, credit unions serve precisely the type of individual that the specialized microenterprise programs could be graduating. Such a situation suggests that graduation would occur more frequently if the specialized programs were attempting to develop a relationship between their clients and a credit union rather than a relationship between their clients and a bank.

FINANCIAL PARTNERSHIP. The second role—in which credit unions might operate as a financial partner with specialized microenterprise programs and institutions—is more speculative, because credit unions do not have a history of joint ventures with other corporate entities or programs. The typical pattern for credit unions is one of a direct relationship with individual members.

An alternative to credit union systems becoming more active financial partners in the micro- and small-enterprise development community would be for clients of microenterprise programs to become members of local credit unions, with the credit unions providing savings and loan services and the programs providing complementary training and technical assistance services. Because credit unions can accept savings, this is a potentially attractive arrangement: Through partnership with the credit unions, the micro- and small-enterprise programs could offer their members a service that may be even more important to them than access to loans (Gadway, Gadway, and Sardi 1991, 42). Under such an arrangement, credit unions would retain the interest earnings, and an agreement on fees for services between the credit union and the microenterprise program would provide for reimbursement to the institution for nonfinancial services associated with preparing and servicing the loan client.

The absence of adequate liquidity in national credit union systems would again appear to be the major constraint to developing such relationships. In spite of the aggregate numbers, most credit unions in developing countries are not large enough and do not have sufficient resources to service large numbers of new clients. Existing resources force the rationing of credit among existing members; without substantial growth in savings (or outside funding) to finance new loans, credit unions would be hard-pressed to serve a significantly increased membership base. Any increase would need to be achieved without abandoning the fundamental principles that have been the foundation of their success and stability: the common bond, the long-term membership relationship, lending based on an initial savings history, a loan portfolio financed by savings rather than externally provided capital, and a diversified, demand-driven portfolio.

CREDIT UNIONS AS A MODEL

Credit union experiences can be models for programs developed by other micro- and small-enterprise service providers. The credit union movements in the developing world have accumulated considerable experience in the provision of financial services to small-scale savers and borrowers. Among those that might have particular relevance to micro- and small-enterprise development programs are experiences with character-based lending, minimalist credit programs, risk management, savings mobilization, low-cost service delivery mechanisms, financial system development, portfolio management, operational management systems, and relations with donor agencies.

NOTES

1. In the traditional credit union model, the base-level cooperatives are the only institutions providing direct services to individuals. In Latin America, this model has been modified somewhat as second-tier institutions have initiated programs of savings mobilization and direct lending, often in competition with their member base-level credit unions.

2. This bears some similarity in concept to the solidarity groups discussed in Chapter 7.

3. Nonaffiliated credit unions do exist in developing countries, but with several notable exceptions, they tend to be small, locally oriented institutions serving discrete memberships.

4. Three of the countries—Malawi, Togo, and Bolivia—were selected because WOCCU has projects with a resident adviser in each of the countries, facilitating data collection. Data from Ecuador were available as a result of a microenterprise sector assessment conducted in 1990; data on credit unions in the Dominican Republic were collected as part of a credit demand analysis conducted for another project. In addition, the chapter makes use of information collected in the studies of the Cameroon Cooperative Credit Union League (CamCCUL) and the Malawi Union of Savings and Credit Corporations (MUSCCO) during 1989 and visits to credit union movements in Ecuador and the Dominican Republic.

5. These figures refer only to credit unions that are affiliated with WOCCU.

6. Most of the observations and conclusions presented in this section are based on the author's personal observations from twenty years of working with the credit union movements of Africa, Latin America, the Caribbean, and the United States. Other information was drawn from records compiled by WOCCU, a select bibliography of credit union experiences in micro- and small-enterprise development, and conversations with credit union professionals.

7. "Minimalist" is used in microenterprise literature to refer to programs that provide credit without attempting to integrate it with training, technical assistance, or other services to support the business enterprise receiving the credit.

8. In the remaining sixteen countries the percentage of loans financed by savings ranged from 88 to 99 percent (WOCCU 1990, 33–34).

9. Several observers have concluded that the frozen nature of share savings, accompanied by a policy of automatically extending share loans up to the amount of savings, has frequently been used by members to effectively withdraw their shares. By borrowing up to their share limit and not repaying the loan, the members have withdrawn their savings. To the extent that this is practiced, credit union statistics overstate the amount of true savings and loans outstanding in the system.

10. Donor and government subsidies have often been granted to the national leagues, but most of the credit unions themselves cover expenses through operational income.

11. Ratios as high as seven to ten times savings are also possible, but credit risk rises proportionately.

12. This conclusion is supported by the experiences of the Bank Rakyat Indonesia Unit Banking system, as discussed in Chapters 2 and 11.

CHAPTER 9

The Village Bank Methodology: Performance and Prospects

Sharon L. Holt

T HIS CHAPTER PRESENTS a preliminary investigation into the village banking methodology.[1] Its main objectives are to define this particular community-based savings and loan model, document its achievements to date, and suggest future policy directions.

THE VILLAGE BANK MODEL

Village banks are community-managed credit and savings associations. They are established to improve members' access to financial services, build a community self-help group, and help members accumulate savings. Village banking has been evolving since the mid-1980s to fit both local conditions and the operating procedures of the agencies that have implemented the methodology.

Most agencies have based their village banking programs on the model designed by John and Marguerite Hatch and presented in "The Village Bank Manual" (1989). This manual attributes poverty, especially for women, to low perception of personal capabilities and opportunities, limited access to external resources, and low or nonexistent personal savings. Village banks provide the tools to enable people to break out of poverty, including loans for income-generating activities, incentives to save money, and a mutual support group of thirty to fifty members.

The financial operation of village banks begins when sponsoring agencies lend seed capital to newly established village banks, which then on-lend the money to their members. All members sign the loan agreement to offer a collective guarantee. First loans typically are for the local equivalent of $50, for a term of four months, to be repaid weekly to the village bank. Loans usually finance short-term working capital investments. Village banks charge commercial rates of interest

156

—rates in most programs range between 1 and 3 percent per month. At the end of the sixteen weeks, the village banks repay the sponsoring agency with interest. The loan money that comes from, and is repaid to, the sponsoring organization makes up the external account.

When members repay their first loan on time, they can get a second loan. The amount of the second loan is determined by the savings a member has accumulated during the first loan period through weekly contributions. The methodology anticipates that members will save a minimum of 20 percent of the loan amount per cycle. The previous loan plus accumulated savings determines the size of each following loan. A person saving $10 on an initial $50 loan and $12 on a second $60 loan would be eligible for a third loan of $82 ($10 + $12 + $60).

Members' savings stay in the village bank and are used to finance new loans or collective income-generating activities. No interest is paid on savings; instead, members receive a share of profits from the village bank's relending activities or other investments. The internal account is made up of these savings, interest from loans made with member savings, fines charged to members, profits from village bank investments, and installment payments to the external account. The village bank determines the terms and regulations for all internal account investments. The external account acts as a catalyst to stimulate the development of the internal account and of members' personal savings.

Members work toward building sufficient savings to reach the external account maximum loan limit of $300 in three years. After achieving this level of savings, a member graduates from the program. The $300 loan limit is designed to prevent wealthier members from gaining disproportionate access to village bank capital. The model assumes that $300 is a sufficient sum to allow for self-financing of income-generating activities. The model also anticipates that the village bank will continue to function, financing its operations with members' savings.

THE ORGANIZATIONAL STRUCTURE

The organizational structure of the village banking model consists of the sponsoring agency and the village banks. Sponsoring agency promoters organize the village banks. The manual assumes that village banking requires very limited administrative overhead. The promoter is responsible for training and organizing village bank members and each bank's governing committee. The manual suggests that, during a month-long trial and training period, the village banks have four weekly meetings to organize, elect directors, start the savings process, establish bylaws, and plan for the bank's inauguration. After the initial month, the manual foresees a drop in visits by promoters. Village banks must learn to conduct most meetings without outside assistance.

A village bank consists of its general membership and a committee. Membership is based on self-selection. This is crucial, since members guarantee one another's loans. Further, members are required to go through a trial period before obtaining a loan. The optimal size of a village bank—from the point of view of self-management and effectiveness of the group guarantee—is considered to be between thirty and fifty members.

Village banks are managed by an elected committee of at least a president, a secretary, and a treasurer. Committee responsibilities include convening meetings, approving loans, supervising loan payments, receiving savings deposits, lending out or investing savings, and keeping up-to-date records. Full attendance at meetings is stressed, as is members' input in decision making. According to the manual, greater member participation reduces the chances that resources will be co-opted by elites and facilitates planning by pooling resources and knowledge.

SOCIAL COMPONENTS

The social goal of village banking is to reduce poverty in families by increasing the incomes of women (see Acharya and Bennett 1982). The model anticipates that female participation in village banks will enhance social status and intrahousehold bargaining power (see Bennett 1990).

To meet social objectives, the village banking model defines three main strategies. First, it targets poor women as clients. Second, village banks act as self-help groups that provide mutual support to their members, since women's poverty is thought to stem in part from a lack of self-confidence (see Kropp et al. 1989). Third, the model seeks to build local capacity to manage village banks in a participatory manner, with the hopes of empowering the poor in other areas as well (see Chambers 1983; Korten and Alfonso 1983; Hirshman 1984; Cernea 1985; Lewis 1988).

OBSERVATIONS ON THE MODEL

The village bank model possesses characteristics that make it appealing to both sponsoring agencies and clients. For lenders, it reduces risks by imposing joint repayment liability on the members, tying loan levels to savings deposits, starting with small loans, and increasing loan amounts as a member builds a credit history. By transferring many of the administrative aspects of providing financial services to the village banks, an implementing agency minimizes its own transaction costs in the longer term. The simplicity of the financial mechanism and the relatively small amount of capital it requires may also be desirable to sponsoring agencies.

Organizationally it also has appeal. The methodology calls for very limited administrative overhead. Although it demands some training to establish each bank, it is a "minimalist" financial service model. The model does not require coordination with agencies such as commercial banks, government ministries, or apex institutions, and it allows for direct interaction with communities.

Borrowers may be attracted to the methodology for a number of reasons. First, as community banks with simple procedures and loans that are available immediately, village banks reduce members' noninterest costs of borrowing. Second, village banks allow members to overcome collateral requirements, which are particularly severe for women. Third, village banking offers both savings and credit services. Finally, the model provides a forum in which the community can interact for social or productive purposes.

But the appealing aspects of the model are also its weaknesses. It is unclear whether the forms of risk management used in village banking, such as small initial loans and group guarantees, are sufficient to ensure financial viability. The model's low-cost, highly decentralized institutional structure may suffer from the lack of an intermediate-level institution necessary to absorb excess savings, provide access to capital when local demand for funds exceeds supply, perform occasional supervisory duties and audits, and undertake responsibilities such as leveraging capital from a bank. The model advocates a minimalist service delivery methodology, yet targets the most disadvantaged and difficult-to-reach group. It is precisely this group that may require both financial and nonfinancial inputs such as business training to help develop its businesses beyond subsistence levels (Mann, Grindle, and Shipton 1989).

ADAPTATIONS OF THE BASIC MODEL

The village banking model has been adapted by different organizations to fit varying contexts. No program follows a completely "pure" version of village banking as set out in the manual.

FINANCIAL ADAPTATIONS

Most sponsoring agencies have kept the basic financial structure of internal and external accounts that grow simultaneously with members' savings levels. Some programs, however, have departed from the

$300 limit and the $50 starting point. Loan installment payments, loan maturities, and meeting schedules all vary. For the Foundation for International Community Assistance (FINCA)/Northern Mexico, a four-month loan cycle appears to match the market and trading-based activities of bank members. At the Cooperative for American Relief to Everywhere (CARE)/Guatemala and Freedom from Hunger Foundation (FFH)/Thailand, loans are for six months because they go mostly for livestock raising or textile weaving, activities that turn over less quickly than trading. At FINCA/Costa Rica, loan maturities vary between eighteen and sixty months. These longer cycles probably reflect a number of factors, including larger loans and the fact that the program is much older than the others.

Some programs have opted for noncommercial interest rates. Save the Children (SCF)/El Salvador lends to its banks at a heavily subsidized rate of 3 percent; Catholic Relief Services (CRS)/Thailand lends at 12 percent, below the government-regulated commercial rate of 17 percent. FINCA/Costa Rica gives subsidized loans to new banks at the rate of 18 percent, but then increases the rate to between 21 and 30 percent as banks develop. These amounts are still below the commercial rate of 36 percent. In contrast, CARE/Guatemala charges 24 percent, above the government-regulated commercial rate of 16 to 18 percent.

INSTITUTIONAL ADAPTATIONS

Strongly influenced by the Grameen Bank, FFH adapted the organizational structure of the village bank to include solidarity groups. FFH requires potential borrowers to organize themselves into solidarity groups of four to seven borrowers. These groups then join together to make a village bank. Liability for the loan is then transferred to this smaller unit. If the solidarity group does not repay the loan, however, the entire village bank is liable.

Older village banks in the FINCA/Costa Rica program have introduced their own organizational changes. In banks with many participants (one, for example, has 163 members), committee members take on the tasks of bank teller and manager. Financial transactions do not take place at weekly meetings in front of the whole membership. Instead, members go to the treasurer to make transactions on an individual basis.

FINCA/Costa Rica has also introduced a three-level village bank classification system. Banks are categorized by their stage of development, and more developed banks are eligible for larger loans and receive different types of assistance from FINCA.

Most institutional changes have come at the sponsoring agency level. CRS/Thailand works through three local nongovernmental organizations (NGOs). This additional institutional layer requires institution-building efforts, which increase costs. CRS project management must monitor the village banks and the NGOs.

FFH's programs and CARE/Guatemala use commercial banks as sources of funds, as places to keep village banks' accounts, or both, although neither program has established a formal partnership with the commercial banks. In the FFH/Thailand program, the Bangkok Bank, a local commercial bank, makes loans directly to each village bank. These loans are backed by a 25 percent guarantee from FFH, a 50 percent guarantee from the Friends of Women's World Banking, and a 25 percent guarantee from the Bangkok Bank. During the second phase of the program, the Bangkok Bank is supposed to assume direct supervision of community promoters and village banks. FFH's staff or a local NGO partner provides technical assistance, primarily on hunger-related issues.

Commercial banks offer CARE/Guatemala's village banks a place to keep their savings and lending accounts. In contrast to FFH, individual village bank members—not just the committee—go to the commercial banks to make financial transactions. CARE anticipates that the village banks may be able to graduate to commercial banks as a source of funds after they have established a strong financial history and built up savings in the commercial banks. Few instances of this type of graduation have taken place to date, however.

Additional institutional adaptations of the model emphasize coordination with other organizations to fulfill advisory, technical assistance, or marketing support functions. FFH/Thailand's national advisory committee provides advice, technical assistance, and government and private-sector support to the village banking initiative. FFH/Thailand and FFH/Ghana get assistance from government health extension workers. FINCA/Costa Rica has developed an even broader network of collaborating institutions. In addition to its national advisory board, it has thirty-five different private firms giving economic, technical, or marketing assistance to specific village banks. In this way, FINCA/Costa Rica provides its clients with nonfinancial assistance without having to pay for it directly.

BROADENING SERVICE DELIVERY

FINCA/Costa Rica, FFH, and CARE have altered the model to include a technical assistance or education component. CARE's promoters have had training so that they can deliver extension messages regarding pig and poultry raising. CARE extension workers develop subgroups of four or five women for joint investment in agricultural innovations. CARE also helps link the village banks to sources of education on nutrition and other health-related issues. CARE finds this additional assistance necessary to help women entrepreneurs develop their businesses beyond subsistence levels.

FFH entered village banking with the underlying aim of reducing malnutrition. In FFH's experience, providing solely nutrition information was not enough to attract regular active participation by poor people. The financial services portion of the program was developed to entice participation and improve poor people's ability to generate income for food. Educational messages are aimed at promoting the use of credit for income generation, food security, and improved nutrition. Thus, the objectives of FFH's programs are slightly different from the goals of the others, requiring higher costs and more intensive interaction with villagers.

LARGER SCALE AND LONGER TIME FRAME

The newest village banking initiative studied, FINCA/El Salvador, is designed to serve both village banks and individuals in rural and urban areas.[2] The El Salvador project is much larger in terms of funding and expected beneficiaries than the others. It is budgeted at $14.9 million over seven years and anticipates establishing 240 village banks (7,200 women) and reaching 240 individual borrowers in the first year alone. In contrast, CRS/Thailand budgeted $1,067,488 to reach thirty-four banks over three years. CARE/Guatemala operated for its first two-and-a-half years as a pilot project on $64,000 to reach a target of nine village banks.[3] FFH/Thailand anticipates reaching seventeen banks in the first two years. After that, if there is confidence that the design is working, it will decide how much to expand. After two years of operation, FINCA/Northern Mexico has formed thirty-eight banks. Larger projects typically require greater administrative support. Therefore, the larger projects put more emphasis on designing administrative components than the pilot efforts.

FINCA/Costa Rica, with 3,825 beneficiaries in 153 banks, lies somewhere between the smaller projects and FINCA/El Salvador. FINCA/Costa Rica acts as an intermediary and maintains a permanent relationship with its village banks. Neither banks nor individuals graduate. FINCA/Costa Rica continues to play a supervisory role, to link village banks to other sources of support, and to provide technical support in finance and management. It employs a staff and data management network to support large numbers of village banks.

DOCUMENTING ACHIEVEMENTS: VILLAGE BANKING IN PRACTICE

Village banking's achievements in practice are analyzed here according to financial, organizational, and social categories.

REPAYMENT

Repayment is a critical issue for financial services programs. If high repayment levels are not achieved, programs have no chance of sustaining themselves. Moreover, repayment can be an indicator of the financial health of a lending institution.

EXTERNAL ACCOUNTS. For the most part, the repayment rates in village banking programs' external accounts have been high. All programs except one have repayment rates above 90 percent. Table 9.1 illustrates that the pilot programs (FFH/Thailand and Ghana, CRS/Thailand, and CARE/Guatemala) have managed to maintain rates of 100 percent. FINCA/Costa Rica and FINCA/Northern Mexico have achieved rates of 98 and approximately 92 percent, respectively. SCF/El Salvador has a considerably lower repayment rate of 52 percent.

Programs that have invested heavily in village bank training and the administrative oversight of the banks have been the most successful at maintaining high repayment rates. SCF reported that defaults were highest in its older banks, where it invested the least in the village banks' setup and training. In the first year of funding, when village banks received the least training and supervision, 43 percent of SCF/El Salvador's banks failed. This figure dropped to 23 percent in 1986–87, to 16 percent in 1987–88, and eventually to zero in 1988–90. In 1990, two of the FINCA/Northern Mexico program's oldest banks, which had the least training and supervision, defaulted after two years. Repayment rates at FINCA/Costa Rica increased as the program gained experience, altered its training methodology, and slowed its expansion.[4] Repayment rates went from 92 percent in 1986 to 98 percent in 1990.

The four pilot projects studied gained from the other programs' experiments and started emphasizing training and, to a much lesser extent, supervision. All programs now incorporate a four-week trial and training period. The administrative investment clearly pays off in terms of repayment, but it escalates program costs substantially.

Highly subsidized interest rates may also influence repayment. SCF, which charged community banks only 3 percent a year, had the lowest repayment rate, only 52 percent. Highly subsidized interest rates can indicate to borrowers that the credit is a gift or welfare transfer that does not have to be repaid. Moreover, they encourage inefficient investment by borrowers.

A village-level study of FINCA/Costa Rica indicated that village banks with formal, written membership requirements and screening measures in their bylaws have greater success in disciplining their members to repay on time and in keeping less creditworthy individuals from joining the village bank (Wenner 1989). Savings also appeared to play an important role in reducing external account delinquency. If a village bank has accumulated sufficient savings in its internal

Table 9.1   Seven Village Bank Programs

	FFH/Thailand	CRS/Thailand	FFH/Ghana	CARE/Guatemala	FINCA/No. Mexico	FINCA/Costa Rica	SCF/El Salvador
Start date	7/89	/89	4/90	4/88	3/88	/85	/85
No. of banks	11	13	10	9	38	153	100
Total no. members	220	719	293	334	680	3,825	1,528
Avg. no. members per bank	20	55	29	37	19	25	15–25
Percent women	99.5	100	100	100	100	25	57
Repayment rate (%)	100	100	100	100	92[a]	98[b]	52
Annual interest rate (external) (%)	23	12	36	24	36–48	18–25	3
Annual interest rate (internal) (%)	24	24–36	60–120	24	60	30	36
Loan maximum ($)	300	300	NA	150[c]	300	2,000	62
Initial loan ($)	60	60	NA	50	50	140	NA
Maturity (months)	6	4	NA	4–6	4	18–60	24–36
Community involvement	No	No	NA	Yes	Some	Yes	NA
Subgroups	No	No	NA	Yes	Some	Yes	NA
Agribased economy	Yes	Yes	NA	Yes	No	Yes	Mixed
Total savings ($000s)	0.88	7.3	2.7	24.4	31.8	NA	NA
Savings/loans (%)	5	16	15	29.1	47.8	11.2	NA
Deposit annual interest rate (%)	9	NA	0	11	0	7–15	NA

NA = not available.
[a] Approximate figures.
[b] Some of these funds may still be recoverable.
[c] The loan limit is 750 quetzals, which once equaled $300 but dropped to $150 with rising inflation.

account, it will use these funds to repay FINCA and cover a member's late external payments when necessary. The tardy borrower(s) then must repay the internal account, sometimes with a penalty.

Sociocultural factors can also have an impact on repayment, as evidenced by lower repayments at FINCA/Northern Mexico and SCF/El Salvador, which operate in areas that have highly transient, migratory populations—in the case of El Salvador, exacerbated by the country's civil war.

Experience suggests that risk-reducing features of the methodology can be effective insurance against default. However, risk-reduction measures must be accompanied by sufficient training and administrative oversight.

INTERNAL ACCOUNTS. Programs' records of the internal accounts are lax compared to those maintained for the external accounts. Evidence suggests that repayment in these accounts is characterized by a different dynamic. Internal repayment records of village banks in CRS/Thailand, FINCA/Northern Mexico, and FINCA/Costa Rica appeared to have a number of incidents of arrears and rather ad hoc rescheduling.

In the FINCA/Northern Mexico program, delinquencies in the internal accounts had negative consequences for the external account. FINCA/Northern Mexico had adopted a policy of relending external loan installment payments in addition to members' savings in the internal accounts to generate more interest income on loans. In a number of instances, village banks could not meet their external account payments on time because internal loans had fallen into arrears. Although the external account loans were eventually repaid, the "abuse" of the internal accounts led the project manager to discontinue the practice of lending out installment payments.

Other programs have had completely different problems with the internal accounts. At FFH/Thailand and CARE/Guatemala, internal accounts have not yet (or just barely) begun to operate, making the issue of repayment premature. After over two years of lending, San Vicente Pacaya Bank in Guatemala has lent only $624. The reason does not seem to be lack of demand but rather unfamiliarity with the internal accounting mechanisms by members, committee representatives, and probably the staff. In countries with high inflation (Guatemala's reached 85 percent in 1990), failure to circulate internal account monies swiftly results in a severely decapitalized loan fund. Moreover, if internal monies are not re-lent, members never learn how to manage locally mobilized capital.

Two lessons can be drawn from these disparate experiences. First, the risk-management mechanisms integral to the external accounts appear to be less applicable to the internal accounts. Second, the experiences broadly suggest that internal accounts are more difficult to manage than external accounts, since the fund base and loan sizes are less fixed. This instability has had opposite effects in different programs. In the programs with little external supervision of internal accounts, it has led to arrears and rescheduling. In the programs with tighter controls, particularly CARE/Guatemala and FFH/Thailand, the lack of stability in the internal accounts has resulted in very few funds being lent.

FINCA/Costa Rica's experience offers a possible solution. The village banks in Costa Rica also engage in rescheduling and use internal account monies to repay FINCA when necessary. FINCA/Costa Rica's village banks have contingency plans for problems that may emerge in the internal accounts that are similar to those found in informal financial markets. For example, at San Gerardo de Rivas Bank, borrowers who fall into arrears must pay the consequences in terms of high interest rates (5 percent per month) to the account.

The experience of FINCA/Costa Rica suggests that flexibility in repayment is tolerable if it is planned and well managed. But this, in turn, requires relatively sophisticated management and members' compliance. Moreover, even after banks have become relatively independent, their accounts should be checked periodically. At FINCA/Costa Rica, accounting controls take two forms: Promoters and government agencies do periodic audits of village banks, and the banks keep FINCA updated by sending regular reports and internal audits to the headquarters staff. As in the case of the external accounts, supervision (or administration) is crucial and does not necessarily jeopardize autonomy.

LENDING LEVELS AND THE SIGNIFICANCE OF $300

A review of lending levels involves two questions. First, is $300 an appropriate limit across cultural contexts? Second, is the loan ladder, with its $300 limit and three-year time frame, an accurate reflection of client and village bank needs?

A number of village banking programs have abandoned the $50 starting point and the $300 limit as being inappropriate for the local context. CRS/Senegal's program starts at $67 and caps at $500; FINCA/Costa Rica begins at $140 and increases to $2,000. In these countries, $300 was not a sufficient sum. In Guatemala, loan limits dropped from $300 to $150 as a result of inflationary pressures. The variation in loan sizes across projects suggests a need for flexibility across regions and for programs to comply with local needs. The practical experience includes loans ranging from $30 to $2,000. This roughly corroborates Liedholm and Mead's (1987, 38) review of available evidence, which indicated that the overall initial capital requirements for small businesses ranged from around $49 in Sierra Leone to $1,104 in Jamaica.

Although $300 is not a universally applicable standard, village banks may nevertheless need loan limits in order to dissuade elites from viewing the village bank as an attractive source of resources to attempt to control. Other restrictions such as meeting schedules, small initial loan sizes, and strict installment payment requirements also help ensure that only the needy participate. No village banks visited appeared to be dominated financially by elites, although village banks frequently have members with a broad range of income levels. Eliminating loan limits could also expose village banks to riskier loans.

Loan limits may have to change as members build up savings and banks develop greater management capacity. The experience of the Asociación Juntas de Pacuar village bank of FINCA/Costa Rica demonstrates what happens to investment patterns in village banks over time. The bank started in 1986, with loans up to $150. By 1990, the bank had 163 members and offered loans from about $150 to just over $2,000. The loans also varied in maturities; a few loans had terms as long as four years, but the majority remained short term.

In communities where there are increasing economic activities and market opportunities, village bank members and the community itself are likely to experience a growing demand for loans. The experience of Costa Rica suggests that the $300 limit, three-year time frame may not conform to local needs and capacities that grow over time. Sponsoring agencies should be prepared to respond to this need while being careful to maintain poor people as clients.

SAVINGS

Unlike many other financial service programs targeted at poor people, village banking includes savings as an integral part of its methodology. Members are expected to save a minimum of 20 percent per cycle. Some programs have reached this goal, but others have not. Savings as a percentage of loans varies from a low of 5 percent in the FFH program in Thailand to a high of almost 48 percent at FINCA/Northern Mexico. The level of savings has important implications for the timetable of the program. In programs with low savings, reaching the $300 loan and savings level will take years.

Savings are high in programs where there is considerable demand for liquidity. The village bank members in northern Mexico, for example, demand liquidity for trading and selling (typically clothes, cosmetics, or food)—activities that turn over quickly and require considerable working capital. In contrast, FFH/Thailand members use their loans for livestock raising and fertilizer for crop production, activities that turn over only once every five to seven months. This decreases the demand for liquidity, as investments are tied up in physical assets for longer periods. Two additional factors have also diminished FFH/Thailand members' incentive to save. First, FFH/Thailand's project started relatively slowly, which probably reduced members' confidence in the security of their future loans and, therefore, savings levels. Second, FFH members may not feel that their savings are easily accessible, since the internal account has not yet begun to lend. Once the internal account begins to operate and members gain confidence in their community bank, savings may grow.

The rate paid on deposits has little correlation with savings levels. FFH/Thailand has the highest real deposit rate (around 6 percent) but the lowest level of savings (5 percent). In contrast, CARE/Guatemala has a high level of savings (29 percent) but a highly negative real deposit rate; in 1990, inflation in Guatemala was 85 percent. Similarly, FINCA/Northern Mexico boasts the highest savings level (48 percent), but the project offers no interest on savings. This finding appears to contradict the prevailing belief that savings must yield a good return to attract depositors (Otero 1989b; Vogel 1990), though it corroborates much of what is discussed in Chapter 2 on savings in Indonesia. Two explanations are possible. First, the fact that village bank members probably have very few alternatives for storing their savings in liquid assets may mean that they are willing to pay for a deposit facility. Their other options may be highly risky (money under the mattress) or illiquid (livestock or jewelry). A second explanation is that village bank members are just using their savings as a means of obtaining larger loans. The low or negative return on savings could be viewed as an additional cost of the loan.

Another issue is the relationship between providing access to savings deposits and using those funds for relending in the internal account. In the village banking programs, savings are frequently tied up in loans. This reduces the incentive for clients to put their emergency savings into such an account. The alternative is to not lend savings and keep them readily accessible.

The village banks in Costa Rica emphasize using savings for loans. Regulations vary, but the system established at Playa Linda Bank is typical. Members are paid an annual interest of 15 percent on savings, which are then lent at 30 percent. Members do not have access to their savings; rather, they have to borrow at 30 percent. This helps work the money and capitalize the fund. If members quit, they can get 50 percent of their savings immediately and 50 percent after three months. Under this scenario, savings play mainly a liquidity or leveraging role, enabling members to gain access to larger loans. With this type of savings incentive structure, Costa Rica has achieved an 11.2 percent savings level.

Savings are more readily accessible at the village banks in Guatemala. Members can withdraw their savings at the end of a cycle. There is also considerable membership turnover, as there is in other village banks. In addition, savings are seen as secure because they are kept in commercial banks. These factors diminish the committee's ability to use the internal accounts for loans. It is never clear how much money must be available to meet the demands for withdrawals. With this savings incentive structure, savings as a percentage of loans has reached 29 percent.

PROGRAM COSTS

Low cost is an attribute often claimed for the village banking methodology. Examining costs in practice has proved to be complicated, because programs do not keep comparable records of accounts: Some programs include costs that are not incorporated into other programs; local costs of labor and other inputs vary substantially across regions; and programs are in different stages of development. The pilot projects are clearly more costly than more established initiatives, because considerable funds are invested in start-up costs and monitoring. Nevertheless, preliminary observations are available from four programs.

The two pilot projects that include education components, FFH/Thailand and CARE/Guatemala, are more costly than their minimalist, non-pilot counterparts, FINCA/Northern Mexico and FINCA/Costa Rica. The estimated 1990 costs for CARE and FFH were $44,282 and $50,284, respectively, compared to only $33,161 for FINCA/Northern Mexico and $16,344 for one zone in FINCA/Costa Rica.[5] The smaller pilots spend more to reach fewer clients. FFH/Thailand and CARE/Guatemala spent approximately $231 and $133 per beneficiary in 1990, respectively; the nonpilot FINCA/Northern Mexico program spent only $48 per client.[6]

Personnel expenses account for a high percentage of program costs, ranging from over 87 percent at CARE/Guatemala to 46 percent at FINCA/Costa Rica. FINCA/Costa Rica's relatively low percentage can be explained by the fact that their more experienced promoters can manage many more banks—between fifteen and twenty—than promoters in other programs. Most of the programs do not show cost of funds. Only the FFH program in Thailand must pay commercial interest rates for its funds. The rest either are wholly grant funded (CARE/Guatemala, FINCA/Northern Mexico) or rely on grants and highly concessional loans (FINCA/Costa Rica).

FINANCIAL SELF-SUFFICIENCY

Can village banking be financially self-sustaining at the program level? Analyzing the expenses of the program together with the income generated by the external accounts permits an examination of this important question.[7]

Several factors complicate the income calculations and projections for the village banking programs. First, since many of the programs—

FFH/Thailand, CARE/Guatemala, and CRS/Thailand—were still in their pilot stages when analyzed, their costs are atypically high and their income low. Second, even the older programs have introduced changes that skew annual income flows and make it difficult to determine average income. Third, few programs keep detailed, disaggregated data on costs and income, and projections are based on the assumption that the banks will conform to the idealized loan ladder. Such projections depart substantially from reality. Given these limitations, it is impossible to do an income analysis using real income data or project projections. Available data can be extrapolated, however, to provide information on the conditions necessary for a project to break even. The lack of detailed data meant that this analysis could be made for only three programs—CARE/Guatemala, FINCA/Northern Mexico, and FFH/Thailand.[8]

The analysis is based on estimating actual income from available repayment, interest rate, and portfolio size information. Estimated income can then be compared with costs. A variety of scenarios can be constructed that show what level of performance would be required to achieve financial self-sufficiency.

The CARE/Guatemala income analysis shows that with a 24 percent interest rate, a 97 percent repayment scenario, and a forty-eight bank portfolio, the project could not break even. The project would cost $52,137 a year but would generate only $38,287 in revenue. Under a 79 percent repayment scenario and a 24 percent interest rate, income would cover only half the costs. With a higher interest rate of 36 percent, the project would break even and even generate a profit under certain scenarios. If the project had forty-eight village bank clients and a strong portfolio with 97 percent repayment, it would generate $57,431 in gross income, which would exceed annual costs. If CARE charged 36 percent interest and maintained a 94 percent repayment rate, it would approximately break even.

At the time of the study, the project was far from achieving these goals, since it had only nine village banks and charged 24 percent annual interest. The program has since expanded its portfolio. By the end of the first quarter of 1991, the project had twenty-eight banks and maintained very high repayment rates. This analysis strongly suggests that in addition to increasing its client base, the CARE program should consider raising its interest rates to cover costs.

Similarly, the FINCA/Northern Mexico program could make a profit only if it charged a 48 percent annual interest rate. With a portfolio of thirty-eight banks and a cumulative annual repayment rate of 94 percent, it could generate $35,519 in interest income and earn a $2,357 profit. If the program charged less than 48 percent interest or if its repayment rate fell below 94 percent, it would have to be subsidized.

Currently, FINCA/Northern Mexico charges 36 percent annually for its larger banks (above fifteen members) and 48 percent for smaller banks (below fifteen members). Therefore, of the three programs, it is probably the closest to financial self-sufficiency.

The FFH/Thailand program is the most costly and represents the higher end of the cost scale even among FFHs worldwide village bank portfolio. Even if the program had forty-two banks, a strong portfolio (97 percent repayment), and an annual interest rate of 48 percent, it would still require a subsidy of about 3 percent of total expenses. Only if the program charged 60 percent annual interest could it break even. At the time of the study, the program was charging 24 percent annual interest to eleven village banks, although FFH/Thailand anticipated a considerable expansion in its portfolio. But even with this expansion, the financial methodology adopted here suggests that if the program is to approach financial self-sufficiency, it will have to increase its interest rates considerably or, alternatively, lower its costs.

Clearly, financially sustainable interest rates will vary across programs and regions. For smaller programs or programs with large educational investments, the interest rate may have to be higher to achieve full cost recovery. Larger programs will probably be able to cover their costs at lower interest rates if they are operating in areas where village banks have big memberships, serve literate clients, and are close together. Nevertheless, this limited cross-program study indicates that average programs will have to charge around 36 to 48 percent in annual interest and have a portfolio of about forty banks to break even. Although these interest rates seem high, they most likely fall far below prevailing informal interest rates, which are probably the only other source of credit available to village bank clients. For programs that are providing educational messages and technical assistance, full cost recovery may not be an operational goal. Nevertheless, even these programs should work toward keeping their financial operations sustainable.

Programs need to adopt more accurate and precise financial accounts and projection methodologies. This will require improved tracking of their own costs and income and better records of the income-generating history and potential of their different village bank clients. Also, programs should begin to collect better data on village banks' internal accounts so that a financial analysis can be done of their operation.

ORGANIZATION AND MANAGEMENT ISSUES

Organization and management determine whether the sponsor can create effective village-level organizations. Two factors contribute to the development of a strong local-level organization—bank membership and leadership.

Village banks vary in size—the largest one studied had 163 members and the smallest had only five. Most banks have between twenty and forty members. Smaller banks are easier for members to operate but are more financially vulnerable and more expensive for the implementing organization. Village banks and implementing agencies can ameliorate the problems of small banks, however. To compensate for the higher expense, for example, FINCA/Northern Mexico charges higher interest rates to banks with fewer than fifteen members.

The ability of a bank to manage itself takes precedence over all else. If a bank is unable to resolve conflicts or manage its accounts, it does not matter how many local resources it has mobilized or how inexpensive it is to serve. Recognizing these limitations, San Vicente Pacaya Bank in Guatemala limited its membership to thirty-five women. FFH has found that the optimal number for its village banks is approximately thirty; this permits the development of group solidarity and good management practices.

The optimum, of course, is to have a well-managed larger bank, but this option is not always possible. Larger banks (fifty to a hundred members) are viable alternatives only when there is a high degree of stability and solidarity in the community, accompanied by strong leadership and bookkeeping skills. Also, the larger the membership, the greater the demands on the committee and village bank meetings. For example, to cope with such demands, Juntas de Pascuar Bank in Costa Rica (with 163 members) is training one of its members to become the paid, full-time treasurer and manager.

A second issue affecting village banks is variation in membership. At banks in Guatemala, membership turnover between cycles sometimes reaches one-quarter of all members. Membership fluctuations follow production cycles. In Durazno Bank, some of the women are seasonal traders who commute to Guatemala City markets. They use village bank credit in December and January. Then they drop out, since the bylaws do not permit them to miss meetings regularly. At San Vicente, the seasonality is based on agriculture.

Women typically leave when they see the time demands of bank membership overtaking the benefits of being a member. Many members participate in the bank for a few cycles, withdraw, then return as their work and household schedules permit. This flexibility is undoubtedly viewed as a positive attribute from the perspective of the members, but it may cause difficulties both for village bank leaders, who have to manage highly variable accounts, and for the sponsoring agencies trying to anticipate project income and credit needs. Variation in membership can also be a reflection of a lack of bank unity or an absence of effective membership-selection criteria.

In contrast to what the model anticipates, village bank projects are unlikely to have banks with a stable membership of fifty over three years, with each member steadily increasing his or her loan size with each cycle. Sponsoring agencies should anticipate such fluctuations and adjust their financial projections accordingly.

VILLAGE BANK LEADERSHIP

Village banks depend on strong leaders, especially during their first few cycles. Typically, village bank leaders are respected members of the community. In Thailand, for example, the village headman's wife is commonly selected as president; in Guatemala, it is typically a prominent woman from a local church. For the all-women groups particularly, committee members may have little or no experience with activities such as running meetings or keeping accounts.

The mechanical functions such as keeping accurate accounts and minutes can be difficult, especially in areas where literacy and numeracy rates are low. None of the banks visited had a fully satisfactory accounting system. Bank operation can be improved through simplification of financial tables, training for the committee in accounting procedures, and improved risk-management procedures. As village bank financial resources increase, pressure grows on village bank leaders to keep accurate and transparent accounts. A second set of management problems involves dealing with rumors (such as that bank management is siphoning off funds or lending savings to themselves), ensuring that members pay their fines, resolving conflicts between members, and determining how to allocate internal account resources. Most programs have provided training sessions for bank leaders to build their management skills. These initiatives are especially important for women's programs.

In FINCA/Costa Rica, male members controlled most committee positions. Yet this problem appeared to decrease as village bank promoters pushed for women's inclusion and leadership in banks. This suggests that the sponsoring agency has an important impact in countering domination by any one group. This is one argument in favor of village banks maintaining a relationship with an outside organization.

Many banks have faced difficulties with leadership turnover. As programs mature, the issue of regularized changes in leadership becomes increasingly important. Over time, as bylaws are more clearly written and patterns are established, there is typically less pressure on the leadership. If these patterns are not institutionalized, banks may become too dependent on one leader.

SPONSORING AGENCY ORGANIZATION
AND MANAGEMENT

Though not emphasized in the village banking manual, sponsoring agencies provide fairly extensive support to the village banking programs. A sponsoring agency's personnel includes promoters, accountants, managers, and support staff. In addition, the agencies require data management systems for tracking the progress of their village bank clients. Training of staff and village bank leaders and members has proved to be an important component of successful projects.

The central issues regarding promoters are whether they should be professional staff or come from the villages (community promoters), and how many village banks one promoter can manage effectively. In most programs, promoters have some postsecondary training. In the programs with education components, the promoters typically have some expertise in either agriculture (CARE) or public health (FFH). FINCA/Northern Mexico has a mixed staff of community and professional promoters.

Although there is a basic assumption that community workers will be less expensive and more effective than their professional counterparts, in reality the picture is less clear. Community promoters require considerable accounting and management training; they need information on how to interact with banks, transfer money, and move money safely. They do not always have the clout to pressure communities to comply with regulations and repayment schedules. For instance, when FINCA/Northern Mexico ran into repayment difficulties with its banks in Agua Prieta, the project manager had to step in to resolve the issue.

Promoters constitute a quarter to a third of program costs. Consequently, programs strive to achieve a low promoter-to-bank ratio. At well-established FINCA/Costa Rica, promoters can handle fifteen to twenty banks. CARE/Guatemala and FFH/Thailand, with education or technical assistance components, have one promoter for every six or seven banks.

In addition to promoters, the village banking programs require promoter coordinators, accountants, administrative assistants, and managers. Even the most streamlined program, FINCA/Costa Rica, has a sizable staff with ten people in the field and seven headquarters. At the other end of the staffing continuum, CARE/Guatemala has a total of eight staff members working on nine village banks.

THE SOCIAL DIMENSIONS

Village banking programs vary their financial services, training, and methods for building community banks to fit the local context.

For example, in Costa Rica, village bank members are generally numerate and literate. This is reflected not only in their bookkeeping but also in their ability to send fairly sophisticated financial reports to headquarters. Similarly, Costa Rica has a comparatively well-developed infrastructure and government service network. FINCA/Costa Rica relies heavily on government and private agencies for support in providing agricultural, marketing, and financial and technical assistance to its banks, thus reducing FINCA's own costs. This is not a viable alternative in all countries. In Guatemala, for example, illiteracy rates are much higher, and the government does not offer the same types of services.

Where communities are relatively stable and cohesive, such as in rural Guatemala and Costa Rica, village banks are relatively easy to establish. For FINCA/Northern Mexico, working in the transient-filled slums of Tijuana and Mexicali, establishing and maintaining banks are much more difficult. This situation can jeopardize the effectiveness of local sanctions as an incentive for repayment and lead to extreme fluctuations in bank membership. To compensate for these factors, banks in regions with highly migratory populations may have to spend more time building up relations among members before they begin to lend.

WHO IS BEING SERVED?

The village banking model expressly seeks to serve the poorest of the poor, especially poor women. A sample study of thirty-six FINCA/Costa Rica village banks found that the average member was male and had an annual income of $987 in 1987, a small farm (twenty hectares), and about a fifth-grade education (Wenner 1989, 14). The 1986 poverty line for Costa Rica was estimated to be about $1,310 annually, which suggests that the average village bank member was poor. But on average they were not extremely poor. The poverty line for extremely poor was estimated to be $637 in 1986 (World Bank 1990b, 75).

CRS/Thailand and FFH/Thailand projects have had similar experiences. A review of the landholdings of village bank members shows that the bulk of members held land in amounts ranging from eight to twenty *rai*,[9] suggesting that the majority of village bank members in these two village banks were poor. But a number of members held fifty or sixty *rai* and were probably fairly well-off by local standards. Conversations with members of the community showed that well-respected, better-off women were asked to join by promoters and others not because their capital was needed but to add legitimacy to the village banks. It is unclear whether a bank with a membership exclusively of very poor people from a community could be viable; such a membership may lack a critical mass of resources and have a scarcity of management skills.

Women constitute 100 percent of the membership in the CRS/Thailand, FFH/Ghana and Thailand, FINCA/Northern Mexico, and CARE/Guatemala projects; 82 percent in FFH/Mali; 57 percent in SCF/El Salvador; but only 27 percent in FINCA/Costa Rica. In the programs that allow only women, sponsors fear that if men were allowed to join, they would dominate the group and reduce the potential for building solidarity among women. Women are more likely to participate when loans start small (around $50), maturities are relatively short (four to six months), and meeting schedules are relatively demanding (weekly or biweekly). The effectiveness of this type of targeting may result from a number of factors. Women may be so desperate for funds that they are the only ones willing to comply with these restrictions. Or these terms may respond better to women's credit needs for small amounts lent for short terms. In the programs with larger loans and longer maturities, women's participation is relatively low.

In some cases, the high percentage of women has been used to justify limited supervision of village banks, on the assumption that women are more responsible financial clients than men. In practice, this assumption has turned out to be misleading. When provided with the proper training and incentives, women can be strong clients, as illustrated by 100 percent repayment rates in CRS/Thailand and FFH/Thailand. But the experience in FINCA/Northern Mexico illustrates that women are capable of slipping into arrears, and the experience with FINCA/Costa Rica illustrates that programs with a majority of male clients can also achieve high repayment rates. The main characteristics distinguishing strong village banks from weak ones include strong village bank solidarity, leadership, and financial management. To the degree that gender influences these variables—and it does—it has proved important.

COMMUNITY EMPOWERMENT

Although not a major focus of the village banking model, it is evident that, in practice, fostering the development of participatory local organizations improves a community's ability to gain access to resources and affects local decision making. Generally, as village banks develop, they place an increasing amount of their time and money into community projects. For example, Banco Superación de la Mujer in northern Mexico has made community investments in raffles, a small food stand, and children's uniforms. San Vicente Pacaya Bank in Guatemala is attempting to get a loan to undertake a villagewide drainage system. At FINCA/Costa Rica, there have been countless examples of banks starting cooperative stores, hotels, restaurants, or other forms of cooperative ventures.

In addition, well-established village banks can be conduits for communities to express their common needs to outside agencies and for other service agencies to interact with communities.

PROBLEMS AND PROSPECTS

This section explores the problems and prospects that village banking efforts may face as they move from their pilot experiences to becoming more mature programs.

THE PROSPECTS FOR GRADUATION

Some of the village bank design documents assume that village banks will graduate to more formal financial institutions. Graduation could involve individual clients or the village bank as a whole.

Few programs studied have had individual clients graduate to formal commercial banks. For example, after two years of operation, eight women, or 2 percent of participants, in the CARE/Guatemala project graduated. Banks are not equipped to lend to such clients, nor are borrowers able to invest the time and expense needed to interact with a commercial bank.

Another possibility involves graduating village banks (not individual customers) to commercial banks. Both CARE/Guatemala and FFH/Thailand village banks have established relationships with local commercial banks, first by placing their joint savings in bank accounts. The bank in Thailand also provides loans (guaranteed by donors) to the village banks. Both programs anticipate that village banks will graduate to these commercial banks as a source of loan capital after they have gone through about six cycles of operation. They expect that the banks will accept the village banks' credit histories and savings accounts as sufficient evidence of creditworthiness.

Although to date there is no history of this kind of graduation, there is reason to believe that village banks have a better chance of graduating than individual entrepreneurs have had. Lending to groups decreases transaction costs for both borrowers and lenders. Lenders have greater incentives to make larger and therefore cheaper group loans, while time-consuming transactions for borrowers are confined to committee members.

But even group lending may have difficulty overcoming all the constraints. For example, collateral requirements and interest rate ceilings may discourage commercial banks from lending to village banks. Village banks may be able to overcome the collateral constraint by maintaining a high savings-to-loan ratio in the participating commercial bank as a hedge against default. Even if these constraints were overcome, however, questions remain regarding supervision or audit of village banks and whether it is desirable to link community groups to formal systems in countries where the formal financial sector is not functioning well.

FINANCIAL VIABILITY

If graduation does not turn out to be a viable option, projects could work to establish the village banks as independent, sustainable institutions. The village banking methodology assumes that the community-managed village banks themselves will be sufficiently strong financially to continue to operate as local savings and loan associations beyond the life of the project. In addition, it assumes that the interest earned by the sponsoring agency will be sufficient to cover the costs of starting up new banks.

No village banking program has had experience with a single village bank becoming financially self-sufficient. This is not especially surprising. Financial intermediation requires a certain scale of operation and dispersion of loans and savings to function effectively (Huppi and Feder 1990).[10] This scale and dispersion are unlikely to be achieved in one village bank.

Village banks operate in communities where the majority of the participants are involved in similar productive activities. In rural areas, these activities are primarily agricultural; in urban areas, they are typically trading or small-scale production. The result is that at the beginning of the agricultural production cycle, for example, there is excess demand for loans, and at the end there is a surplus of savings. This synchronization is further aggravated by the related concentration of risks. If drought or flood affects the village, all clients will face similar pressures to go into arrears or default. Independent village-level institutions would have difficulty responding to the synchronization of demand or risks (Binswanger and Rosenzweig 1986).

Currently, the sponsoring agency's provision of external loans alleviates these bottlenecks. If village banks continue to operate after the sponsoring agency withdraws, they will probably look more like traditional rotating savings and loan associations or some type of periodic, small-scale credit union. If the legacies of village banking projects are traditional rotating credit associations or similar organizations, the question arises whether the considerable investment involved in setting up a village bank is a cost-effective way to achieve this outcome.

Financial self-sufficiency is more likely to be achieved at a sponsoring agency level. As defined here, a program would be considered financially self-sufficient if it covered—through fees and interest charges—its operating costs, including loan loss reserves, the cost of funds, and inflation, to maintain the real value of the loan capital (see Chapter 1).

In their discussion of a financial systems approach in Chapter 1, Rhyne and Otero identify four levels of financial self-sufficiency. Using these definitions, no program studied here has become financially self-sufficient. All the village banking programs studied are at either level one (CARE/Guatemala and CRS/Thailand, both pilot projects) or level two (FINCA/Northern Mexico, FFH/Thailand, and FINCA/Costa Rica). The projects' preliminary investments in financial self-sufficiency involved working toward developing links between village and commercial banks, government agencies, or private investors (FINCA/Costa Rica, CARE/Guatemala, and FFH/Thailand) or establishing a confederation of village banks that would raise funds from its membership for operational costs and a central fund, which would alleviate excess demand and supply constraints (CRS/Thailand). Despite these efforts, even FINCA/Costa Rica—which has been operating since 1985—relies on concessional and grant funds to finance staff positions, equipment, and some of its capital lending base.

Although projects acknowledge financial sustainability as an objective, those studied have yet to introduce many of the mechanisms that would allow them to meet this goal. For example, interest rates are rarely associated with costs, and programs do not keep sufficiently detailed accounts of their financial operations. With the possible exception of FINCA/Northern Mexico, programs do not set interest rate levels on cost-recovery principles. To set interest rates at a cost-recovery level, programs would have to keep detailed records of their operating and technical assistance costs and costs of funds. Currently, only FFH/Thailand keeps such detailed accounts.

Projects have made only limited efforts to become financially sustainable. The original village bank methodology conceived of the sponsoring agency as initiating village banks but not becoming a permanent partner. The village bank manual anticipates that clients will graduate after three years or that the village bank will continue to operate without assistance from the sponsoring agency. Therefore, sponsoring agencies have not focused on the establishment of permanent, intermediate institutions. If, indeed, village banks or village bank clients did graduate or become independent after three years, projects could justify long-term subsidies. But, as discussed above, no village bank and few village bank clients have graduated to commercial lending institutions, and no village bank has become financially self-sufficient.

The final factor that may inhibit financial self-sufficiency is sponsoring agencies' limited access to funds for a capital lending base. The savings they generate stay in the village banks for relending in the internal accounts. Only one project (FFH/Thailand) has access to nondonor money for lending. Clearly, dependence on donor capital is not commensurate with genuine financial viability.

APEX INSTITUTIONS

If projects are to become financially self-sufficient, they must establish intermediate or apex institutions that provide village banks with a source of funds, a secure place for surplus deposits, auditing, and general technical services. CRS/Thailand and FINCA/Costa Rica have taken steps toward establishing apex institutions.

CRS/Thailand is considering a confederation model, although this has yet to be fully conceptualized or implemented. The international credit union network, which has many years of experience with confederate systems, could provide a model. Alternatively, sponsoring agencies could pursue a strategy of linking village banks to the existing credit union network.

FINCA/Costa Rica offers an alternative apex model, assuming for itself the role of a permanent financial intermediary. FINCA/Costa Rica plays a supervisory role, auditing the village banks once or twice a year—sometimes in collaboration with government agencies—and ensuring that local elites do not capture a disproportionate share of the funds. It also provides loans to village banks from interest income, soft loans, and grants. FINCA/Costa Rica has been quite successful at serving its 153 banks as an intermediary. The central challenge it faces involves moving away from donor funds to more stable commercial sources of funds.

EXPANDING VILLAGE BANKING PROJECTS

To date, village banking projects have reached only a small number of clients. The majority of programs serve under 800 people. With the exception of FINCA/El Salvador, which was not operating when this study was done and has over 25,000 clients, FINCA/Costa Rica is by far the largest program, reaching just over 3,500 people. The factors constraining NGO growth identified by Tendler (1989) in her study of the Ford Foundation's livelihood and employment generation programs are also applicable to village banking. Her reasons included low levels of funding, NGOs' sometimes adversarial relationship with government or more formal institutions, their high costs per beneficiary, a tendency not to see large scale as a priority goal, and the smallness and homogeneity of NGOs, which can give them a qualitative advantage in responding to local needs.

If village banking programs do not overcome the constraints that are keeping them small, they will be unable to play a significant role in poverty reduction. Yet scaling up will require tradeoffs. Sponsoring agencies are likely to have to decrease the specialized attention they currently give to their village banks (by standardizing procedures) and begin to intermediate funds between village banks and commercial banks, raise interest rates, put less investment in technical assistance, and make greater investments in financial and institutional self-sufficiency.

COMMUNITY MANAGEMENT

The village banking methodology puts considerable emphasis on community management and participation. For cooperatives to be successful, members must feel that they have a sense of ownership in the organization (Huppi and Feder 1990). Lacking a stake, the incentives for members to contribute to the association's operations, repay loans, or contribute savings are significantly reduced. Village banking programs have been very successful at building a sense of ownership. Some of the factors that have contributed to this success include village banks' self-selection of their members, the community-managed and participatory nature of sponsoring agencies' management training for village banks, and members' resource contributions to the organization.

SUPERVISION AND RISK MANAGEMENT

The village banking model does not anticipate outside supervision after initial training and does not discuss risk. Village bank staff frequently view membership participation and management as adequate substitutes for outside auditing and other forms of risk management. There is the basic assumption that communities will be almost self-regulating. This is especially true in the all-female programs, since women are perceived as more responsible than men (Hatch and Hatch 1989). At the extreme, outside supervision (for example, auditing) is seen by some project staff as a threat to community authority and participation. This philosophy has translated into a policy of minimal supervision of the internal accounts, which are interpreted as available for communities to manage as they see fit.

The result of this lack of attention to risk is that projects have begun to experience theft and financial mismanagement. In FINCA/Northern Mexico, for example, one bank disbanded when the loan funds and savings were stolen. In other banks, treasurers have unlawfully borrowed from group funds for personal expenses. There are also numerous examples of mismanaged accounts resulting in arrears and rescheduling. The experience with theft and financial mismanagement raises two concerns. One is the need for improved oversight and risk-reducing strategies, and the other is the adequacy of management skills in the community.

Although risk can never be eliminated, it can be significantly reduced. Risk management or depositor protection involves the full disclosure of information about the solvency and liquidity of the deposit-taking institution, typically by licensed external auditors (see Chapter 3). But in projects in which the majority of participants are illiterate, disclosure of information is difficult.

Village banks should pursue nontraditional methods of risk management. Examples include monthly cross-checking of accounts by different village bank members and keeping savings in commercial banks, where they require at least three signatures to be withdrawn. External auditors might also audit village bank books once or twice a year. A reserve fund or insurance program for members' savings could be established.

Of the village bank programs studied, FINCA/Costa Rica possesses the most advanced risk-reduction practices. Village banks send their own internal audits to the central office once or twice a year. In addition, government agencies or FINCA staff conduct an annual external audit of village bank internal and external accounts. These procedures have significantly reduced incidences of mismanaged funds. Risk-reducing strategies that involve oversight need not jeopardize local participation or autonomy. Indeed, FINCA/Costa Rica's village banks were by far the most independent banks visited. Therefore, the participation versus supervision dichotomy posited by some project managers appears to be false.

The second issue that arises in association with mismanaged funds is local ability to keep accurate accounts. If village banks are to become effective local savings and loan cooperatives, they must have treasurers who can keep accurate accounts. Teaching these skills to illiterate or semiliterate people is possible, but it requires creative approaches and a larger time commitment than is currently envisioned by village bank project staff.

This examination of village banking leads to some encouraging conclusions. First, the model shows promise in its ability to reach poor people, particularly women, who are traditionally excluded from formal financial services. Second, village bank projects have been fairly successful at mobilizing local resources, including members' savings successful at mobilizing local resources, including members' savings and human resources (labor). Third, many of the older village banks meet expectations regarding community participation and have begun to benefit from investments they have made in public goods, such as roads and cooperative ventures. Finally, for the most part, village banks have maintained high repayment rates in their external accounts.

But this preliminary study has also exposed some substantial shortcomings and divergences between the model and the field. These problems affect primarily the financial operation and management of village bank projects.

Village bank operations are much more diverse and complex than the original village bank model expected. Members are not on a three-year path to financial independence, and financial self-sustainability has not been achieved at the community level. Membership turnover is common, and track records on savings and loans do not reflect even or constant growth. This variation has made village bank accounts difficult to manage. Moreover, there is little evidence that clients' financial needs stop after they have saved $300 or that this sum allows them to graduate to commercial banks. These findings indicate that the three-year, $300 timetable does not accurately describe village bank clients' financial behavior or needs.

Similarly, village banks need considerably more training, supervision, and monitoring from sponsoring agencies than the model anticipated. Although village banks' demand for these inputs declines substantially over time, evidence from the older programs indicates that it does not stop after three years. Moreover, if sponsoring agencies are interested in establishing sustainable financial institutions, they must greatly improve their accounting and management information systems.

These findings have serious implications for the design, implementation, and sustainability of village banking projects. Projects interested in fostering sustainable financial systems for their clients must put greater emphasis either on encouraging village banks to graduate to more formal institutions or on establishing apex institutions that can provide funds to village banks, absorb their excess savings when necessary, and offer supervisory and training services. Meeting these objectives will probably require projects to grow substantially and introduce more stringent and standardized operating and financial procedures.

The village bank projects studied show promise, particularly in their ability to reach the poor. But much remains to be done, especially in the areas of financial management and institutional development, before village banking programs will be able to reach significant numbers of clients or attain financial sustainability.

NOTES

1. Village banking was pioneered by the Foundation for International Community Assistance (FINCA), a U.S.-based nonprofit organization that specializes in rural credit. The chapter is based on field visits to project sites in Thailand, Guatemala, Costa Rica, and Mexico administered by FINCA and other U.S.-based nonprofit organizations that use the model. In Thailand, visits were made to village banking initiatives introduced by the Freedom from Hunger Foundation (FFH) and Catholic Relief Services (CRS). In Guatemala, Costa Rica, and Mexico, projects sponsored by CARE and FINCA were visited. Information from SCF/El Salvador, FINCA/El Salvador, and FFH/Ghana is also incorporated into the study, although field visits were not made to those sites.

2. Loans made through the village banks range from $50 to $300; individual entrepreneurs are eligible for loans of between $500 and $3,000.

3. CARE/Guatemala received a $455,000 grant to expand its operations to forty communities in Chiquimula beginning in 1991.

4. Between 1985 and 1988, the number of FINCA/Costa Rica village banks grew by 700 percent.

5. These figures are cost estimates based on financial returns from three quarters in 1990. Data limitations made it impossible to do a cost breakdown of the total Costa Rican program.

6. Information on cost per beneficiary for FINCA/Costa Rica's program was not available.

7. Wenner (1989, 17–18), in his study of village banks in Costa Rica, calculated the private and social rates of return on thirty-six banks. Only eleven banks (30 percent) showed a positive private rate of return, but this figure increased to eighteen banks when a social rate of return calculation was used. Wenner's calculations, however, did not assess differences in family welfare such as changes in household nutritional status or investment in children's education.

8. For a complete review of the financial methodology used here, see Chapter 9.

9. One *rai* is equivalent to 0.16 hectare.

10. In Chapter 8, Magill discusses how small credit unions with small client bases can have only a minimal impact on their clients because they are unable to generate sufficient resources to provide meaningful levels of credit to significant numbers of people.

CHAPTER 10

Transformation Lending:
Helping Microenterprises Become
Small Businesses

Larry R. Reed and David R. Befus

PITY THE SUCCESSFUL microentrepreneur. Farisai is one. She paid
back every short-term working capital loan she ever received and
enlarged her business in the process, but her success disqualifies her
from receiving more loans from the microenterprise development
agency that supported her. Rodrigo is another. He could triple his production and number of employees, but neither the bank nor the nonprofit credit program he borrowed from before will provide him a loan
for purchasing the equipment he needs to expand.

Farisai and Rodrigo are caught in what economist Hugo Pirela
Martínez calls "the gray area of microenterprise development." Too
big for credit programs that provide only short-term working capital,
yet still too small to meet the minimum loan amounts or collateral requirements of formal financial institutions, these enterprises find their
growth curtailed by a lack of credit available in amounts and terms that
meet their expanding needs. Growing microenterprises find that "their
success has made them too steep a risk for both the informal and formal
finance sectors. They are lost in the gray area, a true structural gap in
which thriving businesses stagnate, their potential for generating further income and employment curtailed" (Pirela Martínez 1990, 33).

The irony is that, according to the U.S. Agency for International Development (USAID), growing enterprises such as those owned by Farisai and Rodrigo "may offer the greatest potential for reaching the
poorest of the poor by creating jobs and for generating the greatest developmental impact by transforming marginal enterprises into sustainable businesses" (Boomgard 1989, 63).

Although USAID and Pirela Martínez both recognize the potential of
enterprises operating in the "gray area," neither can point to successful examples of programs that support the growth of these enterprises.
USAID's stocktaking report states, "The question of how to reach the
enterprise whose needs cannot be satisfied by the minimalist strategy
remains unanswered" (Boomgard 1989, 67).

185

This chapter seeks to answer this question by reviewing five programs that engage in transformation lending, that is, they make loans and provide services to support the transformation of microenterprises into small businesses. These five programs not only succeed at providing loans and other services that aid microenterprise transformation but also cover all or nearly all their expenses with earned income.

TRANSFORMATION LENDING: A DEFINITION

The term *transformation lending* first appeared in the USAID microenterprise stocktaking report, which divided the microenterprise programs it reviewed into three levels: enterprise formation, enterprise expansion, and enterprise transformation. The key characteristic of enterprise transformation is that it seeks to turn larger microenterprises into small enterprises by providing working capital and fixed-asset loans (average size, $3,000),[1] combined with training (Boomgard 1989).

For purposes of this chapter, a microenterprise has ten or fewer workers (often members of the owner's family); produces simple, unsophisticated products based on traditional technology; and faces intense competition as a result of low barriers to entry. Small enterprises have ten to fifty workers (many hired from outside the family), produce relatively more complex products involving some sort of innovation in technology, and work in a less competitive environment because of higher barriers to entry. Thus, microenterprise transformation involves:

- Changes in the means of production and increases in productivity,

- Increases in sales income sufficient to support the addition of new employees,

- Changes in the relationship between the business owner and employees,

- Increases in assets, and

- Increases in specialization.

Transformation lending is the provision of a mix of credit and services whose purpose is to assist microenterprises increase their assets and productivity and become small businesses, thereby increasing their sales, income, and number of employees. Transformation lending does not equate with either graduation into the formal financial sector or legal incorporation. Achieving these standards requires vastly different levels of cost and effort in different countries, which makes them difficult to use as across-the-board measurements. For example, a microenterprise owner in Indonesia can receive a loan from a commercial bank for as little as $13.50. In other countries, commercial banks will provide loans no smaller than $10,000 and require collateral equal to three times the value of the loan. In this chapter, transformation is defined by increases in assets, productivity, and employment rather than the legal status of the enterprise or its source of financing.

THE NEEDS OF A TRANSFORMING MICROENTERPRISE

Most microenterprises start as highly integrated firms. They grow or collect raw materials or purchase unprocessed goods in bulk and sell them to end users (for example, basket makers and vegetable hawkers). Many microenterprises find that they can increase their productivity by restricting themselves to a smaller number of activities within the production and distribution system. They may purchase raw materials from a wholesaler instead of growing or collecting them themselves. They may sell to marketers instead of selling directly to end users (Mead 1992).

With this increased specialization comes many other changes in the operation of the business:

- *Personnel.* The enterprise moves from primarily family labor to more hired labor with defined roles. Personnel management and labor relations become concerns of the business owner.

- *Marketing.* Transforming businesses must secure stable markets for their increased production. This often entails expanding beyond small neighborhood markets, selling to formal businesses, and clearly defining the enterprise's comparative advantage.

- *Technology.* New and larger markets often require higher production quantities and more stringent quality standards. To meet these requirements, microenterprises upgrade their technology. Workers in the enterprise need to acquire skills appropriate to this change in technology (Jean, Hyman, and O'Donnell 1990).

- *Supply.* With new equipment in place and a larger work force, the enterprise cannot afford to let supply disruptions idle operations. It needs secure, long-term sources of supply.

- *Credit*. The greater reliance on processed and purchased raw materials creates an increased need for working capital credit. The need for tools and equipment creates an increased need for fixed-asset credit.

- *Cash management*. With increased raw material expenses, more hired labor, and higher investment requirements, transforming businesses must be able to make distinctions between business and household funds.

This review of the needs of transforming enterprises has two key implications for credit programs seeking to support microenterprise transformation. First, these programs must provide credit for both working capital and fixed-asset needs. Fixed-asset loans must be made in amounts large enough to purchase equipment and over terms long enough to match the payback period of the equipment.

Second, credit alone will not cause a microenterprise to transform. Changes in business management, production processes, marketing channels, and sources of supply are also needed. Some microenterprise owners will already have the skills and knowledge necessary to make this transition. Others will be able to locate mentors or training courses to help them improve their skills and manage the transition. Still others will need specialized training or other targeted interventions before they will be able to transform their enterprises. The type and amount of services a transformation lending program provides will depend on which of these microenterprises it targets.

A REVIEW OF FIVE TRANSFORMATION LENDING PROGRAMS

This section describes five programs involved in transformation lending (see Tables 10.1 and 10.2 for comparisons). The program descriptions are based on reviews of published documents and internal reports rather than field visits.

BANK RAKYAT INDONESIA'S UNIT DESA SYSTEM

Bank Rakyat Indonesia (BRI) is one of five state-owned banks in Indonesia. It is one of Indonesia's largest banks, with total assets of $6.5

Table 10.1   Comparison of Program Methodology, Training, and Performance

	ADEMI	IDH	NDF/J	ACEP	BRI Unit Desa
Year started	1983	1979	1981	1986	1984
Year of data	1989	1991	1990	1991	1990
Program methodology					
Loans to groups	No	Yes	Yes	No	No
Loans to individuals	Yes	Yes	Yes	Yes	Yes
Maximum loan size	$5,000	$10,000	$35,000	$20,000	$13,500
Maximum loan term (months)	24	36	120	16	36
Average loan size	$544	$683	$6,870	$2,877	$414
Average loan term (months)	6	14	48	8	11
Effective interest rate[a]	74%	29%	32%[b]	31%	32%[b]
Training					
Training program	Yes	Yes	Yes	No	No
Training costs as % of total	3%	8%	24%	0%	0%
Program performance					
Number of loans made/year	7,619	778	562	1,373	1,379,000
Amount of loans/year (000s)	$4,142	$531	$3,861	$3,950	$578,437

Sources: BRI: Boomgard and Angell (see Chapter 11); ADEMI: Lewin (1991); IDH: IDH (1992); NDF/J: NDF/J (1992); ACEP: Rofe (1992).
[a]Effective interest rate includes commissions and fees charges and is calculated using the average loan term for each program.
[b]Program uses tiered interest rate structure; number given is the average rate.

Table 10.2 Comparison of Financial Performance, Organizational Structure, and Impact

	ADEMI	IDH	NDF/J	ACEP	BRI Unit Desa
Financial performance					
Loan portfolio (000s)	$2,119	$618	$4,505	$2,570	$535,040
Interest and fee income (000s)	$945	$119	$1,015	$423	$159,700
Total expenses (000s)	$643	$119	$946	$370	$133,760
Earnings (000s)	$302	$0	$70	$53	$25,940
Cost/$ in portfolio	0.30	0.19	0.21	0.14	0.25
Income/$ in portfolio	0.45	0.19	0.23	0.16	0.30
Return on average assets	14.6%	0.0%	1.1%	1.8%	3.5%[a]
Average cost of capital	8.0%	0.5%[a]	3.0%	0.0%	12.0%
Arrears rate	10.2%	20.3%	11.0%	NA	5.1%
Default rate	1.2%	7.1%	2.1%	2.0%	1.2%
Organizational structure					
Number of branches	20	5	4	14	3,628
Loan officers	70	14	23	14	10,950
Loans/loan officer	109	56	24	98	126
Loan portfolio/loan officer	$30,271	$44,143	$195,870	$183,571	$52,825
Impact					
Jobs created/year[a]	2,011	1,452	2,675	1,301	540,127
Amount loaned/job created	$2,060	$366	$1,443	$3,036	$1,071
Loans to women	35%	74%	NA	23%	25%

NA=not available.
[a]Estimates.

billion and a loan portfolio of over $4.7 billion. BRI operates the Unit Desa system, which is the world's single largest supplier of credit and savings facilities to microenterprises.[2] From 1984 to 1991, the BRI Unit Desa system made 10.1 million loans. In 1991, the system had 1.8 million loans outstanding totaling $746 million. It also held 8.6 million savings accounts and had $1.3 billion in savings on deposit.

LOAN TYPES AND SIZES. The Unit Desa system operates a lending program known as KUPEDES (Kredit Umum Pedesaan). The KUPEDES program provides two types of loans: working capital loans and investment loans. These differ only in the length of the loan terms; working capital loans range from three to twenty-four months; investment loans can have terms up to thirty-six months. Eighty-five percent of the loans made in the KUPEDES program are working capital loans. Loan sizes range from $13.50 to $13,500. Only proven clients who have made full and timely payments on previous loans can receive the maximum amount. The average size loan in 1991 was $414.

LOAN APPRAISAL AND SECURITY. Loan appraisal involves simplified procedures for assessing the profitability of the business and the value of collateral. Unit Desa loan managers visit business sites and within two hours complete simple cash flow and balance sheet calculations. From these appraisals, the loan managers determine the appropriate loan size.

The heart of the KUPEDES credit program is a progressive lending system that rewards timely repayments. Borrowers who make every loan payment on time automatically qualify for a repeat loan of double the previous loan's size. Each late payment reduces the maximum size of the next loan, and borrowers who make their final payments more than two months late cannot qualify for another loan. All borrowers must demonstrate that they have sufficient assets to cover the value of their loans in the form of land, buildings, other property, or the assignment of wages.

INTEREST RATES. BRI uses a two-tiered interest schedule, charging a flat interest rate of 1.5 percent a month on loan amounts up to Rp 3 million and 1.0 percent on amounts above Rp 3 million. The effective annual rate for a twelve-month loan ranges from 31.7 percent on loans under Rp 3 million to 22.7 percent for the maximum loan of Rp 25 million. The KUPEDES program also charges a prompt-payment incentive fee of 0.5 percent per month, which it refunds to borrowers who make all their payments on time.

LENDING PERFORMANCE. The Unit Desa system currently makes 115,000 loans a month totaling $50.3 million. Past-due loans equal 5 percent of the portfolio, and loan losses are 1.2 percent.

SAVINGS. The Unit Desa system offers three different savings programs paying interest ranging from 9 to 15 percent, based on the amount deposited. The most popular of these programs, SIMPEDES

(Simpanan Pedesaan), allows savers to make unlimited withdrawals. The Unit Desa system has three and a half times more savers than borrowers, and at the end of 1991, total savings on deposit exceeded total loans outstanding by more than $500 million.

TRAINING. The BRI Unit Desa system does not include a training component for either borrowers or savers.

ORGANIZATIONAL STRUCTURE. The Unit Desa system is organized around village units staffed by four people—a general manager, a loan officer, a cashier, and a bookkeeper. As loan volume increases, the Unit Desa adds staff until it reaches ten employees. After that, the Unit Desa is split in two. If there is significant lending activity in outlying areas, the Unit Desa sets up a village post consisting of a cashier and a bookkeeper. In 1990, BRI had 2,893 Unit Desa and 735 village posts, employing almost 15,000 people. The average Unit Desa maintains a portfolio of 475 loans with outstanding balances totaling $185,000.

FINANCIAL STRUCTURE. Savings on deposit, loans bearing market rates of interest, and a grant from the government of Indonesia make up the loan fund of the Unit Desa system.[3] Since 1989, savings have exceeded outstanding loans. The Unit Desa system pays an average cost of capital of approximately 12 percent.

PROFITABILITY. Prior to the introduction of the KUPEDES lending system, BRI suffered large losses in the Unit Desa system. The KUPEDES program broke even eighteen months after its introduction and has been making money ever since. Profits from the Unit Desa system have quadrupled since 1985, reaching Rp 36.9 billion ($20.3 million) in 1989.

ADEMI[4]

The Asociación para el Desarrollo de la Microempresa, Inc. (ADEMI) in the Dominican Republic began operations in 1983 with support from ACCION International, a U.S.-based private voluntary organization. ADEMI aims to create jobs and increase incomes in the informal sector by providing credit to microenterprises. From 1983 until the end of 1991, ADEMI made 36,377 loans for a total value of $20 million.

LOAN TYPES AND SIZES. ADEMI currently provides both working capital and fixed-asset loans to individual microenterprises. Loans for working capital have terms of one to twelve months, and fixed-asset loans can have terms up to twenty-four months. Loans for working capital range from $50 to $500; loans for fixed-asset purchases range from $800 to $5,000.

LOAN APPRAISAL AND SECURITY. Loan advisers visit potential applicants several times before helping them complete a three-page application form. Loans are approved first by the loan adviser, then by the operations manager, and finally by the finance manager. Clients receive small (average, $135) short-term (one to three months) loans initially. Loan amounts and terms increase as the borrower successfully repays previous loans (average loan size for repeat loans is $508). Successful borrowers can stay with ADEMI indefinitely, and many have received over twenty loans from the organization. ADEMI provides fixed-asset loans, which it reviews with more scrutiny, for borrowers who have demonstrated their creditworthiness through several loan cycles.

INTEREST RATES. ADEMI charges a commission of 8 percent on a loan, paid in advance. It also charges a flat rate of 2.8 percent per month, which combines charges for interest and advisory services. ADEMI's effective annual rate equals 74 percent. It operates in a relatively inflationary environment, unlike BRI.

LENDING PERFORMANCE. At the end of 1991, ADEMI had 8,930 loans outstanding totaling RD$57 million (U.S. $4.5 million), with an arrears rate of 6 percent. ADEMI made 60 percent of these loans to manufacturing businesses, 24 percent to trade, and 16 percent to services and others.

SAVINGS. ADEMI does not operate a savings program but encourages its borrowers to open savings accounts with commercial banks.

TRAINING. ADEMI provides demand-driven technical assistance, responding to needs expressed by borrowers. Loan advisers provide training informally as they monitor loans. If a loan adviser cannot solve a problem, he or she brings in outside consultants in areas such as production, marketing, and accounting. In 1989, direct training expenses by ADEMI made up only 3 percent of the total budget.

ORGANIZATIONAL STRUCTURE. ADEMI's organizational structure delegates considerable responsibility to the loan advisers, giving them the authority to select and approve loans. Each loan adviser processes fifteen loans a month. The average adviser's portfolio consists of 90 to 140 borrowers and $30,000 in loans. ADEMI provides bonus payments to loan advisers based on the performance of their portfolios. Advisers can increase their salaries by up to 50 percent through these bonuses. In 1989, ADEMI had a staff of ninety-six, seventy of whom were field officers.

FINANCIAL STRUCTURE. ADEMI finances its loan portfolio primarily out of borrowed funds. At the end of 1989, ADEMI had borrowed nearly RD$10 million (U.S. $1.67 million), with an average cost of funds of 10 percent.

PROFITABILITY. Since 1986, ADEMI's income from interest and fees has exceeded its operating expenses. Since 1988, ADEMI's interest and fee income has exceeded all expenses, including depreciation and loan write-offs. In 1989, grant income made up only 5 percent of ADEMI's total income.

INSTITUTO DE DESARROLLO HONDUREÑO[5]

The Instituto de Desarrollo Hondureño (IDH) began in 1978 with funding and technical support from Opportunity International, a U.S.-based private voluntary organization. IDH initially focused on transformation lending and gradually expanded its program to include a poorer clientele.

LOAN TYPES AND SIZES. IDH now operates three distinct lending programs:

1. *Individual loans.* Loans up to $10,000 are made to individuals for working capital or fixed assets, with terms up to two years. They average $900, with a payback period of fifteen months.

2. *Group loans.* Loans are made to other organizations (cooperatives and community development organizations) seeking to assist people in very poor communities start businesses. Each group has at least sixty members. Loans average $200 a person, with terms of two years.

3. *Community banks.* Loans are made to groups of about thirty people located in the major open market of Tegucigalpa. Loans to the community banks average $120 a person and are paid back in three months.

LOAN APPRAISAL AND SECURITY. Individual loans require significant investigation prior to disbursement, including an application form consisting of several pages. Community bank loans require very little documentation. With group loans, the social welfare organization receiving the funds does all the identification and screening of potential clients.

All loans require some form of guarantee, which may be collateral or a qualified cosigner (including joint guarantees by group members). Clients who "graduate" from the group loan or community bank programs can qualify for individual loans.

INTEREST RATES. IDH charges 24 percent interest on individual loans plus a 3 percent commission, giving it an effective rate of 27 percent. It also charges 24 percent to community banks. IDH charges a subsidized rate of 5 percent on group loans, based on a condition established by the donor agency providing the funds for these loans.

LENDING PERFORMANCE. In 1991, IDH made 700 individual loans, sixty community bank loans, and twelve group loans, giving it a total of over 3,000 clients. IDH lent $530,000 in 1991 and had an outstanding portfolio of $618,000. That year, IDH had an arrears rate of 20 percent and a default rate of 7 percent, though its longer-run performance was better.

SAVINGS. The community bank program incorporates savings by the community, using the village bank methodology explained in Chapter 9. The individual loan program has no savings component.

TRAINING. IDH offers training in basic business management and technical areas such as sewing, carpentry, baking, and agriculture. Borrowers attend courses on a voluntary basis and pay fees that cover the direct cost of providing the training. IDH opens these courses to the general public as a means of earning revenue and attracting qualified loan candidates.

ORGANIZATIONAL STRUCTURE. IDH employs nine project supervisors to oversee the individual loan program, four supervisors for the community banks, and one supervisor for the group loans. In both the individual loan and community bank programs, each project supervisor manages an average portfolio of $55,000; the group loan supervisor manages over $100,000 in loans. IDH operates from a central office in Tegucigalpa and four branch offices.

FINANCIAL STRUCTURE. IDH's loan capital comes from grants from international and local donors, reinvested earnings, and subsidized loans from the Inter-American Development Bank (IDB). IDH pays an average cost of capital of less than 1 percent.

PROFITABILITY. IDH's total expenses exceeded its operating income (interest, fees, and commissions) by $15,000 in 1991. Donated funds to subsidize the expansion of the community bank and group loan programs more than made up for this deficit, keeping IDH solvent. However, this excess of income over expenses is not sufficient to cover the devaluation of the loan fund due to inflation.

NATIONAL DEVELOPMENT FOUNDATION OF JAMAICA[6]

The National Development Foundation of Jamaica (NDF/J) was founded in 1981 with the assistance of the Pan American Development Foundation, a U.S.-based private voluntary organization. NDF/J defines its mission as promoting the growth of the small-enterprise sector through the provision of nontraditional credit, training, and technical services. NDF/J began lending in Kingston and has branched out into other urban and rural areas of Jamaica. From 1981 to 1990, NDF/J made 3,361 loans totaling $6.7 million.

LOAN TYPES AND SIZES. NDF/J lends to individuals and groups for working capital and fixed-asset purchases, in amounts up to $35,000 and for periods up to ten years.

LOAN APPRAISAL AND SECURITY. NDF/J's screening process includes an initial interview, a three-page loan application, and an appraisal by a field officer. A borrower may receive a large first loan from NDF/J if he or she can meet the screening requirements. Over time, NDF/J has come to rely more on hard collateral and loan guarantees in assessing the security of a loan (Stroh 1986). NDF/J's field officers provide follow-up with borrowers, conducting regular monitoring visits to advise borrowers and assess the performance of the business.

INTEREST RATES. NDF/J interest rates depend on the sector of the business: 23 percent for agriculture, 32 percent for manufacturing, and 36 percent for trade and services (effective rates).

LENDING PERFORMANCE. During 1990, NDF/J made 604 loans totaling J$28 million (U.S. $2.6 million). NDF/J's loan portfolio at the end of 1990 totaled J$50 million (U.S. $4.6 million). Fifty-six percent of NDF/J's loan portfolio has gone to businesses in the service and commerce sector, 22 percent to manufacturing, and 21 percent to agriculture. Loan losses totaled 2.1 percent of the portfolio in 1990, a marked decrease from a high of over 7 percent in 1985. NDF/J officials reported an arrears rate of 11 percent at the end of 1991. They also reported that smaller loans (under U.S. $500) had the highest delinquencies (38 percent at the end of 1991) and required more time and services from loan monitors.

SAVINGS. NDF/J does not operate a savings program but does encourage its borrowers to save at commercial financial institutions.

TRAINING. Training has always been a key component of NDF/J's program. It operates a separate Technical Services and Training (TST) unit that provides a six-hour training program covering NDF/J's policies and basic business management for all new loan recipients. In addition, all loan recipients qualify for up to twenty hours of one-on-one business counseling services from TST.

NDF/J also conducts seminars on entrepreneurship, provides specialized agricultural training, and carries out surveys of borrowers broken down by gender or economic subsector. NDF/J recently added a business development program to help small enterprises expand their markets both locally and internationally. NDF/J charges a consulting fee for these services and markets them to all small enterprises on the island, including nonborrowers.

ORGANIZATIONAL STRUCTURE. NDF/J operates from a head office, four branch offices, and six sub-branches. All lending activity takes place in the branch and sub-branch offices. NDF/J operates two distinct divisions: Banking Operations and Technical Services and Training.

NDF/J field officers make loan appraisals and present loans for approval. Business counselors provide ongoing monitoring of the loans and consult with the borrowers. Loan approvals may be made by the branch manager, operations manager, executive director, or credit committee of the board, depending on the size of the loan.

FINANCIAL STRUCTURE. Borrowed funds at rates ranging from 1 to 10 percent make up 45 percent of the NDF/J portfolio. This gives NDF/J an average cost of capital of 3 percent.

PROFITABILITY. In 1989, NDF/J earned enough from interest income to cover the expenses of the credit program.[7] In 1990, earned income (including income from the endowment fund) exceeded all expenses by about U.S. $70,000 and covered 69 percent of training expenses. NDF/J's income covers its operating costs but not the cost of inflation on the loan portfolio. A recent analysis conducted by Peat Marwick concluded that NDF/J would need to increase the size of its portfolio by 22 percent annually in order to maintain financial viability.

AGENCE DE CREDIT POUR L'ENTERPRISE PRIVEE[8]

The Agence de Credit pour l'Enterprise Privee (ACEP) in Senegal began operations in 1986 as the small-scale enterprise component of a USAID-financed community and enterprise development project. USAID established the program to provide commercial loans to small and medium-sized Senegalese businesses. By the end of 1993, ACEP was expected to be converted into a permanent financial institution.

After operating the program for three years, USAID determined that Senegalese small enterprises could effectively use credit to expand their businesses, but that the program would need to expand substantially to achieve financial viability. This led to a reorganization of the program, a move of the office from Kaolack (in the interior) to Dakar, the establishment of a branch network, and the hiring of a new expatriate director.

LOAN TYPES AND SIZES. ACEP makes loans to individual enterprises for both working capital and fixed-asset purchases. It lends mainly to existing enterprises with proven track records, though in rare cases it does provide loans for start-up costs. ACEP lends up to $12,000 for first-time borrowers and $20,000 for subsequent loans, with loan terms no longer than sixteen months.

LOAN APPRAISAL AND SECURITY. Branch managers take loan applications, visit business sites, and make recommendations on loan approval to the ACEP loan committee. The loan committee, made up of the ACEP director, the head of the legal department, and the regional managers, makes all loan approval decisions, which require unanimous approval.

Borrowers must secure their loans with collateral, guarantees, or both. ACEP accepts real property, equipment, accounts receivable, and personal assets as collateral. ACEP also accepts third-party guarantees from individuals or institutions. All ACEP borrowers and guarantors must take out a life insurance policy for the amount of the loan with ACEP as the beneficiary. Borrowers with payments over five days late must pay a penalty of 2 percent a month on the amount in arrears plus an administrative fee equivalent to $10.

INTEREST RATES. ACEP charges the maximum interest rate allowed by the Senegalese government, which is 16 percent. In addition, ACEP charges a 1 percent origination fee. This translates to a 28 percent annual rate. For use of accounts receivable as collateral, ACEP charges an extra 3 percent commission to cover the additional risk involved.

LENDING PERFORMANCE. In fiscal year 1991, ACEP made 1,373 loans totaling $3.9 million. Since 1986, ACEP has made 2,142 loans totaling $7.8 million to 1,710 different businesses. In fiscal year 1991, ACEP's average loan size was $2,800 and the average loan term was eight months. Fifty percent of ACEP's loans go to agribusiness, 27 percent to general commerce, 17 percent to manufacturing, and 6 percent to agriculture. ACEP's loan write-offs in 1991 amounted to 2 percent of its outstanding portfolio.

SAVINGS. ACEP does not operate a savings program but expects to introduce savings services once it becomes a formal financial institution.

TRAINING. ACEP does not operate a training program.

ORGANIZATIONAL STRUCTURE. ACEP has fourteen branch offices in five regions (Kaolack, Fatick, Louga, Thies, and Dakar). Branch offices generally contain only one employee operating from a storefront office. Branch managers produce the loan applications, monitor client enterprises, and follow up on clients. On average, each branch manager generates $280,000 in loans each year and maintains a portfolio of 100 clients. ACEP provides its branch managers with an annual bonus equal to 5 percent of the profits generated by their branches.

The regional manager supervises the branches and reviews loan applications. Each regional office contains a cashier's office where clients make their loan payments, although branch offices located far from the regional office may accept payments as well.

FINANCIAL STRUCTURE. At the beginning of 1992, donated funds made up ACEP's entire loan portfolio. ACEP has begun the process of converting itself into a credit union owned by the proprietors of small-scale enterprises in Senegal. It plans to fund future growth with the savings of the credit union members as well as continued donations.

PROFITABILITY. In fiscal year 1991, ACEP earned $423,077 in interest and fee income and incurred $370,237 in operating expenses, giving it a profit for the first time. Earned income amounted to 40 percent of operating expenses in 1989 and 50 percent in 1990. These expense figures do not reflect two subsidies: ACEP does not pay the salary of its director or any cost of capital.

KEY LESSONS

This review of five credit programs gives us new insight into how lending institutions can support the transformation of microenterprises into small businesses. Some of the key lessons are discussed below.

FINANCIAL VIABILITY

Microenterprise lending programs can serve the needs of transforming enterprises in a financially viable way. Liedholm and Mead (1987, 105) stated, "Those projects that have attempted to provide long-term, fixed asset lending to small firms have, with few exceptions, proved to be both unfruitful and high in administrative costs." In contrast to that assessment, this chapter presents three programs that provide fixed-asset loans in combination with working capital loans and whose income meets or exceeds operational expenses. According to the typology of self-sufficiency levels developed in Chapter 1, one program (IDH) operates at level two, two programs (ADEMI and NDF/J) operate at level three, and one (BRI) operates at level four.

CREDIT DELIVERY

Successful transformation lending programs have characteristics in common with all successful providers of credit. No matter what target group a credit program seeks to serve, it must obey certain principles of cost-effective credit delivery. These characteristics of successful credit programs include:

- *Simple, streamlined procedures.* All five programs have developed standardized lending procedures that speed the process of loan analysis and approval.

- *Good information systems.* All five programs maintain computerized information systems that provide regular and timely reports on loan repayments, arrears, income, and expenses.

- *Loan costs commensurate with loan income.* The five programs vary widely in number of loans per loan officer (24 to 156) and loan portfolio per loan officer ($30,000 to $195,000). Those programs with smaller loan portfolios per loan officer (BRI, ADEMI, and IDH) have the simplest screening and monitoring procedures. Those programs with more extensive screening, monitoring, or training programs (NDF/J and ACEP) offset these costs with higher average portfolios per loan officer.

- *Decentralized program structures.* All five programs operate from several branches. With the exception of ACEP, branch offices make most or all of the loan decisions.

- *Positive interest rates.* All five programs charge rates equal to or above those charged in the formal financial sector.

LENDING PRACTICES

Successful transformation lending programs have developed methodologies that differ from those of programs that provide only short-term working capital. Common lending practices among the five programs include:

- *Loans to individuals.* Three of the five organizations make loans only to individuals. Two make both group and individual loans, but individual loans predominate.

- *Variable terms.* The organizations provide longer terms for fixed-asset than for working capital loans—from sixteen months to ten years.

- *High loan ceilings.* Maximum loan amounts ranged from $5,000 to $35,000.

- *Higher collateral requirements for larger loans.* All five programs require some form of formal collateral from recipients of fixed-asset loans.

Evidence from these five programs and others shows that lending methodologies aimed at transforming enterprises do not work well for standard microenterprise lending, and vice versa. NDF/J reported that loans under $500 require more staff time and have the highest arrears rates (38 percent versus 11 percent overall). IDH found that the procedures it used for screening and approving individual loans were too costly and time-consuming when making small working capital loans. It employed two different group lending methodologies for reaching poorer clientele.

ADEMI found the solidarity group methodology too costly and time-consuming when it began targeting growing manufacturing firms. It scrapped group lending altogether. Other solidarity group lending programs have found that the group methodology does not work when successful borrowers need to purchase fixed assets. For these clients, they make individual loans in larger amounts with longer payback periods (see Chapter 7). Transformation lending policies exist on a continuum between microenterprise lending techniques and the techniques of commercial banks.

CLIENTELE

Although the methodologies may differ, one institution can still serve both expanding and transforming firms. BRI, ADEMI, and IDH serve both expanding and transforming microenterprises. For BRI and ADEMI, expanding firms make up a majority of their clientele. These three organizations serve both sectors by moving clients through a gradual progression from one type of loan product to others. IDH does this by operating three distinct lending programs, with graduates from the two group lending programs becoming eligible to participate in the individual loan program.

IDENTIFICATION METHODS

Transformation lending programs have developed two different methods for identifying microenterprises that can successfully undergo transformation. For a transformation lending program to be successful, it must develop cost-effective means of identifying microenterprises capable of undergoing transformation. The five programs reviewed here employ two different methods for doing this. We call these two methods "gradual growth" and "high hurdles."

BRI and ADEMI (and to some extent IDH) employ the gradual growth method. Borrowers move through a succession of loans of increasing size until they qualify for longer-term fixed-asset loans. When a borrower qualifies for a fixed-asset loan, he or she has already demonstrated an ability to use credit effectively, which decreases the risk to the lending institution.

NDF/J and ACEP utilize the high hurdles method. They have higher collateral requirements and employ more extensive screening procedures for first-time borrowers than the other programs. Borrowers can qualify for a long-term fixed-asset loan immediately, without repaying a series of smaller loans first. Thus, approved applicants of ACEP and NDF/J have already demonstrated sufficient money management skills to have acquired the assets needed to qualify for a loan. They must also have sufficient business knowledge to present a rudimentary business plan that shows good potential for success.

The gradual growth methodology seeks to work with all microenterprises, supporting the credit needs of those enterprises experiencing growth. The high hurdles methodology seeks to work with only a very small percentage of the microenterprise universe—those larger microenterprises that are growing. The appropriateness of either methodology depends on the goals of the lending institution, its target beneficiaries, and the availability of credit to various sectors of the microenterprise community. Gradual growth does a much better job of providing credit to the smallest microenterprises and to women and of supporting their growth over time. High hurdles lending institutions that seek to serve more women or a poorer clientele must often develop additional lending methodologies for these clients. IDH has done this by creating two group lending programs. ACEP has begun testing group loans as a means of increasing the number of female borrowers.

TRAINING PROGRAMS

Targeted training programs may support microenterprise transformation, but they are not necessary parts of successful transformation lending. Two of the programs we reviewed offer no training programs (BRI and ACEP). Another two (ADEMI and IDH) offer only voluntary training, charge for their training services, and spend a small proportion of their total budget on training. Only NDF/J requires training, provides free training, and spends a large portion of its budget (24 percent) on training.

BENEFICIARIES

Lending institutions can support microenterprise transformation and still reach a large number of beneficiaries at low cost. To get some comparison among programs that emphasize job creation to varying extents, we have defined the beneficiaries of a credit program as those receiving loans and those who gain employment in new jobs created in enterprises that receive loans. The total estimated number of new beneficiaries per year in these five programs range from 2,230 (IDH) to over one million (BRI). The loan portfolio per beneficiary ranges from $277 (IDH) to $1,392 (NDF/J). The three institutions that use the gradual growth method serve significantly more beneficiaries per dollar in the portfolio than do the two high hurdles institutions. Gradual growth institutions had at least one beneficiary for every $500 in the portfolio; it took $950 or more to serve one beneficiary in the high hurdles institutions.

GROWTH

Preliminary evidence shows that transformation lending programs support growth in assets, employment, and productivity of microenterprises, helping them to transform into small businesses. Earlier we defined microenterprise transformation as an increase in assets and productivity to the level of a small business, accompanied by a concurrent increase in sales, income, and number of employees. Preliminary evidence from these five programs suggests that this sort of transformation does take place. For example:

- IDH reports high levels of job creation per dollar lent (one new job for every $366 lent). The fact that IDH uses stringent criteria for defining job creation makes this statistic even more impressive.

- ADEMI reports high levels of increase in labor productivity among the larger firms it supports (Poyo, Hoelscher, and Malhotra 1989).

- BRI reports that, among multiple borrowers, employment and household income grew in real terms and grew most rapidly in those businesses receiving larger loans (Sutoro and Haryanto 1990).

Although it indicates that transformation takes place, this evidence remains sketchy. Determining the full scope of business transformation among the microenterprises supported by these programs will require further study.

AREAS FOR ADDITIONAL RESEARCH

This chapter has helped show that we know more than was previously thought about how to support the transformation of microenterprises into small enterprises. However, the review also points out gaps in knowledge. This section reviews key areas of transformation lending that need additional research.

TRAINING. The five programs showed significant differences in their approaches to training, yet all demonstrated an ability to assist microenterprise transformation. Additional research may tell us whether training programs play an important role in the transformation process and, if so, what types of training are most important.

SUBSECTOR ANALYSIS. The countrywide surveys of microenterprise cited earlier all report that rates of growth among microenterprises vary widely by economic subsector. Other studies suggest that the raw material, equipment, and capital requirements of transforming businesses vary by subsector (Mead 1992). Additional study in this area might help microenterprise credit institutions target their transformation lending programs to specific subsectors.

IMPACT. All five programs reviewed had studies or statistics to demonstrate their impact through increases in income, assets, profits, or employment generation in the businesses assisted. None of these studies compared the performance of borrowers to a control group of nonborrowers, however, so it is impossible to determine whether the reported increases were due to the lending program or to other factors (see Chapter 6 for more on evaluation methods). Nor did the studies examine the processes involved in transformation identified above, such as changes in labor relations, markets, or technology. Most of the studies also dealt only with current or recent borrowers and could not address critical long-term results.

NOTES

1. All dollar amounts are U.S. dollars unless otherwise indicated.

2. The BRI Unit Desa system is described more fully in Chapters 2 and 11.

3. The grant from the government came in 1984 and makes up only 4 percent of the current loan portfolio.

4. This section draws heavily on Lewin (1991); Poyo, Hoelscher, and Malhotra (1989); ACCION (1991); and ADEMI documents.

5. This section is based on IDH's annual reports and internal documents and interviews with IDH staff.

6. This section draws heavily on NDF/J annual reports and interviews with NDF/J staff. Other sources are noted in the text.

7. NDF/J attributes some costs to the TST unit that might be considered costs of the credit program. For example, NDF/J includes 60 percent of the salaries of the project development, loan monitoring, and collections officers in the TST unit (Wieland, Stearns, and Salas 1990).

8. This section is based on Rofe (1992) and interviews with the ACEP director.

PART III

A Closer Look at Successful Microenterprise Finance Experiences

PART III EXAMINES case studies of four microenterprise finance institutions representing three regions of the world: Asia, Africa, and Latin America. Each of these cases documents movement toward greater scale and financial self-sufficiency. In Chapter 11, Boomgard and Angell document what is probably the most successful institution serving microenterprises in the world. Bank Rakyat Indonesia's Unit Desa system (or Unit Banking system) serves 2 million borrowers and 8 million savers. Its loans are fully financed by its savers, and it is a significant source of profit for its parent bank. This chapter attempts to explain the factors that led to its success and reflects on the prospect that similar systems can be established in other countries.

In Chapter 12, Glosser describes the transformation of PRODEM, a very successful solidarity group program in Bolivia, into BancoSol, the first private commercial bank specifically devoted to microenterprises. The creators of BancoSol were pioneers, facing head-on many of the issues raised in the earlier chapters on regulation and institutional development. With BancoSol, other nongovernmental institutions wishing to become financial institutions have a model to follow, and the mainstream banking world has an example as well.

Chapters 13 and 14 both review the evolution of nongovernmental programs using the solidarity group methodology—one in Colombia using the ACCION model, and one in Kenya using a modified Grameen Bank model. Both programs faced the challenge of introducing greater financial sophistication into programs run by NGOs and of confronting the conflicts between businesslike and social welfare approaches to microenterprise finance. Each group found that in order to bring older-generation organizations along, they had to introduce new programs or organizations based on the best available methods. The achievements of these organizations using the new techniques far surpassed those of the older programs and helped demonstrate that improvement in financial viability was possible without sacrificing social goals.

CHAPTER 11

Bank Rakyat Indonesia's Unit Desa System: Achievements and Replicability

James J. Boomgard and Kenneth J. Angell

IN 1984, THE government of Indonesia wagered on an ambitious experiment in modern economic development. The challenge was to transform 3,600 rural branches of a state-owned bank from highly bureaucratized, heavily subsidized conduits for agricultural credit into self-sustaining, profitable commercial financial intermediaries. Few would have accepted the odds of such a venture. But, quietly and without great fanfare, the Unit Desa system of Bank Rakyat Indonesia (BRI) has fulfilled and surpassed even the most optimistic predictions of what might be accomplished.

In 1984 when the experiment began, the BRI Unit Desa system lost more than $24 million; in 1989 the system earned a profit of more than $25 million. From 1984 through June 1990, approximately 7.9 million loans were made from the Unit Desa. There are currently 1.8 million loans outstanding, valued at $615 million. The system makes 115,000 loans each month with a value of $50 million. The average loan size is currently $437. The long-term loan-loss ratio is 3.26 percent.[1] Savings on deposit increased from $26 million in 1983 to $647 million in June 1990 in 6.7 million accounts. There is an excess of savings over loans of $58 million. The system is, for all practical purposes, fully self-sustaining without any remaining external subsidy. By any standards, these are remarkable accomplishments.

Compared with other programs serving microenterprises, the Unit Desa system stands alone in its achievement. For example, as of 1990, the Grameen Bank in Bangladesh had a (cumulative) total of 800,000 members (borrowers and savers) served by 700 branches. Grameen adds approximately 25,000 new members per month. Its outstanding portfolio of $32 million was financed mostly from external sources, with savings accounting for roughly 42 percent. Although Grameen may reach a relatively poorer population than BRI, it requires considerable external subsidies to do so. The Badan Kredit Kecamatan (BKK) system in central Java serves one large province in Indonesia and has an outstanding portfolio of $12.7 million in just over 500,000 loans. Savings account for approximately 20 percent of outstanding loans. Asociación para el Desarrollo de la Microempresa, Inc. (ADEMI) in the Dominican Republic is a nongovernmental lending program that serves microenterprises with loans that average $450. Approximately 10,000 loans are made a year. ADEMI does not mobilize savings.

The success of the BRI Unit Desa system has implications for a broad array of development issues—financial policy, rural credit, microenterprise, donor cooperation, and technical assistance. This chapter extracts some of the most important lessons learned from the project for the broader audience working on these issues.

FROM PROGRAM CREDIT TO FINANCIAL INTERMEDIATION: THE ORIGINS OF THE UNIT DESA SYSTEM

In the early 1980s, the Indonesian financial sector was a textbook example of tight regulation, state domination, subsidization, and fiscal orientation. Central planning, buoyed with oil dollars, allowed the evolution of a financial system designed almost exclusively to channel subsidized resources from the government budget to priority sectors of the economy. Chapter 3 describes some of the negative consequences of such a regulatory framework.

The financial sector was (and is) dominated by a central bank (Bank Indonesia) and five state-owned banks, each with primary responsibility for selected priority sectors. BRI provides financial services for rural development and is one of Indonesia's largest banks. As of 1989, it had total assets of over $6.5 billion, a net loan portfolio in excess of $4.7 billion, and pretax profits over $62 million. BRI's extensive network is said to be the second largest in the world. The bank employs nearly 35,000 people.

BRI's Unit Desa system had its origin in 1970, when BRI was charged with servicing the financial requirements of the Indonesian rice intensification program, BIMAS (an acronym for Bimbingan Massal, or Mass Guidance).[2] Under the improved national BIMAS program, each 600 to 1,000 hectares of irrigated rice in Java and Bali and every 2,000 hectares in the outer islands were to be provided with a new bank called the BRI Unit Desa (village unit), intended to channel credit directly to participating farmers. More than 3,600 Unit Desa were established between 1970 and 1983. Most of these were located in subdistrict (*kecamatan*) capital towns and served an average of eighteen villages.

BIMAS credits reached their peak in the mid-1970s. Thereafter, interest in the program declined rapidly as farmers began to experience problems with pests, flooding, and drought or discovered more convenient ways to acquire needed inputs. Bad crops strapped borrowers with debt to be repaid from other income sources. Those who defaulted were barred from further borrowing.

With participation and repayment falling in the late 1970s and early 1980s, the government alternated between selective debt forgiveness and heavy-handed debt collection. Campaigns to enlist farmers in marginal growing areas in the outer islands temporarily boosted participation but further weakened repayment. The number of farmers participating fell by 60 percent between 1975 and 1983, and the percentage of loans never re-paid rose from 5 percent to more than 20 percent. Those who remained in the program were the richest farmers, who sought cheap credit, and the poorest ones, who were driven to borrow by their poverty. In October 1983, the government effectively killed the BIMAS program by limiting par-ticipation to only those farmers cultivating less than one hectare of land.

While BIMAS was the primary activity of the Unit Desa until 1984, BRI was also asked to manage several other programs through the Unit Desa infrastructure. In 1974, Kredit Mini was established as a grant-funded program to make subsidized loans of up to Rp 200,000 (then U.S. $482) to individuals involved in rural enterprise. Kredit Midi was established in 1980 with subsidized liquidity credits for graduates of Kredit Mini; it provided loans of up to Rp 500,000 (then U.S. $797). Both programs charged interest of 12 percent a year and were financed by 3 percent liquidity credits from Bank Indonesia. Savings were intro-duced into the Unit Desa system in 1976. Funds were mobilized with the national savings program instrument (TABANAS). Interest rates were initially set at 12 percent and later raised to 15 percent. In spite of the negative spread, TABANAS balances in the Unit Desa system reached Rp 38 billion (U.S. $37 million) at the end of 1984.

Throughout the 1970s and early 1980s, the Unit Desa performed well as institutions, but, as a result of the structure of their programs, they were able to cover only a fraction of their operating costs from revenues. Capital for BRI came in the form of cheap (3 percent) liquid-ity credits from Bank Indonesia. Administrative cost subsidies from the Ministry of Finance initially covered 40 percent of all Unit Desa costs and later all their operating losses. Finally, the government of Indone-sia and Bank Indonesia covered 75 percent of BIMAS loan losses.

THE TRANSFORMATION OF
THE UNIT DESA SYSTEM

Faced with growing annual Unit Desa losses, a defunct program, and elimination of the BIMAS subsidies, BRI and the government had to make some critical decisions. Falling international oil prices were eroding oil revenues, which financed more than 60 percent of the government budget. New forms of subsidy were unlikely. Closing the BRI Unit Desa would have eliminated formal banking in about 90 percent of the country. Moreover, there were nearly 14,000 trained Unit Desa employees; abandonment of the system would have been a massive waste of human as well as physical resources.

A potential solution was well understood in some circles. Although there were a number of hurdles to the transformation of the Unit Desa system, the most critical were legal and political restrictions on interest rates. The Ministry of Finance, and particularly its Center for Policy and Implementation Studies (CPIS), pressed for a significant liberalization of bank regulations. One effect of financial liberalization would be to permit operation of a commercially viable general rural credit scheme through the BRI infrastructure. In July 1983, the minister of finance granted BRI authority to charge "break-even" interest rates for a general rural credit scheme, KUPEDES (an acronym for Kredit Umum Pedesaan). In January 1984, KUPEDES was inaugurated.

The decisions that laid the groundwork for the transformation of the Unit Desa system represented a significant policy shift within the government toward the financial sector and some major market-oriented initiatives by the state-owned BRI. The liberalization freed banks to set their own interest rates on commercial loans and savings (except for TABANAS) (Patten and Rosengard 1991, 72). BRI responded to the new regulatory environment by adopting three significant policy changes to revitalize the Unit Desa system:

1. Transformation of the Unit Desa from BIMAS conduits to full-service rural banks.

2. Internal treatment of Unit Desa as semiautonomous profit centers rather than simply as postings in BRI's overall accounts.

3. Evaluation of the Unit Desa based primarily on their profitability rather than on hectares covered or money lent.

The primary lending vehicle for the new Unit Desa system was KUPEDES. KUPEDES drew from the experience with the grant-funded Kredit Mini and Kredit Midi programs but differed fundamentally in that it was financed by BRI borrowing at interest rates that reflected the cost of funds (market savings rates). This, in combination with lending rates that allowed a positive margin, provided a built-in incentive to mobilize resources from savers. Thus, the groundwork was laid for the creation of a viable rural banking system.[3]

ORGANIZATION AND OPERATIONS

The Unit Desa system, although an integral part of BRI's operations, functions as a separate profit center. The foundation of the Unit Desa system is a network of branch banks in villages throughout Indonesia, generally located at the subdistrict (*kecamatan*) level.[4]

The standard Unit Desa has a four-person staff consisting of a general manager, a loan officer, a bookkeeper, and a cashier. Staff members generally have a high school or college education. Each Unit Desa has only one manager, but the number of personnel at a Unit Desa can range from a minimum of four people up to ten. Once the volume of Unit Desa operations requires eleven staff members, the Unit Desa is split into two and another one is established.

Village service posts, comprising two-person teams (a bookkeeper and a cashier), are attached to those Unit Desa that have significant business activity in outlying areas but insufficient transactions to justify the creation of another fully staffed Unit Desa. A post collects savings and loan payments and receives loan applications but does not make loans. When a post generates sufficient transactions, it is converted into a Unit Desa. As of June 1990, the Unit Desa system had 2,893 Unit Desa, 735 posts, and almost 15,000 employees.

The branch network of BRI, the most extensive of any bank in Indonesia, consists of 312 branches and covers the whole country. Branches are full-service retail banking outlets. Although the branches have primary responsibility for the day-to-day supervision of Unit Desa operations, the Unit Desa are only part of the branch activities. Each branch has at least one Unit Desa business manager for every four Unit Desa; the manager routinely visits the Unit Desa and monitors operations, cash balances, and financial controls. In those branches where there are more than ten Unit Desa, a Unit Desa officer is assigned to oversee the business managers. As of June 30, 1989, there were 837 business managers and 138 Unit Desa officers. Although the Unit Desa itself collects data and compiles standard monthly reports, Unit Desa operational and financial data are consolidated and analyzed at the branches. The regional offices oversee the operation of the branches and are located in the capitals of fifteen of the twenty-seven provinces of Indonesia.

BRI's head office is in Jakarta. One full department, the Business Unit Desa, oversees the Unit Desa system. BRI's board of managing directors is the main authority for establishing Unit Desa policy. BRI senior management is assisted on Unit Desa and rural banking–related matters by a team of advisers from the Harvard Institute for International Development (HIID), who are financed with U.S. Agency for International Development (USAID) and World Bank assistance. These advisers report directly to the president director and coordinate daily with the Business Unit Desa Department.

FUNDING AND RESOURCE MOBILIZATION

Funds available to the Unit Desa system are provided from several sources—grants, liquidity credits, donor loans, and savings mobilization. As of March 31, 1990, total resources available to the Unit Desa system amounted to Rp 1,497 billion (approximately U.S. $809 million).

Equity consists of the proceeds of the government's grant of Rp 66.7 billion in liquidity credits to BRI for the Kredit Mini program, which was reallocated for funding KUPEDES loans in 1984. BRI distributed this grant among the Unit Desa in the form of an equity contribution of Rp 19 million for each Unit Desa and Rp 5 million for each post. Each newly established Unit Desa is similarly funded with an initial equity contribution of Rp 19 million.

The availability of this grant means that the Unit Desa continue to be slightly subsidized. Other sources of funds for the Unit Desa carry market interest rates. The grant is limited to the amount that was already available when KUPEDES began and is a declining percentage of the total resources used.

The liquidity credit from Bank Indonesia has three components: the conversion of Rp 43 billion in liquidity credits originally provided by Bank Indonesia to the Kredit Midi program; an initial Rp 100 billion of liquidity credits made available to BRI for KUPEDES lending to reach the break-even point; and an additional injection of Rp 50 billion of liquidity credits to support the growth of KUPEDES beyond the break-even point. Bank Indonesia charges BRI an interest rate of 12 percent a year on these amounts, which is approximately the average rate of interest on all BRI interest-bearing accounts. The outstanding balance of the liquidity credits at the end of March 1990 was Rp 159 billion.

In 1987, the World Bank approved a loan to the government of $101.5 million. The purpose of the loan was to replace Bank Indonesia in providing further liquidity credits for KUPEDES lending. The availability of the World Bank funds was limited to 10 percent of the amount lent or 50 percent of the increase in a quarter, with an upper limit of 65 percent of the increase in outstanding loans. The upper limit dropped to 60 percent in the second year of the loan agreement. The interest rate to BRI for these funds is the average rate on all BRI's interest-bearing accounts. The loan is to be repaid semiannually over fifteen years, beginning in January 1993.[5]

In 1989, the Exim Bank of Japan provided BRI with a loan of Rp 50.7 billion for "local currency costs" (the 40 percent of the increase in loan amount outstanding not covered by the second year of the World Bank loan agreement) for KUPEDES. Like the World Bank loan, the Japanese loan charges interest to BRI that is equivalent to the average rate on all BRI's interest-bearing accounts. Repayment of the Japanese loan is to be made semiannually over fifteen years commencing in September 1991.

The most important source of funds for the Unit Desa system is deposits, which have experienced rapid growth. In 1989, the Unit Desa became a self-funding system when deposits exceeded total loans outstanding. The growth of Unit Desa deposits over time and a comparison with the growth of the loan portfolio are shown in Table 11.1.

Excess savings are placed with BRI branches, where they earn an 18.6 percent transfer fee for the Unit Desa. The BRI branches use the Unit Desa deposits as a source of liquidity for other lending programs. Although deposits exceed loans, BRI continues a strong drive to increase savings deposits. BRI has not been able to utilize reinvested profits to finance KUPEDES lending. Profits from the Unit Desa system are taken into the general accounts of BRI at year end.

THE KUPEDES LOAN PROGRAM

The Unit Desa system has one credit instrument, KUPEDES (general rural credit), which is available for any creditworthy individual or enterprise. Key aspects of the KUPEDES loan program are presented below.

LOAN PURPOSE. Loans may be used for any productive enterprise. Loans for consumption purposes, although not encouraged, are permitted. Although conditions of the World Bank loan state that no more than 5 percent of the total portfolio is to consist of consumption loans, there is no effective way to prevent a borrower from using a loan for consumption purposes.

Most loans are used for working capital, but not necessarily for the purpose stated in the loan application. Borrowers often have multiple enterprises and borrow for whichever is regarded as the most creditworthy. Funds are borrowed and diverted to agriculture or other uses. The majority of KUPEDES loans are listed as being for trade. Most loans are for twelve months with monthly installments.

BORROWER ELIGIBILITY. The main criterion for loan approval is the creditworthiness of the borrower. KUPEDES loans are essentially character loans. Borrowers are required to provide proof of income sources and/or a certification of their business activities. Most loans have a cosigner, who is normally the applicant's spouse. Borrowers are classified into five categories on the basis of their repayment record, and this classification establishes the limit for a subsequent loan (Table 11.2).

COLLATERAL. Indonesian banking law and practice mandate that all bank loans be backed by some form of collateral. Although buildings or

Table 11.1   Unit Desa Deposits as a Percentage of Loans Outstanding (Rp billion)

	1984	1985	1986	1987	1988	1989	*March* 1990
Loans outstanding	111	229	334	429	539	846	993
Loan growth (%)	—	106	46	28	26	575	17[a]
Deposits	42	85	176	288	493	959	1,055
Deposit growth (%)	—	101	107	64	71	95	10[a]
Deposits/loans (%)	38	37	53	67	92	11	106

Source: Bank Rakyat Indonesia, Head Office.
[a] These figures reflect growth in the first quarter of 1990.

any other property (including assignment of wages) may be accepted, most borrowers use land (including house plots). The Unit Desa holds the land certificate, which would enable it to take possession of the property in the event of a default. The documentation of collateral for each loan, however, is more for the purpose of establishing the borrower's serious intent to repay than to provide basis for legal action or an alternative source of loan repayment. BRI rarely acts to recover this collateral, as legal proceedings are costly and take many months.

LOAN MATURITY. The KUPEDES program involves two types of loans—working capital and investment. The only difference between the two loans is in the length of the loan. Working capital loans (90 percent of the total) range from three to twenty-four months. Investment loans can go up to thirty-six months. Repayment schedules can include grace periods of three to nine months. Working capital loans also have the option of single balloon payments for three- to twelve-month maturities. Grace periods and single-payment loans are discouraged, however, as such loans are thought to have lower repayment rates.

LOAN SIZE. The minimum KUPEDES loan is Rp 25,000 (about U.S. $13.50). Since 1987, few loans of less than Rp 100,000 (U.S. $54) have been made. Based on 1989 average salary levels, a loan size of about Rp 120,000 covers the staff time to approve a loan, collect the installments, and pursue borrowers who default. The maximum KUPEDES loan amount was initially set at Rp 1 million and was gradually increased to Rp 25 million (approximately U.S. $13,500) by May 1990. This upper limit is generally available only to repeat customers who have promptly and fully repaid previous loans. The average balance outstanding has risen steadily and was Rp 468,000 (U.S. $252) in June 1990. The average loan size is Rp 1,088,000, and no loan is less than Rp 200,000.

INTEREST RATES. A key element in the development of KUPEDES was the market-based approach to interest rates. This approach focused on

Table 11.2 KUPEDES Borrower Classification

Rating	Criterion	Subsequent Loan Ceiling
A	All payments made on time	Increase of 100 percent over previous loan amount
B	Final payment on time, one or two installments late	Increase of 50 percent over previous loan amount
C	Final payment on time, three or more installments late	No increase of loan amount
D	Final payment late, but paid within two months of due date	Reduction of 50 percent of previous loan amount
E	Final payment more than two months late	No new loan

establishing rates that would ensure sufficient amount and prompt delivery of credit and adequate profitability for the financial intermediary. The underlying assumption was that for small borrowers, convenience and access to credit are more important than the interest rate. The KUPEDES interest rate is not a market rate but rather one that covers funding and operating costs, including adequate loan loss provisions, and permits the Unit Desa system to earn a reasonable profit. The market rate for credit in the villages is much higher than the KUPEDES rate.

On loans of Rp 3 million or less, the interest rate is 1.5 percent a month, calculated on a flat-rate basis on the original loan principal. For loans of more than Rp 3 million, the (flat rate) interest rate structure is two-tiered: 1.5 percent a month on the first Rp 3 million of the original loan principal, and 1.0 percent a month on the amount exceeding Rp 3 million. The effective annual interest rate is 31.7 percent for loans of Rp 3 million or less and ranges from slightly less than 31.7 percent to 22.7 percent for a maximum loan of Rp 25 million.

These rates are much lower than rates charged by informal lenders, which often exceed 10 percent a month. They are lower than rates charged by commercial banks lending to large rural enterprises; the typical interest rate is 20 to 25 percent a year. They are above the rates charged on most government-subsidized loans at 12 percent a year, but such loans are not regularly available. One of the attractions of the KUPEDES program to borrowers is that funds are always available.

In addition to the basic interest rate, there is a prompt-repayment incentive fee of 0.5 percent a month (also flat rate), collected monthly. This is essentially an up-front penalty for failure to pay loan installments on time. The fee is refunded to the borrower semiannually if all repayments are made on time.

DEPOSIT PROGRAMS

Three instruments are used to gather savings deposits: SIMPEDES, TABANAS, and SIMASKOT. (For a fuller description of BRI savings programs, see Chapter 2.)

SIMPEDES (Simpanan Pedesaan, or village savings program) was introduced by BRI as a Unit Desa savings instrument in 1985. SIMPEDES interest rates, calculated on the basis of minimum monthly balances and compounded, are zero on balances of less than Rp 25,000; 9 percent on balances from Rp 25,000 to Rp 200,000; 14.4 percent on balances between Rp 200,000 and Rp 750,000; and 15 percent on balances above Rp 750,000. The saver is permitted unlimited withdrawals, which is considered the key factor behind the success of the program. As an additional incentive for the SIMPEDES program, savers receive coupons for a lottery held every six months for prizes. By far the majority of Unit Desa deposits are placed under SIMPEDES.

The other two instruments, TABANAS and SIMASKOT, are aimed at the smallest savers and urban savers, respectively.

Unit Desa also offer time deposits and demand or checking accounts. The time deposits have maturities ranging from one month to one year. Checking accounts are held primarily by local government agencies.

It is interesting to note that the growth in the number of savers in the Unit Desa system has sharply outpaced the number of borrowers. This is not surprising; in rural areas, at any one time, more people tend to be savers than borrowers. At the end of 1989, the Unit Desa had almost four times as many savers as borrowers.

INTERNAL CONTROLS

The Unit Desa system has never had a complete annual internal audit. In 1989, only 542 of the 2,844 Unit Desa were individually audited. The lack of audits is due to the large number of Unit Desa and staffing constraints of BRI's Internal Audit Department, which audits all BRI's regional and branch offices annually. BRI recognizes that branch supervision does not replace the internal audit function and is taking steps to increase the number of audit staff.

External auditing at BRI is performed by the government's Agency for Financial and Development Supervision, which audits all BRI's regional and branch offices and a random sample of Unit Desa.

PERFORMANCE OF THE UNIT DESA SYSTEM

FINANCIAL PERFORMANCE

Since 1984, the Unit Desa system has registered impressive growth (see Table 11.3). Between 1984 and 1989, total assets increased 617 percent from Rp 0.18 trillion to Rp 1.29 trillion (U.S. $695 million). Savings deposits increased dramatically, in particular SIMPEDES, from Rp 40.2 billion in 1986 to Rp 926.6 billion (U.S. $509 million) in 1989. The outstanding KUPEDES portfolio increased from Rp 111.0 billion to Rp 845.6 billion (U.S. $456 million).

Financial analysts use four quantitative measures for evaluating banks: profitability, liquidity, capital adequacy, and asset quality. Each of these measures is analyzed below for the Unit Desa system.

PROFITABILITY. The Unit Desa system has shown favorable profitability trends and ratios. Before the introduction of KUPEDES, the system had large losses (as much as 50 percent of its expenses), which were covered by direct and indirect subsidies. The KUPEDES program reached the break-even point eighteen months after its start and has generated steadily increasing profits ever since. The Unit Desa profits (before tax) have almost quadrupled, rising from Rp 9.8 billion in 1986 to Rp 36.9 billion (U.S. $20.3 million) in 1989. Pretax profits for the first six months of 1990 were a record Rp 29.8 billion (U.S. $16.1 million).

In 1989, two policy changes resulted in a significant increase in personnel and administrative expenses. First, all Unit Desa staff were upgraded to full BRI employee status, with the consequence of higher salary and employee benefit expenses. Second, senior management determined that all training costs for Unit Desa personnel were to be charged as expenses against the Unit Desa system. The policy changes resulted in approximately Rp 17 billion in additional expenses. Despite the added expenses, the profit of the Unit Desa system was satisfactory and showed an increase in absolute terms.

One effect of these policy changes was that as of January 1990, Unit Desa operating expenses and costs of funds are no longer subsidized. The upgrading exercise had the further benefit of improving the morale of the Unit Desa staff.

Return on average assets (ROAA) increased steadily from 1986 to 1988, rising from 2.7 percent to 4.9 percent. The ROAA declined in 1989 to 3.6 percent due to the added expenses. An ROAA of 1 percent is considered favorable by international standards.

LIQUIDITY. The Unit Desa system has adequate liquidity provided from internal savings mobilization as well as from external funding sources of Bank Indonesia and donor organizations. In 1989, the Unit Desa system became a self-funded organization with deposits surpassing

Table 11.3   Performance of the BRI Unit Desa System (Rp billion)

	1985	1986	1987	1988	1989	March 1990
Total assets	300.5	427.9	511.9	736.2	1,291.2	1,458.4
Average assets	—	364.2	469.9	624.1	1,013.7	1,374.8
Cash and short-term assets	62.8	97.2	97.2	215.7	452.6	469.6
Gross loans[a]	243.8	345.0	429.0	538.8	845.6	992.5
Average loans	—	294.4	387.0	483.9	692.2	919.1
Loans past due	4.8	15.0	24.6	40.2	45.7	50.4
Loan loss provisions	10.5	20.6	21.3	34.2	39.7	44.9
Transfers to loan loss provisions	2.4	10.1	6.2	25.3	25.8	8.4
Loan losses	—	—	5.5	12.4	20.3	3.2
Deposits and borrowings	227.3	351.6	412.5	619.6	1,151.9	1,336.3
Income (loss)	(.9)	9.8	22.5	30.6	36.9	12.1
Key ratios of asset quality						
Past-due loans/gross loans	2.0%	4.3%	5.7%	7.5%	5.4%	5.1%
Loan loss provisions/gross loans	4.3%	6.0%	5.0%	6.3%	4.7%	4.5%
Net loan losses/average loans	—	—	1.4%	2.6%	2.9%	1.2%[b]
Profitability						
Return on average assets	—	2.7%	4.8%	4.9%	3.6%	3.5%[b]
Liquidity						
Cash and short-term assets/total assets	20.9%	22.7%	19.0%	29.3%	35.1%	34.2%
Gross loans/deposits and borrowings	107.4%	98.3%	109.2%	92.4%	76.9%	74.3%
Percentage growth						
Total assets	—	42.4%	19.6%	43.8%	75.4%	51.8%[b]
Gross loans	—	41.5%	24.4%	25.6%	56.9%	69.5%[b]
Deposits and borrowings	—	54.7%	17.3%	50.2%	85.9%	64.0%[b]
Income	—	—	129.6%	36.0%	20.6%	31.2%[b]

Source: Bank Rakyat Indonesia.
a In 1985 and 1986, gross loans included KUPEDES and previous loans of Kredit Mini and Midi programs.
b Annualized figures.

loan requirements. The large number of savings accounts provides a stable source of loanable funds.

CAPITAL ADEQUACY. It is not possible to gauge the capital adequacy of the Unit Desa system, as it is part of BRI. Capital for the system is maintained with BRI. Although each Unit Desa is capitalized with Rp 19 million, all their profits are transferred to BRI. Similarly, the equity that Bank Indonesia provided for the Unit Desa system in 1984 is housed in BRI.

ASSET QUALITY. The quality of the KUPEDES loan portfolio is good. Loan growth has been strong. Annualized loan growth for 1990 was expected to be over 50 percent.

Although Unit Desa age the past-due loan installments, this is not reported to the branch or head office. The only past-due loans reported are those that are overdue beyond the final installment date. Therefore, it was not possible to determine the amount of nonperforming loans in the loan portfolio. Typically, nonperforming loans are those that are more than ninety days past due. Past-due loans are in and of themselves not as problematic as nonperforming loans. Nonperforming loans are more likely to have to be charged off against loan loss reserves.

Total amounts past due as a percentage of loans outstanding, although rising for several years from 2.0 percent in 1985 to 7.5 percent in 1988, declined in 1989 to 5.4 percent. The quality of the portfolio improved during the interim three-month period to March 31, 1990, to 5.1 percent. The level of past-due loans, which includes nonperforming loans, is satisfactory; the downward trend in this ratio is favorable. The arrears problem appears to be largely concentrated in a relatively small number of branches and village units, where heightened management attention is needed.

In the fourth quarter of 1989, the loan loss reserve policy was modified to incorporate both general and specific reserves. Previously, loan loss provisions were maintained at 6 percent of loans outstanding or 100 percent of all loans more than three months beyond the final due date. Under the new policy, provisions for loan losses are maintained at 3 percent of total loans outstanding, plus 50 percent of loan amounts overdue up to three months beyond the final due date, plus 100 percent of amounts overdue more than three months beyond the final due date. Although the new, more conservative policy resulted in changes in reserves for individual Unit Desa, the overall loan loss provisions were unchanged. At the end of March 1990, loan loss provisions were Rp 44.9 billion.

The ratio of loan loss provisions to loans fluctuated from 4.3 percent in 1985 to 6.3 percent in 1988. In 1989, the ratio dropped to 4.7 percent. This is considered to be adequate coverage in view of the loan loss reserve policy.

Loan losses have increased steadily since loan write-offs were instituted in 1987. Although the increase in loan losses is to be expected in a rapidly growing loan portfolio, the increase in the ratio of loan losses to average loans is a negative trend. The ratio, which increased from 1.4 percent in 1987 to 2.6 percent in 1988 and 2.9 percent in 1989, is still in the acceptable range, but continued growth could be of some concern, particularly with the significant increase in the loan ceiling on individual loans.

Although the overall ratio of past-due loans to total loan portfolio is satisfactory, the percentage of borrowers with at least one payment overdue has increased. On average, the percentage of borrowers with overdue loans is about twice the percentage of the amount of the past-due loans compared to the total loan portfolio.

The growing number of borrowers in default makes it difficult for loan officers to follow up properly on each overdue loan and still attend to their other responsibilities. Proper follow-up with delinquent borrowers is necessary so that the past-due loans do not deteriorate into uncollectible loans. BRI will have to put together a mechanism such as loan collection teams at the branch or regional level to assist Unit Desa with large numbers of delinquent borrowers.

The asset quality of the Unit Desa loan portfolio is considered to be satisfactory on the basis of the declining past-due ratio, the conservative loan loss reserve policy, and the acceptable level of loan losses.

MONITORING LOAN PORTFOLIO QUALITY. Various corrective actions on overdue loans are taken at different stages. When a loan installment is missed, the loan officer from the Unit Desa meets with the delinquent borrower. When the final installment of the loan is more than six months in arrears, legal action may be instituted. When the final installment of the loan is more than twelve months in arrears, the loan is written off.

BRI senior management emphasizes the importance of loan portfolio quality. Each Unit Desa makes monthly reports to its branch on various loan portfolio quality measures. Emphasis is placed on the amount of principal paid to date as a percentage of the total amount of principal due to date. If the percentage of borrowers paying their installments on time remains above 95 percent, the Unit Desa is considered to be operating in a satisfactory manner. If the percentage declines for two successive months, the Unit must collect installments rather than increase lending. If the percentage falls below 95 percent, the branch manager takes disciplinary action against the Unit Desa manager.

OPERATIONAL PERFORMANCE

LENDING OPERATIONS. From 1984 to 1990, the Unit Desa disbursed about Rp 3.4 trillion in KUPEDES loans (almost U.S. $1.9 billion at the end-1989 exchange rate). The total number of loans made during this period was 6.4 million. Average loan size increased almost threefold from Rp 287,000 in 1984 to Rp 777,000 in 1989. (The consumer price index rose approximately 50 percent during that period.) The number of annual loans made during this same period more than doubled from 0.64 million to 1.4 million. The average loan maturity increased from twelve months over 1988–89 to the current level of around sixteen months.

DEPOSIT OPERATIONS. Since the introduction of the SIMPEDES program in 1985, deposit growth has outpaced loan growth in every year. The rapid growth in SIMPEDES, accounting for over 70 percent of total Unit Desa deposits as of March 1990, has been the major factor in total deposits exceeding loans in the Unit Desa system. Savings deposits have proved to be the most stable source of deposits in the Unit Desa system.

GEOGRAPHICAL DISTRIBUTION. As of December 1989, 75 percent of KUPEDES loans outstanding and two-thirds of total Unit Desa savings were on the islands of Java and Bali. These figures parallel Indonesian demographics, as more than 60 percent of Indonesia's population lives on Java and Bali, and the level of economic activity there is relatively higher than on the other islands. About 85 percent of the Unit Desa profits were generated on Java and Bali. Almost all the outer islands show lower portfolio quality than Java and Bali.

THE UNIT DESA AND BRI

The Unit Desa system generates a significantly higher return on average assets than does BRI as a whole. This profitability makes the Unit Desa system extremely important for BRI. Although the total assets of the Unit Desa are less than 10 percent of BRI's total assets, in 1987, 1988, and 1989, the Unit Desa accounted for 30 percent of BRI's total net income (before taxes). In 1990, the Unit Desa were expected to account for close to 50 percent of BRI's pretax income.

FUTURE RISKS

In spite of its success, the challenge of developing the Unit Desa system is not over. There are a number of factors that could undermine its progress. Not least among these is that pressures for growth, expansion of savings, and short-term profitability could overextend the human resource capacity of the organization and dislodge the system from its foundation—character-based, progressive lending.[6] This could place the portfolio at risk and jeopardize the orderly development of the Unit Desa system. Alternatively, maintenance of profitability through increased loan size may distance the Unit Desa from the poorer segments of the population. It is difficult to estimate the significance of these concerns, but it is important for BRI to continue to monitor these issues as the system matures.

DEVELOPMENTAL IMPACT OF UNIT DESA FINANCIAL SERVICES

PROFILE OF UNIT DESA CUSTOMERS

Unit Desa customers are sometimes referred to as "middle-level" rural Indonesians. Although this description contains an element of truth, it is misleading. The rural population served by the Unit Desa system is far more homogeneous than the population at large, and it is certainly more uniform than the urban population.[7] Unit Desa clients are middle level by comparison with clients of the provincial-based rural financial institutions (RFIs), such as the BKK in central Java.

The provincial systems are generally thought to reach the poorest of creditworthy rural Indonesians. There are several reasons to presume that the Unit Desa system serves a better-off group. The Unit Desa are commonly located in the *kecamatan* capital town, while the provincial systems reach into the villages. The Unit Desa lending instrument, KUPEDES, requires collateral, while the RFIs lend exclusively on the basis of character references. The average loan size of KUPEDES is in the $400 range, several times larger than the RFI average of less than $100. To the extent that these indicators are accurate predictors of the target population, then middle level is a reasonable description of the Unit Desa clientele.

Nevertheless, the term *middle level* is also misleading. Survey-generated profiles of Unit Desa borrowers and RFI customers suggest that there is much less difference between the two groups than is generally assumed.[8] For example, 73 percent of KUPEDES borrowers come from landless and near-landless families. By comparison, Goldmark and Rosengard's (1983) study of the BKK found that 53 percent of those surveyed owned no land at all, only 5 percent more than KUPEDES borrowers. Also, the income distribution profile of KUPEDES borrowers is approximately the same as that of the rural population. National survey data for 1987 placed 16.4 percent of the rural population below the poverty line as defined by the World Bank. Sutoro and Haryanto (1990) found that 15.1 percent of KUPEDES borrowers fell below the poverty line at the time of their first loan.

There are some differences between RFI and KUPEDES clients, however. The participation rate of women in the Unit Desa system is relatively high by Indonesian banking standards but low in comparison with what might be achieved. Just under 25 percent of KUPEDES borrowers are women, although evidence from Sutoro and Haryanto's in-depth survey suggests that the percentage of loan-financed enterprises owned and operated by women may be slightly higher. In contrast, more than 60 percent of BKK borrowers are women.

IMPACT ON ENTERPRISES SUPPORTED BY KUPEDES LENDING

The assumption of the designers and supporters of the Unit Desa system was that provision of efficient financial services would stimulate the growth of productivity and employment in rural Indonesia (USAID 1986, 18). There are at least five main ways this can occur: (1) Lending may increase net income and employment in borrowing enterprises; (2) deposit facilities may increase the productivity of household assets; (3) financial intermediation may improve economic efficiency or resource allocation by decreasing the cost of transferring financial resources from savers to investors; (4) successful Unit Desa performance can reduce the costs of entry for new purveyors of financial services; and (5) Unit Desa operations may influence the policy environment in which financial institutions operate. There is evidence that all these results have occurred.

From an enterprise development perspective, KUPEDES would be classified as an enterprise expansion program (see Boomgard 1989). Expansion programs generally offer financial inputs rather than technical assistance or training to client firms. As such, they do not necessarily seek major changes in the performance of their clients. A typical expansion program thus has a relatively small impact when measured on a per firm basis. Nevertheless, some expansion programs can have tremendous overall impact because of the large number of firms they assist and the low cost per enterprise assisted. The fact that the Unit Desa system has reached millions of enterprises means that the total program benefits can be presumed to be immense.

In the case of the Unit Desa system, one obvious direct impact is often overlooked—the development of 2,800 profitable branches with total employment of more than 13,000 people. By the standards of most enterprise development programs, these numbers alone are substantial.

It is not a simple matter to document the effect of access to financial services on enterprise value added, employment, or household income. Among the most serious issues is not knowing what would have happened in the absence of the service. Given the broad array of both formal and informal financial services available in rural Indonesia, there are serious institutional attribution questions. Moreover, the fungibility of finance makes it extremely difficult to trace the flow of money through a household in order to attribute changes in the performance of an enterprise to the availability of financial services. (See Chapter 6 for further discussion of evaluation methods.)

Sutoro and Haryanto (1990) offer some insight into the impact question, but the study's measurements are based entirely on information collected from borrowers during one interview. It is not possible, therefore, to compare the performance of borrowers with that of similar nonborrowers. In addition, since the study interviewed only individuals who had taken multiple KUPEDES loans, the sample is biased toward the most successful program clients. Those who may not have qualified for repeat loans, for whatever reason, were excluded. Finally, one-shot interviews for collecting retrospective household or enterprise financial information are notoriously inaccurate. The following presents what we do know from the Sutoro and Haryanto study:

- The average KUPEDES borrower interviewed had participated for three years and had taken three loans averaging Rp 466,000 or U.S. $251 at 1990 exchange rates.

- The profits earned by the enterprises for which the loans were taken grew in real terms at an annual rate of 24.6 percent during the average three years of program participation. The reasons for this growth were increased sales, in part because of increased ability to buy inventory or to produce; purchase of inputs at more advantageous prices; and reduction in work stoppages due to improved cash flow.

- Total income of borrower households grew over a similar period at an annual rate of 20.7 percent. According to World Bank data reported by Sutoro and Haryanto, average rural per capita incomes increased by 3.8 percent a year between 1984 and 1987. This comparison is indicative, but because entirely different methodological approaches were used, few conclusions can be drawn.

- Total employment in borrower enterprises increased at an annual rate of 18.2 percent in terms of employees and 22.5 percent in annual labor hours. Employment increased for both unpaid family workers and wage employees. Wage employment increased faster than use of family labor. Wage rates increased at a real rate of 2.9 percent a year.

DIFFERENTIAL IMPACT BY LOAN SIZE

Sutoro and Haryanto (1990) also analyzed the impact of KUPEDES loans by loan size. Several interesting conclusions emerged from this breakdown.

- Loan size was a strong predictor of both net enterprise income and total household income. This finding suggests that poorer groups are reached through smaller loans.

- During the three years of borrowing, enterprise income rose most rapidly with loans in the Rp 250,000 to Rp 500,000 range; household income rose most rapidly for the largest borrowers. The evidence is not sufficiently conclusive, however, to justify targeting.

- Total enterprise employment increased with loan size, but only as loans exceeded Rp 1 million.

- During the three years of borrowing, the share of enterprise income distributed as wages exhibited broad variations. The wage share rose for the smallest loan size but declined for larger loans. Presumably, this was because of the relatively more capital-intensive enterprises of the larger borrowers.

Equally interesting are the perceived benefits accruing to borrowers in different loan size groupings. Both large and small borrowers reported increased income and sales and ranked them as the first and second most important benefits, respectively. Avoiding work stoppages due to shortages of working capital was ranked highly by both groups. After these three, however, rankings began to change. Smaller borrowers clearly tended to benefit more from what might be called basic needs—savings, school, food, and clothing. Larger borrowers also considered these important but reported more impact on middle-class acquisitions—particularly the purchase of appliances, furniture, and vehicles. Launching new enterprises was important for both groups of borrowers but more so for the larger borrowers. Larger borrowers perceived greater benefits than smaller borrowers in their ability to use KUPEDES loans to purchase land and capture lower interest payments.

IMPACT OF SAVINGS AND FINANCIAL INTERMEDIATION

Presumably, growth in individual savings improves the asset position of customers, but no attempt has been made to document the impact of savings or intermediation on customers. The clear benefit of

Unit Desa savings is financial intermediation due to the integration of the units with the financial markets and the more fluid movement of capital to those best able to use it.

DYNAMIC BENEFITS: PROMOTING ENTRY INTO RURAL FINANCIAL MARKETS

The Unit Desa system has shown that providing financial services to rural areas can be profitable. This has encouraged the creation and expansion of other banks and financial institutions in rural areas, thus reaching more of the rural population, providing the rural population with alternative financial services, and lowering the cost of financial services through competition. Competition is expected to increase throughout the 1990s.

POLICY BENEFITS: INFLUENCING POLICIES THROUGH PROJECTS

The success of the Unit Desa system in providing profitable, non-subsidized financial services to the rural poor has strongly influenced Ministry of Finance regulations for banks. In January 1990, new banking regulations sharply reduced subsidized lines of credit from the central bank and required all banks, public and private, to ensure that at least 20 percent of their lending activities were directed to the rural areas. These regulations clearly show the influence of the Unit Desa system not only in establishing the demand for financial services in the rural areas but, more importantly, in proving that these services can be provided without subsidies.

ACCOUNTING FOR THE SUCCESS OF THE UNIT DESA SYSTEM: LESSONS AND REPLICABILITY

WHAT CAN BE LEARNED FROM THE UNIT DESA SYSTEM?

The BRI Unit Desa system is a rare example of a successful financial institution that profitably reaches the enterprising poor. Its success can be attributed primarily to the fact that the BRI Unit Desa system has been permitted to adhere to the fundamentals of banking and finance enough of the time to become operationally effective and financially viable. At the system level, the Unit Desa success reinforces several critical points.

- Nonrestrictive interest rate policy has been an absolutely essential precondition to the success of the Unit Desa system. Without the freedom and will to set rates on savings and lending, the Unit Desa system would not have become self-sustaining and profitable.

- Institutional development and developmental impact cannot be separated. There will be no impact without a viable institution; there will be no institution without perceived value.

- Getting incentives right for borrowers, savers, employees, and managers has been a key ingredient. Competitive interest rates and reasonable liquidity induce savings; payment incentives and the opportunity for more credit induce repayment; fair salaries, benefits, and performance incentives induce staff to perform efficiently; and profit-center accounting induces effective management.

- Provision of financial services as opposed to targeted credit offers greater opportunities for developing a large customer base, a self-financed capital base, and institutional self-sustainability.

- The demand for liquidity is far more important to most rural citizens than the demand for credit. Savings mobilization is just as important as credit in meeting the financial needs of the rural population.

- Low-income rural people make good and profitable financial clients.

REPLICATING THE UNIT DESA SYSTEM

The Unit Desa system offers an attractive model for replication in other developing countries. There are, however, strong differences of opinion about its replicability. There are four conditions under which a risk taker might consider trying to replicate a Unit Desa–type system:

1. If there is a reasonably sound institutional home for such a system with an interested, powerful, and dynamic leader.[9] The institution should probably be a licensed and regulated financial institution. Nongovernmental organizations (NGOs) are not likely to have the capacity for expansion and financial intermediation without first becoming such

institutions. The institution should also have the authority and will to establish reasonable performance incentives for employees.

2. If interest rates can be set at commercially viable and cost-based levels. This may be achieved through general financial policy or through specific exceptions for a particular program.

3. If the institution or external donors are able to provide long-term, expert technical assistance and selected risky capital investment subsidies. External technical assistance is essential to keep the program on track in the face of the forces that have thwarted previous efforts to do good. Risk capital is required to allow decision makers to invest in the development of the system when outsiders are demanding quick returns.

4. If everyone is patient.

Other valuable preconditions for replication include high population density; a social ethic that allows a character-based reference system; a large pool of educated, unemployed youth, which allows staffing with talented but relatively low-cost local personnel; a good-quality, extensive physical infrastructure, including roads and communications, which allows for a density of economic activity that corresponds to the density of population; and economic growth. It is difficult to know how limiting these restrictions might be.

Replication of any institution from one context to another is a complex and challenging task. The BRI Unit Desa system has achieved such remarkable results that much more attention should be devoted to understanding what might be replicated and how.

NOTES

This chapter is based on an evaluation carried out in 1990.

1. An alternative measure of the long-term loss ratio that accounts for collections of loans written off, amounting to approximately 25 percent of total write-offs, was reported by BRI as 2.75 percent at the end of August 1990.

2. A detailed description of BIMAS can be found in Robinson and Snodgrass (1987).

3. Further details on the factors that influenced these key policy changes can be found in Patten and Snodgrass (1987).

4. There is not a Unit Desa in every village. When the number of Unit Desa reached its peak of 3,626 in 1984, there were about 63,000 officially registered villages in Indonesia. Most village units transact around 90 percent of their loan and deposit business with five or six nearby villages. At its peak, the Unit Desa system covered about one-third of the villages in Indonesia.

5. In July 1990, the World Bank approved an additional loan of $125 million to BRI for the Unit Desa system. The loan will provide funds for liquidity credits for increased KUPEDES lending, capital expenditures, and technical assistance.

6. Character-based lending relies on individual credit histories and community recommendations for lending decisions. Portfolio risk is generally managed through small initial loan limits that can be progressively increased with successful repayment records.

7. The distinction between urban and rural in Indonesia is not always obvious, particularly on the islands of Java and Bali. In general, it is probably appropriate to reserve the term *urban* to refer to Jakarta and the provincial capital cities. The *kabupaten* (district) capitals are more difficult to classify but more closely resemble rural towns than the major urban centers. The *kecamatan* (subdistrict) capital towns are quite clearly rural by Indonesian standards, even though in other contexts they may appear more urbanized than the term *rural* generally connotes.

8. This section draws heavily on Sutoro and Haryanto (1990). The study is based on a sample survey drawn from the loan records of sixteen selected Unit Desa in four provinces. The sample was designed to be representative in terms of location, rural income levels, and loan activities. Information on RFI clients is taken from a study of central Java BKK customers by Goldmark and Rosengard (1983).

9. The importance of the leader of the institution cannot be underestimated. Kamardy Arief, president director of BRI throughout the 1980s, was responsible for much of the success of the Unit Desa system. He came to BRI in 1983 as the reform package for KUPEDES was being completed. He strongly supported the Unit Desa system, worked to keep the Unit Desa program uncluttered, and made good use of the technical advisers.

CHAPTER 12

The Creation of
BancoSol in Bolivia

Amy J. Glosser

BANCO SOLIDARIO, S.A., or BancoSol, started operations in Bolivia in February 1992 as the first private commercial bank in the world that caters specifically to microentrepreneurs. BancoSol was the brainchild of many individuals and institutions, including several leaders from the Bolivian business community, the Calmeadow Foundation, and ACCION International. It grew directly out of the success of PRODEM (Fundación para la Promocion y Desarrollo de la Microempresa), a nonprofit microlending program. This chapter outlines the process that led to the creation of this bank, in the hope that others will explore the possibility of creating such a bank in other places.

PRODEM

In 1984, ACCION International, a U.S.-based nongovernmental organization (NGO) operating throughout Latin America, recruited a group of effective and influential Bolivians to spearhead the creation of a microenterprise development program and serve as the board of directors. Thus, in 1986, PRODEM was created as a joint venture between prominent members of the Bolivian business community, who provided seed capital and leadership, and ACCION International, which provided the technology and methodology for the program.

By offering access to credit and training, PRODEM aims to broaden employment opportunities, encourage investment in microbusinesses, and increase the level of income generated by the sector. PRODEM's credit program uses the solidarity group lending methodology discussed in detail in Chapter 7. PRODEM's short-term loans, with an average size of $273,[1] provide working capital for small-scale production, commercial activities, and services. The training component consists of brief seminars designed to introduce clients to the concept of credit, how it works, and how it can help their businesses. Basic marketing, administration, and accounting are also included. PRODEM's initial funding came from the U.S. Agency for International Development (USAID) PL 480 program, the Bolivian Fondo Social de Emergencia (the Social Emergency Fund), the Bolivian private sector, and the Calmeadow Foundation. By the end of 1988, PRODEM's successful track record opened the door to new funders and larger grants. In 1989, USAID provided more than $3.1 million, which was to be spent over a four-year period through 1993.

In 1988, PRODEM opened a branch office in El Alto, a city bordering La Paz with a population of nearly 400,000 people, most of whom can be classified as urban poor. By the end of that year, PRODEM's fifteen employees had helped finance loans to more than 13,300 microbusinesses. In 1989, PRODEM opened its second regional headquarters office in Santa Cruz, increasing the number of employees to thirty-five by the end of the year. Throughout 1990 and 1991, growth continued and the number of microentrepreneurs served by PRODEM more than doubled. By the close of 1991, there were 116 employees in the four main offices and seven branch offices. PRODEM's portfolio rapidly grew to over $4 million, increasing the number of new clients it was able to serve. PRODEM's average loan size steadily increased as a greater percentage of the clients became repeat borrowers who had access to larger loans. With an overall average loan size of $273, PRODEM has provided loans equivalent to more than $27,592,000, and the default rate has consistently been close to zero. Only $1,650 has not been recovered since 1987.

Seventy-seven percent of PRODEM's clients are women. Most of them are market vendors who sell vegetables, fruit, prepared food, or consumer goods. But half of PRODEM's portfolio is lent to the microproduction sector that includes shoemakers, tailors, and bakers. The remaining clients provide services such as shoe repair or mechanics.

Many factors have contributed to PRODEM's success, but three stand out as particularly important: powerful information systems, an organization-wide commitment to total quality, and investment in employees. Each of these plays a critical role in the low staff turnover rates and very low rate of default among clients.

PRODEM's custom-designed information system tracks loans, payment dates, and accounting records. With this system, PRODEM's credit officers can learn within one day which groups are delinquent and immediately pay them a visit.

The second important factor is the continued commitment to the total quality of the portfolio. Both clients and credit officers believe that the program belongs to them and that only through hard work by both clients and employees can the program survive.

The third factor contributing to PRODEM's success has been its focus on employees, particularly at the credit officer level. The credit officer is the primary contact point with the client. Many loan officers come from the same ethnic background as clients and speak the clients' local dialects. Credit officers who make it through the competitive selection process undergo three months of intensive training. In addition, they attend a yearly "Management and Communications" seminar where the topics vary, depending on the officer's number of years of service to the organization. Each credit officer is responsible for about a $70,000 portfolio and between 180 and 350 clients.

RATIONALE FOR THE CREATION OF A BANK

Several factors prompted PRODEM's leadership to consider an alternative structure for the lending program. As an NGO, PRODEM was unable to expand at the desired rate to meet the overwhelming demand for credit. More important, PRODEM was legally restricted from offering full financial services to its clients, particularly savings services. Last, PRODEM's leadership sought to create a market-driven approach to microlending. These three factors are intricately linked.

MEETING THE DEMAND FOR CREDIT

PRODEM's mandate includes program expansion to meet a greater percentage of the unmet demand for credit. To expand, PRODEM required additional financing. As a private nonprofit organization, PRODEM's financing came primarily from three sources: income from lending activity, subsidized loans, and donations. The interest income and fees from the lending operation were sufficient to cover operational costs and finance minimal expansion for offices that had been in existence for more than thirty months. Thus PRODEM could have achieved sustainability and even grown slightly as more of its offices became profitable. To expand operations significantly, however, PRODEM had to obtain funds to increase its loan portfolio and cover losses until the income from the new loans equaled the costs of operation. Its only option was to seek grants and subsidized loans from foundations and international donor agencies. Furthermore, PRODEM quickly realized that funding sources were becoming finite. Even with a successful fund-raising effort, PRODEM would not achieve the desired level of growth and expansion. The problem was that the demand for credit from the microenterprise sector far exceeded what any donor or group of donors could supply.

As an NGO, PRODEM was legally restricted from seeking alternative sources of funding such as client savings, commercial debt, shareholder investment, and loans from the Central Bank of Bolivia. Yet only with access to these sources of funds could PRODEM realize the desired level of expansion.

CAPTURING SAVINGS

Two critical reasons motivated PRODEM to seek ways to capture client savings legally: the need for a constant and increasing flow of resources to finance expansion, and the desire to offer clients access to full financial services. In 1988, PRODEM adopted a mandatory savings component of 5 percent of each loan. These funds were placed in individual accounts that drew market interest rates. Clients had free access to their funds once they paid off their loans and wished to leave the program. PRODEM was not actually offering deposit facilities, since clients could not deposit and withdraw funds on demand. Instead, the arrangement was seen more as a refundable fee that accompanied the lending program. A small portion of these funds was used to finance an increase in the loan portfolio when donations or subsidized loans had been made to PRODEM but not disbursed. When the program was instituted, the compulsory savings account was small and relatively easy to manage. But as PRODEM grew and accumulated more clients, total savings increased and had reached more than $1 million by the close of 1991. At this point, it became clear both legally and financially that PRODEM had to find another means of managing this aspect of its program.

The second motivation to capture savings stemmed from the desire of PRODEM's board of directors to offer full financial services to its clients. As Rhyne and Otero argue in Chapter 1, access to savings is as important as credit for the poor. The directors of PRODEM recognized that offering credit was only half the equation for its clientele and that savings were critical for the development of microentrepreneurs' business and socioeconomic progress. Savings, the board insisted, are important for people at all levels, not only for enterprise development but also for old age, ill health, weddings, or basic security. The PRODEM program, however, served only those who demanded resources and ignored the potential clients who had excess resources and needed a safe mechanism to save. As PRODEM's compulsory savings increased, its leadership realized that this account combined with voluntary savings would be a viable source of funds for expansion. Experience with banks in other countries, such as the Bank Rakyat Indonesia (BRI) described in Chapters 2 and 11, shows that microentrepreneurs and the poor have a great propensity to save when provided with safe, accessible mechanisms.

In Bolivia, where the annual inflation rate lingers between 10 and 20 percent, savers look for a safe place to store currency where, at a

minimum, it can retain its value. Many of PRODEM's clients are excluded from traditional formal-sector financial institutions because the
minimum-deposit limits are too high, institutions are not conveniently
located, and literacy is required. Furthermore, potential clients of PRO-
DEM do not have confidence in formal institutions. Past bank scandals
and fraud throughout Bolivia have left many people with little reason
to entrust a formal institution with their savings. The result is that
many of Bolivia's poor are left with no alternative but to store the value
of their currency in assets such as livestock, inventory, or consumer
products or to save it without the benefit of an interest-bearing account. These methods of storing currency are risky and demonstrate
the need for a safe, reliable, and convenient savings mechanism.

The PRODEM board concluded that as a financial institution PRODEM
could engage on a massive scale in the transfer of resources from those
who have an excess to those who wish to accrue debt. Thus, PRODEM
would become an intermediary as opposed to a lending operation. In
addition to savings and credit for working capital, PRODEM's leadership saw great demand for other services. As a financial institution,
PRODEM could offer a variety of services, such as loans for investment
capital, housing, and education; term deposits; and dollar accounts.

BEYOND SUSTAINABILITY: A MARKET-DRIVEN APPROACH

A third reason to create a bank came from PRODEM's objective to go
beyond sustainability and create a market-driven approach to development. PRODEM was sustainable; with its start-up costs covered by loans
or donations, it was able to function at a profitable level and attain
slow growth. However, a significant expansion of operations would require outside sources of funding to finance new offices, cover losses
until these branches became profitable, and expand the lending portfolio at existing offices. Thus, PRODEM's leadership faced a choice.

By paying for its funds through interest on savings deposits, dividends, bonds, interbank loans, and other forms of financing available
to financial institutions, PRODEM would accomplish expansion and become completely independent from donated funds. In creating a market-driven approach to development, PRODEM's leadership sought to
establish a long-term economic solution to what they viewed as an economic challenge—not a social problem. They determined that PRODEM
would no longer have beneficiaries of its programs; instead it would
serve clients with whom it had a mutual relationship. It would no
longer transfer resources from donors to beneficiaries; instead it would
transfer capital among its clients. PRODEM would no longer have
donors but investors, who asked only for a given return on their funds.

The directors of PRODEM saw the creation of a successful, profitable venture as a way of opening a system that had been closed to a large segment of the population of Bolivia. If this proposed bank became profitable, others in Bolivia and elsewhere would replicate the process and increase the quality and quantity of services available for the poor.

The directors sought an alternative to the NGO model, which traditionally addressed microentrepreneurs' lack of access to formal credit as a social rather than an economic issue, and chose to create a for-profit bank. Helping to bring PRODEM's directors to this conclusion were successful microenterprise banking experiences in other parts of the world. For example, the Grameen Bank in Bangladesh, although neither a private institution nor a profitable one, illustrates the potential to provide financial services to the poor on a massive scale. As of the close of 1991, Grameen had more than 1,000 branch offices and served more than one million clients. BRI, discussed at length in Chapters 2 and 11, is a public venture that has proved to be profitable. With more than 3,600 branch offices, it has an active portfolio of 1.8 million loans valued at $615 million. Savings deposits amounted to $647 million in 1990.

COBANCO—THE TRANSITION

Once PRODEM's leadership decided to create a bank, they formed a separate steering committee called COBANCO (Comite Promotor del Banco para la Microempresa) to carry out the transition process. Its objectives were to:

- Generate a financial feasibility study of the proposed bank.

- Promote the project among financial institutions and potential national and international investors.

- Inform local authorities about the project and coordinate activities with the Superintendencia de Bancos (SIB), including legal registration, the issuing of stock, and the presentation of investment documents.

- Negotiate with USAID and other donors to transfer funds from PRODEM to the bank.

- Coordinate the organization and design of new operating plans for the bank and PRODEM.

COBANCO existed for two years and four months with financing from ACCION International, the Calmeadow Foundation, and PRODEM board members. The work of COBANCO can be divided into four parts: the feasibility studies, raising equity, the legal process, and the operational transition.

FEASIBILITY STUDIES AND BANK STRUCTURE

In the process of completing a feasibility study, COBANCO moved through five different versions that showed the evolution of the planners' thinking. The first two studies provided preliminary outlines of the project that were thorough enough to survey the opinions of potential investors and various constituencies in and out of Bolivia. COBANCO was cautious in its presentation, fearing political fallout from the concept of making profits by lending money to the poor. For the most part, however, constituencies embraced the idea, but investors were slow to come forward. The first two feasibility studies called for bank financing by concessionary loans and donations. The COBANCO team believed that raising funds from unknown commercial sources would be difficult and therefore sought to enlist the support of familiar sources of funds. Also, at this stage, the planners themselves doubted the bank's ability to generate enough profit to cover the costs of commercial financing.

By March 1990, COBANCO had completed a third feasibility study that contained the idea of obtaining concessionary loans at a rate of 3 percent a year. COBANCO leadership used this feasibility study as their main tool in presenting the idea to potential investors at a series of meetings in Washington, D.C. These meetings represented a turning point in the formation of the bank. Several multilateral lending and financing institutions interested in investing in the bank agreed that COBANCO should change its approach.[2] Instead of concessionary financing, the bank should adopt a market-oriented investment strategy and obtain commercial debt for a commercial bank. Furthermore, the participants at the meeting encouraged COBANCO to use another means, such as PRODEM, to finance some of the costly operational aspects that the bank should not bear.

The Washington meetings led COBANCO to write a fourth version of the feasibility study, which stated:

One of the most basic issues in the establishment of this type of bank concerns how the development costs of the operation should be funded. In order to make good quality loans, the micro-credit bank must devote significant effort in the areas that commercial banks do not have to. . . . In order to clearly differentiate between the two types of activities, and the costs associated with these activities, the promoters of this project are proposing to operate with two distinct entities—a bank and a redirected PRODEM—which working together will accomplish both

the financial and the social objectives of the various participants.
(PRODEM 1990)

With the creation of the bank, PRODEM would concentrate its efforts
on developing rural credit programs in Bolivia's secondary cities and
small towns. It would research and develop financial products for BancoSol and its own offices, such as loans for investment capital, agriculture, housing, health care, and education. PRODEM would function as a
support entity for BancoSol but would also continue to operate existing
offices that were not yet profitable and open new offices in other cities.
Once these offices became profitable, they could be sold to BancoSol. In
addition, PRODEM would assist the bank directly by covering costs associated with consultants, training, and staff development.

This arrangement between the bank and PRODEM allowed the proposed bank to forgo concessionary loans in exchange for PRODEM's
contribution to areas that would otherwise drain funds from the bank's
operating budget. This partnership between the NGO and the bank presented a choice to potential funders, depending on their nature and
mission: either contribute to the development activities of PRODEM or
invest in the credit and savings operation of the bank.

The need for concessionary loans was further decreased when it became possible for PRODEM to sell a large portion of its portfolio to the
new bank in exchange for shares. This arrangement would provide the
bank with a large start-up subsidy—nearly half of its paid-in equity capital to be used as its lending portfolio—and nearly 20,000 clients. Thus,
unlike other commercial banks, the proposed bank would start out as
the largest bank in the country in terms of the number of clients served.

Once COBANCO became committed to the idea of a commercial venture, the Inter-American Investment Corporation (IIC) and the International Finance Corporation (IFC) conducted a joint appraisal mission in
Bolivia. Their interest represented another turning point in the process
of the bank's creation; the multilateral lenders were beginning to show
their support for the project and their financial commitment.

The final version of the feasibility study was written one year after
the Washington meetings and provides an accurate picture of BancoSol
as it now exists both financially and operationally. Much of the content
of the study addressed various requirements of the SIB for incorporation of the bank, such as a list of investors and a thorough cost analysis. In addition, the final version shows that the bank will become
profitable within three years as opposed to the previously estimated
five years.

Two key issues elicited the most debate during the design of the
bank: the structure of the entity and the bank's interest rates.

OPERATING STRUCTURE. The COBANCO team considered various structures for the proposed financial institution. They investigated the

possibility of creating a *casa bancaria*—a type of financial institution recently created in Bolivia—instead of a full-service commercial bank. *Casa bancarias* are similar to banks in that they can make loans and capture savings, but they have much less flexibility. For example, they are unable to engage in international transactions, offer checking accounts, participate in the capitalization of other businesses, or offer credit for the buying of bonds, securities, or businesses. Although the establishment of a *casa bancaria* requires its founders to raise less equity, its operational capacity is restricted. In the short term, the limitations associated with a *casa bancaria* were not problematic, but in the long term, a full commercial bank would prove to be more flexible.

INTEREST RATES. COBANCO first drafted an interest rate policy that stated that the bank would charge a rate enabling it to cover all costs and make a reasonable profit within the allotted time period. Under this policy, the rate would be higher than that already charged by PRODEM—4 percent a month. But even PRODEM's rate was criticized as too high by several constituencies. Some potential investors in the bank, both national and international, expressed concern that the bank's image and their image as investors would be tarnished if the bank charged such a high rate. Many pointed out that the effective annual rate charged by PRODEM was more than 20 percentage points higher than the rates charged by other commercial banks.[3] Still others noted that NGOs and lending programs charged lower rates than PRODEM.

The bank planners responded by pointing out that the proposed bank was different from other commercial banks as well as from NGOs involved in microcredit. The costs of operation are much higher for a bank that caters to microentrepreneurs. The average loan size for the proposed bank would start at $273; for most other banks, the average loan size exceeded $135,000. PRODEM's average loan term was only twenty-two weeks, which further added to the cost of the lending operation. Furthermore, a microcredit bank must invest substantial funds in the education of each client, teaching him or her about the bank, how it works, how credit can work for the client, the procedures for paying it back, and so on. The proposed bank would have to pay commercial rates for the money it borrowed; NGOs could charge lower rates because the funds they received were cost-free or subsidized. In addition, the proposed bank had many additional costs of operation that stemmed from the formalization process associated with a bank. Unlike NGOs, a bank requires complex management information systems, security systems, and other operational and technical features that increase its costs of operation.

COBANCO decided that the interest rate had to be high enough to cover costs, including the cost of funds. In order to create a sustainable and independent institution, the only alternative was to charge above commercial rates to ensure profitability. COBANCO determined that the bank would adopt PRODEM's rate of 4 percent a month for at least the first year of operation. Beyond this, the bank would aim to adopt a fluctuating interest rate policy similar to that of other banks in the country, which depends on rates charged by competitors and the changing costs of operation.

PURSUING INVESTORS AND SELLING EQUITY

The pursuit of investors began early in the process of establishing the bank. One of COBANCO's first initiatives in selling equity was to arrange for the transfer of funds from PRODEM to the bank in exchange for shares. Out of PRODEM's $5 million in assets, about $2.5 million of its loan portfolio was earmarked for transfer. This process required renegotiating three grants and one soft loan that had been made to PRODEM and had not yet expired. The largest grant, for $1.8 million, came from USAID and was supposed to be used strictly for PRODEM's lending portfolio. After complex negotiations, USAID approved the proposal based on the notion that the USAID funds donated to PRODEM were no longer classified as U.S. government funds after they had been lent once and repaid. As a result of this agreement and another one with the second donor organization, the Bolivian Social Emergency Fund, PRODEM used its portfolio to purchase 44.2 percent of the bank's stock.

PRODEM's investor relationship benefits not only the bank, which received substantial equity investment and was able to commence operations with a sizable portfolio and more than 20,000 clients, but also PRODEM, which will receive dividends once the bank becomes profitable. It is projected that the dividends will be sufficient to finance PRODEM's operations after ten years of bank operations. Until then, however, PRODEM must raise funds to accomplish its redirected objectives.

Unlike other commercial banks in Bolivia, BancoSol has many non-Bolivian investors. Several different reasons motivated their investment in this bank. Most decided to participate in the venture because of its blend of profitability and social merit. COBANCO emphasized to potential investors motivated by social welfare concerns that BancoSol represents a unique opportunity for development of the financial and microenterprise sectors and, unlike other microlending programs, represents a market-driven solution. For local investors, the motive may have been more political. By investing in the progress of one's own country, especially in projects that benefit the poor, one invests in stability for the future. As for the multilateral investors, BancoSol represented an opportunity to diversify their portfolios with alternative-development, private-sector projects.

Several of the non-Bolivian investors became active in the creation of the bank and in the promotion of the project to other investors. The Calmeadow Foundation of Canada, in addition to its substantial financial investment, provided technical assistance and helped to encourage others to buy shares. The IIC was influential both in the design of the bank and in recruiting other investors. In addition, IIC's commitment to the project provided a "seal of approval," which fostered a sense of the bank's credibility within the international community.

Bolivian investors own less than one-fourth of the bank's equity. Nearly all this investment comes from businesses associated with PRODEM and with BancoSol board members. Other than the five "organizers" of the bank who made token investments as mandated by the SIB, BancoSol has no individual investors.

By December 1990, COBANCO had commitments for nearly $5 million of equity financing, exceeding the threshold of $3.2 million required to start the process of legal incorporation.

LEGAL PROCESS

The legal incorporation of the bank centered on the SIB, which monitors all banks in the country. In 1990, the SIB reestablished its control over the banking system after being heavily criticized in the 1980s as corrupt and ineffective. Today, the SIB is regarded as one of the most effective supervisory systems in Latin America. It enforces the rules and regulations of the banking industry and monitors the day-to-day operations of the sector as laid out by the general law of banking.

With legal assistance, COBANCO worked closely with the SIB to prepare the necessary documentation about the feasibility of the project, the investors, and the five "organizers" or founders of the bank who would assume legal responsibility for the entity. Seven months after these documents were formally submitted, the SIB approved the application. The next step for COBANCO was to obtain authorization to operate. COBANCO had to demonstrate that BancoSol was ready to commence operations. The SIB made several site visits to the bank to verify the quality of the accounting systems, the security apparatus, and the bank personnel. In February 1992, eleven months after COBANCO submitted the application, the authorization to operate was granted and BancoSol officially opened to the public.

The process of incorporation proved to be lengthy and tedious for several reasons. First, the law that governs the financial community was written in 1928 and is antiquated. As a result, the process of incorporating and establishing a financial entity is designed for traditional banks with locations in the center of the business district, national investors, and a traditional method of operation. Second, because the projected bank was different from all other banks in the country, the SIB was especially cautious in its acceptance of the project. COBANCO had difficulty convincing the SIB that the project was feasible because, despite its high interest rates, it involved small loans, nontraditional collateral through solidarity groups, and an unconventional clientele. COBANCO anticipated this difficulty and selected the founders based on their prestigious reputations and significant experience in the banking sector in order to enhance the credibility of the venture. Third, COBANCO encountered delays in the process because of its nontraditional group of investors. The documentation and information required by the SIB are based on conventional investors and are difficult to apply to the foundations and multilateral institutions that invested in BancoSol. Last, the SIB was not accustomed to NGOs as investors. Therefore, the quality of PRODEM's investment and its relationship to the bank were thoroughly investigated.

OPERATIONAL TRANSITION

Operationally, the most important aspect of the transition was the comprehensive formalization process of what had been PRODEM's operating procedures. In order to conform to SIB requirements, all the systems from PRODEM had to be redesigned to incorporate the necessary formality, efficiency, and thoroughness. For example, PRODEM's systems were based on monthly reports for its donors that stressed statistics that are unimportant in banking, such as total number of clients served, total number of projects financed, or percentage of female clients. The SIB required reports about lending activity, deposit activity, and current balances every day, week, fifteen days, month, quarter, and year. Second, as an NGO, PRODEM's systems did not incorporate taxation. A third difference stemmed from the fact that PRODEM had many sources of funding and had to keep their accounts separate. For a bank, the sources of funds are irrelevant. According to the chief operating officer of BancoSol, "money is simply money for the bank."

Anticipating the need for extensive changes, COBANCO initiated much of the operational transition well before BancoSol opened. Once the decision was made to create the bank, PRODEM took over the teller operations from the two banks contracted to serve PRODEM clients. This enabled PRODEM to offer better and more controlled services to its clients as well as to devise systems, train personnel, and prepare teller operations for BancoSol. COBANCO began to hire staff for the bank; they tested their ideas, devised new systems, and developed methods for the bank while working at PRODEM. Many of those who were hired came from the traditional banking sector, and many PRODEM employees in the areas of accounting, computer systems, and administration joined the newly assembled team for the bank.

SYSTEMS. Much of the work carried out at PRODEM before the creation of the bank centered around systems design. Two examples were a new accounting software program based on the SIB's reporting requirements and a passbook savings software program. Both were similar to systems used in other Bolivian banks. Installing the systems at PRODEM enabled BancoSol to commence operations with somewhat proven and functioning systems and with employees who were familiar with the new programs.

SECURITY. Each branch of the bank was required to have in place an alarm system with video cameras, additional guards, and, for regional offices, a safe. Unlike PRODEM, the bank was required to hire a secure transport company to transfer money from branch offices to the regional office.

CREDIT PROGRAM. Few operational changes occurred in the credit program—the crux of the banking operation. The number of clients per credit officer and the size of each credit officer's loan portfolio were increased for greater efficiency and to enhance prospects for profitability. For the most part, however, according to the general manager of the bank, BancoSol's credit program is merely PRODEM with a different name.

STAFF TRANSITION. PRODEM made a large investment in preparing its employees for the transition, both technically and ideologically. PRODEM determined that its staff would fill as many bank positions as possible. Since the bank's systems were more sophisticated and intricate, PRODEM offered several seminars and training sessions aimed at increasing the skill level of its employees.

In addition to technical training, PRODEM invested substantially in the ideological and psychological aspects of the transition for its employees. As an NGO, PRODEM emphasized a commitment to improving social welfare; BancoSol, although equally committed to the same values, also had to be motivated by profits. These almost conflicting ideologies influenced the culture of each organization. PRODEM's atmosphere was familial, supportive, and casual. In contrast, banks must be formal and hierarchical. Compared to other banks, BancoSol's corporate culture still resembles PRODEM's, but there is a difference between the two. To help bridge this gap for employees, PRODEM held a series of motivational seminars that addressed the tension between ideologies for all levels of the organization. Some of the transition seminars were specifically targeted toward the credit officers. Although their jobs changed very little, it was through the credit officers that the concept of the bank was communicated to the clients. If the credit officers were not committed to the ideology behind the bank, the client base would surely deteriorate.

PRODEM also hired several new employees from the banking sector; they brought new skills and a profit orientation to the other employees who made the transition from PRODEM. The new employees also went through the transition seminars to gain a better understanding of how and why BancoSol was different.

CLIENT TRANSITION. In December 1991, once all the preparations were made, the clients were informed of the transition. Through daily seminars, the credit officers explained the reasons for the creation of the bank and the transition procedures. With a bank, clients would have a permanent source of loans, access to a variety of financial services, and an overall improvement in the quality of service. Nearly all the clients were immediately pleased by the idea, especially since the interest rate charged by the new bank was the same as PRODEM's. Many clients commented that they would finally have a bank that understood and catered to their needs.

COSTS OF THE TRANSITION. The transition proved to be a costly venture. The additional systems, software, security, personnel, training, consultants, travel, transition seminars, and renovations were very expensive. COBANCO and PRODEM spent nearly $560,000 on the transition process, excluding renovations and the purchase of fixed assets.

THE BANK

BancoSol officially opened its doors to the public on February 10, 1992, in the San Pedro barrio of La Paz, about five blocks from the original PRODEM office. By August 1992, six BancoSol offices were functioning, all in the region of La Paz and El Alto. With one exception, these offices were originally PRODEM offices that were converted to BancoSol. This conversion enabled the bank to minimize expenditures by having PRODEM cover the costs associated with opening new offices. All the offices are strategically located in or near a market district and all are modestly designed, taking care not to intimidate the clients. At the end of 1992, PRODEM added a second regional office in Santa Cruz and one more branch office. The bank plans to keep up its rate of expansion as more PRODEM offices become profitable and are acquired by the bank and as the bank itself opens new offices.

SERVICES OFFERED

When it opened, BancoSol offered its clients only two services: solidarity group loans and compulsory savings. By the close of 1992, BancoSol planned to offer both savings and credit in U.S. dollars or in accounts that are in bolivianos but tied to the dollar. This is an important addition to the bank, since much of the Bolivian economy functions in U.S. dollars. At other commercial banks, over 70 percent of the savings accounts are held in U.S. dollars and 20 percent are in accounts tied to the dollar. Future plans also include diversification of the types of loans offered to include credit for investment capital, housing, and health care.

SAVINGS. In addition to the compulsory savings program, which was transferred from PRODEM, BancoSol has begun to offer voluntary savings, including time deposits and demand deposits. Like other commercial banks, each client with a savings account receives a passbook in which all transactions are logged. Unlike other banks, BancoSol's interest rate paid on savings does not fluctuate. As of June 1992, the rate paid was 20.4 percent, which was slightly lower than market rates. BancoSol is the only bank in the country with no minimum amount required to open an account. It has more than $1 million from compulsory savings, and the average size of a savings account is about $100; the average size at other banks ranges from $500 to $5,000.

BancoSol is in the process of developing a strategy to mobilize savings not only from the current client base but from the informal sector in general. The bank plans to conduct a thorough evaluation of the market, devise a product that serves the special needs of the sector, and prepare for the implementation of the program by training the appropriate personnel. Prior to this effort, BancoSol has maintained conservative projections, assuming that by 1994 the amount of voluntary savings will total more than $1.4 million and compulsory savings will grow to roughly $5 million.

CREDIT. BancoSol's credit program is strikingly different from credit services offered by other Bolivian private commercial banks. In understanding these differences, it is important to keep in mind that NGOs, not other commercial banks, are BancoSol's competition. Most BancoSol clients do not have access to other banks. Nonetheless, since BancoSol functions as a bank, a comparison can be helpful in explaining its structure.[4]

The interest rate for loans at BancoSol is 4 percent a month, with an effective rate of 55 to 57 percent a year. Other commercial banks' effective rates, unregulated by the government, fluctuated between 28 and 31 percent a year as of June 1992. At $277 (and even at the expected 1997 average of $900), BancoSol's average loan size is dwarfed by the average loan size at other banks, which ranges from $35,000 to $120,000. BancoSol's minimum loan is $80 and its maximum is $5,000. At other commercial banks, the minimum is $3,000. A majority of BancoSol's loan recipients are women (70 percent); at other banks, women make up less than 40 percent of the loan recipients. Last, BancoSol's loan portfolio, combined with PRODEM's, is valued at $5.2 million; other banks' portfolios range from $80 million to $128 million.

In addition, BancoSol's credit officers are very different from their counterparts at other banks. At BancoSol, most credit officers come to the bank with a bachelor's degree or the equivalent in the social sciences; at other banks, most credit officers have degrees in business. Sixty-five percent of the credit officers are women at BancoSol, but only 20 to 40 percent of loan officers at other banks are women. The most striking difference, however, is that at BancoSol, the starting salary for a credit officer is the equivalent of $180 a month; at other banks it is about $400 a month. The BancoSol salary structure is on a par with that of NGOs and other organizations in the development field.

THE LOAN PROCESS. The method by which BancoSol makes loans is very different from that used by other commercial banks.[5] The process begins with borrower identification, whereas in traditional banks the borrowers are self-selecting. Commercial banks encourage loan applications through promotional information targeted to specific industries or to individuals with specific income levels. At BancoSol, officers undertake extensive fieldwork, survey local neighborhoods, and get to know potential clients. These potential clients attend promotional sessions to learn the process of obtaining credit from the bank.

Once clients have been identified, each bank conducts a credit evaluation. At a traditional bank, loan officers assess project cash flows and ask for guarantees of two or more times the loan value, typically in the form of urban property. At BancoSol, the solidarity group acts as the key screening mechanism and is a substitute for collateral; community members choose to be in a group with others who are creditworthy and on whom they can rely to make timely loan payments.

Loan monitoring at traditional banks consists mostly of quarterly reviews of unaudited financial statements, annual reviews of audited statements, and annual site visits. At BancoSol, loan officers meet with each solidarity group on a weekly basis, and each officer is recognized and accepted as a regular presence in the community with which he or she works. All loan repayments are collected on Mondays, and the computerized reporting system identifies late payments by Monday evening. Groups that miss payments are visited on Tuesday by their loan officers, who identify the problem and determine when payment will be made.

One of the most striking differences between BancoSol and other commercial banks is the payback rate. In a typical month at BancoSol, approximately 12 percent of all loan payments are made in advance, 67 percent are made on time, and 21 percent are late. Of these late payments, 89 percent are made within one day of the due date and 99 percent are made within three days of the due date. Thus .04 percent of BancoSol's portfolio is in arrears beyond thirty days; at other banks, the average is 4.42 percent of the gross loan portfolio.

FINANCIAL STRUCTURE

ASSETS. The quality of BancoSol's assets is strong due to its very low default rate on loans. Seventy-two percent of the bank's assets for 1992 was its loan portfolio, a figure that is almost on a par with the industry standard (76 percent).[6] (See Table 12.1.) Since all BancoSol's profits come from its lending operation, it would be beneficial to increase this percentage.

Eighteen percent of the bank's assets were fixed assets in 1992. Although this percentage will decrease by 1994 to 13 percent, it is still relatively high compared with the industry average (4 percent). BancoSol invests much less in dollar amounts in its fixed assets when compared with other banks, but this amount represents a high percentage of its asset base because BancoSol's assets are small.

EQUITY. As a result of PRODEM's sizable investment, BancoSol's equity represents from 37 to 46 percent of its total assets; the industry average is 7 percent. This indicates that BancoSol is very well capitalized but also that it is not efficient at using its equity investment to leverage debt. BancoSol intends to reduce the proportion of equity investment to assets to roughly 20 percent, which is still well above the industry average. This will allow BancoSol to leverage debt, but not to the extent that the bank assumes unnecessary risk.

BancoSol's equity will be used to finance operational losses until the bank becomes profitable, to purchase liquid investments and fixed assets, and to meet the minimum equity requirements of the SIB. BancoSol issued common shares of stock, which were purchased privately. The only written contract that exists with the shareholders is a simple form that outlines their financial commitment to the venture. With IIC, however, BancoSol has a more complicated shareholder's agreement that includes an exit mechanism calling upon local investors to buy IIC's shares at predetermined prices under standard terms and conditions for multilateral lending institutions. This ensures that IIC will make a return on its funds.

It is hoped that the borrowers of BancoSol will have an opportunity to purchase shares in the bank. This could be financed by international investors who wish to sell their equity.

Part of the bank's initial strategy is to invest up to 40 percent of the bank's equity in fixed assets in order to diversify the bank's holdings and limit the bank's risk from currency instability. This includes investment in land and buildings, computer equipment, and office furniture.

LIABILITIES. The liability structure consists of loans from development organizations, interbank loans, client savings, and the issuing of bonds. The liabilities section of the balance sheet may change slightly as the bank replaces its expensive forms of debt with less expensive

Table 12.1   BancoSol Balance Sheet (projections)

	December 1992	December 1993	December 1994
Assets			
Current assets			
Legal reserves	$ 560,846	$ 717,195	$ 1,332,804
Cash on hand	181,481	249,735	316,403
Certificates of deposit	0	0	1,850,793
Total current assets	$ 742,327	$ 966,930	$ 3,500,000
Loan portfolio	$ 9,096,296	$12,521,428	$15,875,661
Less loan loss provision	(16,931)	(34,127)	(50,793)
Net portfolio	$ 9,079,365	$12,487,300	$15,824,868
Fixed assets	2,258,684	2,445,026	2,875,132
Net deferred costs	491,798	385,978	333,068
Total assets	$12,572,174	$16,295,234	$22,533,068
Liabilities			
Current liabilities			
Voluntary savings	$ 159,259	$ 515,873	$ 1,473,809
Compulsory savings	1,851,322	3,069,576	5,191,005
Other short-term debt	3,433,598	665,344	0
Fixed-term deposits	1,587,300	3,703,703	6,348,943
Total current liabilities	$ 7,031,479	$ 7,954,496	$13,013,750
Long-term liabilities	$ 800,265	$ 800,265	$ 800,265
Total liabilities	$ 7,831,744	$ 8,754,761	$13,814,022
Equity			
Paid-in capital	$ 5,137,520	$ 7,619,044	$ 7,619,044
Reserves	6,613	47,619	165,608
Retained earnings	(403,703)	(126,190)	934,391
Total equity	$ 4,740,430	$ 7,540,473	$ 8,719,043
Total liabilities and equity	$12,572,174	$16,295,235	$22,533,068

alternatives. The bank has acquired an additional loan for $1 million at 9 percent annually, and one more loan is in the process of negotiation. In order to balance these hard currency loans with local currency and limit the bank's exposure to exchange rate risk, BancoSol may issue a bond in bolivianos once prospective buyers have been identified. The bank will pay a market interest rate on these bonds of 30 percent a year.

The debt strategy for BancoSol is to replace more expensive debt such as bonds and interbank loans with client deposits. In 1992, 25 percent of the bank's liabilities were client savings; by 1994, client savings are projected to represent almost 50 percent of the bank's liabilities and 42 percent of the bank's lending portfolio. BancoSol will also introduce certificates of deposit (CDs), which carry an interest rate of roughly 20 percent a month in bolivianos, thus further increasing the extent to which the bank will be financed from deposits as opposed to commercial debt. By 1994, CDs are expected to represent almost half of the bank's liabilities. Other short-term debt, such as interbank loans, will be reduced to zero. The bank's long-term liabilities will remain constant. BancoSol's long-term loans were transferred from PRODEM and come from the USAID PL 480 program.

INCOME. BancoSol's income statement for 1992–94 shows that the bank will make a profit by 1993, which it will almost double by 1994 (see Table 12.2). More than 96 percent of the bank's income will come from its lending portfolio and less than 4 percent from interest-bearing accounts. At other banks, between 70 and 85 percent of their income comes from lending operations, with the remainder coming from interest-bearing accounts and fees associated with financial services other than credit.

The income statement also reveals that administrative costs for BancoSol are a very large percentage of its total costs of operation when compared with the rest of the industry. Administrative costs are more than 80 percent of the total, and the industry standard is about 20 percent. The huge difference between these percentages stems from the high costs associated with microlending. As the number of clients increases relative to the number of credit officers, efficiency will improve, although costs will always be high.

CHALLENGES FOR BANCOSOL

OIL AND WATER

BancoSol's initial experience in creating a private commercial bank out of an NGO was successful. One of the main reasons for its success was its ability to combine the two potentially conflicting operating models of an NGO and a for-profit venture. To quote the BancoSol chief financial officer, "at times it's like mixing oil and water."

The conflict shows itself as BancoSol struggles to define its corporate culture. On one side is the culture from PRODEM, which can be

Table 12.2   BancoSol Income Statement (projections)

	December 1992	December 1993	December 1994
Income			
Interest earned			
Loan portfolio	$ 2,152,116	$ 5,483,597	$ 7,221,957
Legal reserves	17,196	38,888	69,312
Certificates of deposit	10,052	0	219,576
Total interest earned	$ 2,179,364	$ 5,522,485	$ 7,510,845
Costs of funds			
Savings deposits	$ 210,582	$ 544,709	$ 1,010,052
Other short-term debt	245,767	374,074	19,841
Debt—PL 480	167,989	192,063	192,063
Fixed-term deposits	96,296	555,555	1,142,857
Total costs of funds	$ 720,634	$ 1,666,401	$ 2,364,813
Financial margin	$ 1,458,730	$ 3,856,084	$ 5,146,032
Costs of operation			
Administrative spending			
Personnel	$ 539,153	$ 1,210,585	$ 1,551,058
Contracted services	22,222	46,560	52,910
Communications	44,179	89,682	115,079
Maintenance	21,957	69,576	97,090
Other expenditures	87,301	263,942	325,925
National and branch office costs	766,134	1,058,201	1,269,843
Depreciation	118,518	170,634	206,878
Total administration	$ 1,599,464	$ 2,909,180	$ 3,618,783
Loan loss provision	16,931	17,195	16,666
Total taxes	192,063	327,248	421,428
Miscellaneous	47,883	87,301	108,465
Total operating costs	$ 1,856,341	$ 3,340,924	$ 4,165,342
Net profit/loss	($ 397,611)	$ 515,160	$ 980,690

categorized as informal, relaxed, and lateral. Much of this culture remains. For example, the bank's credit officers and general manager work
as tellers on days when checks are disbursed and payments collected;
the staff is on a first-name basis, from the guards and messengers to the
vice presidents; and BancoSol's employees do not punch time clocks.
On the other side is the formality and more traditional atmosphere

associated with the financial sector, which is slowly infiltrating Banco-Sol's corporate culture. The shift in culture has been influenced by BancoSol's profit orientation, by its commitment to formality and efficiency, and by BancoSol employees who came from the formal financial sector. For example, although no dress code exists, the staff is choosing to wear more professional attire.

PROFITABILITY

The critical question is whether BancoSol can achieve profitability. Many factors influence the answer. The first factor is whether BancoSol will be able to significantly expand its credit program and maintain the quality of its portfolio. Some BancoSol employees and outside observers have expressed concern about potential competition for BancoSol. Many NGOs run microlending programs in Bolivia. Despite varying degrees of success, the programs generally offer interest rates that are lower than BancoSol's. Although BancoSol believes that its clients are loyal and support the idea of a permanent bank geared to their needs, it remains to be seen whether this competition is formidable enough to interfere with the growth of BancoSol. Furthermore, as BancoSol expands, it will move beyond the clientele to which it is accustomed. BancoSol's clients have shown a high degree of motivation and commitment in joining the program. As BancoSol casts its net further into the informal sector, it may find potential clients with the same level of commitment or it may find that quality of the portfolio diminishes as more clients join the program. Last, BancoSol plans to diversify its lending operation with loans for investment capital, housing, and health care. The question remains whether BancoSol can capture a greater market share with this diversification, and whether it can maintain its high payback rates for these types of loans.

BancoSol projections show that client savings will be a main source of financing for the growth of the institution. Thus, in the near future, BancoSol must develop and launch a locally designed plan to capture these resources. Although there are many indications that the poor have a high propensity to save when provided with a safe, convenient mechanism, BancoSol has yet to develop this mechanism.

By 1994, BancoSol intends to increase its loan portfolio, total assets, and total equity by 45 percent, with a 6 percent average increase in the number of new clients per month. As a new entity, how well can BancoSol manage this growth, maintain efficiency, and attain profitability? As the bank grows, the pressure to increase costs may escalate. For example, BancoSol constantly faces pressure to increase its salaries, which are substantially lower than those at other commercial banks, and it may have difficulty attracting and keeping qualified personnel at salary scales that allow it to be profitable.

Beyond the management of growth, however, are doubts about whether BancoSol can maintain its commitment to the microenterprise sector and still reach the desired levels of profitability. Since smaller loans are more expensive to make, BancoSol will face pressure to increase its average loan size in order to stay profitable. BancoSol leadership has strongly stated its commitment to keeping the microentrepreneur the focus of the bank. This commitment is sure to be tested again and again.

NOTES

1. All dollar amounts are U.S. dollars.

2. The Inter-American Development Bank (IDB), the International Finance Corporation (IFC), the Inter-American Investment Corporation (IIC), the United Nations Capital Development Fund (UNCDF), the U.S. Agency for International Development (USAID), the Canadian International Development Agency (CIDA), and the World Bank participated in a review of COBANCO's proposal.

3. PRODEM's effective rate is 69 percent; other banks' rates fluctuate between 35 and 50 percent.

4. Two Bolivian banks in particular were used in this comparison: a high-end bank with many corporate clients, and a large bank serving the middle market.

5. The following comparison of credit procedures was adapted from a project appraisal prepared by the Inter-American Investment Corporation (1990).

6. Industry data come from the SIB (1992).

CHAPTER 13

The Association of Solidarity Groups of Colombia: Governance and Services

Arelis Gómez Alfonso with Nan Borton and Carlos Castello

ORIGINS AND OBJECTIVES

The origins of the Association of Solidarity Groups (Asociación Grupos Solidarios de Colombia, or AGS) go back to 1982 when ACCION International began to promote the solidarity group methodology in Colombia. (See Chapter 7 for a full discussion of the methodology.) At that time, the Carvajal microenterprise methodology was widely accepted among private and public organizations.[1] Four organizations—Fundación Mundial de la Mujer (FMM), Cali; Fundación Familiar (FF), Cali; Centro de Desarrollo Vecinal (CDV) of Cartagena; and Cooperativa Multiactiva de Desarrollo Social (CIDES), Bogotá—began working together with the solidarity group methodology in 1983.

In the same year, the first national plan for microenterprise development also began operations. Created by the government at the initiative of Fundación Carvajal, the plan was implemented by those organizations operating microenterprise programs under the Carvajal approach. Solidarity group programs were not recognized as valid, and the ACCION-assisted institutions were excluded.

After three years of operation, the four solidarity group organizations decided to form a centralized institution. In 1987, the group obtained legal status as AGS. Its governing body was a general assembly made up of legal representatives of the affiliated institutions, which set policies for AGS. Its staff consisted of an executive director, who was also the ACCION country director, and a technical group of five. The goal of AGS was to strengthen the operational capabilities of its affiliates in order to scale up their programs. Its objectives included:

• Technical assistance to members in methodological, operational, and evaluative aspects of the solidarity group and *famiempresa* (individual loan) programs.

- Fund-raising at both national and international levels.

- Program promotion with the private and public sectors.

- Staff training.

- Service provision in areas such as software development.

By the end of 1988, the creation of AGS was considered very successful by the membership. After intense lobbying efforts, AGS was welcomed by the government of Colombia as part of the national plan. This achievement did not provide financial resources but gave AGS and the solidarity group methodology public recognition, legitimacy, and participation in every discussion on microenterprise development.

THE AGS NETWORK'S OUTREACH

Between August 1983, when the first program got under way, and March 1991, AGS members made loans to nearly 40,000 microentrepreneurs, 56 percent of whom were women. The seventeen programs disbursed about 184,000 loans for a total of $27.6 million, charging market rates.[2] The average loan amount was $150. Cumulative savings of program beneficiaries totaled $600,000, and about 18,000 people received training.

In March 1991, the combined loan portfolio amounted to $2.6 million and the late payment rate stood at 6.5 percent of outstanding loans (loans in arrears thirty days or more). Nine of the seventeen programs had reached operational self-sufficiency, meaning that interest income and other fees charged to clients covered the costs of operation.

AGS PROGRAM COMPONENTS

AGS's services are provided to its membership at no cost and can be classified in four main categories: program methodology, institutional strengthening, promotion of new programs, and financial intermediation.

TECHNICAL ASSISTANCE AND SERVICES

Methodology services include training and technical assistance to member institutions in the implementation of solidarity group and *famiempresa* programs. Training and technical assistance are provided in savings mobilization, promotion techniques, credit policies, credit analysis, business assistance to microentrepreneurs, training content, and pedagogy. These services are mainly for new members.

Institutional strengthening concentrates on such areas as board composition and role, organizational structure, planning, staff management, financial management, cost control, portfolio management, and loan collection. Important aspects of institutional strengthening include technical assistance in proposal writing and in developing negotiating skills.

During the past few years, AGS has promoted systematized accounting, portfolio management, program monitoring, and evaluation. In support of these efforts, computer equipment is provided to all members, and two employees of AGS are devoted full time to software development and technical assistance activities.

FINANCIAL INTERMEDIATION: THE AGS COOPERATIVE

During the first years of operation, AGS's role in financial intermediation was oriented toward fund-raising for the programs. Financial resources for operational expenses were given as donations. A revolving fund provided soft-term credit at an interest rate of 18 percent; the market rate was as high as 48 percent. AGS also provided technical assistance to member agencies in negotiating lines of credit from formal-sector financial institutions and in preparing proposals for international donors.

With the growth in both membership and program outreach during 1987–89, AGS realized that significant expansion programs were not possible based on international grants. It also realized that there were local financial resources that could be tapped through an appropriate financial mechanism. For instance, lines of credit made available by the national plan, with resources from the Inter-American Development Bank (IDB) and the World Bank, were channeled through commercial or cooperative banks and financial corporations. Most important, the mandatory savings feature of the solidarity group program gave AGS potential access to an average of $200,000 in monthly savings from its network (40,000 beneficiaries saving a minimum of $5 a month). This meant that the long-term future of the solidarity groups and *famiempresa* programs would be tied to their capacity to mobilize domestic resources through financial intermediation. The question remained what mechanism would best serve the objectives of AGS and its membership.

The creation of a savings and loans cooperative was an appealing option. Because cooperatives were perceived as development institutions, entrance to the cooperative movement was accessible. There was no minimum capital requirement, nor was previous experience in managing loans and savings required. Moreover, the cooperative movement was a well-developed network that could open a wide range of financial possibilities to AGS. Most important, cooperatives had the legal right to mobilize savings.

In 1990, AGS created the Cooperativa Grupos Solidarios de Colombia (AGS-COOP). Its main objective is to mobilize the country's internal savings to finance program expansion. A distinctive characteristic of AGS-COOP during its initial years (1990–93) was that its membership was made up of institutions, not individuals. This structure was chosen in order to keep decision making in the same hands that controlled AGS and to maintain a unity of objectives, particularly continued focus on microenterprise development. With this structure, the savings of program beneficiaries cannot be legally mobilized, as they are not direct members. In the second phase (1993 and after), the cooperative will become open. To achieve open status, AGS-COOP must have capital of $300,000 and three years of experience in managing savings and loans. Then it will be entitled to accept deposits from the public and to manage the savings of all the beneficiaries of the solidarity groups and *famiempresa* programs.

RESOURCE MOBILIZATION AND SERVICES. AGS-COOP currently operates two lines of credit for its associates: the capital resources line and the rediscount line. The capital resource line was created with the $30,000 start-up capital pooled by AGS members for the creation of the cooperative. Loans under this line are provided on relatively soft terms. The interest rate is presently 23.4 percent, paid quarterly (the effective rate is around 33 percent); in contrast, the prevalent market rate is 38 percent, with an inflation rate of 25 percent as of May 1991. The members relend these resources at a nominal rate of 42 percent, plus commissions. Loan terms usually range from one to thirty-six months for amounts up to five times the member's participation in the cooperative's capital. For every loan, it is mandatory for the borrower-associate to capitalize 10 percent. This regulation is aimed at increasing the cooperative's capital to $300,000 to meet the requirements of an open cooperative. Additional funding for the capital resources credit line will come from donations.

The rediscount line operates with funds obtained from cooperative banks and financial institutions through the rediscount line of the government-owned Banco de la Republica. The funds are re-lent to AGS members at 33.07 percent interest for on-lending to microentrepreneurs. The average loan term is three years.

Along with the provision of credit, AGS-COOP offers associates technical assistance in managing the funds received. The cooperative also assists the members in negotiating credit from financial institutions, particularly commercial banks. In the near future it will place deposits in financial institutions to guarantee credit to members for up to four times the amount deposited. Meanwhile, it accepts returns equivalent to what is paid to savings accounts. Under these conditions, lines of credit for $350,000 have been approved. As part of its services, AGS provides collateral for its members, including acting as a cosigner for commercial loans to FF, Corporación Acción por Tolima/Ibague (ACTUAR/Tolima), Corporación Mundial de la Mujer Colombia/Bogotá (CMMC/Bogotá), and Corporación Acción por Bogotá (ACTUAR/Bogotá).

Once the cooperative becomes open and program beneficiaries start making monthly savings deposits, it will open a third credit window for short-term loans to associates. Interest rates on savings deposits are expected to be higher than those of commercial banks. By 1995, AGS-COOP expects to mobilize $375,000 in monthly savings from its projected network of 75,000 beneficiaries.

AGS-COOP also contemplates a role in managing excess liquidity that members may maintain as reserves for bad loans and current accounts that earn no interest at the bank. AGS-COOP will create a liquidity fund in the form of certificates of deposit (CDs) to be placed in the fiduciary market. It will pay interest to the associates on their CDs and open a fourth line of credit with these resources. CD holders will be able to receive short-term loans at market interest rates for amounts up to three times the value of the deposits.

ADVANTAGES OF AGS-COOP SERVICES. AGS-COOP services, from the associates' perspective, offer many advantages over other financial sources. The two major advantages are access and opportunity. Credit from the financial markets in Colombia is often unavailable due to restrictions placed on banks by monetary authorities. AGS loans are readily accessible to its members. Because AGS closely monitors and maintains updated information on each program, the transaction period is kept to a minimum; it averages three days from submission of a loan application. In addition, AGS-COOP loans are repaid in up to three years as opposed to the prevalent short-term loans of the shallow financial markets. Collateral is flexible and negotiable.

AGS-COOP credit, however, has several drawbacks. Funds available under the different lines of credit are limited. For example, ACTUAR/Bogotá alone could absorb all the available funds, although the cooperative has sixteen other programs to serve as well. Another limitation from the associates' perspective is that, in the rediscount line, the spread is only 3 to 5 percent. Although this is true in nominal terms, in effective terms it ranges much higher, as most program portfolios rotate three to four times a year. Another limitation is that the rediscount line features high effective interest rates.

Nevertheless, the smaller and newer programs, particularly those implemented by institutions that are not financially strong, will not be ready for financial intermediation for some time. They will need grants or soft loans to achieve operational self-sufficiency and enough of a net worth for financial institutions to consider them good credit risks. This is the case for at least half the programs. For them, the cooperative will be particularly important, as it will lend to small and new programs; the banks will not.

EVOLUTION OF AGS MEMBER ORGANIZATIONS

AGS member organizations fall roughly into three generations, depending on when they joined the association. Table 13.1 shows changes in program performance by measuring changes in levels of operation, program efficiency, and portfolio quality. The performance of the third-generation members (1987–90) is far more impressive than that of the first-generation ones (1983–85). This reflects the experience developed by AGS in the selection of partners and provision of technical assistance, as well as improvement in operational techniques. Members from the first generation, with six to seven years in operation, account for only 13 percent of the total program clients.[3] In contrast, third-generation members, with one to three years in operation, account for 70 percent of the total.

Some of this disparity appears to be linked to differences between organizations created by AGS and organizations already operating solidarity group programs when they joined AGS. In the creation of AC-TUAR/Bogotá, ACTUAR/Quindio, and ACTUAR/Caldas, AGS carefully applied all the lessons learned from the first two generations of members: (1) build strong boards; (2) concentrate efforts on one main program; (3) develop an efficient technology for credit analysis, delivery, and follow-up; (4) develop a strong managerial capacity; and (5) develop supportive management information systems (MIS). By December 1990, ACTUAR/Bogotá, after only two years in operation, accounted for 59 percent of the AGS program beneficiaries in the June–December period and maintained a healthy portfolio.

Program performance also differs based on the characteristics of the implementing organization. The ACTUAR group has strong boards, entrepreneurial management, and a strong focus on credit. The FMM/Popayan group also has strong and aggressive boards, but its efforts are dispersed in the provision of an array of services. The Fundación Banco Mundial de la Mujer Colombia (FWWBC)/Cali group focuses mainly on credit but has less aggressive boards and management. A fourth group is made up of those organizations with a more charitable orientation such as Centro de Desarrollo Vecinal (CDV)/ Cartagena and Corporación Fondo de Apoyo de Empresas Asociativas/Nacional-Bucaramanga (CORFAS). The performance of the ACTUAR group is far more impressive than that of the fourth group for all the indicators.

ADDITIONAL IMPACT OF AGS

AGS has given the membership and its programs a more entrepreneurial approach to development. As a result of these efforts, 90 percent of the programs operate at or near self-sufficiency. Before joining AGS, Fundación para el Desarrollo Industrial, Comercial y Artesenal de le Guajira/Riohacha (FUNDICAR) had been disbursing ten loans a year; under the solidarity group program, it began disbursing ten loans a day. Programs that had a welfare approach, such as FF, CORFAS, and PISINGOS, are now operating with positive interest rates. The semipublic CDV is going through a process of privatization with the assistance of AGS. The professionalization of the institutions and their staffs constitutes an important contribution of AGS.

AGS has also helped change attitudes toward positive interest rates at the national level. The network's statistics have given the government, the private sector, and international donors empirical proof that it is possible to operate a development credit program with market interest rates. After AGS became part of the national plan, all microenterprise credit programs, including those under the Carvajal methodology, adopted the market interest rate approach of the AGS network.

The impressive aggregate results at the national level have given the solidarity group and *famiempresa* methodologies credibility and legitimacy before the public. Acceptance into the national plan for microenterprise development in 1987 gave AGS public recognition and made its programs eligible for IDB funding, starting in 1991.

STAGES IN THE DEVELOPMENT OF AGS

AGS has moved through a series of growth stages marked by differences in objectives, the role of ACCION, type of membership, services provided, and orientation of those services. These stages reflect both the evolution of its individual members over time and the particular dynamics of a member-owned service organization.

During stage one (1983–84), ACCION played the central role in providing services and leading the group. The main objectives during this stage were teaching and monitoring the solidarity group methodology and promoting more businesslike management. Financial services consisted of seed capital donations for revolving funds and operational expenses. No service fees were charged for training or technical assistance.

There were no selection criteria in choosing partner organizations. Those willing to try the solidarity group methodology were automatically welcome. As a result, membership was heterogeneous; AGS sought no

Table 13.1   Performance of AGS Member Organizations

Program, Year Joined	Avg. Increase in No. Clients/Yr.	% Increase/ Total	Avg. No. Loans/Yr.	% Arrears	Cost per $ Loaned	Self-Sufficiency Rate (%)
CIDES/Bogotá, 1983	288	2	2,221	—	.06	92
WWB/Cali, 1983	509	4	3,949	17	.17	86
FF/Cali, 1983	369	3	3,047	7	.08	106
CDV/Cartagena, 1983	268	2	2,711	11	.05	102
CIDES/Manizales, 1984	142	1	933	8	.13	65
CORFAS/Bucaramanga, 1985	343	3	1,213	34	.35	64
Average Increase		2.5			.14	85.8
ACTUAR/Antioquia, 1985	905	8	1,332	6	NA	NA
FMM /Popayan, 1985	296	3	3,282	9	.07	111
CMMC/Medellín, 1985	347	3	1,099	13	.07	65
FMM/Bucaramanga, 1987	201	2	815	7	.16	95
FMSD/Barranquilla, 1987	936	8	4,526	9	.04	171
Average Increase		4.8			.06	88.4
ACTUAR/Tolima, 1987	1,256	11	4,352	6	.04	301
PISINGOS/Bogotá, 1988	456	4	1,400	3	.05	139
ACTUAR/Bogotá, 1988	3,469	30	6,025	3	.12	99
CMMC /Bogotá, 1989	435	4	1,003	5	.02	589
ACTUAR/Caldas, 1989	355	3	616	8	.05	158
ACTUAR/Quindio, 1990	445	4	788	6	.16	63
FUNDICAR Guajira, 1990	462	4	1,458	0	.04	194
FMSD/Cartagena, 1990	39	0	220	3	.55	15
Average Increase		7.5			.12	194.7
Total or Average	11,521	5.2	40,990	NA	.12	132

NA = not available.

common institutional values or goals, only a common operating philosophy. The methodology tied the group together, but members' interest in working with ACCION was increasingly fund-driven. Programs were small. Self-sufficiency was constrained by low credit volume, inadequate managerial skills, and lack of an entrepreneurial vision at the board level.

In stage two (1985–87), ACCION still played the leading role in the group, but decision making became more collective. AGS concentrated on strengthening the programs' management and self-sufficiency, improving program performance, and obtaining recognition and legitimacy in the eyes of the government.

A number of new members joined at this stage. Selection criteria were still undefined, but ACCION had learned the benefits of working with organizations with strong private-sector and financial support. For these organizations, interest in joining AGS was mainly methodology-driven as opposed to fund-driven. They had to cover their operating expenses. Some contributed the seed capital for the revolving fund from their own resources. This fact by itself established a generational difference between the members joining in the first and second stages. The programs in this second group all operate with market interest rates and have a stronger orientation toward achieving self-sufficiency and large outreach.

Stage three (1987–90) began with the formal creation of AGS in September 1987. Objectives were to scale up program operations, strengthen AGS and its services, and become accepted as members of the national plan. ACCION assumed a lower profile in decision making, which became institutionalized through a board of directors. As expanding operations required high levels of financial assistance, AGS became more aggressive in financial intermediation. AGS created a credit fund for the affiliates and carried out active fund-raising for the programs at both national and international levels.

Membership expansion saw a new trend during stage three. Eligibility criteria for membership were established and, with the lessons learned from two generations of members, AGS embarked on the creation of organizations and the promotion of new programs within existing ones.

The programs were in different stages of development, and adjusting the services to the different needs became a difficult task for AGS. Limited human and financial resources forced AGS to concentrate on those members with the highest growth potential—most of which were newer members. New stars arose—ACTUAR/Bogotá, Fundación Mario Santo Domingo (FMSD)—among the young programs, and old stars resented the displacement and the decreased access to services.

AGS specifically sought out these new members to carry out its own objectives—scaling up, professionalization, and visibility. The older members began to express their dissatisfaction through the AGS board of directors. Under these circumstances, a potentially lethal dynamic of board members versus AGS staff became possible. A resolution had to be reached to make AGS services more responsive to the needs of all members. The creation of the cooperative and AGS's growing skill in financial intermediation have been key to a successful resolution. AGS still has a skill—brokering funds for loans—that the members do not and cannot have. This makes AGS very useful to them and will quell some of the discontent.

Stage four began with the creation of AGS-COOP in 1990. Objectives in this stage are to concentrate fully on scaling up operations through the mobilization of local resources and savings.

Ties to AGS are once again fund-driven rather than methodology-driven, particularly for the older members. Most have already outgrown the need for methodology-related services, so the cooperative and its financial services have become the bond holding the group together. AGS, in turn, has become the technical assistance arm of the cooperative. Members are highly satisfied with the creation of the cooperative and perceive it as the "motor" that will speed up the expansion of their programs.

THE AGS MODEL: STRENGTHS AND WEAKNESSES

PARTICIPATION AND BOARD STRUCTURE

The governing structure of AGS, including the board, is in the hands of the affiliates' executive directors. This structure has been instrumental in ensuring that the services provided by AGS respond to the needs of the membership. It has also facilitated communication and a close relationship between AGS and its membership.

Nonetheless, the fact that the directors are making decisions that directly affect their own organizations has had a negative impact on the objectivity of the process. The governing structure of AGS, like that of many membership organizations, is weak because the beneficiaries of the services provided by AGS are the same agencies that control the institution. The executive directors are both judge and jury. Policy decisions seldom take into account a larger vision beyond the parochial concerns of the members. A typical example is the strong opposition of some board members to increasing the interest rates charged by AGS and implementing fees for services. The growth of the organization and its long-term sustainability have been sacrificed in favor of cheap money and free services for the membership.

The executive directors are accountable to their own boards. Therefore, while acting as AGS board members, they cannot make decisions without previous authorization from their own boards. The result has been a slow decision-making and implementation process. For example, when the AGS board was discussing the creation of the cooperative, most members could not decide to make the initial $600 contribution without the consent of their own boards.

MEMBERSHIP EXPANSION

The rapid growth in membership has been a source of tension in AGS. With a larger number of members and limited and slowly growing resources, the older members have become resentful of newer ones. Also, the heterogeneity in membership and the variety of views and approaches have resulted in vast differences among members in the size and soundness of their programs. These differences challenge AGS's technical capabilities. It is difficult to serve such a variety of points of view and program needs.

Finally, there are no technical criteria or mechanisms for disaffiliation of those members that are not in tune with the AGS approach. In fact, AGS is not satisfied with the performance of several members, but no action has been taken partially because of the lack of criteria. Meanwhile, AGS devotes too much time and too many resources to "inefficient" members.

SERVICES

The quality of AGS services is high, and so is the quality of the staff. The membership regards them as among the most important assets of AGS. Timing in providing services is good as well. AGS responds quickly and effectively to the problems that members face. Methodology transfer to new programs is done efficiently and is supported with manuals, guidelines, and systems for every aspect of the programs' operations.

Some services have become outdated, however. Technical assistance demands are heavy for new programs, and older ones face new and complex problems in their attempts to scale up. The result is that AGS staff members are spread too thin, and some of the services offered are not particularly relevant to the larger or older programs.

ACCION'S ROLE IN AGS

Ties to ACCION have given AGS access to international resources, experience, and innovations that have helped programs learn faster. At the national level, ACCION has given AGS credibility and support among the government, private-sector, and donor agencies. The perception of the membership is that AGS would not have been nearly as successful without ACCION. ACCION's presence has been instrumental in ensuring that the services provided by AGS are of high quality. It has also contributed to keeping objectivity and a technical perspective in the board's decision making. Technically, ACCION has given direction, quality, and coherence to the work of AGS and its members. Financially, it has provided the means to achieve them. These last two factors have made ACCION's presence crucial to AGS growth and sustainability.

Nonetheless, ACCION's presence in AGS has been so strong that it has inhibited the membership from identifying with AGS. The members identify AGS and its directors with ACCION to the point that most refer to AGS and ACCION interchangeably. The fact that ACCION's country director was also the executive director of AGS has contributed to this confusion.

FINANCIAL SERVICES AND AGS-COOP

With the creation of the cooperative, AGS set in motion a financial strategy for innovative types of intermediation. The cooperative's main strength lies in the capacity to mobilize local resources, especially the savings of the programs' beneficiaries.

The cooperative has united two sectors—microenterprise and cooperative—that have worked separately in the past. In the microenterprise sector, AGS-COOP seeks a source of social and productive development; in the cooperative movement, it seeks a well-developed network of financial institutions that opens a wide range of financial possibilities to AGS. It also seeks to devise innovative ways to attract resources from its affiliates and to develop comparative advantage over the banking system by offering attractive interest rates and quick disbursement.

In coordination with the members, the staff developed complex criteria for allocating resources based on technical grounds, including quality and risks of the credit portfolios, each program's prospects for growth, and financial perspectives of the implementing agency. Some members believe that such criteria provide an advantage to certain institutions that, due to "external" reasons (quality and interest of board members, location, and so forth), are relatively successful at scaling up. In reality, those factors are mostly the result of a good program implemented by a solid institution.

SUSTAINABILITY

At present, AGS depends partly on outside funds to cover its operational expenses. Support for this purpose has come from several North American organizations. ACCION has covered the salaries of the AGS executive director and operational director, as well as some travel expenses. Part of the income comes from the interest charged to members and returns on a fund made up of monthly balances of grant funds.

As of March 1991, income from interest on loans covered 69 percent of AGS operational expenses. This figure does not include ACCION's subsidies for the salaries of the directors, which, if considered, would reduce the self-sufficiency rate to 34 percent.

With respect to the creation of AGS-COOP in 1990 and a more aggressive role in financial intermediation, AGS projected that income generated from interest on loans would fully cover the running costs of both AGS and the cooperative by 1993.

Problems with AGS self-sufficiency are related partly to its participatory governance structure: Program policies are dictated by the membership itself at the board level. Currently, all technical assistance services are provided free of charge, including those involving credit line negotiation on behalf of the members and proposal writing.

Finally, AGS members see AGS as an instrument to subsidize programs. Cheap resources represent a direct subsidy available to the programs through AGS. AGS provides them with a substantial margin (presently 24 percent a year) on part of their credit portfolio at the expense of the purchasing power of AGS assets in real terms.

LESSONS FOR REPLICABILITY

The experience of AGS demonstrates that apex organizations can be an excellent strategy for institutional strengthening of development organizations, program expansion, and channeling of financial resources. The successes and problems encountered by AGS in its development provide important lessons.

EVOLUTION IN THE ROLE OF THE APEX INSTITUTION

AGS has evolved from concentrating on methodology implementation to concentrating on financial intermediation, as it adjusts to the changing needs of its members. As the programs become stronger and operations scale up, needs evolve; the need for increased technical capacity to manage the program changes to a need for increased financial capacity to expand it. This change led AGS to create the cooperative.

Institutional capacity building accompanies every stage, although the needs in this area change significantly according to program evolution, becoming increasingly sophisticated as time goes on. The evolution of needs corresponds roughly to the stages in institutional development described in Chapter 4.

Time between stages can vary, depending on how strong the organizations are, the amount of resources available, the experience of the apex institution in implementing the methodology, the development of the management information system, and the degree of homogeneity in the membership.

A COMMON PHILOSOPHY

To maximize impact, an apex organization should be created by institutions with a common development philosophy and a similar methodology. The focus on solidarity group and *famiempresa* programs was the key factor behind the creation of AGS and its success. It allowed AGS to develop specialized services and to adapt those services to the changing needs of its membership. Later, the focus on expansion served the same purpose.

The process of developing a common philosophy starts with those who make program policies and those who implement them: board and staff members. There must be an educational process involving board members and staff of member institutions if they are to develop a philosophical consensus. Issues that have been important for AGS member education and consensus building include scaling up of operations, with all its implications for operational and financial self-sufficiency; interest rate policies; the role of training and business assistance; and the importance of limiting programs to those directly related to income generation. The key here is that the institutions must share a vision about their roles as development agencies.

Political clout is one of the main assets of an apex organization. A group of many institutions joined by a common development philosophy and a similar methodology has stronger political influence than a single institution with regional subsidiaries. AGS members are able to influence local politicians and bring regional pressures to bear at the national level.

SELECTION OF PARTNERS

Well-defined eligibility criteria are essential in the selection of members. The experience of AGS demonstrates that choosing members solely on the basis of willingness to participate is ineffective in promoting the solidarity group program. High performance is evidenced among those members whose objectives are more fully aligned with those of AGS, whose management is based on efficiency, whose target population is well defined, and who have an approach that concentrates on the provision of a few specialized, related services.

Organizations do not move easily to self-sufficiency and expansion if they do not start with those as operational objectives. The process of changing a charitable organization into an businesslike one consumes time and resources, particularly when the change is the result of a donor requirement rather than an organizational conviction.

It is important to limit the number of partners to those with the highest potential in terms of management, outreach, and effectiveness and to avoid a multiplicity of partners that do not add to an overall program of wide scope. This is an instrumental factor in determining the cost-effectiveness of the apex organization, particularly when financial resources are limited.

AGS's most successful member organizations rate high in the seven characteristics of nongovernmental organizations (NGOs) defined in Chapter 5 as essential for moving into financial intermediation, which include strong boards, commitment to scaling up, well-defined lending technology, and effective financial management.

SUPPORT SYSTEMS

Any scaling-up attempts of an apex organization need to be supported by well-developed monitoring systems. The ability of AGS to closely monitor and evaluate program changes has been essential in providing effective services to the membership and in learning better ways to operate programs.

An apex organization can provide technical assistance and training to members in data-collection, monitoring, and evaluation mechanisms. The apex organization can also play a role in teaching the NGOs the use of program statistics as key tools in management, decision making, and leveraging financial resources from donors. Computerization of management information systems is instrumental in increasing productivity and in managing and monitoring program expansion. Critical tasks in accounting, portfolio management, impact evaluation, and staff performance appraisal and in developing effective internal control systems are enhanced by the use of computers.

SERVICES

An apex organization can best seize the opportunity for economies of scale, and thus cost efficiency, with a group of institutions with common problems. It can minimize the technical assistance, training, and supervision costs involved in implementing the programs. The apex organization can provide these and other services less expensively than can each individual institution. Experience has shown that such services are essential to institutional strengthening and scaling up of operations. Problems emerge, however, when members evolve to a point where they need specialized assistance beyond the competence of a small staff.

FINANCIAL INTERMEDIATION

An apex organization can play a key financial intermediation role, tapping both local and external financial resources, which is difficult for NGOs to do separately. In the case of AGS-COOP, this role now includes facilitating access to credit from financial institutions and will include mobilizing program beneficiaries' savings. The mobilization of domestic resources is particularly important as external financial resources become scarce.

An apex organization has significant advantages in raising both national and international resources. Most donor agencies interested in supporting microenterprise programs prefer to provide large grants through an apex organization rather than limited financing through small programs. Donors are increasingly recognizing that it is desirable to promote the creation of umbrella organizations that can serve the needs of several implementing agencies and provide funders with a vehicle to allocate scarce development resources more efficiently. This is particularly true in countries such as Colombia, where the allocation system favors national institutions that have some clout in the public and private sectors.

ROLE OF EXTERNAL AGENCIES

An external agency can play a catalytic role in the development of apex institutions. The role played by ACCION in the case of AGS was crucial in assuring financial support and transferring know-how to the programs. AGS required large initial subsidies while it developed experience and the capacity to generate internal resources. ACCION was able to mobilize these resources. As an organization becomes more aggressive in financial intermediation and closer to self-sufficiency, its dependence on subsidies and attachment to an outside agency tend to disappear.

PARTICIPATION

Apex organizations with participatory governance structures face problems of conflicting interests. The dual "judge and jury" role played by the AGS board members negatively affected objectivity in decision making and AGS's own growth. Satisfied members tend to seek out their own benefits, and dissatisfied ones tend to act out their grievances in their role as governors rather than in their role as members.

An apex organization should explore the alternative of expanding its board with representatives from the private sector who are not connected in any way with its affiliates. Criteria and mechanisms for resource allocation among members must be developed so that when the board makes such decisions, the existing conflicts of interest can be resolved.

NOTES

1. This approach to microenterprise development emphasizes training as the microentrepreneur's most important need, in contrast to ACCION's approach of emphasizing credit.

2. Figures represent average yearly exchange rates for 1983 to 1989 and monthly rates for 1990 and 1991. All dollar amounts are U.S. dollars.

3. Figures are calculated on the basis of average number of clients per year.

CHAPTER 14

The Juhudi Credit Scheme: From a Traditional Integrated Method to a Financial Systems Approach

Albert Kimanthi Mutua

THIS CHAPTER RELATES the experiences gained by the Kenya Rural Enterprise Program (KREP) in developing effective microenterprise credit programs. It reviews some of the factors that limit the ability of nongovernmental organizations (NGOs) to function as financial intermediaries and reports on some key aspects of the design of the Juhudi Credit Scheme.

THE KENYA RURAL ENTERPRISE PROGRAM

KREP was established in 1984 by World Education Inc. with funding from the U.S. Agency for International Development (USAID). In 1987, the project was locally incorporated as a Kenyan NGO. KREP's mission is to serve as a catalyst for empowering low-income people, encourage them to participate in the development process, and enhance their quality of life, all through microenterprise development. Its goals are to generate employment and increase income.

In the beginning, KREP's strategy for developing microenterprises worked through the promotion of Kenyan NGOs' credit programs. The objective at that time was to build the institutional capability of as many Kenyan NGOs as possible. KREP provided the NGOs with grants, training, and technical assistance. In a period of four years, KREP supported about a dozen credit programs, most of which were add-ons to existing social welfare programs. Over time, it became clear that NGOs involved in social welfare programs found the transition to sustainability-focused lending difficult to make. It also became obvious that the "integrated" method of developing microenterprises, which combined traditional methods of making loans with intensive entrepreneur training and technical assistance, had limited impact on the beneficiaries, was costly, and could be sustained or expanded only through grant funding.

In 1989, KREP changed its strategy. First, the program selected four of the most promising NGOs: the Council for International Development's Promotion of Rural Initiatives and Development Enterprises, Ltd. (PRIDE) program, Tototo Home Industries, the National Council of Churches of Kenya, and the Presbyterian Church in East Africa (PCEA) Chogoria Hospital. Second, the focus of lending and the method of credit delivery were changed from the integrated to the "minimalist" approach, described in detail below. Third, KREP changed the terms of the financial assistance it offered NGOs, from 100 percent grant to 70 percent loan and 30 percent grant. Finally, to address self-sufficiency concerns and to put into practice what it had learned over the years, KREP launched its own direct lending program, the Juhudi Credit Scheme. KREP pursued these two tracks—working with NGOs and establishing the Juhudi scheme—simultaneously, using the minimalist methodology with both. The experience of each is recounted here.

LESSONS FROM NGOs

The change from the integrated to the minimalist approach improved the impact and cost-effectiveness of the programs significantly. The seven NGOs assisted by KREP lent only K Sh 15.7 million (U.S. $560,714) to 2,500 borrowers over a three-year period using the integrated credit delivery system. Start-up and operating costs totaled about $540,000. The average cost of disbursing and administering each loan for the NGOs was $213, or 96 cents for every shilling lent. With repayment rates averaging 78 percent, the programs were losing 22 cents of loan principal for every shilling disbursed. Interest revenues averaged 25 cents per shilling lent. The only way these programs could continue operating was by gaining access to more grant funds.

Results under the minimalist approach portray a brighter picture for the four KREP-assisted NGOs and for Juhudi, all of which adopted a new group-based method of lending to individuals. Over the initial period of about sixteen months, the five programs lent $1.5 million to 6,079 borrowers. The cost per shilling lent declined, on average, from 96 cents to 25 cents, and repayment rates improved from 78 to 95 percent. Revenues generated through credit activities covered about 60 percent of operating costs. In addition, a total of $253,000, or 16 percent of the total amount lent, was mobilized in the form of borrowers' savings.

From these results, it is clear that a financial systems approach to microenterprise development—which emphasizes institutional sustainability as a crucial element in providing credit services—is the most effective way of giving poor entrepreneurs access to financial services (see Chapter 1). Although remarkable improvements have been made by the institutions that adopted the minimalist approach, there are still a number of issues that need to be resolved before we can assert conclusively that NGOs can become effective financial intermediaries.

CAN EXISTING WELFARE PROGRAMS IMPLEMENT EFFECTIVE CREDIT PROGRAMS?

One major concern is whether microenterprise credit programs run by traditional welfare NGOs can succeed. Although the Kenyan NGOs that adopted a financial systems approach have made significant improvements, they are faced with the problem of balancing the objectives of welfare and sustainability-focused credit programs. This tension threatens expansion of their schemes, as management attention is split between credit and welfare programs.

Welfare-oriented NGOs traditionally have approached development from a very broad perspective. Usually, welfare programs focus on alleviating poverty by providing a number of free or subsidized services. Sustainability-focused programs assume that they are providing a service that poor people want and for which they are willing to pay. When welfare NGOs begin to operate credit programs, their general orientation tends to make them focus on selecting the neediest of clients—the poorest of the poor—rather than on delivering credit efficiently. These differences in focus have been largely responsible for the NGOs' slow transition to financial systems–based lending to poor entrepreneurs.

Kenyan NGOs are struggling with the question of who the target beneficiaries of NGO credit programs should be: the very poorest of people or poor people who are already entrepreneurs? Because NGO welfare programs focus on the poorest of the poor, their credit programs tend to serve the same constituency. When welfare criteria are used to select beneficiaries, the credit programs end up with borrowers who are not entrepreneurs. The poorest people in any community are not likely to be business operators. They are more concerned with the basic needs of survival and would most likely divert loan money to serve more urgent needs. Credit programs should not be overly concerned with strict definitions of beneficiaries. Since credit programs are demand driven, general criteria on who qualifies for credit are sufficient.

Some objectives and activities of welfare programs conflict with the principles of good credit management. This is most evident when both welfare and credit services are provided in the same community by the same organization. For example, in one program, a decision to reschedule loan payments was made because social workers determined that the borrower had domestic problems.

In other cases, credit policies are based on humanitarian reasons rather than workable financial models. For example, NGOs argue for below-market interest rates because they believe that the poorest people cannot afford higher ones. But studies in Kenya and elsewhere have shown that poor entrepreneurs are more concerned with convenience in borrowing than with the price they pay for these services. The biggest obstacle for NGOs in making the transition to a finance-based system thus appears to be the perceptions of the NGOs rather than reality.

It is common for NGOs to start credit programs without proper preparation, such as management information systems or qualified personnel. Many NGO programs are managed by staff who have no experience with credit and are often unable to judge the quality of the portfolios they are managing.

Lack of capacity to manage credit is largely a result of personnel remuneration policies that are not compatible with those in the commercial sector. Generally, welfare-oriented NGOs pay much less than the commercial sector. This limits their ability to recruit and maintain qualified staff. Organizations that are willing to pay competitive salaries for credit staff have a problem justifying a higher salary scale for credit staff than for welfare program staff. In some cases, welfare program staff are asked to double as credit officers, even when the two roles conflict.

Donors are partly responsible for creating this situation. Many credit programs are donor initiated, without much consideration of other essential institutional requirements. Donors often relate that this new methodology has worked marvels in some places and urge an NGO to adopt the process without considering its management capacity. Many NGOs are vulnerable to such suggestions because they survive through grants.

Credit for microenterprise development has, however, become a very specialized operation that relies on sound credit management principles. If these principles are compromised, efficiency cannot be realized. Poor entrepreneurs stand to gain much more from this efficiency than from the current subsidized and costly credit services. The Juhudi Credit Scheme was an attempt to circumvent many of these problems by building a new organization (as a part of KREP) that would have a more commercial orientation and would demonstrate to other NGOs that such an orientation could work.

JUHUDI CREDIT SCHEME

The Juhudi Credit Scheme is a KREP program that provides credit and savings services to poor entrepreneurs. The Juhudi idea was conceived in 1987 when it became apparent that out of the dozen NGOs assisted by KREP, only a few would become significant financial intermediaries. KREP considers the establishment of Juhudi to be a major step toward its own financial self-sufficiency goal and, by extension, toward providing credit services to microenterprises in Kenya on a continuing basis.

Juhudi attempts to provide access to credit on a commercially viable basis. Each Juhudi branch is expected to cover its costs of operations from credit revenues within three years. The branches work toward specific annual operational outputs and maintain their sights on the main goal during implementation. For example, the objectives of a branch are to recruit and maintain a minimum of 1,800 borrowers; organize clients into groups of five members (Watano); combine six Watano groups to form a larger association of thirty members known as Kikundi Cha Wanabiashara (KIWA); mobilize savings by encouraging members to contribute toward a group savings fund, which serves as collateral for loans and broadens the members' business capital base; and advance partially secured loans to KIWA members for the purpose of expanding existing or establishing new enterprises. In addition to these objectives, branches are given targets indicating performance expectations in areas such as the volume and number of loans to be made in a given period, cash flow position, and portfolio quality.

Juhudi's design features several characteristics of the financial systems approach outlined in Chapter 1 and practiced by organizations such as the Grameen Bank. The scheme federates small groups of five members into KIWAs of thirty people to facilitate economies of scale in lending operations. KIWA members are required to add to the savings fund every week and hold regular weekly meetings of all members to perform credit and savings operations. The KIWAs conduct loan appraisal and approval procedures. The program makes small initial loans that are repayable weekly over a one-year loan term. Savings begin before lending: After eight weeks of uninterrupted savings by each KIWA, eighteen members qualify for loans. The remaining twelve members in the KIWA qualify for loans after the first eighteen repay at least four installments without fail, and all KIWA members continue contributing toward the group savings fund without interruption. Once members repay current loans, they qualify for repeat loans, provided the other KIWA members continue to meet their obligations.

To optimize the production capacity of staff and minimize the cost of operations, credit officers are assigned 300 borrowers, all located within approximately a 2.5-kilometer radius, organized into ten KIWAs. The officers spend a great deal of their time recruiting and forming these groups. This approach minimizes travel costs and time and makes it easy for officers to visit clients and businesses regularly. During KIWA meetings, credit transactions are carried out. This allows lending officers to attend to thirty clients without having to travel.

Credit officers supervise the KIWA as it collects savings and loan repayments. Credit officers who meet predetermined targets are rewarded annually with cash bonuses, which are expected to contribute positively to the management of their portfolios.

Juhudi operations are administered through KREP's self-accounting profit centers, known as Area Credit Offices (ACOs). Each ACO is managed by an area credit officer who reports to a credit manager in the head office. Lending and savings operations are supervised by a minimum of six credit officers in each ACO. Each ACO must have a minimum of 1,800 borrowers at any one time.

Each Juhudi branch is considered a commercially viable venture. The start-up capital, provided by the head office, is composed of a loan, repayable quarterly over a seven-year period, and equity. Typically, the loan accounts for about 70 percent of the total capital, which averages $607,000. With this initial capital, every branch is expected to operate as an ongoing enterprise, meeting its obligations from its own resources. Additional loans are provided from headquarters only to expand the branch. In the first three years of operation, members' savings do not form part of the capital but are banked and managed by the KIWA. KREP intends to convert members' group savings into equity or loan capital once a strong relationship has been forged with the borrowers.

Before choosing the location of an ACO or branch, KREP conducts a detailed area study, including a census; classifies enterprises by type, ownership, and size; and assesses the demand for Juhudi services. The ACOs are located in areas that have high concentrations of microenterprises and are close to banking services. One of the weaknesses of the group-based method of lending is that it can work only where the microenterprise population is large enough to support a branch. Unfortunately, enterprises located in towns with few other microenterprises are overlooked. In Kenya, however, there are many commercial centers in towns throughout the country with adequate concentrations of entrepreneurs.

ACCOMPLISHMENTS OF THE FIRST JUHUDI BRANCH

Juhudi's first branch opened in September 1991 in Kibera, the largest slum of Nairobi.[1] This branch started with initial capital of $360,000 and three credit officers, which increased to six a year later. During the first sixteen months, this branch disbursed $450,000 to 1,253 borrowers. Its portfolio stood at $285,000 and was growing at an average rate of $9,000 a month. Repayment reached 98.2 percent, indicating that 1.8 percent of the amount due is past due. Start-up and operating costs totaled $50,000 against revenues of $40,000. Administrative costs were 11 cents for every shilling lent.

PROBLEMS AND FUTURE CHALLENGES

The pace of client acceptance and group formation is perhaps the most deceiving aspect of the group-based method of lending. From a financial standpoint, the faster the organization can recruit borrowers and make loans, the lower the cost of operation and the sooner returns on investment can be realized. However, KREP learned that the "get-rich-quick" idea is a time bomb waiting to explode.

In the beginning, Juhudi was enthusiastic in recruiting borrowers and forming groups as fast as possible. Believing that peer pressure and forfeiture of savings would take care of defaulters, Juhudi provided inadequate time for orientation and training and relied too heavily on self-selection for loan security. With a KIWA formed in two weeks, members could borrow by the sixth week. After most members of the scheme had received loans, problems began to emerge. First, because of reliance on self-selection, a number of borrowers who were not genuine business operators infiltrated the scheme. Second, the rules of the game were not clear to some KIWA members. When it came to forfeiting savings to recover loans in default, some members stopped making the required weekly contributions to the group savings fund. These factors made several groups very fragile, resulting in poor attendance at weekly meetings and a subsequent lack of understanding among the KIWA members. The lesson here is that groups should not be formed in a hurry. Sufficient time must be provided for training, orientation, and assessment of the clients' characters and businesses and for members to get to know one another as coguarantors.

The maximum loan size for first-time borrowers is set at $357. Watano members are expected to appraise and determine the most appropriate amount, subject to the ceiling. Initially, members were not trained in how to appraise loans. It was assumed that since they were business operators, they would be good appraisers. But business needs were not always reflected in the amounts borrowed. Some members borrowed several times what they needed; others borrowed only a fraction of what they needed. Naturally, those that borrowed too much diverted the loans to other purposes and were unable to meet weekly repayments. Borrowers who got less than they needed could not take full advantage of opportunities before their first repayments were due. Juhudi saw a strong relationship between inappropriate loan sizes and loan repayment.

Two important lessons emerged. First, borrowers must be trained in how to appraise loans, particularly the responsibilities and consequences of appraising loans incorrectly. Second, loan appraisal cannot be left entirely to borrowers. Credit officers must play a role in determining the loan size.

When the first branch started operations, loans were guaranteed by the core Watano members in each KIWA. If a Watano defaulted, the remaining twenty-five KIWA members were not affected. This policy contributed to a lack of cohesion among KIWA members. Clients identified with their own Watano group, but not necessarily with other groups in the KIWA. Unscrupulous Watanos found it easy to collude, once all their members had received loans. Further, the peer-pressure mechanism could not be implemented properly, since KIWA members did not have to bother with the affairs of Watanos. As a result, a few Watanos had all five members defaulting, and no mechanism existed to apply pressure.

The responsibility of recovering bad loans from savings is now placed on the entire KIWA, through a three-tiered collateral system. When a borrower defaults, all his or her savings are forfeited toward the loan balance (the borrower is considered the primary guarantor). If a balance remains after this first-level deduction, savings of the remaining four Watano members (the secondary guarantors) are forfeited in equal proportions. Last, if there is any balance remaining after the second-level deduction, it is recovered from the savings of the twenty-five KIWA members in equal proportions.

Once every year, Juhudi borrowers can withdraw up to 10 percent of their savings plus interest earned. KREP considers savings mobilization a process of empowering poor entrepreneurs by facilitating a gradual but steady accumulation of cash assets. Apart from acting as security for loans, savings widen the capital base of businesses as well as meet personal financial commitments. In the long run, KREP—with the consent and collaboration of clients—hopes to use these deposits as capital by converting the fund into equity or loan fund capital.

In addition to savings, the scheme provides for a bad-debts reserve, calculated as 1 percent of the loan repayments received. This reserve covers any portion of bad loans that cannot be recovered from savings. Clients are not told of this reserve. To protect members' savings against write-offs from death and permanent disability, borrowers pay a premium of $1.80 per person per year toward a loan insurance fund.

It is widely believed that microenterprises need mostly short-term working capital to cover current transaction requirements and to purchase supplies. It is also believed that most urban microenterprises operate on a short-term planning cycle. Based on these assumptions, KREP formulated a loan duration policy that required all loans to be repaid in weekly installments over a period not exceeding one year.

These assumptions hold true for the majority of Juhudi borrowers. For the remaining 20 percent, mostly manufacturing enterprises, this policy has a number of shortfalls. A few of the entrepreneurs need loans for fixed capital items, such as tools, which have no immediate returns. The majority have a turnover cb hycle longer than a week. Proprietors operating hawking businesses, however, need very short-term loans (from one to three months), with several repeat loans.

A strong case has been made by borrowers for policies that reflect their financial needs. Because some borrowers had not yet realized any sales when the first installments fell due, they had to use some of the loan to make repayment installments. Some borrowers have specifically requested a three-month grace period, bimonthly repayments, and slightly larger loans (Oketch forthcoming).

KREP is very optimistic about Juhudi's future in microenterprise development. It recognizes that the task of providing credit to the poor, combined with a strategy of self-sustainability, is a difficult one. KREP sees its efforts succeeding if it can maintain:

- A continuous reassessment of the methodology.

- An effective information system that allows problems to be identified and rectified quickly.

- Strict lender-borrower relationships with clients, with an open mind for criticism from clients.

- High morale among credit officers through competitive remuneration incentive schemes aimed at recognizing outstanding performance.

KREP is convinced that consistent hard work, focus on details, and encouraging clients to participate in decision making will bear fruit.

NOTE

1. A baseline survey of microenterprises in this slum found that there are about 7,500 such businesses. See Parker and Aleke-Dondo (1991).

Bibliography

ACCION International. 1990. "Informe, Sexto Taller Inter-Programas, Ino-vacciones Metodológicas y el Desafio de La Masificación." Mazate-nango, Guatemala: ACCION International.

———. 1991. "Informe Anual de Estadísticas." Cambridge, Mass.: ACCION International.

Acharya, M., and L. Bennett. 1982. "Women and the Subsistence Sector: Economic Participation and Household Decision-Making in Nepal." World Bank Staff Working Paper No. 526. Washington, D.C.: World Bank.

Adams, Dale W. 1971. "Agricultural Credit in Latin America: A Critical Review of External Funding Policy." *American Journal of Agricultural Economics* 53(2):163–72.

———. 1973. "The Case for Voluntary Savings Mobilization: Why Rural Capital Markets Flounder." Mimeo. Washington, D.C.: USAID, 19:309–34.

———. 1978. "Mobilizing Household Savings through Rural Financial Markets." *Economic Development and Cultural Change* 26(3):547–60.

———. 1984a. "Are the Arguments for Cheap Agricultural Credit Sound?" In *Undermining Rural Development with Cheap Credit*, edited by Dale W. Adams, Douglas Graham, and John D. Von Pischke, 65–77. Boulder, Colo.: Westview Press.

———. 1984b. "Do Rural Savings Matter?" Studies in Rural Finance, Economics and Sociology Occasional Paper No. 1083. Columbus: Ohio State University.

———. 1984c. "Effects of Finance on Rural Development." In *Undermining Rural Development with Cheap Credit*, edited by Dale W. Adams, Douglas Graham, and John D. Von Pischke, 11–21. Boulder, Colo.: Westview Press.

———. 1988. "The Conundrum of Successful Credit Projects in Floundering Rural Financial Markets." *Economic Development and Cultural Change* 36(2):355–67.

Adams, Dale W., and Delbert A. Fitchett, eds. 1992. *Informal Finance in Low-Income Countries*. Boulder, Colo.: Westview Press.

Adams, Dale W., and Douglas H. Graham. 1981. "A Critique of Traditional Agricultural Credit Projects and Policies." *Journal of Development Economics* 8(3):347–66.

———. 1984. "A Critique of Traditional Agricultural Credit Projects and Policies." In *Agriculture Development in the Third World*, edited by Carl Eicher and John M. Staatz. Baltimore: Johns Hopkins University Press.

Adams, Dale W., Douglas H. Graham, and John D. Von Pischke, eds. 1984. *Undermining Rural Development with Cheap Credit*. Boulder, Colo.: Westview Press.

Adams, Dale W., and G. I. Nehman. 1979. "Borrowing Costs and the Demand for Rural Credit." *Journal of Development Studies* 15:165–76.

Adams, Dale W., and Pablo Romero. 1981. "Group Lending to the Rural Poor in the Dominican Republic: A Stunted Innovation." *Canadian Journal of Agricultural Economics* July: 216–24.

Adams, Dale W., and Robert C. Vogel. 1986. "Rural Financial Markets in Low Income Countries: Recent Controversies and Lessons." *World Development* 14(4):477–87.

Afwan, Ismah. 1991. "A Review of BRI Unit Development (Background, Philosophy and Historical Analysis)." Mimeo. Jakarta: Center for Policy and Implementation Studies (CPIS).

Agabin, Meliza H. 1985. "Rural Savings Mobilization: Asian Perspective and Prospects." *CB Review* 37:7–15.

Aleem, Irfan. Forthcoming. "The Rural Credit Market in Pakistan: The Costs of Screening." In *Agricultural Development Policies and the Economics of Rural Organization,* edited by Karla Hoff, Avishay Braverman, and Joseph E. Stiglitz.

Aleke-Dondo, C., and Albert Kimanthi Mutua. 1990. "Informal Financial Markets in Kenya." Nairobi: Kenya Rural Enterprise Program.

Ardilla Iprosco, Fabio. 1990. "Evaluation of the Omnibus Small Business Enterprise Project." Mimeo. Bogotá, Colombia: Catholic Relief Services.

Arunachalam, Jaya. 1988. "Credit Needs of Women Workers in the Informal Sector, Case Study of Working Women's Forum (India)." Mimeo. Mylapore.

Ashe, Jeffrey. 1985. "*The Pisces II Experience: Local Efforts in Micro-Enterprise Development, vol. 2, Case Studies.* Washington, D.C.: USAID.

Asociación Grupos Solidarios de Colombia (AGS). 1991a. "Balance Comparativo 1989–1990." Mimeo. Bogotá, Colombia: AGS.

———. 1991b. "Balance General a Diciembre 31 de 1990." Mimeo. Bogotá, Colombia: AGS.

———. 1991c. "Consolidation and Promotion of Solidarity Groups Microenterprise Programs." Mimeo. Bogotá, Colombia: AGS.

———. 1991d. "Final Progress Report/Ford Foundation: Institutional Consolidation and Research Project." Mimeo. Bogotá, Colombia: AGS.

———. 1991e. "Institutional Consolidation and Research Project." Final progress report presented to the Ford Foundation. Bogotá, Colombia: AGS.

———. 1991f. "Presupuesto de Operación y Funcionamiento para el año de 1991." Mimeo. Bogotá, Colombia: AGS.

Banco Solidario, S.A. (BancoSol). 1991. "Proyecto de Factibilidad." La Paz, Bolivia.

———. 1992a. "Policy Statement." La Paz, Bolivia.

———. 1992b. "Presupuesto Gestión 1992." La Paz, Bolivia.

Bangladesh Bank. 1979. *Problems and Issues of Agricultural Credit and Rural Finance.* Dhaka: Bangladesh Bank.

Bank Indonesia Jakarta dengan Pusat Penelitian Pembangunan Pedesaan dan Kawasan Universitas Gadjah Mada. 1987. "Mengkaitkan Bank dengan LPSM dalam Mobilisasi Dana dan Penyaluran Kredit Studi Kasus." Yogyakarta: LSM Binaan LPSM Java Tengah dan D. I. Yogyakarta.

Bank Rakyat Indonesia (BRI). 1985. *Bank Rakyat Indonesia dalam Era Pembangunan 90th Anniversary Book*. Jakarta: BRI
———. 1990. "Briefing Booklet: KUPEDES Development Impact Survey." Jakarta: Planning Research and Development Department, BRI.
Bartel, Margaret. 1992. "Financial Ratios: A Tool of Financial Management in Microenterprise Credit Programs." GEMINI Technical Report No. 7. Bethesda, Md.: Development Alternatives, Inc.
Bath, Paquita, and Dinora Mendez de Sanchez, eds. 1990. *The Evolution of a Relationship: A History of OEF International and OEF de El Salvador*. San Salvador: Asociación para la Organización Empresarial Femenina de El Salvador (OEF/ES).
Bennett, Lynn. 1990. "An Approach to the Study of Women's Productive Roles as a Determinant of Intra-household Allocation Patterns." In *Intra-Household Resource Allocation: Issues and Methods for Development Policy and Planning*, edited by Beatrice Lorge Rogers and Nina P. Schlossman. Tokyo: United Nations University.
Benston, George J., et al. 1986. *Safe and Sound Banking. Past, Present, and Future*. Cambridge, Mass.: MIT Press.
Berger, Marguerite, and Mayra Buvinič, eds. 1989. *Women's Ventures: Assistance to the Informal Sector in Latin America*. West Hartford, Conn.: Kumarian Press.
Biggs, Tyler S., Donald R. Snodgrass, and Pradeep Srivastava. 1990. "On Minimalist Credit Programs." Development Discussion Paper No. 331. Cambridge, Mass.: Harvard Institute for International Development.
Binswanger, Hans P., and Mark R. Rosenzweig. 1986. "Behavioral and Material Determinants of Production Relations in Agriculture." *Journal of Development Studies* 22(3):503–39.
Blair, Harry W. 1984. "Agricultural Credit, Political Economy, and Patronage." In *Undermining Rural Development with Cheap Credit*, edited by Dale W. Adams, Douglas Graham, and John D. Von Pischke, 183–93. Boulder, Colo.: Westview Press.
Boomgard, James J. 1989. "A.I.D. Microenterprise Stocktaking: Synthesis Report." A.I.D. Evaluation Special Study No. 65. Washington, D.C.: USAID.
Boomgard, James J., James Kern, Calvin Miller, and Richard H. Patten. 1992. "A Review of the Prospects for Rural Financial Institution Development in Bolivia." GEMINI Technical Report No. 31. Bethesda, Md.: Development Alternatives, Inc.
Bottomley, Anthony. 1975. "Interest Rate Determination in Underdeveloped Rural Areas." *American Journal of Agricultural Economics* 57(2): 279–91.
Bouman, F. J. A. 1977. "Indigenous Savings and Credit Societies in the Third World." *Savings and Development* 1(4):181–214.
———. 1979. "The ROSCA: Financial Technology of an Informal Savings and Credit Institution in Developing Countries." *Savings and Development* 3(4):253–76.
———. 1984. "Informal Saving and Credit Arrangements in Developing Countries: Observations from Sri Lanka." In *Undermining Rural Development with Cheap Credit*, edited by. Dale W. Adams, Douglas Graham,

and John D. Von Pischke, 232–47. Boulder, Colo.: Westview Press.

———. 1989. *Small, Short and Unsecured: Informal Finance in Rural India.* Delhi: Oxford University Press.

Bourne, Compton, and Douglas H. Graham. 1980. "Funding and Viability of Rural Development Banks." *Savings and Development* 4(4):303–19.

Bratton, Michael. 1986. "Financing Smallholder Production: A Comparison of Individual and Group Credit Schemes in Zimbabwe." *Public Administration and Development* 6(2):115–32.

Braverman, Avishay. 1989. "Rural Credit Reforms in LDCs: Issues and Evidence." *Journal of Economic Development* 14:105–21.

Braverman, Avishay, and J. Luis Guasch. 1986. "Rural Credit Markets and Institutions in Developing Countries: Lessons for Policy Analysis from Practice and Modern Theory." *World Development* 14(10/11):1253–67.

———. Forthcoming. "The Theory of Rural Credit Markets." In *Agricultural Development Policies and the Economics of Rural Organization,* edited by Karla Hoff, Avishay Braverman, and Joseph E. Stiglitz.

Brock, Philip L., ed. 1992. *If Texas Were Chile: A Primer on Banking Reform.* San Francisco: Institute for Contemporary Studies.

Brown, David, and David Korten. 1989. "Understanding Voluntary Organizations: Guidelines for Donors." Working Paper Series No. 258. Washington, D.C.: World Bank.

Buzzard, Shirley, and Elaine Edgcomb, eds. 1987. *Monitoring and Evaluating Small Business Projects: A Step by Step Guide for Private Development Organizations.* New York: PACT.

Campbell, Wallace, Ted Weihe, Jim Moriss, Henry Cruz, and Brian Tormey. 1985. *Cooperatives in Chile's Transition to Democracy: Findings from a Study Tour by U.S. Cooperative Representatives.* Washington, D.C.: OCDC.

Carrillo, Bedoya Mariela. 1988. "Evaluación de Impacto del Programa de Expansión de Grupos Solidarios Asesorados por AITEC." Mimeo. Cali, Colombia.

Castello, Carlos. 1991a. "Asociación Grupos Solidarios de Colombia: Definición, Programas y Resultados." Mimeo. Bogotá, Colombia.

———. 1991b. "Informe del Consejo Directivo y la Dirección Ejecutiva a la Asamblea General de la Asociación Grupos Solidarios de Colombia." Mimeo. Bogotá, Colombia: Asociación Grupos Solidarios de Colombia.

Castello, Carlos, Katherine Stearns, and Robert Peck Christen. 1991. "Exposing Interest Rates: Their True Significance for Microentrepreneurs and Credit Programs." Discussion Paper No. 6. Cambridge, Mass.: ACCION International.

Catholic Relief Services. 1991. "Progress Report No. 5. Final Progress Report/CRS." Mimeo.

Center for Women and Development. 1989. "Production Credit for Rural Women Project, An Impact Evaluation Study." Mimeo. Katmandu, Nepal.

Cernea, Michael, ed. 1985. *Putting People First: Sociological Variables in Rural Development.* New York: Oxford University Press.

Chambers, Robert. 1983. *Rural Development: Putting the Last First.* London: Longman.

Chandravarkar, Anand G. 1987. "The Informal Financial Sector in Developing Countries." Occasional Paper No. 2. Kuala Lumpur, Malaysia: South East Asian Central Banks (SEACEN) Research and Training Centre.

Chen, Martha Alter. 1991. *Coping with Seasonality and Drought*. New Delhi: Sage.

Christen, Robert Peck. 1989. "What Microenterprise Credit Programs Can Learn from the Moneylenders." Discussion Papers Series No. 4. Cambridge, Mass.: ACCION International.

———. 1990. *Financial Management of Micro-Credit Programs: A Guidebook for NGOs*. Cambridge, Mass.: ACCION International.

Comprehensive Marketing Systems, Inc. 1990. "Final Report, A.I.D. Project No. 497–0341, Contract between Bank Rakyat Indonesia and Comprehensive Marketing Systems, Inc." Washington, D.C.: Comprehensive Marketing Systems, Inc.

Coopers and Lybrand. 1986. "National Development Foundation of Jamaica." Kingston, Jamaica: Coopers and Lybrand.

Darling, Malcom Lyall. 1978. *The Punjab Peasant in Prosperity and Debt*. 4th ed. Columbia, Mo.: South Asia Books.

De Santis, Dennis, and Paola Long. 1989. "Microenterprise Stocktaking: Cameroon. A.I.D. Evaluation." Occasional Paper No. 23. Washington, D.C.: USAID.

Dominican Republic Credit Union League. 1987. Annual Report. Santo Domingo.

Donald, Gordon. 1976. *Credit for Small Farmers in Developing Countries*. Boulder, Colo.: Westview Press.

Downing, Jeanne. 1990. "Gender and the Growth and Dynamics of Microenterprises." GEMINI Working Paper No. 5. Bethesda, Md.: Development Alternatives, Inc.

Drake, Deborah, and María Otero. 1992. *Alchemists for the Poor: NGOs as Financial Institutions*. Cambridge, Mass.: ACCION International.

Eaton, Jonathan, and Mark Gersovitz. 1981. "Debt with Potential Repudiation: Theoretical and Empirical Analysis." *Review of Economic Studies* 48(2):289–309.

Escobar de Pabon, Silvia. 1990. *Crisis, Politica y Dinamica de los Sectores Semi-empresarial y Familiar: La Paz, Cochabamba, Santa Cruz, 1985–1989*. La Paz, Bolivia: Centro de Estudios para el Desarrollo Laboral y Agrario (CEDLA).

Esman, Milton J. 1972. "The Elements of Institution Building." *Institution Building and Development: From Concepts to Application*, edited by Jonathan Eaton. Beverly Hills, Calif.: Sage.

Esman, Milton J., and Norman Uphoff. 1984. *Local Organizations: Intermediaries in Rural Development*. Ithaca, N.Y.: Cornell University Press.

Farbman, Michael. 1981. "The Pisces Studies: Assisting the Smallest Economic Activities of the Urban Poor." Washington, D.C.: USAID.

Farbman, Michael, and Fred O'Regan. 1989. "Intermediate Assessment, Get Ahead Foundation Cooperative Agreement." Mimeo. USAID/South Africa.

Fernando, Nimal A. 1988. "The Interest Rate Structure and Factors Affecting Interest Rate Determination in the Informal Rural Credit Market in Sri Lanka." *Savings and Development* 12(3):249–67.

Fisher, William, Jeffrey Poyo, and Ann Beasley. 1992. "Evaluation of the Micro and Small Enterprise Development Project in Bolivia." GEMINI Technical Report No. 42. Bethesda, Md.: Development Alternatives, Inc.

Fisseha, Yacob. 1991. "Small-Scale Enterprises in Lesotho: Summary of a Country-Wide Survey." GEMINI Technical Report No. 14. Bethesda, Md.: Development Alternatives, Inc.

Fisseha, Yacob, and Michael A. McPherson. 1991. "A Countrywide Study of Small-Scale Enterprises in Swaziland." GEMINI Technical Report No. 24. Bethesda, Md.: Development Alternatives, Inc.

Floro, S. L., and P. A. Yotopoulos. 1991. *Informal Credit Markets and the New Institutional Economics. The Case of Philippine Agriculture.* Boulder, Colo.: Westview Press.

Freres, Christian. 1989. "Informe Final, Evaluación de Impact, 1989." Bogotá, Colombia: Asociación Grupos Solidarios.

Fry, Maxwell J. 1988. *Money, Interest, and Banking in Economic Development.* Baltimore, Md.: Johns Hopkins University Press.

Fundación WWB Colombia. 1989. *Informe de Actividades Fundación WWB Colombia 1989.* Cali, Colombia: Fundación WWB.

Furubotn, Eirik, and Rudolf Richter, eds. 1989. *The Economics and Law of Banking Regulation.* Stadwald, Germany: University of Saarland , Center for the Study of the New Institutional Economics.

Gadway, John F., Tantri M. H. Gadway, and Jacob Sardi. 1991. "An Evaluation of the Institutional Aspects of Financial Institutions Development Project, Phase I in Indonesia." GEMINI Technical Report No. 15. Bethesda, Md.: Development Alternatives, Inc.

Garavito, Jaime A. "Programa de Grupos Solidarios para Trabajadores Independientes, Evaluación de Impacto." Bogotá, Colombia: Asociación Grupos Solidarios.

Germidis, Dimitri, Denis Kessler, and Rachel Meghir. 1991. *Financial Systems and Development: What Role for the Formal and Informal Financial Sectors?* Paris: Development Centre of the Organization for Economic Co-operation and Development.

Get Ahead Foundation. 1991. "Stokvel Department Quarterly Report." Mimeo. Pretoria, South Africa.

Goldmark, Susan, and Jay Rosengard. 1983. "Credit to Indonesian Entrepreneurs: An Assessment of the Badan Kredit Kecamatan Program." Washington, D.C.: Development Alternatives, Inc.

Gonzalez-Vega, Claudio. 1976. "On the Iron Law of Interest Rate Restrictions: Agricultural Credit Policies in Costa Rica and in Other Less Developed Countries." Ph.D. dissertation, Department of Economics, Stanford University, Stanford, Calif.

———. 1990. "On the Viability of Agricultural Development Banks: Conceptual Framework." Ohio State University Economics and Sociology Occasional Paper No. 1760. Columbus, Ohio.

Grameen Bank Donor Consortium. 1988. "Grameen Bank, Phase III Project, Appraisal Report." Mimeo. Dhaka, Bangledesh.

Grameen Trust. 1990a. Grameen Dialogue No. 1(2). Dhaka, Bangladesh: Grameen Bank.

————. 1990b. Grameen Dialogue No. 1(3). Dhaka, Bangladesh: Grameen Bank.

————. 1990. Computer Unit. Dhaka, Bangladesh: Grameen Bank.

————. 1991. Grameen Dialogue No. 7. Dhaka, Bangladesh: Grameen Bank.

Grown, A. Caren. 1989. "Beyond Survival: Expanding Income-Earning Opportunities for Women in Developing Countries." *World Development* 17(7):937–52.

Guyer, Jane. 1980. "Household Budgets and Women's Issues." Working Paper No. 28. Boston, Mass.: African Studies Center, Boston University.

Guzman, Diego. 1986. "Guía Metodológica: Programa de Capacitación Socio-Empresarial para Grupos Solidarios." Bogotá, Colombia: ACCION International.

————. 1989. "Guía Metodológica: Program de Grupos Solidarios para Trabajadores Independientes." Bogotá, Colombia: ACCION International.

————. 1990, 1991. Trip reports and technical assistance reports for ACCION International affiliates, including Bolivia 1987, Colombia 1986–1990, and Guatemala 1990 and 1991. Asociación Grupos Solidarios de Colombia.

————. 1991. "Asociación Grupos Solidarios de Colombia: Plan Operaciones." Mimeo. Bogotá, Colombia.

Hatch, John K., and Marguerite Sakir Hatch. 1989. "Village Bank Manual for Community Leaders and Promoters." 2d ed. Phoenix: Foundation for International Community Assistance (FINCA).

Higuera Martinez, Claudio. 1989a. "Consolidación de un Ente Movilizador de Recursos para los Programas de Grupos Solidarios y Famiempresas en Colombia." Mimeo. Bogotá, Colombia: Asociación Grupos Solidarios.

————. 1989b. "Estrategia para el Montaje y Desarrollo Empresarial de un Organismo Movilizador de Recursos al Servicio Directo de la Asociación Grupos Solidarios de Colombia." Documento Preliminar sobre la Viabilidad Jurídica de la Nueva Entidad. Definición de Objetivos y Esquema de Modelo Empresarial. Bogotá, Colombia: Asociación Grupos Solidarios.

Hirshman, Albert. 1984. *Getting Ahead Collectively—Grassroots Experiences in Latin America.* New York: Pergamon Press.

Hoff, Karla, Avishay Braverman, and Joseph E. Stiglitz, eds. Forthcoming. *Agricultural Development Policies and the Economics of Rural Organization.*

Hoff, Karla, and Joseph E. Stiglitz. 1990. "Introduction: Imperfect Information and Rural Credit Markets—Puzzles and Policy Perspectives." *World Bank Economic Review* 4(2):235–50.

Holstrom, B. H., and J. Tirole. 1990. "The Theory of the Firm." In *Handbook of Industrial Organization,* edited by R. Schmalensee and R. Willig, 21–45. Amsterdam: North Holland.

Holt, Sharon L. 1991. "Women in the BPD and Unit Desa Financial Service Programs: Lessons from Two Impact Studies in Indonesia." GEMINI Technical Report No. 19. Bethesda, Md.: Development Alternatives, Inc.

Holt, Sharon L., and Helena Ribe. 1990. "Developing Financial Institutions for the Poor: A Focus on Gender Issues." Washington, D.C.: World Bank.

Honduras Credit Union Federation. 1987. Annual Report. Tegucigalpa, Honduras.

Horten, David, and Karl Pillemer. 1983. "Self-Help Groups and Social Movement Organizations: Social Structure and Social Change." *Research in Social Movements, Conflicts and Change* 5:203–33.

Hossain, Mahabub. 1988. "Credit for Alleviation of Rural Poverty: The Grameen Bank in Bangladesh." Research Report No. 65. Washington, D.C.: International Food Policy Research Institute.

Howse, C. J. 1983. "Agricultural Development without Credit." In *Rural Financial Markets in Developing Countries: Their Use and Abuse,* edited by John D. Von Pischke, Dale W. Adams, and Gordon Donald, 134–37. Baltimore: Johns Hopkins University Press.

Huppi, Monika, and Gershon Feder. 1990. "The Role of Groups and Credit Cooperatives in Rural Lending." World Bank, Policy Planning and Research Working Paper WPS284. Washington, D.C.

Instituto de Desarrollo Hondureño (IDH). 1992. "1991 Informe Anual." Tegucigalpa, Honduras: IDH.

Inter-American Investment Corporation (IIC). 1990. Project appraisal. Mimeo.

International Labor Organization/United Nations Development Program Employment Creation Strategy Project. 1989. "The Impact of Unsubsidized Rural Credit Programs on Employment Generation in Indonesia." Mimeo. Jakarta.

Jackelen, Henry L. 1989. "Banking on the Informal Sector." In *Microenterprises in Developing Countries,* edited by Jacob Levitsky. London: Intermediate Technology Publications.

Jackelen, Henry R., and Elisabeth Rhyne. 1991. "Towards a More Market-Oriented Approach to Credit and Savings for the Poor." *Small Enterprise Development* 2(4):4–20.

Jean, Andy, Eric Hyman, and Mike O'Donnell. 1990. "Technology—The Key to Increasing the Productivity of Microenterprises." GEMINI Working Paper No. 8. Bethesda, Md.: Development Alternatives, Inc.

Kamble, N. D. 1979. *Poverty within Poverty: A Study of the Weaker Sections in a Deccan Village.* Bangalore, India: Institute for Social and Economic Change.

Kane, Edward J. 1977. "Good Intentions and Unintended Evil: The Case Against Selective Credit Allocation." *Journal of Money, Credit, and Banking* 9:55–69.

———. 1985. *The Gathering Crisis in Federal Deposit Insurance.* Cambridge, Mass.: MIT Press.

Kelley, Allen C., and Jeffrey G. Williamson. 1968. "Household Savings Behavior in the Developing Economies: The Indonesian Case." *Economic Development and Cultural Change* 16(3):385–403.

Kenya Rural Enterprise Program (KREP). 1991. Programme Report, March-August 1991. Nairobi, Kenya.

Kilby, Peter, and David D'zmura. 1985. "Searching for Benefits." USAID Evaluation Special Study No. 28. Washington, D.C.: USAID.

Kindervatter, Suzanne. 1988. "From Effectiveness to Efficiency: The Challenge of Scale in Assisting Rural Women Pre-Entrepreneurs." In *Technical Assistance and Training: What Difference Does It Make? How Can It Be*

Done Effectively and Affordably? Report of a working session of the SEEP Network. New York.

Klein, B., and K. Leffler. 1981. "The Role of Market Forces in Assuring Contractual Performance." *Journal of Political Economy* 81:815–41.

Korten, David C., and Felipe Alfonso, eds. 1983. *Bureaucracy and the Poor: Closing the Gap.* West Hartford,Conn.: Kumarian Press.

Kropp, E., M. T. Marx, B. Pramod, B. R. Quinones, and H. D. Seibel. 1989. *Linking Self-Help Groups and Banks in Developing Countries.* Eschborn, Germany: Gesellschaft für Technische Zusammenarbeit (GTZ), and Bangkok: Asian and Pacific Regional Agricultural Credit Association (APRACA).

Ladman, Jerry R. 1971. "Some Empirical Evidence in Unorganized Rural Credit Markets." *Canadian Journal of Agricultural Economics* 19(3):61–66.

Lassen, Cheryl. 1988. Keynote address in *Technical Assistance and Training: What Difference Does It Make? How Can It Be Done Effectively and Affordably?* Report of a working session of the SEEP Network. New York.

Lee, Tae Young, Dong Hi Kim, and Dale W. Adams. 1977. "Savings Deposits and Credit Activities in South Korean Agricultural Cooperatives, 1961–75." *Asian Survey* 17(12):1182–94.

Levitsky, Jacob, ed. 1989. *Microenterprises in Developing Countries.* London: Intermediate Technologies Publications.

Lewin, A. Christopher. 1991. "The ADEMI Approach to Microenterprise Credit." GEMINI Special Publication No. 3. Bethesda, Md.: Development Alternatives, Inc.

Lewis, John P. 1988. *Strengthening the Poor: What Have We Learned. Overseas Development Council, U.S.-Third World Policy Perspectives.* No. 10. New Brunswick, N.J.: Transaction Books.

Lieberson, Joseph, and William Doyle. 1989. "Microenterprise Stocktaking: A Statistical Look at A.I.D.'s Microenterprise Portfolio." Washington, D.C.: USAID.

Liedholm, Carl. 1989. "Small Scale Enterprise Dynamics and the Evolving Role of Informal Finance." Seminar on Informal Financial Markets in Development, paper no. 8. Washington, D.C.

———. 1990. "The Dynamics of Small Scale Industries in Africa and the Role of Policy." GEMINI Working Paper No. 2. Bethesda, Md.: Development Alternatives, Inc.

———. 1991. "Dynamics of Small- and Micro-Scale Enterprises and the Evolving Role of Finance." GEMINI Working Paper No. 26. Bethesda, Md.: Development Alternatives, Inc.

Liedholm, Carl, and Michael A. McPherson. 1991. "Small Scale Enterprises in Mamelodi and Kwazekele Townships, South Africa: Survey Findings." GEMINI Technical Report No. 16. Bethesda, Md.: Development Alternatives, Inc.

Liedholm, Carl, and Donald Mead. 1987. "Small Scale Industries in Developing Countries: Empirical Evidence and Policy Implications." MSU International Development Paper No. 9. Michigan State University, East Lansing.

———. 1991. "Dynamics of Microenterprises: Research Issues and Approaches." GEMINI Working Paper No. 12. Bethesda, Md.: Development Alternatives, Inc.

————. 1992. "The Structure and Growth of Microenterprises in Southern and Eastern Africa: Evidence from Recent Surveys." Paper presented at the USAID Eastern and Southern Africa Regional Conference on Small and Micro Enterprise Development.

Liong, Kwan H. 1991. "Rural Savings Mobilization through BRI Unit Banking System: History, Achievement and Prospect." Mimeo. Jakarta: Center for Policy and Implementation Studies.

Lipton, Michael. 1976. "Agricultural Finance and Rural Credit in Poor Countries." *World Development* 4(7):543–53.

Long, Carolyn, Daouda Diop, and James Cawley. 1990. "Report of Program Working Group." In *Towards Partnership in Africa,* edited by Phyllis Ingersoll and Jerry Ingersoll. Washington, D.C.: InterAction and FAVDO.

Lycette, Margaret, and Karen White. 1989. "Improving Women's Access to Credit in Latin America and the Caribbean: Policy and Project Recommendations." In *Women's Ventures: Assistance to the Informal Sector in Latin America,* edited by Marguerite Berger and Mayra Buvinič. West Hartford, Conn.: Kumarian Press.

Maisel, Sherman, ed. 1981. *Risk and Capital Adequacy in Commercial Banks.* Chicago: University of Chicago Press.

Malhotra, Mohini. 1992. "Poverty Lending and Microenterprise Development: A Clarification of the Issues." GEMINI Working Paper No. 30. Bethesda, Md.: Development Alternatives, Inc.

————. n.d. "USAID/Bolivia's Micro- and Small Enterprise Development Program." Unpublished paper.

Mann, Charles K., Merilee S. Grindle, and Parker Shipton. 1989. *Seeking Solutions: Framework and Cases for Small Enterprise Development Programs.* West Hartford, Conn.: Kumarian Press.

March, Katherine S., and Rachelle L. Taqqu. 1986. *Women's Informal Associations in Developing Countries: Catalysts for Change?* Boulder, Colo.: Westview Press.

Marla, Sarma. 1981. *Bonded Labour in India: National Survey on the Incidence of Bonded Labour.* New Delhi: Biblia Impex Private Ltd.

Mashek, Robert. 1989. "The Asociación Grupos Solidarios de Colombia: A Healthy Network." Mimeo. Arlington, Vir.: Inter-American Foundation.

Mauri, Arnaldo. 1977. "A Policy to Mobilize Rural Savings in Developing Countries." *Savings and Development* 1(1):14–25.

McKinnon, Ronald I. 1973. *Money and Capital in Economic Development.* Washington, D.C.: Brookings Institution.

————. 1989. "Macroeconomic Instability and Moral Hazard in Banking in a Liberalizing Economy." In *Latin American Debt and Adjustment. External Shocks and Macroeconomic Policies,* edited by Philip L. Brock, Michael B. Connolly, and Claudio Gonzalez-Vega, 99–111. New York: Praeger.

McPherson, Michael A. 1991a. "Growth and Change in Malawi's Small and Medium Enterprise Sector, 1986–1990." GEMINI Technical Report No. 17. Bethesda, Md.: Development Alternatives, Inc.

————. 1991b. "Micro and Small-Scale Enterprises in Zimbabwe: Results of a Country-Wide Survey." GEMINI Technical Report No. 25. Bethesda, Md.: Development Alternatives, Inc.

————. 1992. "Growth and Survival in Southern African Small Enterprises." Unpublished doctoral dissertation, Michigan State University, East Lansing.

Mead, Donald. 1992. "Microenterprise Development in a Sub-sector Context." *Small Enterprise Development* 3(1): 35–42.

Mead, Donald, Thomas Dichter, Yacob Fisseha, and Steve Haggblade. 1990. "Prospects for Enhancing the Performance of Micro and Small-Scale Nonfarm Enterprises in Niger." GEMINI Working Paper No. 3. Bethesda, Md.: Development Alternatives, Inc.

Meyer, Richard L. 1985. "Deposit Mobilization for Rural Lending." Rome: Food and Agricultural Organization of the United Nations.

Meyer, Richard L., and Carlos E. Cuevas. 1990. "Reducing the Transaction Costs of Financial Intermediation: Theory and Innovations." Paper presented at the International Conference on Savings and Credit for Development, Copenhagen.

Meyer, Richard L., and G. Nagarajan. 1988. "Financial Services for Small and Micro Enterprises: A Need for Policy Changes and Innovation." *Savings and Development* 4(12):363–73.

Miracle, Marvin, Diane Miracle, and Laurie Cohen. 1980. "Informal Savings Mobilization in Africa." *Economic Development and Cultural Change* 28(4):701–24.

Moermanto, R. J. 1991. "The KUPEDES as a Lending Instrument for BRI Unit Banks." Mimeo. Jakarta: Center for Policy and Implementation Studies.

Mosley, Paul, and Rudra Prasad Dahal. 1987. "Credit for the Rural Poor: A Comparison of Policy Experiments in Nepal and Bangladesh." *Manchester Papers on Development* 3(2):45–59.

Muller & Associados. 1991a. "El Sistema Bancario National." Boletin 62. La Paz, Bolivia.

————. 1991b. *Evaluación Economica, 1991.* La Paz, Bolivia.

————. 1991c. "Sector Informal y Crecimiento Economico en Bolivia." Boletin 67. La Paz, Bolivia.

Mundle, Sudipto. 1976. "The Bonded of Palamau." *Economic and Political Weekly* 11(18):653–56.

National Development Foundation of Jamaica (NDF/J). 1990. "1989 Annual Report." Kingston, Jamaica: NDF/J.

————. 1991. "1990 Annual Report." Kingston, Jamaica: NDF/J.

Nisbet, Charles. 1967. "Interest Rates and Imperfect Competition in the Informal Credit Market of Rural Chile." *Economic Development and Cultural Change* 16(1):73–90.

Noponen, Helzi. 1990. "Loans to the Working Poor: A Longitudinal Study of Credit, Gender and the Household Economy." Working Paper No. 6. New Brunswick, N.J.: Rutgers University.

Oketch, H. O. Forthcoming. "A Diagnostic Survey of the Juhudi Kibera Credit Scheme." Kenya Rural Enterprise Program.

Olson, Mancur. 1965. *The Logic of Collective Action.* Cambridge, Mass.: Harvard University Press.

Organización Regional de las Agencias Para el Desarrollo de la Microempresa (ORADME). 1992. "Memoria Anual 1991." San José, Costa Rica.

Otero, María. 1986. "The Solidarity Group Concept: Its Characteristics and Significance for Urban Informal Sector Activities." New York: PACT.

————. 1989a. *Breaking Through: The Expansion of Micro-Enterprise Programs as a Challenge for Non-Profit Institutions.* Cambridge, Mass.: ACCION International.

————. 1989b. "A Handful of Rice: Saving Mobilization by Micro-Enterprise Programs and Perspectives for the Future." Monograph Series No. 3. Washington D.C.: ACCION International.

————. 1989c. "Solidarity Group Programs: Working Methodology for Enhancing the Economic Activities of Women in the Informal Sector." In *Women's Ventures: Assistance to the Informal Sector in Latin America,* edited by Marguerite Berger and Mayra Buvinič. West Hartford, Conn.: Kumarian Press.

Parker, Joan, and C. Aleke-Dondo. 1991. "Kenya: Kibera's Small Enterprise Sector Baseline Survey Report." GEMINI Working Paper No. 17. Bethesda, Md.: Development Alternatives, Inc.

Patten, Richard H., and Jay K. Rosengard. 1991. *Progress with Profits: The Development of Rural Banking in Indonesia.* San Francisco: International Center for Economic Growth and the Harvard Institute for International Development.

Patten, Richard H., and Donald R. Snodgrass. 1987. "Monitoring and Evaluating KUPEDES (General Rural Credit) in Indonesia." Harvard Institute for International Development (HIID) Discussion Paper No. 249. Cambridge, Mass.: Harvard Institute for International Development.

Penny, David H. 1968. "Farm Credit Policy in the Early Stages of Agricultural Development." *American Journal of Agricultural Economics* 12:32–45.

People's Bank of Nigeria. 1991. Brochure. Lagos, Nigeria.

Pirela Martínez, Hugo. 1990. "The Gray Area in Microenterprise Development." *Grassroots Development* 14(2): 33–40.

Polizatto, Vincent P. 1989. "Prudential Regulation and Banking Supervision. Building an Institutional Framework for Banks." Policy, Planning, and Research Working Paper No. 340. Washington, D.C.: World Bank.

Poyo, Jeffrey. 1992. "Relaciones de Agencia, el Banco Agrícola y las Cooperativas Rurales de Ahorro y Crédito." In *República Dominicana: Mercados Financieros Rurales y Movilización de Depósitos,* edited by Claudio Gonzalez-Vega. Santo Domingo, Dominican Republic: Programa Servicios Financieros Rurales, Ohio State University.

Poyo, Jeffrey, David Hoelscher, and Mohini Malhotra. 1989. "Microenterprise Stoc-taking: The Dominican Republic." Washington, D.C.: USAID.

PRODEM. 1988. "Micro-Business Development Bank, Bolivia: Investor's Preview." La Paz, Bolivia.

————. 1988, 1989, 1990, and 1991. "Informes Anuales." La Paz, Bolivia.

————. 1990. "Financing Proposal and Introductory Description for a Commercial Micro-Credit Bank in Bolivia." Mimeo. La Paz, Bolivia.

Rahman, Rushidan Islam. 1988. "Poor Women's Access to Economic Gain from Grameen Bank Loans." Working Paper No. 9/12. National Centre for Development Studies. Dhaka, Bangladesh.

Reserve Bank of India. 1954. *All-India Rural Credit Survey.* Vol. 1, *The Survey*

Report; vol. 2, *The General Report;* vol. 3, *The Technical Report.* Bombay: Reserve Bank of India.

Revere, Elspeth. 1988. "An Impact Evaluation of the Microbusiness Promotion Project." Guatemala City: Community Development Corporation.

Rhyne, Elisabeth. 1991. "The Microenterprise Finance Institutions of Indonesia and Their Implications for Donors." GEMINI Working Paper No. 20. Bethesda, Md.: Development Alternatives, Inc.

Rippey, Paul. 1989. *A Discussion of Association pour la Productivite Burkina Faso.* Oagadougou, Burkina Faso: Asociation pour la Productivite (APP).

Robinson, Marguerite S. 1988. *Local Politics: The Law of the Fishes.* Delhi: Oxford University Press.

———. 1989. "The Framework and Development of the Bank Rakyat Indonesia Unit Banking System, 1970–1994." Mimeo, 2 vols. Jakarta: Center for Policy and Implementation Studies.

———. 1991. "The Bank Rakyat Indonesia, 1970–1990: Strategies for Successful Rural Banking." Mimeo. Jakarta: Bank Rakyat Indonesia and Center for Policy and Implementation Studies.

———. 1992. "Rural Financial Intermediation: Lessons from Indonesia." Development Discussion Paper. Cambridge, Mass.: Harvard Institute for International Development.

Robinson, Marguerite S., and Donald R. Snodgrass. 1987. "The Role of Institutional Credit in Indonesia's Rice Intensification Program." Development Discussion Paper No. 248. Cambridge, Mass.: Harvard Institute for International Development.

Robinson, Marguerite S., and Sudarno Sumarto. 1988. "Savings and Lending in the Unit Banking System." Mimeo. Jakarta: Center for Policy and Implementation Studies.

Roemer, Michael, and Christine Jones, eds. 1991. *Markets in Developing Countries: Parallel, Fragmented and Black.* San Francisco: International Center for Economic Growth and Harvard Institute for International Development.

Rofe, Nicholas. 1992. "ACEP: Agence de Credit pour l'Enterprise Privee." Paper presented at the USAID Eastern and Southern Africa Regional Conference on Small and Micro Enterprise Development.

Roman, L., and P. Orneus. 1988. "Banking in the Informal Sector: A Report on the Self-Employed Women's Association in Ahmedabad, India." Stockholm School of Economics, Minor Field Study, Series 2.

Rose, Martha. 1991. "Credit Unions and Small-Scale Enterprise Development in Ecuador." In *Ecuador Micro-enterprise Sector Assessment: Financial Markets and the Micro- and Small-Scale Enterprise Sector,* edited by Richard Meyer, John Porges, Martha Rose, and Jean Gilson. GEMINI Technical Report No. 9. Bethesda, Md.: Development Alternatives, Inc.

Roth, Hans-Dieter. 1983. *Indian Moneylenders at Work: Case Studies of the Traditional Rural Credit Markets in Dhanbad District, Bihar.* New Delhi: Manohar.

Rubio, Frank. 1991. "Microenterprise Growth Dynamics in the Dominican Republic: The ADEMI Case." GEMINI Working Paper No. 21. Bethesda, Md.: Development Alternatives, Inc.

Santo Pietro, Daniel, ed. 1989. *Accelerating Institutional Development: Roles for US PVOs.* Report of a workshop. New York: Private Agencies Collaborating Together (PACT).

Sartono, Hudi. 1991. "The Rural Banking Unit in Bank Rakyat Indonesia (BRI)." Mimeo. Jakarta: Center for Policy and Implementation Studies.

Sawyer, Susana. 1990. "Training and Technical Assistance in Small Enterprise Development Strategies: An Examination of the Issues for 30 PVOs." Mimeo. Small Enterprise Education and Promotion (SEEP) Network.

Schaefer-Kehnert, Walter, and John D. Von Pischke. 1984. "Agricultural Credit Policy in Developing Countries." Reprint Series No. 280. Washington, D.C.: World Bank.

Schmit, L. T. 1991. "Rural Credit between Subsidy and Market: Adjustment of the Village Units of Bank Rakyat Indonesia in Sociological Perspective." Leiden Development Series No. 11. Leiden: Leiden University.

Sebstad, Jennefer. 1982. "Struggle and Development Among Self Employed Women." Washington, D.C.: USAID.

SEEP. 1989a. "Expanding the Benefits of Small Enterprise Development: A Dialogue." Report of a Joint Forum of the SEEP Network and PACT.

———. 1989b. "Small Enterprise Development and Income Generating Activities Through Indigenous Nongovernmental Organizations: Towards a Strategy." Report to the International Labour Office. New York: Small Enterprise Education and Promotion (SEEP) Network.

Shavell, S. 1984. "On the Design of Contracts and Remedies for Breach." *Quarterly Journal of Economics* 99:121–48.

Shaw, Edward S., and Ronald I. McKinnon. 1973. *Financial Deepening in Economic Development.* New York: Oxford University Press.

Siamwalla, Ammar, Chirmsak Pinthong, Mipon Poapongsakorn, Ploenpit Satsanguan, Prayong Nettayarak, Wanrak Mingmaneenakin, and Yuavares Tubpun. Forthcoming. "The Thai Rural Credit System and Elements of a Theory: Public Subsidies, Private Information, and Segmented Markets." In *Agricultural Development Policies and the Economics of Rural Organization,* edited by Karla Hoff, Avishay Braverman, and Joseph E. Stiglitz.

Sideri, Sandro. 1984. "Savings Mobilization in Rural Areas and the Process of Economic Development." *Savings and Development* 8(3):207–16.

Singh, Karam. 1983. "Structure of Interest Rates on Consumption Loans in an Indian Village." In *Rural Financial Markets in Developing Countries: Their Use and Abuse,* edited by John D. Von Pischke, Dale W. Adams, and Gordon Donald, 251–54. Baltimore: Johns Hopkins University Press.

Snodgrass, Donald R., and Richard H. Patten. 1991. "Reform of Rural Credit in Indonesia: Inducing Bureaucracies to Behave Competitively." In *Reforming Economic Systems in Developing Countries,* edited by Dwight H. Perkins and Michael Roemer, 341–63. Cambridge, Mass.: Harvard Institute for International Development.

Stearns, Katherine, and María Otero, eds. 1990. "The Critical Connection: Governments, Private Institutions, and the Informal Sector in Latin America." Monograph Series 5. Cambridge, Mass.: ACCION International.

Stigler, George J. 1971. "The Theory of Economic Regulation." *Bell Journal of Economics and Management Science,* 2:3–21.

Stiglitz, Joseph E. 1990. "Peer Monitoring and Credit Markets." *World Bank Economic Review* 4(3):351–66.

Stiglitz, Joseph E., and A. Weiss. 1981. "Credit Rationing in Markets with Imperfect Information." *American Economic Review* 71:393–410.

Stroh, Paul. 1986. "National Development Foundation of Jamaica: Lessons Learned Since Inception through July 1986." Washington, D.C.: Development Technologies, Inc.

Sugianto. 1989. "KUPEDES and SIMPEDES." *Asia Pacific Rural Finance* 5:12–14.

———. 1990a. "Development of Rural Agricultural Financial Policy and the Progress and Benefits of BRI's KUPEDES Program." Mimeo. Jakarta: BRI.

———. 1990b. "Transaction Costs at Small Scale Banks Below the Branch Level." Mimeo. Jakarta: BRI.

Suharto. 1985. *Mengenai Bank Perkreditan Rakyat di Indonesia.* Jakarta.

———. 1988. *Sejarah Pendirian Bank Perkreditan Rakyat.* Jakarta.

Superintendencia de Bancos (SIB). 1977. "Requisitos que Exige la Ley General de Bancos de la Republica de Bolivia y Tramites a los Debe Sujetarse la Organization y Instalación de un Banco Privado Commercial Bajo El Concepto de la Ley General de Bancos." La Paz, Bolivia.

———. 1992. "Boletin Informativo." La Paz, Bolivia.

Sutoro, Ann Dunham, and Roes Haryanto. 1990. "KUPEDES Development Impact Survey." BRI Briefing Booklet. Jakarta.

Tendler, Judith. 1983. "Ventures in the Informal Sector, and How They Worked Out in Brazil." AID Evaluation Special Study No. 12. Washington, D.C.: USAID.

———. 1989. "Whatever Happened to Poverty Alleviation?" In *Microenterprises in Developing Countries,* edited by Jacob Levitsky. London: Intermediate Technologies Publications.

Tun Wai, U. 1977. "A Revisit to Interest Rates Outside the Organized Money Markets of Underdeveloped Countries." *Banca Nazionale del Lavoro Quarterly Review* 30(122):291–312.

———. 1980. "The Role of Unorganized Financial Markets in Economic Development and in the Formulation of Monetary Policy." *Savings and Development* 4(4):300–308.

United Nations. 1962. "Measures for Mobilizing Domestic Saving for Productive Investment." *Economic Bulletin for Asia and the Far East* 12(3):1–26.

Uphoff, Norman T. 1986. *Local Institutional Development: An Analytical Source Book with Cases.* West Hartford, Conn.: Kumarian Press.

U.S. Agency for International Development (USAID). 1972. "Spring Review of Rural Credit." Washington, D.C.: USAID

———. 1973. *Spring Review of Small Farmer Credit.* Vols. 1–20. Washington, D.C.: USAID.

———. 1986. "Project Paper Amendment: Financial Institutions Development Project Amendment (497-0341)." Jakarta: USAID/Jakarta.

———. 1991. "Bolivia Project Paper: Micro and Small Enterprise Development." Internal. Washington, D.C.: USAID.

Varian, Hal R. 1989. "Monitoring Agents with Other Agents." Center for Research on Economic and Social Theory Working Paper No. 89-18. Ann Arbor: Department of Economics, University of Michigan.

Vogel, Robert C. 1979. "Subsidized Interest Rates and the Structure of Agricultural Credit in Developing Countries." In *Problems and Issues of Agricultural Credit and Rural Finance,* 27–34. Dhaka: Bangladesh Bank.

———. 1981. "Rural Financial Market Performance: Implications of Low Delinquency Rates." *American Journal of Agricultural Economics* 63(1):58–65.

———. 1984a. "The Effect of Subsidized Agricultural Credit on Income Distribution in Costa Rica." In *Undermining Rural Development with Cheap Credit,* edited by Dale W. Adams, Douglas H. Graham, and John D. Von Pischke, 133–45. Boulder, Colo.: Westview Press.

———. 1984b. "Savings Mobilization: The Forgotten Half of Rural Finance." In *Undermining Rural Development with Cheap Credit,* edited by Dale W. Adams, Douglas H. Graham, and John D. Von Pischke, 248–65. Boulder, Colo.: Westview Press.

———. 1990. "Successful Rural Savings Mobilization: The Incentives Required and the Discipline They Provide." Key Biscayne, Fla.: Inter-American Management Consulting Corporation (IMCC).

Von Pischke, John D. 1978. "Towards an Operational Approach to Savings for Rural Developers." *Savings and Development* 2(1):3–55.

———. 1983a. "The Pitfalls of Specialized Farm Credit Institutions in Low-Income Countries." In *Rural Financial Markets in Developing Countries: Their Use and Abuse,* edited by John D. Von Pischke, Dale W. Adams, and Gordon Donald, 175–82. Baltimore: Johns Hopkins University Press.

———. 1983b. "Toward an Operational Approach to Savings for Rural Developers." In *Rural Financial Markets in Developing Countries: Their Use and Abuse,* edited by John D. Von Pischke, Dale W. Adams, and Gordon Donald, 414–21. Baltimore: Johns Hopkins University Press.

———. 1991. "Finance at the Frontier: Debt Capacity and the Role of Credit in the Private Economy." EDI Development Series. Washington, D.C.: World Bank.

Von Pischke, John D., Dale Adams, and Gordon Donald, eds. 1983. *Rural Financial Markets in Developing Countries: Their Use and Abuse.* Baltimore: Johns Hopkins University Press.

Waterfield, Charles. 1992. "Designing for Financial Viability of Microenterprise Programs: A Simplified Approach." Draft. Mennonite Economic Development Associates.

Webster, Russell, and Timothy Mooney. 1989. "A.I.D. Microenterprise Stocktaking: Malawi." USAID Evaluation Occasional Paper No. 20. Washington, D.C.: USAID.

Wenner, Mark D. 1989. "Screening and Loan Repayment Performance: An Empirical Analysis of a Group Credit Scheme in Southern Costa Rica." A Final Report of Dissertation Finding to the Inter-American Foundation. University of Wisconsin–Madison, Department of Agricultural Economics.

————. 1990. "Group Credit in Costa Rica: An Econometric Analysis of Information Transfer, Repayment Performance, and Cost-Effectiveness." Paper presented at the American Agricultural Economics Association annual meeting, Vancouver, British Columbia, August 4–8.

Wieland, Robert, Katherine Stearns, and Antonio Salas. 1990. "A Review of Small and Micro Enterprises in Jamaica: Prospects for Assisting Them." Arlington, Vir.: Inter-American Management Consulting Corporation.

Wilmington, Martin W. 1983. "Aspects of Moneylending in Northern Sudan." In *Rural Financial Markets in Developing Countries: Their Use and Abuse,* edited by John D. Von Pischke, Dale W. Adams, and Gordon Donald, 255–61. Baltimore: Johns Hopkins University Press.

World Bank. 1983. *Indonesia: Rural Credit Study.* Washington, D.C.: World Bank.

————. 1984a. *Agriculture Credit: Sector Policy Paper.* 2d ed. Washington, D.C.: World Bank.

————. 1984b. "Employment and Income Distribution in Indonesia." World Bank Country Study. Washington, D.C.: World Bank.

————. 1989. *World Development Report, 1989.* New York: Oxford University Press.

————. 1990a. "Costa Rica: Public Sector Spending." World Bank Report No. 8519–CR. Draft. Washington, D.C.: World Bank.

————. 1990b. *World Development Report, 1990.* New York: Oxford University Press.

————. 1991a. *Bolivia: From Stabilization to Sustained Growth.* Report No. 9763–BO. Washington, D.C.: World Bank.

————. 1991b. "Gender and Poverty in India." World Bank Country Study. Washington, D.C.: World Bank.

World Council of Credit Unions (WOCCU). 1987. *Feasibility Study: Establishment of an Apex Cooperative Financial Intermediary in the Philippines.* Madison, Wis.: WOCCU.

————. 1990. "1989 Statistical Report." Madison, Wis.: WOCCU.

————. 1991. "1990 Annual Report and Directory." Madison, Wis.: WOCCU.

Yaron, Jacob. 1991a. "Development Finance Institutions: Is Current Assessment of their Financial Performance Adequate?" Washington, D.C.: World Bank.

————. 1991b. "Successful Rural Finance Institutions." World Bank Discussion Paper No. 150. Washington, D.C.: World Bank.

Index

The New world of
microenterprise finance